Human Geography Today

Human Geography Today

Edited by
Doreen Massey, John Allen and Philip Sarre

Polity Press

First published in 1999 by Polity Press
in association with Blackwell Publishers Ltd

Editorial office:
Polity Press
65 Bridge Street
Cambridge CB2 1UR, UK

Marketing and production:
Blackwell Publishers Ltd
108 Cowley Road
Oxford OX4 1JF, UK

Published in the USA by
Blackwell Publishers Inc.
Commerce Place
350 Main Street
Malden, MA 02148, USA

ISBN 0-7456-2188-0
ISBN 0-7456-2189-9 (pbk)

A catalogue record for this book is available from the British Library and has
been applied for from the Library of Congress.

Typeset in 10 on 11$^1/_2$pt Sabon
by Wearset, Boldon, Tyne and Wear
Printed in Great Britain by MPG Books, Bodmin, Cornwall

This book is printed on acid-free paper.

Contents

Notes on Contributors

John Agnew is Professor of Geography at the University of California Los Angeles. He taught previously at Syracuse University, New York, and has been a Visiting Professor at the Universities of Chicago and British Columbia. His research and teaching are in political geography and international political economy. His most recent book is *Geopolitics: Re-Visioning World Politics* (1998).

John Allen is Head of Geography at the Open University, where he has edited and co-authored such volumes as *Political and Economic Forms of Modernity* (1992), *A Shrinking World? Global Unevenness and Inequality* (1995) and *Rethinking the Region: Spaces of Neoliberalism* (1997). He is currently writing a book on spatiality and power.

Doreen Massey is Professor of Geography in the Faculty of Social Sciences at the Open University. Her books include *Spatial Divisions of Labour* (second edition 1995) and *Space, Place and Gender* (1994). She is co-founder and joint editor of *Soundings: A Journal of Politics and Culture*.

Geraldine Pratt teaches geography at the University of British Columbia and is editor of *Environment and Planning D: Society and Space*. She writes about gender and race in relation to labour issues, and is especially interested in what cultural theory can bring to our understanding of labour market segmentation. She is co-author with Susan Hanson of *Women, Work and Space* (1995).

Sarah Radcliffe teaches geography at the University of Cambridge and researches issues of contemporary social change in Latin America. Her work addresses the gender, racial and social dynamics of political entities and political identities. Recent publications include *Re-Making the Nation: Place, Politics and Identity in Latin America* (1996), written with S. Westwood.

Gillian Rose teaches geography at the University of Edinburgh. She is the author of *Feminism and Geography* and co-editor, with A. Blunt, of *Women Writing Space*. Her current research focuses on the visual spaces and subjectivities of exhibitions, galleries and museums.

David Sibley teaches human geography at the University of Hull. His research has been concerned with a reworking of socio-spatial theory, drawing on psychoanalytical and anthropological conceptions of the social self and human relationships with the material world. He has written on nomadic cultures, childhood, animals in cities and the production of geographical knowledge.

David Slater is Professor of Social and Political Geography at Loughborough University. He is author of *Territory and State Power in Latin America* (1989) and editor of two special issues on *Social Movements and Political Change in Latin America* (1994). He is currently doing research on geopolitical imaginations and global transformations.

Susan J. Smith is Ogilvie Professor of Geography at the University of Edinburgh. Her research and teaching spans a variety of themes in urban, housing and cultural studies, focusing especially on the geographies of inequality and exclusion. Her books include *The Politics of 'Race' and Residence* (1989), *Social Policy and Housing* (1990), *Housing for Health* (1991) and *Children at Risk?* (1995). She is currently working on a project concerned with inequalities in the distribution of cultural resources, and with the relevance of cultural forms to the quality of social life.

Edward W. Soja teaches in the Department of Urban Planning, School of Public Policy and Social Research, at the University of California Los Angeles. His publications include *Postmodern Geographies: The Reassertion of Space in Critical Social Theory* (1989) and *Thirdspace: Journeys to Los Angeles and Other Real-and-Imagined Places* (1996). He is currently working on *Postmetropolis*, in which he looks at an application of ideas developed in *Thirdspace* to current trends in urban restructuring; a critical human geography of contemporary Los Angeles in the aftermath of the Justice Riots of 1992; and an introductory text to the growing new field of critical urban studies.

Nigel Thrift is Professor and Head of the School of Geographical Sciences at Bristol University. His research is in a number of areas including social and cultural theory, technological cultures, time, and the nature of contemporary capitalism. His recent books include *Mapping the Subject* (1995) (co-edited with Steve Pile); *Spatial Formations* (1996), *Money/Space* (1996) (with Andrew Leyshon); and *Shopping, Place and Identity* (1998) (with Danny Miller, Peter Jackson, Beverley Holbrook and Mike Rowlands).

Gill Valentine is Lecturer in Geography at the University of Sheffield, where she teaches social geography, approaches to human geography and qualitative methods. Her research interests include: food and foodscapes; geographies of parenting and childhood; and sexuality and space. She is co-author with David Bell of *Consuming Geographies: You Are Where You Eat* (1997) and *Mapping Desire* (1995); and co-editor with Tracey Skelton of *Cool Places: Geographies of Youth Cultures* (1998).

Michael John Watts is Director and Chancellor's Professor of Geography at the Institute of International Studies, University of California, Berkeley, where he has taught for twenty years. His most recent books are *Globalising Food*, co-edited with David Goodman (1997) and *Liberation Ecologies*, co-edited with Richard Peet (1995). He is currently working on a project on agricultural transformation and post-socialist transitions, and on a book on the poultry industry.

Sarah Whatmore works in the School of Geographical Sciences at the University of Bristol. Her research and teaching focuses on the political and ethical spaces of various networks – including food, property and environmental management – in which the social and material are intricately bound together. She is an editor of *Environment and Planning A*, and a member of the editorial board of *Transactions of the Institute of British Geographers*.

Preface

Although we are slightly wary of the word, this book aims to be something of a manifesto. We want to argue for certain, very broad, ways of doing human geography. Much of the opening chapter is concerned with laying out the bones of this. We have also tried to produce the book in a way which was at least modestly collective. The two things together have enormously increased both the amount of work involved and the complexity of the process of production. Within the geography group at the Open University this has meant our meeting quite frequently over a long period of time. With contributors from beyond the Open University it has meant hoping that they would agree with our initial proposals – for themes and sections and so forth, and the broad propositions about the future of human geography. For all of us it has meant perhaps rather more drafting and redrafting than is usually the case for 'collections'. We know, from many a discussion, that these chapters have often been difficult to write, and not only because of having to respond to comments from the editorial group. Rather, a number of us found it a real test of commitment and imagination to argue for the kind of human geography we are seeking. Producing 'critiques' is so easy by comparison! Our real thanks, then, to all the contributors to this volume.

Within the Open University, we did work very much as a collective – in which Mandy Morris was also involved in the early stages: our thanks go to her too. There was some division of labour, though, with individuals taking organizational responsibility for particular parts, and for writing their introductions. These were as follows: part I Philip

Sarre, part II John Allen, part III Steve Pile, part IV Michael Pryke, and part V Doreen Massey. Ed Hall was also involved throughout the process. All of us at the Open University, though, have discussed everything, so for those errors which remain, etc., you will have to blame us all collectively.

Finally, we should like to thank Rebecca Harkin of Polity, who presented us with the idea in the first place, and with whom it is a delight to work. And thanks too to the secretarial staff at the Open University – to Margaret Charters, who took a leading organizational role, and to Michele Marsh and Doreen Warwick, who helped see the project through to its finished form.

Doreen Massey
John Allen
Philip Sarre
Ed Hall
Steve Pile
Michael Pryke

Acknowledgements

The authors and publisher gratefully acknowledge permission to reproduce the following copyright material:

The Economist: extract from article, 10 August 1996, reprinted by permission of *The Economist*.

Richard Ford: extracts from *Independence Day* (first published in Great Britain by The Harvill Press 1995), copyright © 1995 by Richard Ford, reprinted by permission of The Harvill Press.

A. Game and D. Metcalfe: extracts from *Passionate Sociology* (Sage, London, 1996), reprinted by permission of Sage Publications Ltd.

bell hooks: extracts from *Yearning: Race, Gender and Cultural Politics* (South End Press, 1990), reprinted by permission of South End Press.

T. Ingold: extracts from 'Building, dwelling, living. How People and animals make themselves at home in the world' in M. Strathern (ed) *Shifting Contexts: Transformations in Anthropological Knowledge* (Routledge 1995), reprinted by permission of Routledge.

T.R. Schatzki: an extract from *Social Practices: A Wittgensteinian Approach to Human Activity and the Social* (Cambridge University Press, 1997), reprinted by permission of Cambridge University Press.

Part I
The 'Nature' of Human Geography

1
Issues and Debates

Doreen Massey with the collective

Introduction

This book is founded upon a conviction that the academic discipline which goes by the name of 'human geography' both has much to offer to the wider world of intellectual endeavour and the world which it studies, and harbours within itself at the moment some fascinating debates.

The series of which this book forms one volume allows participants in the various academic disciplines the space to reflect on their current positioning and debates and to consider ways of moving forward. It is, of course, impossible to produce a 'complete survey' (whatever that might be) and there are inevitably many views on how we might move forward. What is reflected here is a specific strategy. First, we have chosen to organize the field and its current and emerging debates in a particular way. The result of this is evident in the foci we have chosen for the parts of the book. And second we have, collectively, tried not to predict the future directions of the discipline but rather to argue in favour of certain broad directions.

The first of these two decisions (how to organize the field and present its debates) involved long discussion. One obvious option, though one discarded fairly early on, was to divide the field into its various subject matters and to proceed along the lines of sections on 'political geography', 'economic geography' and so on. Not only would this be a little boring, we thought, and not only would the lines between the subject areas be extremely difficult to draw, but also and more import-antly their very drawing would deny one of the more productive of recent developments: the interlinking of these fields and their sharing of debates. Any representation will perforce deny some aspects over others and any taxonomy of sections will make distinctions and draw borders which are just as frequently transgressed as respected, but to proceed along the strategy of sub-fields, we felt, would be particularly unhelpful. Perhaps, indeed, one of the many good things which has been happen-ing in human geography is a diminution in the significance of that particular kind of division.

Another possibility was to include separate chapters on class, ethni-city, gender . . . Again we decided against; and this, as with other decisions, was the outcome of long debate. The ellipsis itself gives an indication of one difficulty: the problematic nature of an approach which may have to have recourse to (and arguments over) lists. But there were far more serious issues too. Over the last decade feminist and post-colonial geographies have challenged, and influenced, the nature of theorizing, research and writing, in fields of work throughout human geography. It is our hope that, rather than being confined to 'parts', that challenge and influence is reflected in different ways throughout the book.

Given that the book is not a snapshot but an account of (and an attempt to intervene in) change we could also have focused on major shifts and developments: the cultural turn, the impact of poststructural-ism or postmodernism, for instance. This possibility too we debated at some length, and to some extent it is reflected in the book's final organ-ization. However, these issues in themselves are not peculiarly geo-graphical. Although they are (as everything possibly is) in some sense intrinsically spatial, they are not *specifically* spatial (or geographical in a wider sense). They stem from debates, and political movements, which have their origins primarily outside of geography. We felt that our aim should be, in this volume, to tease out and focus upon debates and movements which reflect, which catch at, the specific differentia of 'human geography'. This is absolutely not because of some commitment to disciplinary boundaries or traditions or what not. Indeed much of what is in this book concerns the nature of the discipline's relationship to other fields of knowledge (more on this later). But there are, as things currently stand, academic disciplines. There are, to put it in a way which is more acceptable and productive, distinct ways of understand-ing the world around us. For us, human geography's take on the world derives from its standing on the ground of the triad of space–place–nature. If there is such a positioning, then it is important to discuss and develop the debates and ideas which are peculiar to it.

Again, we do this out of a particular belief: that this approach has a lot to offer, that the particular take on the world pursued by 'human geographers' can contribute significantly to the studies pursued from the standpoint of other perspectives.

Our strategy, then, was to begin from this particular take on the world. This part and the four which follow all have the specificity of the geographical at their heart. It is through this means that we believe the relationship with other disciplines can be fruitfully two-way: geography can contribute and influence as well as be influenced by. The parts represent 'issues' (in the widest sense) which we believe to be both central to human geography and of a long-term and wider significance. One of those issues is (probably) constantly with us: how to think about space and place must be core to a discipline which pretends to be geographical. Other parts reflect more recent developments – perhaps only ten or fifteen years ago there would not have been a part on 'geography and difference', yet today that conjunction is both one of the key points around which geography and other disciplines interact and a vital moment in a radical rethinking of politics and the political. This present part is an attempt to raise the profile of a range of issues which we believe are likely to be, and we would argue certainly should be, of increasing significance in the future: the relation between the human and non-human worlds. Here again we want to transgress the boundaries denoted by the discipline's title, but this time by exploring its designation as 'human'.

What we aimed to gather together in the different parts of this book, then, was a range of intellectual issues which we believe to be of long standing, which are core to human geography's concerns, and which are important components of the contribution which the discipline can make to knowledge and understanding more generally.

Our second decision was to bring together a book which argued for a particular way of going forward. In that sense the book is more manifesto than prediction but, we hope, a manifesto which is open and enabling rather than regulating. We want to argue the case for particular ways of looking at the world and for particular ways in which human geography can contribute to that project. It is a very broad manifesto and, as will be seen from the chapters which follow, there is plenty of room for debate within it. None the less, we do feel that there are certain things happening in the discipline which are of particular importance, certain developments singularly worthy of promotion, certain ways of setting questions and of conducting intellectual explorations which are likely to be especially productive.

We want this book to be used and thought about. All the contributions (including the editors') have been drafted, discussed, and revised (sometimes more than once) in the light of those discussions. The aim was not to police what we each wrote but rather to produce a volume which cohered around a set of discussions, discussions which we believe to be important for the future direction of human geography – debates which will, indeed, influence its 'nature'. It is for that reason that the rest of this chapter is devoted to outlining the broad elements of these debates, and to indicating how individual contributions in their various ways link in to the issues we want to put on the agenda. It is a chapter which does not only have to be read 'at the beginning' – we hope it can be returned to as a source of reflection. The aim is to stimulate discussion which can continue beyond the pages of the book.

It is perhaps worth saying at the outset, however, that we do not advance these ideas on the grounds that they are simply 'true', in some sense of eternal, distanced objectivity. Rather – and this is a theme around which many of the chapters which follow also circulate – the impetus is that these are ways of looking at the world which are appropriate now, in these times and spaces; they seem to us to offer the most potentially constructive way of approaching the understanding of a world which is (and which is increasingly recognized as being) geographical in all respects.

Theorizing geographically

There has been a long history of debate about the significance of a geographical understanding of the world. It has become an established (though not entirely uncontested) theme tune within our discipline that 'geography matters'. The original case was made by constructing a certain reciprocity between 'the social' and 'the spatial' – while we in a spatial discipline accepted that the spatial was always socially constructed so too, we argued, it had to be recognized that the social was necessarily also spatially constructed. What is more, we argued, the fact and nature of that spatial construction matter; they make a difference. In this volume we essentially take the broad outline of that position as read.

We do, however, in a number of ways wish to exemplify this argument and, more significantly, to push it further. For example, throughout the book there is an active engagement with theories and theorists from other parts of academe. However, what we are concerned to do is not merely to import new ideas into geography but to examine the specificity of their operation within our discipline and to tease out how their use within an explicitly geographical theorizing may modify or develop them. Thus, there has in recent years been much writing introducing to geography concepts and approaches developed initially in other disciplines. What we believe to be necessary is to consider both what the specific meaning of these ideas/authors can be *within geography*, and – perhaps even more importantly – how their manipulation in issues of space/spatiality may make a further contribution to the theories themselves. This work of rethinking the theories as geographical is, we believe, a significant contribution. It means both *really* bringing the approaches into human geography by rethinking them through space–place–nature and contributing *back* to other disciplines what can be learned by articulating the approaches in a specifically geographical manner. After all, if the world really is inextricably geographical, then this must be done. Our argument is that working these theories in an explicitly geographical fashion may radically reconfigure fields which previously had been thought of without that dimension. In pursuing this theme of 'geography makes a difference' we are not trying to carve out an empire for the discipline, or even trying to draw boundaries to give more emphasis to the field in itself (indeed some of us are pretty wary of boundaries). Rather, we are trying to be rigorous about the specific contribution which can be made from a position which emphasizes the perspective of space–place–nature.

This way of thinking runs throughout the book. Thus, Sarah Whatmore takes on the work of actor network theorists, and of related others such as Donna Haraway, and both uses them to problematize our own thinking within geography about the sharp boundaries which we so habitually draw (most significantly here between humans and 'non-humans') and turns the argument around to highlight 'the significance of geography to discerning the world in binary terms' (p. 32). If we want, then, to try to 'glimpse' a 'non-binary world' (p. 26) (and this is a theme which runs through much of the book) then one of the most significant steps must be to rework our geographical imaginations. Indeed Ed Soja argues that what Henri Lefebvre, and also Soja himself, are involved in is a project working towards 'the spatialization of dialectical thinking itself' (p. 268). On this reading, the familiar sequence of thesis + antithesis → synthesis has indeed a ring of sequentiality; it is a binary ordering whose culmination has a temporal logic, or at least a temporal imagination in its figuring. As Whatmore argues, 'recourse to variants of dialectical reasoning' do not 'provide a radical enough basis for critical enquiry ... Far from challenging this *a priori* categorization of the things of the world, dialectics can be seen to raise its binary logic to the level of a contradiction and engine of history' (p. 25). Whatmore and Soja have rather different takes on what to do about this. Whatmore's approach is through a grounded theory which stresses the interconnections and networks that both constitute and link the hybrid entities of the world. She wishes to change the nature of our imaginative geographies. Soja, given that he sees the dialectical sequence as temporal, argues for its spatialization. This 'thirding' 'shifts the "rhythm" of dialectical thinking from a temporal to a more spatial mode, from a linear or diachronic sequencing to ... configurative simultaneities, ... synchronies' (p. 269). What the two authors share, however, is a conviction that the problems of binary thinking are not something which we discover 'outside geography' and then bring into our discipline to wrestle with there. Rather, those problems themselves are, in one way or another – and we may wish to debate how – deeply geographical. They are bound up with ways of spatio-temporalizing the world which are so seemingly 'natural', so habitual, that we had forgotten to think about them. This is one aspect of what we mean by taking seriously the potential significance of a geographical perspective.

There are other aspects, too. Many of the contributors to this book engage with major theorists, or strands of theory, and demonstrate how thinking them through a geographical perspective can craft them in a different way, add something to or remould their originally a-spatial approach to the world. All of the papers in part II, for instance, do this in different ways. Issues of our imaginations of the world, and in particular the work of Edward Said, are already far more explicitly spatial than many of the other 'extra-geographical' theorists addressed in the book. Yet even here the authors show how the debate can productively be pushed further. In his detailed examination of US imperialist imaginations, David Slater pulls more complexities through the work of Said and Homi Bhabha than are usually recognized (the plurality and division of colonial and imperial discourses at their source, for instance, and not only in their effects), and stresses the potential significance of counter-representations, 'alternative visions to the power of already established discourses of governability, [which] often possess a depth and a breadth that goes well beyond concepts of mimicry or mockery' (p. 73).

In the same part, Michael Watts spatializes Stuart Hall's doubled notion of articulation and demonstrates how the centrality of a very 'simple' geography lies at the heart of some of the problems Watts sees in the post-development movement. The construction of a sense of place, and a historical geography, with ur-histories at their heart and internal coherences unquestioned is, he argues, at the root of this problem. A critical geography is therefore essential to understanding and reformulating such a politics. Here, then, a radical geographical imaginary is being used both to criticize certain aspects of the post-development movement and to point towards possibilities for their rethinking. 'Space', and the way we imagine it, are revealed to be among the stakes at issue in the politics of the exchanges between the adherents of development on the one hand and post-development on the other.

But if all these issues in part II – of development and of post-development, of geographical imaginations and so forth – are perhaps in some sense already recognizably spatial, other authors in this volume tackle theorists and streams of theory which would seem to be far removed from such concerns. In part III, David Sibley extends the thinking of Melanie Klein and of Julia Kristeva, by arguing that the objects of object relations theory can be construed also as places, and that places too can be abject. '[G]eography', he argues, 'has a contribution to make to object relations theory' (p. 118), and psycho-social geographies may become part of a larger spatialized psychoanalysis. 'Geography can articulate feelings about space and place which have only been hinted at in the psychoanalytical literature' (p. 118).

And on a different theme again, the whole of part IV wrestles with the intertwining of space and power. John Allen takes on the literature on power and rethinks it in terms of its (varied) relations to spatiality. Stressing the need both for particular versions of theories of power, and for an appreciation of its necessary spatiality, he goes on to present a theorizing of the relation power/space and to indicate some of the ways in which such a thorough spatialization can refashion both theoretical understandings and their implications. John Agnew likewise (though in the converse direction) argues that rethinking spatiality (in this case the spatiality of the nation state) necessitates rethinking also concepts of power. The 'limiting [of the] understanding of the spatiality of power to the territoriality of states' (p. 176), he argues, rested on a particular conceptualization of power as power over, power as coercion, and power in the definition of property rights. Changing understandings of power problematize such confining spatialities and, conversely, increasingly evident changing spatialities problematize the older assumptions about the nature of power. John Agnew, in other words, draws out his argument in careful relation to a specific power/space formation. So too does Sarah Radcliffe in her detailed analysis of the sheer complexities of the spatialities, and of the productiveness of those spatialities, in a whole range of foci (biopolitics, racializations, resistances, and the constructions of the nation state) drawn from research in Latin America. The richness of this analysis, and the intricacy of the intertwining of power and spatiality, are a sure demonstration of how much the analysis of the latter can add to the analysis of the former.

One final example raises yet another strand in this complex field of the ways in which geography might 'matter'. There has of course emerged over many years now, and over the social and cultural sciences generally, an increasing awareness of the potential significance of spatiality and a growing use, in part but not only in reflection of this, of a spatialized vocabulary. We read everywhere of centres and margins, of peripheries and locatedness, and so on. This has been often remarked on, and both appreciation and caution have been expressed within geography itself. Ed Soja, expansively and generously taking in all the various aspects of these developments, calls it 'an unprecedented spatial turn' and reflects that in retrospect it may 'be seen as one of the most important intellectual developments in the late twentieth century' (p. 261). Indeed, in this general sense, it is one of the developments which this book is concerned to further. Within that overall enthusiasm, however, some differentiations can be made and some of them emerge from the contributions to this book. In his chapter, John Allen makes an important distinction between 'vocabularies' on the one hand and 'theories' on the other. He addresses the distinction directly: the 'central line of argument is that despite advances in our spatial *vocabularies* of power, a spatialized *theory* of power requires that we rethink the different modalities of power deployed in traditional accounts' (p. 194). More generally, using a spatial vocabulary is by no means the same as really spatializing one's approach to understanding. It is the latter towards which we are aiming here.

Susan Smith's analysis of the Sienese Palio and the Common Ridings of the Scottish Borders addresses other issues which arise from this recent, widespread, cheerful and promiscuous adoption of spatial vocabularies. It also addresses an issue closer to home: how within geography itself there has on occasions been an over-easy deployment of a vocabulary which not only, perhaps, unnecessarily simplifies and rigidifies, but also is assumed to bear within it a particular set of attendant political connotations. Smith begins by drawing out, and adding to, how geography matters in the constructions of sameness/difference/identity by such writers as Harrison, Bakhtin and Tilley. 'Fairs and festivals make and transform space, and by exploring this we can gain insight into the identities they express and constitute' (p. 136). Geography, then, is injected more integrally into the theories she is using. However, and this is the step which is important in the present argument, that very 'use' of a spatialized theoretical approach in the grounded investigation of the Palio and the Common Ridings thoroughly complicates and disrupts what might have been the predictable reading of the relations between spaces and politics. Reflecting upon 'the currently dominant discourse around cores and peripheries, mainstreams and margins', she argues that it 'could perhaps fairly be said that geographies of difference are currently over-theorised and under-specified' (p. 140). It is unwarranted to assume some automatic association between centre, similarity and boundedness, for instance, or between marginality, dislocation and a radical politics. Michael Watts, of course, is making a similar point in relation to the geographical imaginaries of Ken Saro-Wiwa's version of the Ogoni; and Geraldine Pratt more normatively puts this position through her work with Filipina domestic labourers in Vancouver (more on the latter later).

This is an important area of debate, and not simply for those within geography, for it challenges quite directly the imaginative geographies which have on occasions been imported into the discipline from, for instance, cultural theorists. Susan Smith challenges Homi Bhabha: 'even from this brief sketch, it is apparent that borders are not necessarily places from which something new "begins its presencing" (Bhabha, 1994)' (p. 146). So, not only do the contributors to this volume take on the task of theorizing spatially (and thus radically reworking non-spatial conceptions) but also there emerges an argument that the careful use of a spatialized theoretical approach achieves something else as well, by specifying a greater – and more problematical – complexity in the relations between that impossible-to-separate duo of the social and the spatial. Sarah Radcliffe argues a similar point, that despite advances in the conceptualization of power, 'there is no easy decoding of the spatialities of power. The rejection of the binary of domination/resistance leaves in place the more difficult analytical and methodological aspect of identifying and explaining the different geographies and dynamics of co-existing (and at times contradictory) powers' (p. 238).

Certainly, what all these contributions are pushing for is deeper thought about the meaning and implications of any spatial turn. We must be clear about the difference between really theorizing spatially and more casually wielding a spatial vocabulary. And we must, in turn, examine that spatial vocabulary for its own assumptions and incipient fixities. It certainly on occasions has its ironies. Geraldine Pratt wonders whether the metaphorical spatializing of the social does not on occasions at least risk doing harm precisely by erasing (or potentially erasing) the difference between the social in a general sense and the more explicitly spatial (her example is 'the home' as on the one hand an identity and on the other a place). Such an elision, one might add, might also in consequence erase the very specificity of the spatial, the specifically geographical. That would indeed be an ironic outcome of a lexical revision which supposedly aspired to put space more firmly on to the map. And there is a further irony which returns us to the opening point in this exploration of the potential meaning of 'geography matters'. For the figures in Susan Smith's chapter illustrate another thing: that many of the elements in this newly spatialized vocabulary operate precisely as dualisms (centre/margin) and with their assumptions of political character (domination/resistance) attached. Such an imagination is of course and again spatial. But it is precisely the kind of dichotomized imagination which many of the wielders of this vocabulary have been striving to escape. The 'spatial turn' is, as Ed Soja says, of real significance; the form which it takes may be more significant still.

Relational thinking

The second of our areas of concern, indeed, is what *kind* of geography matters. Thus, we are concerned with the manner in which that triad of space–place–nature is to be conceptualized, both as individual elements and together. Our broad commitment is to what we call 'relational thinking'. Thinking relationally is, in part, an attempt to reimagine the either/or constructions of binary thinking (where the only relations are negative ones of exclusion) and to recognize the important elements of interconnection which go into the construction of any identity. The geographical imaginary of inside versus outside has been strong in Western culture, is being increasingly questioned, and is certainly questioned here. The broad approach of 'thinking in terms of relations' is examined and employed throughout the book: in the debates over the conceptualization of space and place, in the discussion of the nature of power and in the examination of those most profound of Western boundaries: between Nature and Culture, and Body and Mind. Indeed it is in some ways ironic, and has for us been the subject of extended discussion, that this book is entitled *Human Geography*.

'Thinking in terms of relations' is, famously, easier said than done. Sarah Whatmore sets out on this task, showing how it involves, not the establishment/recognition of links between preconstituted 'things', but the relational conceptualization of entities themselves. She argues for an understanding of the world through the real making of the networks through which it is (she argues) constructed; that entities themselves are precarious achievements.

John Agnew's analysis, from the political field, of the current reworking of the significance of the nation state is an example of an aspect of this. What he demonstrates very clearly is how the organization of the world (and the organization of many forms of social science knowledge) into a particular relation between the social and the spatial – the nation state – although so frequently assumed to be 'fixed, as if for all time' (p. 173), is in fact a precarious achievement and one which is being at this very time, as Agnew puts it, 'unbundled'. It is an unbundling, moreover, provoked at least in part by the greater importance, and recognition of the importance, of the porosities of the previous identity. The 'territorial trap' idea of the nation state assumes a space which is bounded, in which there is a fundamental opposition between inside and outside, and where the space is the 'container' of the society (p. 176). That imagination of space in terms of 'blocks' is undermined by a greater degree of interconnection. 'A patchwork of places within a global node and network system therefore coexists with but is slowly eroding the territorial spatiality with which we are all so familiar ... a new geopolitics of power based on global networks and flows is in the offing' (p. 184). And finally, and at the same time, this growing recognition and reality of interrelations reworks the identities of the spatial entities themselves.

Gill Valentine, through an exploration of food, examines the myriad of relational constructions in which it is involved, including personal identity, issues of class and ethnicity, and imaginations of relations at what might be called the global level. She pulls out the way in which such an 'everyday' (p. 48) thing as food is imbricated in so many of the relations which result in our articulation of our cultural place in the world. 'Thus food is one way of acting out a fiction of community and of struggling against imagined forces of disintegration, ... it is also a linking process, a way of expressing cultural unity, of not just composing but also recomposing boundaries' (p. 53). Not just a connection between pre-givens, then, but part of the process of their constitution.

Moreover, such a viewpoint can be brought to space and place themselves. For Nigel Thrift, space can productively be imagined through a 'dwelling perspective' based upon the acknowledged primacy of practices (p. 308), and places, then, are space produced as a *'plenitude of different relations'* (p. 310). In this perspective, places are dynamic, taking shape only in their passing, and always incomplete; in our interconnectedness (which itself both incorporates more of and goes beyond what we commonly include in our references to 'the social') they haunt us and we haunt them. And central to this is embodiment: ' "the materiality of places lives, is inscribed in our bodies" (Game, 1995: 202)' quotes Thrift (p. 314). And in the same part Gillian Rose argues powerfully for a way of imagining space as relational, as constituted by performance. She argues that 'space is ... a doing, that it does not pre-exist its doing, and that its doing is the articulation of relational performances' (p. 248).

There are, however, some major questions lurking beneath the surface of this fairly general formulation. What must immediately be added to the injunction to think in terms of relations is of course that these relations are themselves relations 'of power'. John Allen's chapter addresses this issue at a general level. It teases out some of the ways in which we might understand both spatiality as imbued with power and power as intrinsically spatial: 'spatial assemblages of power'. The nation state, that particular and historical spatial constellation of social relations, was, as John Agnew shows, a product of powerful social forces in the late nineteenth century – and including both the power relations of imperialism and the powerful organizing discourses of the ' "methodological nationalism" [which] came to prevail in political and social thought' (p. 174).

Not abstract relations, then, but practised relations imbued with power. In Sarah Radcliffe's analysis, the role of spatialized powers, themselves drawing on imaginary geographies (for instance of modernity and its others), is analysed in the process of the disciplining of bodies into suitable bearers for a 'modern' future: space/power entailed in the very process of embodiment. Or, to pick up again the nation state, she analyses the relational and mutual construction – once more through spatialized powers – of race and state: for instance, '[t]he constitution of "races" is thus inherently spatial' (p. 229). Finally, Gill Valentine points a number of times to the importance of understanding the nature of this power: in relation to treating different others as 'exotic' for instance or, on the other hand, in constructing a more complex understanding of the interrelatedness of place. As she points out, 'dabbling in difference in the kitchen can ... be dangerous if we ignore some of the ways that acts of consumption are riddled with power' (p. 56), and in this analysis of the potential commodification of difference she picks up on bell hooks's argument that here lies a danger, of 'a consumer cannibalism that not only displaces the Other but denies the significance of that Other's history through a process of decontextualisation (hooks, 1992: 31)' (p. 57).

This raises a further issue about relationality. Such a 'consumer cannibalism' denies the multiplicities of the spatial. Precisely by 'decontextualization', by denying the Other a real history of her or his own, the possibility of genuine alterity, of actually existing alternative stories, is eradicated. Doreen Massey argues that leaving open the possibility for the existence of a multiplicity of stories is precisely one of the potentials held open by really spatializing our analyses and theories. And David Slater's discussion of Latin America points to the utter materiality of this on the world geopolitical stage. In their struggles for liberation, what was at issue for both Simón Bolívar and José Martí was that 'Spanish America ... should not commit the error of regarding Europe or North America as the foreign model to which they should adjust' (p. 73). Fernández Retamar, likewise, points out Slater, 'criticizes the way Latin American culture is taken as an "apprenticeship, a rough draft or a copy of European bourgeois culture"(Fernández Retamar, 1989: 5)' (p. 74). These are precisely cases of what Massey calls the reordering of spatial differences into temporal sequence, where the multiplicities of spatial difference are reimagined as place in the queue. And as Slater says, it leaves 'no doubt about the relation between geopolitical power and modes of subordinating representation' (p. 73).

The multiplicities are in the recognition of the story-telling too. Slater insists also on the importance of recognizing the *theories* of 'the others'; that is, not only are there multiple stories to be told, but there are multiple tellers of stories, reverse discourses and multiple sources of theoretical knowledge. This is part of what is at issue in the case of the Ogoni, what Michael Watts calls the Ogoni's attempt at 'imaginative liberation' (p. 87), and in some of the debates between development and post-development. Watts characterizes anti-development thinking as struggles for sites of alterity, against the postulated homogenizing single story of development. In Watts's analysis what was wrong with the Ogoni's particular strategy was its assumptions about place; its assumption of some authenticity of isomorphism between society and space. In that sense it is an essentializing practice of identity-construction. This is a specific critique of a specific movement. The wider question, which Watts addresses, is whether post-development's attempt (or the attempt of other movements or liberation struggles – Bolívar? Martí?) to establish room for the pursuance of alternative trajectories necessarily falls into this trap. Watts is sceptical of the possibility that 'these identities fall outside of the panoptic gaze of the hegemonic development discourse as new forms of subjectivity which stand opposed to modernity itself' (p. 90). Could others do so? Or are we all ineluctably drawn into the single hegemonic discourse? And if so what does that mean for space? Perhaps the issue is not so much 'outside' or 'inside' as the nature of the relations through which differing stories and voices weave themselves: distinct yet interrelated. Clearly, as on some other issues, there are tensions between our authors here. Where they definitely agree, however, is that space and politics are again intimately interwoven.

This raises another issue. 'Thinking in terms of relations' in its more usual formulations, and particularly in its wider epistemological settings (perhaps most especially poststructuralism), has tended on the whole to point to an essential openness and fluidity of the spatial and, in a subsequent move, to applaud that openness and fluidity politically. Geraldine Pratt, indeed, identifies it as a new hegemonic position in which hybridity and mobility are constantly identified, and then valued entirely positively. The complexities of all this, and the lack of fit between 'goodies' and 'baddies', in some wider political sense, and the kinds of spatialization on which they draw, have already been pointed to.

Gillian Rose draws out in precise terms the nature of the relations implied in thinking space through the body, through desire, and through fantasy, a thinking not in terms of bounded others but as a desire to be in relation *to*. For Teresa de Lauretis, as Rose explains, 'the spatial articulates (sexual) difference and desire. "Difference" becomes "distance" from the self. Yet this distance and its placing "outside the self" is not an interval . . . It is not a distance measured in the space between the sovereign phallocentric subject and his bounded other' (p. 256); it is not a gap between bounded things but the production of two.

Yet, of course, boundaries and bounded entities remain with us and indeed continue constantly to be built and maintained. David Sibley's explorations of psychoanalysis, indeed, although they do reveal ambiguities and pulls in different directions, none the less argue for the power of this tendency. And Geraldine Pratt argues that precisely at the moment that boundaries are blurred, they are reconstructed. The fact of boundaries and boundednesses may be likely to stay with us.

Pratt, moreover, would push this further. In ways which interestingly cross-cut with the arguments of Susan Smith she problematizes the idea that, in abandoning one geographical hegemony, we should now instate another: 'why, we may ask, search for one correct geometry to articulate contemporary configurations of identity, difference and geography?' (p. 153). First of all, she argues that anyway the establishment of identity necessarily involves exclusion: 'non-essential identities are nevertheless boundary projects; identities are constructed through identifying who one is not' (p. 154). This is a different position from those who would argue that identity-construction could be (not necessarily is) pursued through the specificity of *relations to* rather than the counterpositions of *distinctions from*. And in further specifying her position, Pratt links it up to work in radical democracy: 'identities are always defined through difference, through the construction of a "constitutive outside" (Mouffe, 1992). A "we" is inevitably defined through the identification of a "them" ' (p. 156). One response to this can be that, in some sense, this type of thinking is also 'relational'. Even counterpositional boundaries involve 'relations' in some way even if – see Slater – they are the inert, imposed 'relationality' of dualisms. The problem, however, is that, as Massey argues, this bounding of counterposed identities suppresses the maps of power through which the identities are constructed. Perhaps what all our authors are arguing is that these relations be made explicit, be exposed to view. What we, as critics, ought to be doing, argues Pratt, is 'keeping the process of boundary construction in view, as well as tracing the interdependencies of what lies on either side of the boundary' (p. 156). At issue here, primarily then, is the best way to approach this strategy of exposure.

The geographical imagination and the material world

One theme which emerges through the volume is the significance of imaginative geographies – of the geographical imagination. It runs from the cosmologies of our (human) positioning in relation to nature and to an inorganic other, through the framing of our selves and our relations to others, through the politicized imaginings of geopolitics, to what we might call 'conceptual geographies': the binary pictures of dualisms, the mental images of relational space, the isomorphisms of space and society that went to make up the Western 'modernist' creation and generalization of the nation state. The geographical imagination is a highly significant part of (see later) that 'real world' which we socially construct, and has immense influence upon the ways in which people act within it. 'Geographers', as academics, are by no means the only group responsible for constructing either hegemonic or critical geographical imaginations, but our influence is – or could be – important. It is one element of the responsibility of being a geographer.

Much has already been woven into the previous discussions about the nature of the geographical imaginary. A few points are, however, worth drawing out more explicitly. First, there is the evident fact that the construction, maintenance and relative power of particular geographical imaginations is a terrain of contestation. Thus, for instance, David Slater, Sarah Radcliffe and Michael Watts all stress the importance (and complexities and difficulties) of the construction of alternative (anti-hegemonic) geographical imaginaries in struggles within the Third World. Slater analyses the reverse discourses of liberation struggles and more recent attempts at resistance to US domination. Radcliffe points to the use of 'geography itself' (symbols, places, the drawing of alternative maps) in political struggles over the meaning and constitution of nationhood and who should count within it as full citizens. Watts does this too, in the case of the Ogoni, but he also points to two other aspects of this issue. On the one hand there is the rendering of the non-West by the non-West itself (for instance, the Ogoni imaginative construction of other Nigerian peoples). This is not a geographical imagination which is simply some product of the West's global power but one which draws more importantly on the history of post-colonial Africa itself. On the other hand, there is the rendering by the non-West of 'the West itself'. Watts's opening paragraph, a fable told to him by a Zairean friend, is immensely thought-provoking. Its characterizations of the US and various national European productions made us all laugh out loud. Yet what is being told here is in fact more sobering: that the West is in return imagined (and in sometimes accurately derisive terms) by its Others. As this more important point is absorbed and reflected upon, one becomes yet more sober, for the continuing and overwhelming power of the West is embodied in that very ability to respond with the laughter of recognition. What confidence such a response reflects. The other way around, such an imagination might more probably and more legitimately be responded to with anger at a demeaning – and therefore in that context subordinating – caricature.

And yet, and again, the picture is always also more complicated. Just as Watts feels impelled to take issue with some post-development imaginations so too David Slater, while insisting upon the overwhelmingly dominant directions of the power of such imaginations, none the less points out that we must also accept 'the idea that the less powerful can also be implicated in othering, and distanc[e] ourselves from the proclivity to blame the powerful for everything' (p. 80). It reflects back again to the cautionary words of Susan Smith and Geraldine Pratt about the ways in which the politicization of our geographical imaginations can all too easily become simplistic and rigidified.

The second issue here is also a word of caution. Thinking in terms of relations is frequently advocated on the grounds of its ability to undermine essentialist thinking. And that is as true of elements of our geographical imaginations (locality, nation state) as of others. Moreover, an important aspect of non-essentialist thinking is that it recognizes the fact of construction. Things are not given, they are products of processes in particular times and places. That is a position, too, which resonates through this book. It involves a recognition both of the specificity of things (both things theorized and theories themselves) and of the need to analyse the process of their construction through timespace. This process of construction, however, has most frequently been characterized as 'social' construction and, perhaps correlatively, has come to have rather dematerializing implications. It is not that form of the argument which we wish to pursue here. Any understanding of the produced-ness of things must also recognize (and include within that produced-ness) their material embodiedness. Only in that way can we retain our commitment to questioning the binary opposition between 'the natural' and 'the social'.

A similar dematerialization could also flow from an emphasis on geographical imaginations which worked entirely within what it might itself imagine as the realm of the discursive. Over and over again the contributors to this volume work against that kind of prioritization and the categorical distinction on which it is based. Many of the chapters, and in a wide range of settings, address the issue of embodiment, for instance. Gill Valentine's analysis of food moves brilliantly within the integral relations of geographical imagination and material embodiment.

Sarah Radcliffe's chapter analyses particular constructions of the raced body and the supposedly modern body. The point here is that, in all these analyses, drawing on geographical imaginations is itself integral to the processes of embodiment. As Radcliffe says, 'Embodiments are the outcome and the effect of . . . a disciplining which results from the co-ordination of space, place and society by groups invested with power . . . such practices of power are constituted in the context of certain geographies – both imagined and material – around which discursive and practical alignment is constantly attempted' (p. 227). In the context of slightly different lines of argument, Thrift urges 'a *relational material-ism*' (p. 317) and Whatmore a '*materialist semiotics*' (p. 29).

There is, finally, a third argument which must be made here. If we bring together 'thinking in terms of relations' with the geographical ima-gination of our position as 'intellectuals' (that is, those in a powerful posi-tion in the business of representing the world – part of whose business, in other words, is imagined as 'representation') then further disruptions follow. Sarah Whatmore, for instance, stresses our inextricable situated-ness and its effect on the character (and the nature of the claims) of our own geographical imaginations. Here 'situatedness' refers not so much to the specificity of our positionings as inevitably particular intellectuals, but rather to the inevitable embeddedness of the practice itself. We can only think, or even 'represent', as part of our more general 'being in the world'. It is with this fundamental insight that she moves towards what she calls 'hybrid geographies'. Gillian Rose, too, wishes to challenge some of the certainties implied in the currently dominant imagination of the intellectual. She wants to work towards radically unstable notions of space, towards challenging 'the phallocentric prerogative of interpreta-tion' (p. 249), and to work around the limits of discourse.

Much of Nigel Thrift's contribution addresses these issues directly. He urges us to move from a 'building perspective' to a 'dwelling per-spective'; that is, away from a textualist imagination of the world in which 'representation' is somehow a separate layer outside and above 'the real' and where it is representation which comes to have priority and power. In its place he argues for a 'Non-representational theory . . . anchored in an irreducible ontology in which the world is made up of billions of . . . encounters, . . . consisting of multitudinous paths which intersect' (p. 302). This is an approach which tries to make more 'rela-tional' the very positioning of the *theorist in relation* to the world. It is, also, 'a very modest view of the role of theory which is intent on seeking *relational* rather than representational understandings' (p. 304). One implication, then, of some of the arguments made in the contribu-tions which follow is that a radical rethinking of the nature of the intel-lectual (the human geographer too) might also be placed on the agenda.

Locating the book

All of this raises the question of the necessary embeddedness of this volume itself. At the beginning of this chapter we referred to being a human geographer as a form of positionality. Moreover, a number of contributors to the book also try to deepen our notion of situatedness, in the sense of raising up for interrogation the way in which we may imagine our relation to the world. But there is one further element to this situatedness: this volume is 'human geography today' edited and written from within the Western First World. This is not a self-criticism, nor is it a characteristic which it would have been possible simply to change. There has been much cynicism recently expressed about Western academics' inclusion of a few gestural 'voices from the periphery'. (As also in the case of gender and sexual 'minorities', academics, like the middle class living in the inner city, can on occasions treat subordinated others as exotica.) And inclusion can mean an assumption of incorporation, much like the 'cannibalism' of which Gill Valentine writes, which will not put the effort in, or else is too quick in its desire to overcome differences, so that real alterity, the independence and autonomy (always of course themselves constructed 'in relation'), are erased. What is important is to recognize 'partiality' (situatedness in this sense), to take responsibility for it, and to recognize its implications. One of those is that the Western world and the dominant voices are not the only ones producing theory. David Slater makes a powerful case: that the recognition of our own situatedness means really recognizing the ability of 'the Rest', for instance, to 'theorize back' (p. 67) at the West. His argument touches on many elements of the discussion which we have already rehearsed. He posits that recent developments within the Western academy have 'frequently not been accompanied by a diversification or globalization of the *sources* of theoretical knowledge' and that this might be 'a serious handicap in our attempts to globalize the arenas of knowledge and understanding' (p. 79). Greater knowledge will by no means ensure agreement (just as – see the chapter by Doreen Massey – the exposure of our interrelatedness does not mean that the world suddenly becomes benign), but it might enable us 'to think seriously, as Western authors and social scientists, of our own position' (p. 80) and, through a recognition of our singularity in a wider interrelatedness, open up our own identities as agents of knowledge.

When we wrote the proposal for this volume, to send to potential contributors, we wrote in terms of 'something which has been called "an emancipatory geography"'. We already recognized, then, the limits of this formulation. A commitment to some form of liberatory emancipation (a term itself open to all kinds of interpretation from far left to far right of the political spectrum) does not in any way uniquely determine either one's theoretical approach or one's methodology. Relational thinking, querying binaries, recognizing specificity and bringing back nature and the body are all presented here, not on the grounds of containing some absolute eternal truth (a proposition which would anyway in most cases be thoroughly contradictory), but because of their ability to raise awkward, destabilizing questions of the hegemonic power structures of our times and places, and to lend weight to a variety of counter-discourses. Yet even that position is made more complex by the analyses in some of the contributions to this book. The hegemony includes ourselves; we too need to be destabilized; the relationship between politics and space, which is certainly integral, is about as complicated as it could possibly be. Doing human geography then, like Nigel Thrift's non-representational theory, is '*a practical means of going on*' (p. 304). It is also, necessarily, of the world and a part of making it; as such it carries both real responsibilities and creative potential.

References

Bhabha, H. (1994) *The Location of Culture*. London and New York, Routledge.

Fernández Retamar, R. (1989) *Caliban and Other Essays*. Minneapolis, University of Minnesota Press.

Game, A. (1995) 'Time, space, memory, with reference to Bachelard'. In M. Featherstone, S. Lash and R. Robertson (eds), *Global Modernities*. London, Sage, 192–208.

hooks, b. (1992) 'Eating the Other'. In *Black Looks: Race and Representation*. London, Turnaround, 21–39.

Mouffe, C. (1992) 'Feminism, citizenship, and radical democratic politics'. In Judith Butler and Joan Scott (eds), *Feminists Theorize the Political*. New York and London, Routledge, 369–84.

2

Hybrid Geographies: Rethinking the 'Human' in Human Geography

Sarah Whatmore

> This place
> we have not seen before
> these old woods
> your hands
> touching knowledge.
>
> Susan Griffin, 'Knowledge'

Introduction

The Enlightenment antinomy between nature and society marks a pervasive tension in the institutional configuration of scientific knowledge and authority including that of geography, not least through the discipline's complicity in the project of empire (Livingstone, 1992). But it is Margaret Fitzsimmons's critique of what she calls a 'peculiar silence on the question of nature' (1989: 106) which provides the most telling indictment of its implications for the more critical aspirations of contemporary human geography. In the pages of *Antipode*, she called the (then largely Marxist-inspired) community of 'radical' geographers to account for theorizing space without nature in all but a few isolated cases.[1] Fitzsimmons identified three contributory factors in their failure to 'come to grips with the theoretical problem of Nature' (1989: 107): the institutional separation of human and physical geographies, the ontological separation of nature and space in human geography, and the urban bias of the intellectual culture which shaped 'radical' concerns.

Critical human geography has since witnessed a reawakening of debate on 'the question of nature'. This has been animated by intellectual impulses which have broadened the horizons of 'critical' work beyond the compass of Marxism, most significantly through poststructuralist, feminist, post-colonial and environmentalist projects. Wider political and policy imperatives have added further impetus to interest in the environment on the research agendas of the social sciences (and humanities) at large. This mass trespass over the manicured lawns of natural science challenges the categorical cordon that has marked off the 'non-human world' and the grounds for understanding it. Yet, even as these energies put the importance of the question of nature for social science beyond dispute, so a new form of enclosure threatens with the proliferation of 'environmental' sub-disciplines such as environmental sociology (Hannigan, 1995), environmental anthropology (Descola and Palsson, 1996), environmental history (Bird, 1987) and environmental politics (Dobson and Lucardie, 1995).

Across the disciplinary spectrum a tendency to 'add nature in' to already entrenched constellations of 'critical' social science has produced an equally unhelpful cul-de-sac. This takes the form of a dogged impasse between versions of 'social constructionism', in which 'Nature' is treated as an artefact of the social imagination, and versions of 'natural realism', in which 'nature' consists of substantive entities and objective forces (Soper, 1995). The first of these positions is broadly associated with modes of critical enquiry labelled postmodern and linked with the so-called cultural turn in the social sciences, in which the question of nature rapidly becomes reformulated as an exclusively epistemological one about the 'socially constructed nature of scientific enquiry or technological enterprise' (Robertson et al., 1996: 2). Here, Nature is the always already crafted product of human interpretation. Critical analysis of this inescapably mediated Nature becomes fixed on the social hierarchies and discursive conventions and devices of Nature's inscription by (and in) landscape paintings, TV nature programmes, computer models and so on. Unsurprisingly, since an important strand of this critical effort has been focused on their story-telling powers and practices, such work has provoked outright hostility amongst the science establishment (Gross and Levitt, 1994).

More significantly for those laying claim to a 'critical' positionality, such work has been met with deep scepticism amongst environmental (Soulé and Lease, 1995) and social (Redclift and Benton, 1994) scientists, whose own stakes in this same intellectual territory and in projects of ecological and/or socialist salvation are founded, in different ways, on a 'crucial distinction ... between material processes and relations on the one hand and our understandings of, and communications about, those processes on the other' (Dickens, 1996: 83). Here, 'nature' in the raw can, and must, be recognized as ontologically separate from the 'Natures' of social representation in order to sustain the possibility of (and their own pretensions to) a singular analytic-diagnostic truth – an account of society's relationship with nature that uniquely corresponds to a real, objective world. In human geography these battle lines are variously rehearsed and interrogated in recent papers by Demeritt (1996), from a broadly poststructuralist perspective, and Gandy (1996), from a critical realist perspective.

There is undoubtedly a generous measure of caricature in this embattled depiction of the treatment of Nature/nature in social theory which serves primarily to reaffirm intellectual prejudices and identities. Only the most vulgar of 'postmodern' accounts (and there are some) suggest that the world is – to borrow Sheets-Johnstone's evocative phrase – 'the product of an immaculate linguistic conception' (1992: 46). Accounts that get lumped into the 'social constructionist' category are much more diverse than their detractors acknowledge (the textual emphasis of the deconstructionist current as against the performative emphasis of various theories of embodied practice, for example: see Conley, 1997). In most cases, some interval between the moments of 'reality' and 'representation' is sustained; it is just that it is deemed ineluctably opaque. Equally, only the crudest of 'natural realist' accounts (and again, there are some) refuse to recognize the contingency of knowledge claims about 'real-world' entities and processes. This label eclipses the richness of Marxist-inspired analysis (dialectical materialism, critical realism and political ecology to name a few: see Castree, 1995). It is just that such accounts share an inclination to exempt themselves from the representational moment, by variously claiming a privileged correspondence between concept and object, logic and process.

Ironically, this categorical insistence on an either/or, constructionist/ realist approach to the question of nature itself echoes the binary mode of thinking that sets up an opposition between 'the natural' and 'the social' as the absolute and only possibilities in a purified world of black and white. For all their loudly declared enmity, these analytic encampments are similarly premised on the acceptance, however unrecognized, of the *a priori* separation of nature and society. As Bruno Latour has put it:

> Critical explanation always began from the poles and headed toward the middle, which was first the separation point and then the conjunction point for opposing resources ... In this way the middle was simultaneously maintained and abolished, recognized and denied, specified and silenced ... How? ... By conceiving every hybrid as a mixture of two pure forms. (Latour, 1993: 77–8)

This same nature/society binary informs more everyday geographical imaginations and environmental sensibilities rehearsed in pervasive distinctions between 'built environments' (the social pole) and 'natural environments' (the natural pole), with hierarchies of human 'settlement' in between marking inverse gradations of social/natural presence and absence. From the conventions of cartographic colour coding to the protocols of land-use planning or of environmental designation, numerous professional and policy practices impress this binary imaginary upon the fabric of the world (Carter, 1996). With its celebration of 'wild(er)ness', configured as both species and places marked out precisely by their distance from humankind, much environmentalist rhetoric is also complicit in this purification of the spaces of society and nature (Cosgrove, 1990). As Tim Ingold has observed, 'Something [ ] must be wrong somewhere, if the only way to understand our own creative involvement in the world is by taking ourselves out of it' (1995a: 58).

Human geography thus finds itself at an important juncture in its critical engagement with the question of nature, in which neither the 'bracketing off' of an environmental sub-field common in other disciplines, nor the threadbare promise of a reintegration of physical and human geography, will suffice. Nor, in my view, does recourse to variants of dialectical reasoning centred on the ways in which nature and society interact provide a radical enough basis for critical enquiry (see, for example, Harvey, 1996). Far from challenging this *a priori* categorization of the things of the world, dialectics can be seen to raise its binary logic to the level of a contradiction and engine of history.[2] Rather, any critical engagement with the 'question of nature' must begin, as Donna Haraway argues, by building theories whose 'geometries, paradigms and logics break out of binaries . . . and nature/culture modes of any kind' (1991: 129). This, of course, is more easily said than done.

Geographers have already taken up the challenge of exploring what Taussig has called the 'desperate places' in between the 'real' and the 'ideal', the 'natural' and the 'social', the 'objective' and the 'subjective', the 'human' and the 'non-human' (1933: xvii). Examples range from studies of urban wildlife (Wolch et al., 1995) and technological 'subjects' (Bingham, 1996) to computer-simulated environments (Light, 1997) and domestication (Anderson, 1997). These forays share, I suggest, a concern to re-cognize the 'human' in 'human geography' and thereby to signal a rather different agenda for critical geographical thinking about the question of nature, which, in various ways, seeks 'to accommodate the nonhumans in the fabric of our society' (Latour, in Crawford, 1993: 262). This 'hybrid' geographical enterprise, as I have called it in the chapter title, is concerned with studying the *living* rather than abstract spaces of social life, configured by numerous, interconnected agents – variously composed of biological, mechanical and habitual properties and collective capacities – within which people are differently and plurally articulated.

Such an agenda attunes geography to a broader chorus of 'critical' voices in the social sciences searching for ways out of the impasse between 'constructionist' and 'realist' accounts of 'nature'. The kinds of hybrid space being opened up include the 'virtual ecologies' of computer simulation (Wark, 1994), the 'artefactual nature' of Oncomouse (Haraway, 1997) and the 'quasi-objects' which bring socio-technologies to life (Serres and Latour, 1995). These efforts are tentative and unco-ordinated but can be traced through a broad spectrum of contemporary social theory, ranging from feminist challenges to scientific objectivity (such as Haraway, 1991) to rethinking the importance of embodiment amongst cognitive scientists (such as Varela et al., 1991). Amidst these unsteady glimmerings, Katherine Hayles suggests that 'it is possible to glimpse ... the shape of an answer ... [in] a common emphasis on interaction and positionality' (Hayles, 1995: 43). The opening epigraph offers one such glimpse of a non-binary world that signals many of the themes and ideas that follow, but in language more redolent of the sensory texture of what this might mean than the vernacular of social science seems able to approach. In the next section I sketch out what I see as some key dimensions of a hybrid geography which recognizes agency as a relational achievement, involving the creative presence of organic beings, technological devices and discursive codes, as well as people, in the fabrics of everyday living. I then focus on the spatial implications of this kind of approach, illustrated through a consideration of contemporary (re)configurings of wildlife – a category of 'non-humans' most thoroughly outcast from the conventional compass of social life, social science and human geography.

From social actors to actant networks

Through exclusively social contracts, we have abandoned the bond that connects us to the world ... What language do the things of the world speak that we might come to an understanding of them contractually? ... In fact, the Earth speaks to us in terms of forces, bonds and interactions ... each of the partners in symbiosis thus owes [   ] life to the other, on pain of death.

Michel Serres, *The Natural Contract*

The relational conception of social life that I want to outline here takes up the 'common emphases' on positionality and interaction identified by Hayles amongst the disparate theoretical efforts to disrupt the binary terms in which the question of nature has been posed. I take these emphases to imply an epistemological insistence on the situatedness of knowledge and a 'modest' ontological stance rooted in the everyday practice or performance of *ordering*, as against some abstract order attributed to a colossal logos outside or above the social fray.[3] At its most basic then, the hybrid geography that I am proposing implies a radically different understanding of *social agency* in the senses both that agency is decentred, a 'precarious achievement' (Law, 1994: 101) spun between social actors rather than a manifestation of unitary intent, and that it is decoupled from the subject/object binary so that, as Nigel Thrift has put it, 'the "material" and the "social" intertwine and interact in all manner of promiscuous combinations' (1996: 24).

My elaboration of these themes draws particularly on the work of Michel Callon, Bruno Latour, John Law, Michel Serres and others which goes under the label of actor (or actant) network theory (ANT) and is beginning to make a mark on geography (for a review see Murdoch, 1997). It also reflects a strong feminist strand of work on science, technology and the body which Haraway has recently termed 'a lumpy community of modest witnesses' (1997: 268), concerned with 'the interactions of humans and non-humans in the distributed networks of technoscience' (1997: 141). I have explored the ethical dimensions of a relational understanding elsewhere (Whatmore, 1997). Here I want to emphasize three interwoven aspects of such an understanding – the processes and properties of hybridity, collectivity, and corporeality – and their implications for reconfiguring the purified spaces of 'nature' and 'society' as fluid socio-material networkings.

The concept of hybridity as it is deployed by writers like Latour and Haraway seeks to implode the object/subject binary that underlies the modern antinomy between nature and society and to recognize the agency of 'non-human' actants – acknowledging their presence in the social fabric and exploring ways of making it register in the vocabularies of social analysis. For ANT the erasure of 'non-human' agency is an effect of particular, and partial, configurations of social practice and discourse rather than a categorical presumption. This decoupling of human/agency is denoted by the (variable) use of the term 'actant', as distinct from the more conventional 'actor', signalling a methodological commitment to treating any distributions of authority and intentionality amongst actants as practical achievements to be elucidated (Callon and Law, 1995: 490).

Actant networks then mobilize, and are constituted by, a multiplicity of different agents, or 'actants', human and non-human, technological and textual, organic and (geo)physical, which hold each other in position. This hybridized conception of agency admits states of being which fall somewhere between the passive objects of human will and imagination which litter the social sciences, and the autonomous external forces favoured in natural science accounts. Latour follows Serres in designating these in-between states of being as 'quasi-objects', which are as 'real as nature, narrated as discourse, collective as society [and] existential as being' (1993: 89). An actant network is thus simultaneously an assemblage of actants, whose activities are constituted in and through their connectivities with heterogeneous others, and a network that performs as a more or less durable (extensive in time) and more or less long (extensive in space) mode of ordering amongst its constituent parts. Crucially, in terms of the modest ontological stance of ANT, such modes of ordering, however extensive their reach, are neither as obdurate as a social 'structure' nor as volatile as a social 'actor's' change of mind. No more, and no less, than their performance, they represent 'patterns or regularities that may be imputed to the particulars that make up the recursive and generative networks of the social. They are nowhere else. They do not drive those networks. They aren't outside them' (Law, 1994: 83).

This extension of the compass of social agency beyond the human/subject, through the notion of hybridity, has two immediate corollaries for the elaboration of a relational conception of social life. One concerns the implications of a decentred notion of agency or, in terms of ANT, the inherently collective nature of networking – what Callon and Law (1995) call the 'hybrid collectif'. The other pursues the implicit break with the logocentric presumption that agency is an exclusively human attribute, predicated on particular cognitive and linguistic competences, a move associated with what Thrift calls 'non-representational' theories of the social (chapter 15, this volume). Each requires some brief elaboration.

The notion of the hybrid collectif implodes the inside/outside binary which discerns social agency as an internal property of discrete, unitary individuals (including corporate individuals). Agency is reconfigured as a relational effect generated by a network of heterogeneous, interacting components whose activity is constituted in the networks of which they form a part (Law and Mol, 1995: 277). 'Non-human' agents are vital to this conception of a network's collective capacity to act 'because they attach us to one another, because they circulate in our hands and define our social bond by their very circulation' (Latour, 1993: 89). Not to be confused with the more established notion of a social collectivity (that is, an already existing ensemble of people acting in concert), the whole point of speaking of a 'collectif', as Callon and Law (1995) insist, is that it erodes the divisions and distinctions that are taken to reside in the order of things – a world of purified monads and the dualisms that keep them segregated. From this perspective 'the inside-and-outside [becomes] an active category, created by the actors themselves not [one] already defined' (Latour in Crawford, 1993: 257).

How then is the social 'agency' of the hybrid collectif to be understood? The answer provided by Callon and Law is that agency in ANT is an:

> effect [   ] generated in configurations of different materials . . . [that] also . . . take the form of attributions . . . which localise agency as singularity – usually . . . in the form of human bodies. Attributions which endow one part of the configuration with the status of prime mover. Attributions which efface the other entities and relations in the collectif or consign these to a supporting and infrastructural role. (1995: 503)

In other words, the property of collectivity does not preclude inequality (non-equivalence) amongst heterogeneous actants but rather insists that the distribution of power within a network can only be understood as a relational effect, conditioning the performance of any particular actant (including humans). This represents the point of greatest tension between ANT and conventional social theories: a refusal to equate agency (the capacity to act or to have effects) with intentionality, premised on narrow linguistic competences. The agency of the hybrid collectif is a bold attempt to shift the weight of this logocentric bias to recognize other, material, forms of signification, by which the specific capacities and properties of entities from X-rays to viruses make their presence felt. This brings us to the third dimension of relationality which, for the sake of abbreviation, I have referred to as corporeality.

The broader significance of the body in social theory has been associated with the elaboration of various theories of practice which reassert, against the lexical cast of the cultural turn, the corporeal properties that condition the very capacities of cognition and communication that are the hallmark of conventional notions of social (human) agency.[4] In ANT, effort has focused on driving 'a wedge between re-presentation and language' (Callon and Law, 1995: 501) by extending the register of semiotics beyond its traditional concern with signification as linguistic ordering, to all kinds of un-speakable 'message bearers' and material processes of inscription, such as technical devices, instruments and graphics, and bodily capacities, habits and skills (Serres, 1995b). This *materialist semiotics* has two important implications for the kind of relational understanding of social life that I am advancing. On the one hand, it reinforces the hybrid and collective dimensions of this understanding by re-embodying human *being*, recalling our place as organisms and acknowledging our varied and changing embeddedness in the material properties and presences of diverse others (Ingold, 1995b). On the other hand, it disrupts the binary construction of 'reality' and 'representation' which, as I suggested earlier, has dogged discussion of the question of nature.

The privileging of language as a precondition and hallmark of social agency rests on and reproduces a worn-out distinction between language and the world, in which the world is treated as an external referent and language as a medium which represents 'it' in a more or less transparent manner (Callon and Law, 1995: 499). To admit that the relationship is much more opaque and unruly does *not* mean that there is nothing beyond the text; that nothing else matters. Rather it is to refuse the Cartesian designification of nature which simultaneously denies 'animals any linguistic capacities at all and [defines] language strictly as the reflection of the conscious mind' (Senior, 1997: 67). Instead of reality, on the one hand, and a representation, on the other, ANT recognizes chains of translation of varying kinds and lengths which weave sound, vision, gesture and scent through all manner of bodies, elements, instruments and artefacts – so that the distinction between being present and being represented no longer exhausts, or makes sense of, the compass and possibility of social conduct (Latour, 1994).

The relational understanding of social life that I am working towards, as will by now be apparent, involves no small imaginative shift, but rather a series of manoeuvres each of which disconcerts the categorical infrastructure on which the edifice of conventional social theories is built, and which has become insinuated in less formal ways of making sense of 'who' (what) constitutes our social worlds. My own sense of the theoretical space opened up by these manoeuvres is at best tentative. And, like Marilyn Strathern (1996), I do not think that one can, or ought to, look to ANT to provide some sort of ready-made compass. None the less, there are useful beginnings here for journeys out of the impoverished wor(l)d of N/nature, which make it possible to explore the ways in which the entities, capacities and processes conventionally preassigned to the spheres of the 'natural' and the 'social' are mutually conditioned and constituted in the everyday business of *living* in the world. These manoeuvres do not preclude the analytical possibility of still obtaining nature and society as an outcome of specific modes of ordering (networkings), but they do insist that 'there is no longer any reason to limit the ontological varieties that matter to two ... At last the middle kingdom [can be] represented' (Latour, 1993: 79).

Theoretical ventures in this vein must confront, and cannot succeed without disrupting, the spatial configurations of the nature/society binary that litter contemporary environmental thinking and practice. These configurations inhere in the boundaries, at once real and imagined, erected to keep the things of 'nature' and of 'society' in their proper place. Even Latour's metaphor of the 'middle kingdom', for example, is haunted by the territorial grammar that pervades these geometric habits of mind. Re-cognizing nature not as 'a physical place to which one can go' (Haraway, 1992: 66) but as an active, changeable presence that is always already in our midst challenges spatial, as well as, social (pre)dispositions.

Geographies in/of motion

Wildness (as opposed to wilderness) can be found anywhere: in the seemingly tame fields and woodlots of Massachusetts, in the cracks of a Manhattan sidewalk, even in the cells of our own bodies.

W. Cronon, *Uncommon Ground*

The analytic device of the network, freighted with the hybrid, collective and corporeal properties that I have outlined, has immense significance for (re)imagining the geographies of social life. Thus far, geographers have focused on its implications for understanding globalization (Thrift, 1995; Whatmore and Thorne, 1997), economic geographies (Murdoch, 1995; Thrift and Olds, 1996), and the spaces of socio-technologies (Bingham, 1996; Hinchliffe, 1996). All these efforts seek to disrupt the geometric configuration of the world as a single grid-like surface – a *tabula rasa* which invites the inscription of general theoretical claims as omnipresent, uni-versal rationalities. In contrast, they elaborate a *topological* spatial imagination, emphasizing the *simultaneity* of multiple and partial space-time configurations of social life, and the *situatedness* of social institutions, processes and knowledges as always contextual, tentative and incomplete, however long their reach (Thrift, 1995).

This fluid geographical vocabulary betokens a shift in analytical emphasis from reiterating fixed surfaces to tracing points of connection and lines of flow (Mol and Law, 1994). This means not ignoring the effects of established contours and boundaries that mark the social landscape but, rather, recognizing that these spatial parameters inhere in a host of socio-technical practices – such as property, sovereignty and identity – that are always in the making, not in some *a priori* order of things. The significance of this shift is that it unsettles any account which is inclined to render messy, fragile networks as slick, consolidated totalities – like science, capitalism or the state – and recovers a myriad of life-size orderings overshadowed by their heroics (see Gibson-Graham, 1996).

In the above quotation, the environmental historian William Cronon signals some of the implications of this 'topological' imaginary for the question of 'nature' which I want to take up in this section. Playing on Thoreau's famous dictum 'in Wild[er]ness is the preservation of the world', he highlights the significance of geography to discerning the world in binary terms. Just as nature tends to be mapped onto spaces designated 'rural' so wildlife, the embodiment of a purified nature, is associated with those most rarefied of spaces designated 'wilderness'. This co-incidence between 'wild' plants and animals (species) and the 'wild' spaces they inhabit (habitats) pervades Western environmental sensibilities.

It is powerfully evoked, for example, in the protocols of 'global environmental management' which police the place of nature by means of territorial archetypes – like biodiversity reserves – that enact a scientific blueprint of who and what should live there (McNeely et al., 1990). But it is a coincidence that is no less resonant in the political dramatics of radical environmental groups like EarthFirst! or Greenpeace, which reinforce the place of nature by means of iconographic landscapes – like 'the rainforest' – that are framed by/as their televised sites of struggle (Foreman, 1991). Ignorant of their ephemeral status as 'representations', such imagined spaces all too readily become flesh as heterogeneous communities are purified in their name through the sometimes violent removal of people, animals and plants that find themselves on the wrong side of the wire. The ethnic minority Karen people in southern Burma are even now being forcibly ejected by the military government from their traditional lands to make way for the million-hectare Myinmoletkat 'Biosphere' Reserve.[5] In Britain, the ruddy duck recently found itself the target of a bizarre alliance of ornithological and nature conservation agencies intent on culling (that is, killing) its insurgent population here, in order to preserve the genetic purity and species integrity of the 'indigenous' European whiteheaded duck from the ruddy duck's 'aggressive' mating habits (Lawson, 1997). Accommodating non-humans in the fabric of social life requires more intimate, lively and promiscuous geographies than these quarantined fragments of a too precious nature.

The hybrid geographical enterprise that I am proposing unsettles this glib co-incidence of the things/spaces of nature by focusing critical energies closer to home. I cannot imagine, still less claim to know, where all the currents of such geographies of wildlife might lead. But their destination is not, as some would have it, yet another brave new world emerging perfectly formed from the engine of history (or capitalism or modernity) – a 'third nature' of 'cyborg ecologies' forged in the 'machinic totality' of 'contemporary global capitalism' in which *everything* is caught up (Luke, 1996: 11). Rather, such geographies alert us to a world of commotion in which the sites, tracks and contours of social life are constantly in the making through networks of actants-in-relation that are at once local and global, natural and cultural, and always more than human.

In contrast to the universal ambitions of 'third nature' and its forebears, the hybrid geographies that I have in mind are inescapably situated. Their own part in the networks they describe is to be acknowledged, rather than effaced, in terms both of the imprint of researchers and of the words and instruments that extend their ordering presence in time/space (Law, 1994). Refusing any vantage point that purports to take in the world at a glance, they are more modest in the claims they can, and want to, make and, by the same token, are more attendant to the energies of those they make claims about. Conceived of topologically, wildlife is no longer fixed at a distance but emerges within the routine interweavings of people, organisms, elements and machines as these configure the partial, plural and sometimes overlapping time/spaces of everyday living. These humdrum spaces include, amongst others, the mutable fabric of embodiment, the ordinary motions of inhabitation, and the mediating devices that make 'us' present even in 'our' absence.

In place of the rigid contours of the flat maps and species inventories of conservation science, or the objectifying gaze of landscape studies, a topology of wildlife is a much more fluid beast in at least three senses. The first of these senses concerns the *spaces of embodiment*. The mutability of organisms (including humans), in terms of their intrinsic organization and morphological plasticity (Goodwin, 1988), has been somewhat overshadowed by the heady talk of their malleability in the socio-technical networks of genetic engineering; organ transplantation and the like. Yet at the very heart of these artefactual worlds we are reminded by the proliferation of changeling viruses, mutant cells (dis)figuring corporeal stability, and the startling appearance of pink and purple frogs in suburban garden ponds that we are not the only agents in their fabrication.

The second sense of fluidity has to do with the *spaces of motion*. Animals (including humans) and, rather less obviously, plants lead mobile lives – on scales that vary from the Lilliputian travels of a dung beetle to the global navigations of migrating whales and birds. Their mobilities are relational achievements – plant seeds journeying in the bellies of animals; the learning of spatial markers and seasonal routines within creature communities. Moreover, plants and animals have been caught up in socio-technical networks with 'humans' for some 30,000 years, before we recognized ourselves as *Homo sapiens* (Ingold, 1995b). In other words, the categorical boundaries between the wild and the cultivated that we now insist on were unsettled long before the unravelling of DNA. Efforts like the UN Convention on Biological Diversity to fix their place in the world as 'indigenous species' within 'natural habitats' are a no less political regulation of mobile lives than the paraphernalia of passports and border controls.

The third sense in which a topological rendition of wildlife is more fluid concerns the *spaces of relation*. 'Wild' animals and plants whose designation depends on their being forever somewhere else find their place in the world less than secure. The radio collars and tags which adorn the remotest parts of the animal kingdom, no less than their daily exhibition in the wildlife documentaries that occupy TV screens in millions of homes around the world, disturb the geometry of distance and proximity. In place of a straight line from here to there, or a relation rooted in the same spot, the wild and the domestic get swept up in the volatile eddies and flows of socio-technical networks that bring people, living organisms and machines together in new and particular ways (Clark, 1997). Against the technological hyperbole of 'third nature', the novelty of these networks is the *ways* in which they reconfigure humans/animals/artefacts, not that they are unprecedented in actively unsettling these categories.

Conclusion

What happens if we begin from the premise not that we know reality because we are separate from it (traditional objectivity), but that we can know the world because we are connected with it? (Hayles, 1995: 48)

What happens, I have tried to suggest, is an upheaval in the binary terms in which the question of nature has been posed and a recognition of the intimate, sensible and hectic bonds through which people, organisms, machines and elements make and hold their shape in relation to each other in the business of everyday living. This upheaval implicates *geographical* imaginations and practices both in the purifying logic which, like 'ethnic cleansing', fragments living fabrics of association and designates the proper places of 'nature' and 'society', and in the promise of its refusal. That refusal does not lead to a world in which the properties and things ascribed to nature have been comprehensively extinguished by, or absorbed within, the compass of those ascribed to human society. Rather, it requires an acceptance of the world as it is – an always already inhabited achievement of 'heterogenous social encounters, where all of the actors are not human and all of the humans are not "us" however defined' (Haraway, 1992: 67).

Working through the relational conception of social life that I am proposing, geographically, means (amongst other things) looking again at the spatial organization and ethical contours of agency and power within hybrid networks. Their conventional attribution, theoretically and methodologically, to a single (and always human) epicentre – the faceless corporation, scientific laboratory or regulatory authority – has to be destabilized. One aspect of doing this is to re-cognize such 'power-houses' as networks in themselves – fragile achievements of actants-in-relation fraught with daily conflicts, illnesses, misunderstandings, technical glitches and all manner of breakdowns – whose efficacy depends on a host of more diffuse alignments of practices and properties that are not of their ordering. This strategy at least disperses attention through the simultaneous performances of social competences and affordances at different points in a network, and registers the mass of currents rather than single line of force that give it shape (Whatmore and Thorne, 1997). In these terms, the reach and durability of any network performance is less an attribute of an individual's, or organization's, inherent forcefulness than an interactional effect.

As I hope I have made clear, the hybrid geographical enterprise that I have in mind shares little with the totalizing incarnations of a 'third nature' which have begun to appear in geographical writing and elsewhere. Hybrid geographies cannot be other than plural and partial, if they are not to repeat the error of trying to roll the life worlds and inhabited spaces of radically different kinds of subject into one, by virtue of some unacknowledged vantage point outside all and any of them. Rather than passing judgement on a nature that is always at a distance, such geographies have to be situated in terms of the hybrid networks which we (their authors) and they (as portable inscriptions of various kinds) participate in. Finally, and this is harder to put into words, such geographies must strive to find ways of exploring and expressing the kinds of sensible and relational knowledge of these hybrid worlds as pungently as the kind of writing quoted at the start of this paper. This is perhaps the greatest challenge for those of us trained as social scientists: to overhaul our repertoire of methods and poetics in ways that admit and register the creative presence of creatures and devices amongst us, and the animal sensibilities of our diverse human being.

Acknowledgements

This chapter owes much to shared intellectual adventures with colleagues and friends in the Geography Department at Bristol University – notably Lorraine Thorne, Nigel Thrift and Nick Bingham – and elsewhere, particularly Jon Murdoch. I am grateful to Doreen Massey and Philip Sarre for their much-needed encouragement with a piece that I have found challenging to write. The wildlife theme which illustrates some of the key points is the subject of a more sustained research effort in a project with Lorraine Thorne on 'Spatial formations of wildlife exchange', funded by ESRC (award no. R000222113).

Notes

1 The key exception identified by Fitzsimmons was the spate of writings on the transition from first to second nature by Marxist geographers in the late 1970s and early 1980s, most notably Neil Smith's *Uneven Development* (1984) and the special issue of *Antipode* on 'Natural resources and environment' edited by Dick Walker (1979).

2 For a critique of dialectical analysis see Castree (1996) on Harvey's treatment of nature.

3 The 'actant' variant of this 'modest' ontology as it is manifest in actor or actant network theory (ANT: see Callon and Latour, 1981) is reminiscent of Deleuze and Guattari's (1987) 'rhizome' metaphor. Latour comments directly on this link in an interview with Crawford (1993: 262). The description of such ontological stances as 'modest' is first, and best, made by John Law (1994).

4 Of course the cognitive and linguistic competences that conventionally define the fully fledged subject and social actor are patriarchal constructs from which various categories of 'humans' have been, and are still being, excluded. Moreover, the status of these competences as the distinguishing mark of 'humanity' is troubled by the comparable skills of other classes of animals (notably, primates and cetaceous mammals) and broader reassessments of animal cognition (see Ingold, 1988; Noske, 1989).

5 Leading international conservation agencies, including the WWF-UK, the Wildlife Conservation Society in New York and the Washington-based Smithsonian Institute, lent their scientific expertise and credentials to the designation of the Myinmoletkat Reserve and continue to pursue research and conservation programmes there on 'endangered' species like the Sumatran rhinoceros and tiger (*Observer*, 23 March 1997).

References

Anderson, K. (1997) 'A walk on the wild side: a critical geography of domestication'. *Progress in Human Geography*, 21/4: 463–85.

Bingham, N. (1996) 'Object-ions: from technological determinism towards geographies of relations'. *Society and Space*, 14/6: 635–57.

Bird, E. (1987) 'The social construction of nature: theoretical approaches to the history of environmental problems'. *Environmental Review*, 11: 255–64.

Callon, M. and B. Latour (1981) 'Unscrewing the big leviathan'. In K. Knorr-Cetina and A. Cicourel (eds), *Advances in Social Theory and Methodology*. London, Routledge and Kegan Paul, 83–103.

Callon, M. and J. Law (1995) 'Agency and the hybrid collectif'. *South Atlantic Quarterly*, 94/2: 481–507.

Carter, P. (1996) *The Lie of the Land*. London, Faber and Faber.

Castree, N. (1995) 'The nature of produced nature: materiality and knowledge construction in Marxism'. *Antipode*, 27/1: 12–48.

Castree, N. (1996) 'Birds, mice and geography: Marxisms and dialectics'. *Transactions of the Institute of British Geographers*, 21/2: 342–62.

Clark, N. (1997) 'Panic ecology. Nature in the age of superconductivity'. *Theory, Culture and Society*, 14/1: 77–96.

Conley, V. (1997) *Ecopolitics: The environment in Poststructuralist Thought*. London, Routledge.

Cosgrove, D. (1990) 'Environmental thought and action: pre-modern and post-modern'. *Transactions of the Institute of British Geographers*, 15/3: 344–58.

Crawford, T. (1993) 'An interview with Bruno Latour'. *Configurations*, 1/2: 247–68.

Cronon, W. (ed.) (1995) *Uncommon ground: Towards Reinventing Nature*. New York, W.W. Norton.

Deleuze, G. and F. Guattari (1987) (English translation). *A Thousand Plateaus*. London, Athlone Press.

Demeritt, D. (1996) 'Social theory and the reconstruction of science and geography'. *Transactions of the Institute of British Geographers*, 21/3: 484–503.

Descola, P. and G. Palsson (eds) (1996) *Nature and Society: Anthropological Perspectives*. London, Routledge.

Dickens, P. (1996) *Reconstructing Nature*. London, Routledge.

Dobson, A. and D. Lucardie (eds) (1995) *The Politics of Nature*. London, Routledge.

Fitzsimmons, M. (1989) 'The matter of nature'. *Antipode*, 21/2: 106–20.

Foreman, D. (1991) *Confessions of an Eco-Warrior*. New York, Harmony Books.

Gandy, M. (1996) 'Crumbling land: the postmodernity debate and the analysis of environmental problems'. *Progress in Human Geography*, 20/1: 23–40.

Gibson-Graham, J.K. (1996) *The End of Capitalism (As We Knew It)*. Oxford, Blackwell.

Goodwin, B. (1988) 'Organisms and minds: the dialectics of the animal–human interface in biology'. In T. Ingold (ed.), *What Is an Animal?* London, Allen and Unwin, 100–9.

Griffin, S. (1987) 'Knowledge'. In *Unremembered Country*. Port Townsend, Copper Canyon, 22–5.

Gross, P. and N. Levitt (1994) *Higher Superstition: The Academic Left and its Quarrels with Science*. Baltimore, Johns Hopkins University Press.

38   Sarah Whatmore

Hannigan, J. (1995) *Environmental Sociology*. London, Routledge.
Haraway, D. (1991) 'Situated knowledges: the science question in feminism and the privilege of partial perspective'. In *Simians, Cyborgs and Women: The Reinvention of Nature*. San Francisco, Free Association Books, 183–202.
Haraway, D. (1992) 'Otherworldly conversations; terran topics; local terms'. *Science as Culture*, 3/1: 64–98.
Haraway, D. (1997) *Modest Witness@Second Millennium. FemaleMan meets OncoMouse*. London, Routledge.
Harvey, D. (1996) *Justice, Nature and the Geography of Difference*. Oxford, Blackwell.
Hayles, N.K. (1995) 'Searching for common ground'. In M. Soulé and G. Lease (eds), *Reinventing nature? Responses to Postmodern Deconstruction*. Washington DC, Island Press, 47–64.
Hinchliffe, S. (1996) 'Technology, power and space'. *Society and Space*, 14/6: 659–82.
Ingold, T. (1988) 'The animal in the study of humanity'. In T. Ingold (ed.), *What Is an Animal?* London, Allen and Unwin, 84–99.
Ingold, T. (1995a) 'Building, dwelling, living: how animals and people make themselves at home in the world'. In M. Strathern (ed.), *Shifting Contexts. Transformations in Anthropological Knowledge*. London, Routledge, 57–80.
Ingold, T. (1995b) ' "People like us": the concept of the anatomically modern human'. *Cultural Dynamics*, 7/2: 187–214.
Latour, B. (1993) *We Have Never Been Modern*. Brighton, Harvester Wheatsheaf.
Latour, B. (1994) 'Pragmatologies'. *American Behavioural Scientist*, 37/6: 791–808.
Law, J. (1994) *Organising Modernity*. Oxford, Blackwell.
Law, J. and A. Mol (1995) 'Notes on materiality and sociality'. *Sociological Review*, 42/3: 274–94.
Lawson, T. (1997) 'Brent duck'. *Ecos*, 17: 27–34.
Light, J. (1997) 'The changing nature of nature'. *Ecumene*, 4/2: 181–95.
Livingstone, D. (1992) *The Geographical Tradition*. Oxford, Blackwell.
Luke, T. (1996) 'Liberal society and cyborg subjectivity: the politics of environments, bodies, and nature'. *Alternatives*, 21: 1–30.
McNeely, J., K. Miller, W. Reid, R. Mittermeier and T. Werner (1990) *Conserving the World's Biodiversity*. Geneva, IUCN.
Mol, A. and J. Law (1994) 'Regions, networks and fluids: anaemia and social topology'. *Social Studies of Science*, 24: 641–71.
Murdoch, J. (1995) 'Actor-networks and the evolution of economic forms: combining description and explanation in theories of regulation, flexible specialisation and networks'. *Environment and Planning A*, 27/5: 731–57.
Murdoch, J. (1997) 'Towards a geography of heterogenous associations'. *Progress in Human Geography*, 21/3: 321–37.
Noske, B. (1989) *Humans and Other Animals: Beyond the Boundaries of Anthropology*. London, Pluto.
Redclift, M. and T. Benton (eds) (1994) *Social Theory and the Global Environment*. London, Routledge.

Robertson, G., M. Mash, L. Tickner, J. Bird, B. Curtis and T. Putnam (eds) (1996) *FutureNatural: Nature, Science, Culture*. London, Routledge.

Senior, M. (1997) ' "When the beasts spoke": animal speech and classical reason in Descartes and La Fontaine'. In J. Ham and M. Senior (eds), *Animal Acts: Configuring the Human in Western History*. London, Routledge, 61–84.

Serres, M. (1995a) *The Natural Contract* (trans. E. MacArther and W. Paulson). Ann Arbor, University of Michigan Press.

Serres, M. (1995b) *Angels: A Modern Myth*. Paris, Flammarion.

Serres, M. and B. Latour (1995) *Conversations on Science, Culture and Time* (trans. R. Lapidus). Ann Arbor, University of Michigan Press.

Sheets-Johnstone, M. (1992) 'Corporeal archetypes and power: preliminary clarifications and considerations of sex'. *Hypatia*, 7/3: 39–76.

Smith, N. (1984) *Uneven Development*. Oxford, Blackwell.

Soper, K. (1995) *What is Nature?*. Oxford, Blackwell.

Soulé, M. and G. Lease (eds) (1995) *Reinventing Nature? Responses to Postmodern Deconstruction*. Washington DC, Island Press.

Strathern, M. (1996) 'Cutting the network'. *Journal of the Royal Anthropological Institute* (n.s.), 2: 517–35.

Taussig, M. (1993) *Mimesis and Alterity*. London, Routledge.

Thrift, N. (1995) 'A hyperactive world'. In R. Johnston, P. Taylor and M. Watts (eds), *Geographies of Global Change*. Oxford, Blackwell, 18–35.

Thrift, N. (1996) *Spatial Formations*. London, Sage.

Thrift, N. and K. Olds (1996) 'Refiguring the economic in economic geography'. *Progress in Human Geography*, 20/3: 311–37.

Varela, F., E. Thompson and E. Rosch (1991) *The Embodied Mind*. Cambridge MA, MIT Press.

Walker, R. (ed.) (1979) 'Natural resources and environment'. Special issue of *Antipode*, 11/2.

Wark, M. (1994) 'Third nature'. *Cultural Studies*, 8/1: 115–32.

Whatmore, S. (1997) 'Dissecting the autonomous self: hybrid cartographies for a relational ethics'. *Society and Space*, 15/1: 37–53.

Whatmore, S. and L. Thorne (1997) 'Nourishing networks: alternative geographies of food'. In D. Goodman and M. Watts (eds), *Globalising Food: Agrarian Questions and Global Restructuring*. London, Routledge, 287–304.

Wolch, J., K. Wesk and T. Gaines (1995) 'Transpecies urban theory'. *Society and Space*, 13/4: 735–60.

Part II
Imaginative Geographies

Introduction

With the publication in 1978 of Edward Said's pathbreaking text *Orientalism*, the term 'imaginative geography' has taken on a life of its own in geographical writings. It is fair to say that the imaginary as a form of awareness, as a knowledge that does not owe its place simply to the constitution of reason, now occupies a critical role within geographical understanding. It is no longer a devalorized mode of understanding which somehow falls down or buckles at the first hurdle of reason or objective truth. Much of this, of course, is to do with the widespread recognition of the uncertainties of knowledge and their partial character. Asserted spatial truths and knowledges are little more than that: claims to something which is always less than universal or absolute. Within geography, however, this recognition has opened up a particularly rich seam of understanding around the nature of geographical knowledges and their partiality. Why, for instance, certain groups are able to lay claim to particular territories and the spaces of others, and indeed why they may actually feel entitled to do so, owes much to the authority vested in their imaginative stories, descriptions and organizing views. But there is more to the imaginary as a form of knowledge than simply a series of representations, as each of the chapters in this part fully demonstrates.

Perhaps the first aspect to note about the imaginary as a form of geographical knowledge is that it does not amount to a licence to endorse fanciful representations of place or to accept without reflection the boundaries drawn by one person in relation to others. Imaginary geographies are not cursory or fleeting representations in the sense that they are conjured up on a Tuesday and disposed of for something better on a Wednesday. Imaginative geographies are both more elaborate and durable than that. Above all, they draw their robustness from their ability to make it difficult to see or make sense of things in ways other than that represented. There is an apparent obviousness about the way in which, for example, a distant landscape, or the peoples of a close territory, or a particular culinary culture are represented which makes it difficult to contest.

A second aspect to note about the imaginary in relation to the above is that without the power and authority which uses geography both to moralize and to legitimize a particular world view, the confidence of such claims would be severely weakened. Knowledge as a form of power in this instance is precisely what enables some groups, say in the US, to display at one and the same time a familiarity with and a distance from peoples on the other side of the globe and to pass judgements on their actions and lifestyles. Whether it be a 'taken-for-granted' stock of knowledges at the everyday level or the exercise of a geopolitical imagination distributed through scholarly texts and periodicals, narratives and histories, film or various forms of state-sponsored literature, the power of these forms of knowledge lies not only in their creation, but also in their ability to represent what *is* without provoking disbelief.

Geographers have chosen to interpret and to work with these two aspects of imaginative geographies in more or less tight and more or less experiential ways. At one end of the spectrum, there has been the application of power, knowledge and geography through the various discursive practices which shed light on the grids and codes that project a sense of what is 'our' space and what is 'theirs', for example, and who belongs and who does not. The regularity and the authority of the distinctions drawn are similar in this respect to the firm lines drawn between nature and society in many of the situations discussed in the previous chapter. The Foucauldian influence is never far away from this interpretation.

At the looser end of the spectrum, a more social constructionist interpretation has been employed. Moving away from the big geopolitical pictures of nations, territories and states, the immediate qualities which ground our experience and shape our thinking in ways that intuitively make sense produce a rather different set of imaginative geographies. These are by no means the product of a 'local' imagination or less elaborate in their construction, but they are less monumental in form. They take the form of situations and knowledges where, for example, the dramatization of distance between people or the proximity of relationships and the connections drawn can only be made sense of through a restricted number of meanings. It becomes difficult to imagine them in any other way than that represented. A string of normalizing practices and judgements comes into play which meshes with what 'we already know' and makes it difficult to think outside of them.

The stress here, as before, is upon the difficulty of making sense of the world in ways other than those given to us. For it is always possible to think through such imaginary constructions rather than think with them, contesting their authority and pointing out their provisional character. As a form of power/knowledge with material effects their construction cannot be so easily dismissed, however. The starting point, as each of the following chapters exemplifies, is perhaps to understand the work of construction that goes into the production of such geographical knowledges.

3

Imagined Geographies: Geographical Knowledges of Self and Other in Everyday Life

Gill Valentine

Introduction

In the 1990s geographers have become increasingly preoccupied with how knowledge is constructed through a geographical lens. Drawing on the work of the Palestinian social theorist Edward Said, geographers have begun to reflect on how we are responsible for 'inventing' places. In his now classic book *Orientalism*, Said (1978) argues that just as we make our own histories, so too we make our own geographies. In a rich and detailed study he demonstrates that the Orient is not just 'there', but rather that the traditions of thought and imagery which give it a reality are a European invention – a product of the European imagination. He draws on the French philosopher Gaston Bachelard's concept of the 'poetics of space' to explain how space becomes endowed with meaning to dramatize the distance and difference between what is close and what is far away. By exploring the discourse of the 'Mystic Orient', Said shows how the Orient has been contained by and represented through this dominant framework and how this has served to legitimize European hegemony. Indeed he argues that the European sense of self is predicated on 'the Other'. Said describes this as an imaginative geography, although he is also keen to emphasize the very real material foundation of European dominance – namely imperialism.

The notion of an imaginative geography – albeit deployed in a rather different way – is also found in the work of Benedict Anderson.

Anderson (1983) argues that nation states are imagined communities – that they are not based on territory but rather are mental constructs. In support of this claim, that nations are 'imagined' not 'real', he argues that members of even the smallest nation will never know their fellow members, yet all still have an image of a shared identity; and that this sense of comradeship or collective identity is sustained despite the level of exploitation and injustice between fellow citizens. Anderson's work carries some overtones of Said's imaginative geography, in that he too is concerned with how we imagine space and its boundaries, how we imagine whose space it is, and how we construct 'self' and 'other'. Anderson's concept of 'imagined community' has been employed by geographers to understand 'community' at a local scale. Writing about the working-class neighbourhood of Poplar, Gillian Rose defines an imagined community as 'a group of people bound together by some kind of belief stemming from particular historical and geographical circumstances in their own solidarity' (Rose, 1990: 426).

The importance of these imaginative geographies is not only, as May argues (1996: 57), that they 'overlay a more tangible geography and help shape our attitudes to other places and people', but more importantly, that they are fundamental to our understanding of space itself and how we construct our sense of self and other. While imaginative geographies have been the subject of analysis at a collective scale in relation to the 'nation' and the 'local', it is equally important to understand how they are produced and reproduced in everyday life as a result of individual as well as collective actions. Yet the 'everyday' by its very nature is difficult to grasp. Its very 'normality', its very 'taken-for-granted-ness', 'all-around-us-ness', makes it elusive to pin down, to take stock of and think through all the ways in which we deploy geographical knowledge. For this reason this chapter is a bit of a fraud, for rather than tackle the 'everyday' head on, it side-steps some of its complexity by focusing instead on just one of the many – but perhaps also one of the most mundane and taken-for-granted – 'everyday' acts we all engage in – eating – in order to think about what we mean by geographical knowledge in our everyday lives. Specifically it considers how we imagine the personal space of our bodies; how we mobilize a sense of sameness with others and also how we gauge or negotiate difference and distance.

Imagining personal space

Adrienne Rich (1986: 212) has famously argued that 'the body is the geography closest in'. It is also therefore perhaps the first space that we imagine and endow with meaning. In *Phenomenology of Perception*, Merleau-Ponty (1962) describes the relationship between the lived body and its world. He argues that the body is the original subject that constitutes space – that there would be no space without the body. He goes on to suggest that through movement and orientation we create a link between our bodies and the outlying space, so that we organize our surrounding space as a continual extension of our own being.

Eating is one of the ways that the spatiality of our bodies is brought into being. Through the act of eating we imagine ourselves as both spatial and positioned in space. This is most evident in relation to women's experiences of food and eating. Discourses in the media, fashion industry, medicine and consumer culture map our bodily needs, pleasures and possibilities to create geographical and historically specific bodily 'norms'. In particular the development of consumer culture and the parallel growth of the media and advertising industries in the twentieth century have been credited with developing discourses of self-improvement and the body beautiful (Featherstone, 1991). In the late twentieth century we are surrounded by images of ideal bodies against which we are invited to measure our own.

Studies suggest that while Western bodies may actually be getting fatter, women's ideal body shapes in North America and Europe are getting thinner and ideal weights are in decline (Stephens et al., 1994). Lupton (1996) has given the name 'the "food/health/beauty" triplex' to the process by which popular discourses are eliding representations of slim female bodies with health and sexual attractiveness (although there is some evidence that men too are being sexualized and eroticized through advertisements and magazines: see for example Mort, 1988; Bocock, 1993).

Individuals, particularly women, are expected to be self-disciplined (that is, through diet and exercise) enough to produce their bodies in a culturally desirable way. As a result many women are unhappy with their own bodies – feeling guilty about eating, and regularly skipping meals (Charles and Kerr, 1986; Bordo, 1993). Studies repeatedly show that women overestimate their weight, size and shape, with between one half and one quarter of women whose weight is 'normal' for their height imagining themselves to be overweight – to be taking up too much space (Stephens et al., 1994). Food and eating are therefore important components in the way that many women imagine their own geographies. Writing about the general feminine style of body comportment, Iris Marion Young (1990: 146) argues that 'For many women as they move in sport, a space surrounds us in imagination that we are not free to move beyond; the space available to our movement is a constricted space.' And she goes on to claim that women lack confidence and underestimate their bodily abilities, stating that they 'often live [their] bod[ies] as a burden which must be dragged and prodded along and at the same time protected'. These imagined constraints are also apparent in relation to food and eating. Many women imagine their bodies as a burden to be struggled with, feeling that the space available for them to occupy is constricted.

The failure to contain the space of the body – to bring into being the imaginative geography of the self – fills some women with loathing for this 'other' that is their body. Millman's (1980) study of women who are overweight found that many were so ashamed of and disgusted by their bodies that they would not even look at themselves in the mirror. One of her interviewees explains: 'I feel so terrible about the way I look that I cut off connection with my body. I operate from the neck up. I do not look in mirrors' (Millman, 1980: 195).

Berger and Luckmann (1971) describe the experience of self as about both being and having a body. They argue that 'On the one hand, man [*sic*] *is* a body, in the same way that this may be said of every other animal organism. On the other hand, man [*sic*] *has* a body. That is, man [*sic*] experiences himself [*sic*] as an entity that is not identical with his body, but that, on the contrary, has that body at its disposal. In other words, man's [*sic*] experience of himself [*sic*] always hovers in the balance between being and having a body, a balance that must be redressed again and again' (Berger and Luckmann, 1971: 68). This Cartesian mind–body split is evident in accounts of women with eating disorders. In *Life Size*, a fictional account of anorexia by Jenefer Shute (1993), the main character, Josie, aims to minimize the space her body takes up. She questions how she can justify the amount of space she occupies in the world and is critical of the way those around her greedily occupy too much space. Josie imagines her own body as insatiable and out of control and strives to control and discipline it until she can attain a pure mind, by doing away with her body altogether.

Food and eating are important not only in the way we imagine the space we occupy but also in the way we are positioned in social space – how we imagine ourselves, or rather our bodies, in relation to others. Moral judgements about 'good' and 'bad' eating habits rapidly slip into judgements about 'good' and 'bad' people (Backett, 1992). Numerous studies have demonstrated that fat people in the West are imagined to be lazy, self-indulgent and untrustworthy (Dejong, 1980; Dejong and Kleck, 1986). These discourses operate through processes of shaming. To be fat is a visible stigma, it is a marker of a weak character who lacks self-discipline and self-control, so that when our bodies start taking up more space and we can no longer fit into our clothes, we feel shamed – shamed not only by the surveillant gaze of disapproving partners, children, friends and colleagues, but also by our own guilty gaze, into 'doing something about it'. In this way, what Foucault termed 'docile bodies' are produced which fit into and serve prevailing relations of domination and subordination.

Consequently, these discourses about the space an ideal body should take up can have very real material consequences for our everyday lives if we do not produce our bodies in the appropriate way. The fat body is not welcome in many places, from work environments – New York City Traffic Department is one of many institutions to have sacked employees for being overweight (Schwartz, 1986) – to public transport and the beach (Schwartz, 1986; Cline, 1990). Patients can be denied treatment because they are considered to be too self-indulgent to deserve help or to be too lacking in self-discipline to be able to maintain a healthy lifestyle. Children are bullied at school for being slow or lazy. People walk out on their spouses and lovers because they are too sexually unattractive. The fat body is 'other'. In this way, the material realities of what being 'other' can mean (for example, unemployment, loneliness, ill health and so on) can also force individuals to try to produce the space of their bodies in a more culturally desirable way – to become 'docile bodies'.

Thus what we eat and how we manage our bodies shape both how we imagine ourselves as spatial and how we can be positioned in social space. Our bodies actively constitute space and project spatial relations and positions in accordance with our own intentions (for example, in terms of how we feed and discipline them and therefore how much space they take up). At the same time, because our eating and bodily performances are inhibited or constrained by moral representations about how we should or should not look, and how much space we should or should not take up, then so too our bodies' spaces are lived as constituted.

Imagining sameness

In our everyday lives we constantly position ourselves in relation to others. The performance and regulation of shared eating habits and practices of the self are two important ways that we can imagine our cultural place in the world. In all human societies, from all the potentially edible nutritional items only some are actually classified as 'appropriate' to eat (Douglas, 1966). Many foods are classified by different societies or different faiths as 'polluting' or as morally impure. For example, Hindus do not eat cows, while dogs and foxes are not eaten in contemporary Western societies despite being eaten in many other cultures.

These definitions depend on the value and status different social groups assign to animals, plants and so on (Douglas, 1966; James, 1990). The importance of these classifications and rules governing the production and consumption of foods, and what we should or should not do, lies in the fact that they play a fundamental part in our imaginings of self and other at a range of scales, dramatizing the distance between the two.

Food taboos position us in social and cultural space in this way by making it difficult, if not impossible, for us to think about ourselves in any other way. For example, the rules about not eating human flesh are so strongly engrained in us that transgressions of these cultural imaginings are considered revolting, often triggering the body to vomit in disgust. Food, because it is invasive or intrusive, threatens the integrity of the self. There is a risk that we might, by eating the 'wrong thing', transform the self from within – for example, cannibals are supposed to take on the characteristics of the victims they devour (Fischler, 1988). Thus in the same way that moral judgements about how much we eat can slip into judgements about whether we are 'good' or 'bad' people, so too judgements about what we eat can also be used to draw conclusions about our moral worth. To break cultural rules or taboos about 'edible foods' can mark individuals out as social or religious outcasts. Shame and fear of others' disgust at our eating habits are therefore powerful disciplinary mechanisms that serve to (re)produce shared eating habits and shared imaginings of the self.

Imagining our cultural place in the world through food is not only about the operation of moral power – about what we should or should not eat – it is also about cultural power; in other words about taste. Food is just one form of consumption which marks some bodies out as distinctive from others. The French sociologist Pierre Bourdieu (1984) described the knowledge we have about which foods to choose, which cutlery to use and how to look after our bodies as 'cultural capital', arguing that practices of the self, such as eating, betray people's origins or *habitus* (internalized form of class conditioning). Bourdieu based his claims on a survey of 1,000 French citizens, arguing that there were strong class distinctions between what they ate, methods of food preparation and manners. In the 1990s in particular, food snobbery or what Diane Simmonds (1990) terms foodie-ism became an important way that people imagine a sense of shared identity with those who share the same taste.

Social etiquettes constructed around dining out play an important part in (re)producing and regulating this sense of social sameness (Finkelstein, 1989; Visser, 1986, 1991). 'The restaurant makes dining out a mannered exercise, disciplined by customs in a framework of prefigured actions' (Beardsworth and Keil, 1997: 119). While those who know how to behave in such social environments may feel socially comfortable, and even derive pleasure from demonstrating a shared social knowledge, those who are less familiar with the social etiquettes of particular restaurants can feel 'out of place' in these socially regulated environments; although, of course, discourses about taste are less powerful at regulating our eating habits than those about 'edible foods'. It is easier to imagine, and indeed to eat, in ways that transgress our class identities than it is to eat in ways that transgress our shared cultural classifications of 'edible foods'. Indeed, eating fish and chips, a so-called 'working-class' food, on the street is a 'naughty but nice' transgression (Valentine, 1998) for the new service class (even being appropriated by fashionable restaurants in 1996 as part of what the food writer Nigel Slater dubbed the year of the gastro-yob), while saving up to eat out at an expensive restaurant on a special occasion – eating above your social station – can provide a rare taste (in both the culinary and social sense of the word) of how 'the other' half lives.

Gillespie (1995: 198) argues that taste is also 'one of the most significant markers of ethnicity in plural societies'. In a study of British Asian students she found that most of those who took part in her research ate Indian food in the parental home but chose to eat 'English' or 'Americanized' foods at school. In the students' eyes 'Western' food had more cultural capital than Indian food, which they described as 'village food'; a distinction Gillespie compares with Bourdieu's description of French rural peasants' food as low-status food.

Other studies suggest that for first-generation migrants food is an important way of imagining or remembering 'home' and preserving a shared identity. Lupton's (1994) study of food memories found that some participants used food as a way to articulate a nostalgia for their 'homeland'. As Kalcik (1984: 59) writes, 'food links people across space and time, so that it helps create a bond with past members of the group as well as living ones'. Indeed, migrant groups commonly take their food habits with them, altering the culinary habits of host nations through the twin processes of acculturation and hybridization (see for example Gili, 1963; van Otterloo, 1987; Kalcik, 1984). Thus food is one way of acting out a fiction of community and of struggling against imagined forces of disintegration, but it is also a linking process, a way of expressing cultural unity, of not just composing but also recomposing boundaries.

The importance of food sharing or commensality therefore lies in the fact that it is a powerful way of imagining connectedness and symbolizing and mobilizing 'community' action. At the local level, street parties, food festivals, and communal outdoor seasonal events from Ramadan to harvest festivals, the colliery picnic or the pub, are examples where collective acts of consumption (Bell and Valentine, 1997) are used to forge a sense of togetherness between those who live and/or work together. At the same time, while the sharing of butties or the buying of a round may foster social cohesion or a sense of a shared identity, these imaginings of sameness also serve to reproduce social boundaries and emphasize the exclusion of others. Within pubs the drinking practice of 'buying rounds' is particularly important in marking out sameness and difference among drinkers (Hunt and Satterlee, 1986; Bell and Valentine, 1997).

It is also important to think of food as a way of imagining 'communities' beyond the local, beyond the effects of commensality. Concern about where food comes from and the politics of production and consumption are processes through which we articulate a knowledge of and concern for 'other places' while also mobilizing a sense of sameness with like-minded people. For example, vegetarianism (Beardsworth and Keil, 1992) or anti-consumerism are examples of what Brown and Mussell (1984: 11) term 'communities of affiliation', mobilizing people to challenge agribusiness and transnational corporations' practices in countries across the globe through what the people themselves put on their dinner plates (Bell and Valentine, 1997). The campaign against food giant Nestlé because of its manipulative marketing of infant milk formula in developing countries (Chetley, 1986) is a good example of this connectedness between North and South.

The importance of food as a symbol of connectedness in this way is increasingly apparent as global patterns of food availability and trade produce ever more acute gaps between 'rich' and 'poor'. The world-wide charity appeals in the 1980s – Live Aid, Band Aid and USA for Africa – with their calls to 'Feed the World' (the UK song) or 'We are the World' (the US song), articulated a knowledge of and a concern for the globe and a positive will to change it. Nevertheless, the UK song paradoxically also dramatized the distance between donors and recipients, through its bizarre lyric 'Do they know it's Christmas?', with its colonial, Anglocentric emphasis on a Christian religious festival not shared by the largely Muslim Ethiopians the record aimed to help, and through its use of the term 'they' rather than the more inclusive 'we' which features in the US version (Howes, 1990; Bell and Valentine, 1997).

In many different ways, then, when we shop for food or sit down to eat with others we consciously or unconsciously articulate our cultural place in the world. The importance of this lies in the fact that through these performative (and also highly regulated, in terms of moral power – 'what we should eat' – and cultural power – 'what is good taste') acts and practices of the self, we express a common or shared identity with others and caring human relations. In other words we mobilize a sense of 'community' (in terms of class, race, culture, neighbourhood, workplace and even planet). In this way shared identities are imagined through consumption practices in terms of boundedness or contained-ness (Massey, 1992). The danger in doing so, however, is of construct-ing what Massey terms an 'introverted sense of place', or introverted geographies, where imaginings of 'there' and 'here' create a 'them and us' mentality. But at the same time eating is also one of the everyday practices that can serve to challenge the insularities and certainties of our identities.

Imagining difference

The compression of time-space horizons as a result of transport and communication advances have made frontiers and boundaries more per-meable (Harvey, 1990). As barriers of distance have dissolved so there has been a greater collision of different cultures, with the result that encounters between same and other – for some, particularly those in contemporary Western societies (Massey, 1993) – have become more immediate and more intense (Morley and Robins, 1995). Nowhere is this perhaps more obvious in everyday life than on the table. The histo-ries of most basic staples of the Western diet, from tea and sugar to potatoes and chillies, are testament to the historical importance that global interconnections (notably, for example, colonialism) have had on our consumption patterns.

Cook and Crang (1996) argue that consumer commodity geographies are nothing if not complex. On the one hand, Cook and Crang point out that many consumers are ignorant, or at least unaware, of what they term the 'biographies and geographies' (1996: 135) of the food on our plates. On the other hand, they note what Lash and Urry (1994) have termed the 'touristic quality' of contemporary consumption. The development of foodways, encouraged by movements of people, telecommunications revolutions, the food media, cookbooks, restau-rants and so on, offers us the opportunity to get a taste of 'the other'; or, as various advertisements have described it, 'to eat your way round the globe' or 'to discover the world and eat it' (Bell and Valentine, 1997: 189). Wendell Berry (1992: 378), for example, claims 'A signifi-cant part of the pleasure of eating is one's accurate consciousness of the lives and the world from which food comes.' In this way, 'foods do not simply come from places, organically growing out of them, but also make places as symbolic constructs, being deployed in the discurs-ive construction of various imaginative geographies' (Cook and Crang,

1986: 140). The importance of these geographies lies in the fact that they involve the imagining of space and dramatizing of physical and social distance in complex ways and at different (though interwoven) scales.

The availability and use of ingredients and cooking techniques from around the world allow foods to be adapted and reworked in different places (in individual homes but also in the collective space of restaurants, workplace canteens and so on). Thus on the surface food offers us the possibility to break the polarized logic that 'we belong or we don't belong', because it allows us to share in difference while also not claiming a sense of sameness or shared identity. As John Brady (1996) in a paper questioning what it means to eat a doughnut – the most American of all snack foods – in a non-American setting, in his case Berlin, states: 'the doughnut can be deployed in different processes of social identity definition. The doughnut as something typically American is not bound to its American context, but rather can cross borders and take on meanings for individuals outside of a purely American context' (Brady 1996: 3). It can be read, for example, in terms of America's relationship with Germany, food nationalism issues, the changing role of snack foods in contemporary societies and so on (Bell and Valentine, 1997).

Thus foods can articulate an extroverted sense of place 'in which boundaries are seen as contestable and contested social constructions and where here/us is constituted through its connections into the there/them' (Cook and Crang, 1996: 139). The importance of this lies in the fact that in this way foods, cooking and eating can epitomize Massey's (1993) notion of a progressive sense of place, where the crossing of boundaries leads to a complexity of vision, constructing an imaginative geography on our plates where places are no longer internally homogeneous bounded areas, but are spaces of interaction in which local identities are constructed out of resources which may well not be local in their origin.

However, dabbling in difference in the kitchen can also be dangerous if we ignore some of the ways that acts of consumption are riddled with power. Rather than the proliferation of interest in 'exotic' foods (initially fruit and vegetables from Africa and Latin America had 'exotic appeal', but more recently non-European meats such as ostrich have been marked in this way too)[1] stimulating a new level of cultural awareness and support for anti-racism, John May (1996) argues that the consumption of such foods is often both dependent on and helps to reproduce racist imaginative geographies. He uses interviews with people he describes as the 'new cultural class' from Stoke Newington, London, to demonstrate how in their accounts of their taste for 'exotic' food they deploy racist imagery and demonstrate a racist attitude to other cultures. He argues that the whole definition of 'exotic' is a product of the white imagination, stating that:

> notions of the exotic would seem to rest upon [an] *imaginative geography* ... that conflates notions of geographical distance with *social* distance. Exotic food is essentially food that comes from the underdeveloped world and this in turn works to conflate notions of the exotic (that which comes from beyond Europe) with a racialised model of development. This suggests that the associations such foods offer both feed off, and spill over to, the attitudes some white people have towards other minority residents in their area. (May, 1996: 62)

Rather than 'the new cultural class' articulating a genuine interest in different cultures and places, May claims that they use their taste for exotic food to distance themselves from other social groups.

Thus, through the process of consuming 'others' we often try to contain and represent them within our own frameworks, and so control and incorporate difference in a way that makes us feel safe. bell hooks claims that this 'commodification of difference promotes paradigms of consumption wherein whatever difference the Other inhabits is eradicated, via exchange, by a consumer cannibalism that not only displaces the Other but denies the significance of that Other's history through a process of decontextualisation' (hooks, 1992: 31).

Food then remains a complex and important metaphor for the ways that we invent, explore, and more often than not contain difference in our everyday lives. While foods and the acts of cooking and eating offer radical possibilities for ways of imagining very progressive geographies, they also highlight the dangers of imagining other places as an exotic 'Other' which can be contained within our own frameworks.

Conclusion

Throughout our everyday lives we constantly negotiate space, positioning ourselves physically, socially, morally, politically and metaphorically in relation to others. Eating is just one everyday act through which we imagine ourselves as spatial and position ourselves in space. At one level our bodies actively constitute space and project spatial relations and positions in accordance with our own intentions. In this way, through how we feed ourselves and manage our bodies, how we share food with others or how we rework foods from around the globe in our own kitchens, we imagine the space of our bodies (as fat or thin); we imagine a sense of sameness with others (for example, as culturally the same, of the same class, of the same ethnic background, of the same workplace or neighbourhood, even of the same planet); and we imagine a sense of difference (this can be in a progressive, interactive way, or in a narrow-minded, containing or cannibalistic way).

At the same time it is important to recognize that our geographical imaginings are also inhibited or constrained by *moral representations* – about how much space we should or should not take up, what we should or should not eat, and whether we should or should not belong – and by *cultural representations* – about what is 'good taste' or what is appropriate for a person like 'us' to do/eat. These discourses are important because they position us in ways that make it difficult for us to eat and hence imagine ourselves in other ways. They can also produce very real material consequences in terms of social exclusion or discrimination if we transgress them. So in this way our geographies are lived as they are constituted.

In the constitution of our imagined geographies we constantly imagine connections with others. These connections always offer us different possibilities for how to relocate ourselves. On the one hand, connections (in the imagining of self, sameness or difference) can make us more certain in our own identities, and thus foster an insular sense of 'us' versus 'them'. On the other hand, connections offer us new possibilities of sharing in difference through interaction. The important challenge for geography is how we can use geographical knowledge in everyday life not to dramatize the distance between what is close and what is far away, or to contain and incorporate 'the Other', but to produce constellations of relations that are never bounded, never inhibited.

Acknowledgements

This chapter draws on some of the material and ideas that feature in *Consuming Geographies* (1997, Routledge), which I co-authored with David Bell. I therefore owe a special debt of gratitude to David for the ideas, references and inspirations in this chapter which derive from his conversation and writing. I wish to thank the Leverhulme Trust for funding the research project (award no. F118AA) which this chapter draws upon. Many thanks are also due to John Allen and Doreen Massey for their guidance and constructive comments during the writing process.

Note

1 'Exotic' foods are, of course, often appropriated to such an extent that they
   become taken for granted as part of the national diet, losing their 'exotic'

appeal. Tea or curry are historical and contemporary examples of 'exotic' goods which have been subsumed into British culture.

References

Anderson, B. (1983) *Imagined Communities: Reflections on the Origin and Spread of Nationalism*. London, Verso.

Backett, K. (1992) 'Taboos and excesses: lay health moralities in middle class families'. *Sociology of Health and Illness*, 14: 255–73.

Beardsworth, A. and T. Keil (1992) 'The vegetarian option: varieties, conversions, motives and careers'. *Sociological Review*, 40: 252–93.

Beardsworth, A. and T. Keil (1997) *Sociology on the Menu*. London, Routledge.

Bell, D. and G. Valentine (1997) *Consuming Geographies: We Are Where We Eat*. London, Routledge.

Berger, P. and T. Luckmann (1971) *The Social Construction of Reality*. Harmondsworth, Penguin.

Berry, W. (1992) 'The pleasures of eating'. In D. Curtin and L. Heldke (eds), *Cooking, Eating, Thinking: Transformative Philosophies of Food*. Bloomington, Indiana University Press, 374–9.

Bocock, R. (1993) *Consumption*. London, Routledge.

Bordo, S. (1993) *Unbearable Weight: Feminism, Western Culture and the Body*. Berkeley CA, University of California Press.

Bourdieu, P. (1984) *Distinction: A Social Critique of the Judgement of Taste*. London, Routledge.

Brady, J. (1996) 'Delicious doughnuts in Berlin: the dilemma of political community in the age of global capitalism'. *Bad Subjects*, 25 (electronic journal at: http://english-www.hss.cmu.edu/bs/).

Brown, L. and K. Mussell (eds) (1984) 'Introduction'. In L. Brown and K. Mussell (eds), *Ethnic and Regional Foodways in the United States: The Performance of Group Identity*. Knoxville, University of Tennessee Press, 1–14.

Charles, N. and M. Kerr (1986) 'Food for feminist thought'. *Sociological Review*, 34/1: 537–72.

Chetley, A. (1986) *The Politics of Baby Food: Successful Challenges to an International Marketing Strategy*. London, Pinter.

Cline, S. (1990) *Just Desserts*. London, André Deutsch.

Cook, I. and P. Crang (1996) 'The world on a plate: culinary culture, displacement and geographical knowledges'. *Journal of Material Culture*, 1: 131–54.

Dejong, W. (1980) 'The stigma of obesity: the consequences of naive assumptions concerning the causes of physical deviance'. *Journal of Health and Social Behaviour*, 21: 75–87.

Dejong, W. and E. Kleck (1986) 'The social psychological effects of overweight'. In P. Herman, M. Zanna, and E. Higgins (eds), *Physical Appearance, Stigma, and Social Behaviour: The Ontario Symposium*, vol 3. Hillsdale NJ, Lawrence Erlbaum.

Douglas, M. (1966) *Purity and Danger: An Analysis of the Concepts of Pollution and Taboo*. London, Routledge and Kegan Paul.

Featherstone, M. (1991) *Consumer Culture and Postmodernism*. London, Sage.

Finkelstein, J. (1989) *Dining Out: A Sociology of Modern Manners*. Cambridge, Polity Press.

Fischler, C. (1988) 'Food, self and identity'. *Social Science Information*, 27: 275–92.

Gili, E. (1963) *Tia Victoria's Spanish Kitchen*. London, Nicholas Kaye.

Gillespie, M. (1995) *Television, Ethnicity and Cultural Change*. London, Routledge.

Harvey, D. (1990) 'Between space and time: reflections on the geographical imagination'. *Annals of the Association of American Geographers*, 80: 418–34.

hooks, b. (1992) 'Eating the other'. In *Black Looks: Race and Representation*. London, Turnaround, 21–39.

Howes, D. (1990) ' "We Are the World" and its counterparts: popular song as constitutional discourse'. *Politics, Culture, and Society*, 3: 315–39.

Hunt, G. and S. Satterlee (1986) 'Cohesion and division: drinking in an English village'. *Man*, 21: 521–37.

James, A. (1990) 'The good, the bad and the delicious: the role of confectionery in British society'. *Sociological Review*, 38: 666–88.

Kalcik, S. (1984) 'Ethnic foodways in America: symbol and the performance of identity'. In L.K. Brown and K. Mussell (eds), *Ethnic and Regional Foodways in the United States: The Performance of Group Identity*. Knoxville, University of Tennessee Press, 50–65.

Lash, S. and J. Urry (1994) *Economies of Signs and Space*. London, Sage.

Lupton, D. (1994) 'Food, memory and meaning: the symbolic and social nature of food events'. *Sociological Review*, 42/4: 665–85.

Lupton, D. (1996) *Food, the Body and the Self*. London, Sage.

Massey, D. (1992) 'A place called home?'. *New Formations*, 17: 3–15.

Massey, D. (1993) 'Power-geometry and a progressive sense of place'. In J. Bird, B. Curtis, T. Putnam, G. Robertson and L. Tickner (eds), *Mapping the Futures: Local Cultures and Global Change*. London, Routledge, 59–69.

May, J. (1996) ' "A little taste of something more exotic": the imaginative geographies of everyday life'. *Geography*, 81/1: 57–64.

Merleau-Ponty, M. (1962) *The Phenomenology of Perception*. New York, Humanities Press.

Millman, M. (1980) *Such a Pretty Face: Being Fat in America*. New York, Norton.

Morley, D. and K. Robins (1995) *Spaces of Identity: Global Media, Electronic Landscapes and Cultural Boundaries*. London, Routledge.

Mort, F. (1988) 'Boy's own? Masculinity, style and popular culture'. In R. Chapman and J. Rutherford (eds), *Male Order: Unwrapping Masculinity*. London, Lawrence & Wishart, 193–224.

Rich, A. (1986) *Blood, Bread and Poetry*. London, W.W. Norton.

Rose, G. (1990) 'Contested concepts of community: imagining Poplar in the 1920s'. *Journal of Historical Geography*, 16/4: 425–37.

Said, E. (1978) *Orientalism: Western Conceptions of the Orient*. Harmondsworth, Penguin.

Schwartz, H. (1986) *Never Satisfied: A Cultural History of Diets, Fantasies and Fat*. London, Collier Macmillan.

Shute, J. (1993) *Life Size*. London, Mandarin.

Simmonds, D. (1990) 'What's next? Fashion, foodies and the illusion of freedom'. In A. Tomlinson (ed.), *Consumption, Identity and Style: Marketing, Meanings and the Packaging of Pleasure*. London, Routledge, 121–38.

Stephens, D.L., R.P. Hill and C. Hanson (1994) 'The beauty myth and female consumers: the controversial role of advertising'. *Journal of Consumer Affairs*, 28: 137–53.

Valentine, G. (1998) 'Food and the production of the civilised street'. In N. Fyfe (ed.), *Images of the Street: Representation, Experience and Control in Public Space*. London: Routledge, 192–204.

van Otterloo, A. (1987) 'Foreign immigrants and the Dutch at table, 1945–1985. Bridging or widening the gap?'. *Netherlands Journal of Sociology*, 23: 126–43.

Visser, M. (1986) *Much Depends on Dinner: The Extraordinary History and Mythology, Allure and Obsessions, Perils and Taboos, of an Ordinary Meal*. Toronto, McClelland and Stewart.

Visser, M. (1991) *The Rituals of Dinner: The Origins, Evolution, Eccentricities and Meaning of Table Manners*. London, Grove Weidenfeld.

Young, I.M. (1990) *Throwing Like a Girl and Other Essays in Feminist Philosophy and Social Theory*. Bloomington, Indiana University Press.

4

Situating Geopolitical Representations: Inside/Outside and the Power of Imperial Interventions

David Slater

Introduction

It is clear that from the late 1980s onward there has been a quite remarkable growth of interest in the discursive construction of identity, difference and otherness. For Edward Said, whose work has come to be so influential in this domain, the analysis of cultural representations and the critical scrutiny of identity and difference have not infrequently been marked by an absence – the politics of American empire, with its profound implications for so many issues of representation and power. Said (1989: 214), in a commentary on a particular current within anthropology, remarks that in so many of the various writings on epistemology, textualization, difference and otherness, 'there is an almost total absence of any reference to American imperial intervention as a factor affecting the theoretical discussion'. And yet for Said the imperial contest is a cultural fact of enormous political as well as interpretative significance, since it is this specific historical context that acts as a defining horizon for the otherwise overly abstract concepts of 'otherness' and 'difference'. In general, this particular aspect of Said's critical intervention has tended to receive less attention than might have been the case, although clearly, with respect to geographical enquiry, the spatialities of empire in the European context have been the subject of thoughtful reflection (Driver, 1992; Gregory, 1995).

My first point here is that the politics of American empire, taken together with its inscription of a variety of modes of representation of other societies and cultures, needs to be identified as a founding element in the global visions of today. As the world's remaining superpower, the United States in its geopolitical history, which is rooted in the memory and amnesia of inside and outside, and permeated by encounters with internal and external others, provides a crucial ground for any investigation of the meanings and practices of global power. Exploring Said's important proposition, and keeping in focus his own prioritization of the spatial as well as the temporal, I shall begin by drawing out some emblematic continuities in the constitution of otherness. This will then provide a link into a consideration of the ways in which invasive imaginations have been intrinsic to the forms of geopolitical representation that have emerged in the United States. Specifically, I shall discuss salient aspects of the penetration of other spaces, governing visions and the emergence of counter-representations. My examples will largely relate to the US–Latin American context, and in the final section some reflections will be advanced concerning the key significance of alternative agents of knowledge.

Outlines of empire

In many forms of binary opposition which are deployed as a mechanism of classification, there will tend to be a process of demarcation and spatial separation, which is particularly evident in the operation of a will to power over the other. In the geopolitical formation of the United States, in the territorial constitution of its sovereignty, 'internal others' were subjected to a delineation that underpinned and legitimized an accelerating process of territorial expansion and subjugation. At the beginning of the nineteenth century, Thomas Jefferson, in a message to the Senate and House of Representatives, outlined a position on 'the Indian tribes residing within the limits of the United States' that epitomized a recurrent mode of representation and practice. It was argued, for example, that in order to provide an 'extension of territory which the rapid increase of our numbers will call for' two measures were needed. First, these indigenous peoples were to be encouraged to abandon hunting and to devote themselves to the practices of stock raising, agriculture and domestic manufacture, so that the extensive forests they once saw as necessary for their livelihood would be exchanged for the means of improving their farms. Second, by multiplying trading houses among them, and by leading them to agriculture, manufactures and civilization, we would be preparing them ultimately to participate in the 'benefits of our Government', and therefore acting for 'their greatest good'. The appropriation of lands and the establishment of trading houses in the Indian territories were placed in the context of the 'settling and marking of boundaries with the different tribes'. At the same time, further progress in 'new extinguishments of title' was linked to the advancement of 'the geographical knowledge of our own continent', which in turn was contrasted to 'other civilized nations' that 'encountered great expense to enlarge the boundaries of knowledge by undertaking voyages of discovery'.[1]

Resistance to the incursion of a superior civilization was characterized in terms of the presence within the aboriginal population of prejudices, ignorance, pride and the influence of 'interested and crafty individuals', who inculcated a 'sanctimonious reverence for the customs of their ancestors', and portrayed ignorance as safety and knowledge as replete with danger. These were the obstacles to encounter, the problems that faced the spread of Enlightenment and the exercise of reason. The 'ascendancy of habit' was pitted against the 'duty of improving our reason and obeying its mandates' (quoted in Richardson, 1896: 380). In these and related passages, we see the construction of certain 'governing representations' (Norton, 1993), and it is these representations which reflect a clear adherence to the dictates of a civilizing mission and the appropriation of territory. Such an appropriation exemplifies what Deleuze and Guattari (1984: 257) referred to as the process whereby 'civilized and modern societies' deterritorialize with one hand, whilst they reterritorialize with the other. The establishment of a divide, a separation in the evaluation of different peoples and cultures is anchored to a belief in Enlightenment and the possibility of change. Through the diffusion of freedom, reason, science and moral advancement the natives would be transformed into a subordinated, dependent and inferior category of social subjects.

In this context, I want to signal the importance of a certain continuity in a current of representation that can be traced through into the twentieth century and located, for example, in the dichotomies of modernization theory and its prioritization of diffusion. Furthermore, we can also see Jefferson's troublesome and 'crafty individuals' transformed into the Communist subversives who attempt to destabilize and derail the rational and enlightened process of the transition from the traditional to the modern, whilst domestically those same individuals become, in the Cold War period, the 'enemy within', the organizers of 'un-American activities'. These remarks lead us into a general treatment of the influence of ethnocentric assumptions on the framing and formulation of foreign policy and on the overall orientation of American geopolitical interventions.[2] They can also be used as a way of interpreting what Blaut (1993) has referred to as 'geographical diffusionism'.

One of the issues that often overshadows much of the debate on colonial discourse and post-colonial theory concerns the roots of expansion or diffusionism. In traditional Marxist accounts one would invariably find a recurrent emphasis on the economic – the search for new markets, raw materials, cheap labour, or higher profits. In the case of the United States, clearly by the end of the nineteenth century, as the internal frontier reached the point of closure, and as domestic overproduction, agrarian unrest and labour conflicts became more acute, the drive to expand and seek out new territories for economic development became more manifest (Lafeber, 1963). But expansionism could not be understood simply in terms of putatively independent economic pressures. Rather, its meaning and disposition were analysed and justified by a range of writers and politicians who interpreted and gave direction to overseas expansion as part of the nation's destiny. For Frederick Jackson Turner, writing in 1896, expansion had been the dominant fact of American life for three hundred years, and he predicted that this outward movement would continue in the form of a vigorous foreign policy, including the extension of American influence to outlying islands and adjoining countries. Similarly, Josiah Strong, a key spokesman for the American Evangelical Alliance, in his vision of the 'missionary frontier', argued that the Anglo-Saxons with their 'genius for colonizing' would move down upon Mexico and Central and South America, and out over Africa and beyond, bringing Western civilization and Christianity to a backward and heathen world. And again, for Alfred T. Mahan, the development of sea power and access to overseas markets in Asia and Latin America, via the establishment of strategic bases, were closely linked to the concept of 'manifest destiny'. Mahan believed that Western civilization was an 'oasis set in the midst of a desert of barbarism', but he also held the conviction that external threats could be overcome through the spread of progress; those other 'stagnant societies' could be regenerated through American expansion (Healy, 1970: 129–30). Furthermore, at this time, Social Darwinism was another source of expansionist ideology, with Spencer's assertion of the necessity of progress adding a socio-economic orientation to notions of geopolitical predestination (Weinberg, 1963).

An expansion of spatial power, or the establishment of a new spatial-political order, a *Grossraum*, as Schmitt suggested in his analysis of the Monroe Doctrine (Ulmen, 1987), needs a justification, a principle of legitimacy, an ensemble of ideas and concepts that can provide a moral and cultural foundation. Furthermore, in the context of relations with other societies, and specifically in the Americas, remembering Jefferson's notion of the United States having 'a hemisphere to itself', the construction of a geopolitical identity included the positing of difference as inferiority *and* danger. The outside world contained threats to security and to the diffusion of mission. Given the historic differentiation of the New World from the Old, and the support for anti-colonial struggles and the self-determination of emerging nations, threats to security were frequently accompanied by the tendency to separate rulers from the ruled. In the context of revolutionary breaks that were associated with Communist subversion, it was the people who needed to be rescued from their tyrannical government. As a contemporary example, the earlier sections of the Helms–Burton Act of 1996 contain clear references to this distinction. One reads for instance that 'the consistent policy of the United States towards Cuba since the beginning of the Castro regime ... has sought to keep faith with the people of Cuba', whilst 'sanctioning the totalitarian Castro regime'; and further on, 'the Cuban people deserve to be assisted in a decisive manner to end the tyranny that has oppressed them for 36 years, and the continued failure to do so constitutes ethically improper conduct by the international community'.[3]

In this context, discursive continuity can be identified in relation to the desire to protect and guide whilst securing political order. At the beginning of the century the third article of the Platt Amendment, which was written into a 1903 treaty between the United States and Cuba, included the right of the United States to intervene in Cuba to preserve that country's independence. In the present era, the Helms–Burton Act links independence to 'freedom and democracy', and argues for a series of measures which would restore such values to the Cuban people, returning to them their 'right of self-determination'. The policy of the United States should then be 'to recognize that the self-determination of the Cuban people is a sovereign and national right of the citizens of Cuba which must be exercised free of interference by the government of any other country'.[4]

As this particular example demonstrates, the driving force behind geopolitical intervention lies in a profound belief in the rightness of a specific mission that cannot be understood outside of a well-established historical tradition. The mode of representation includes the presumed right to be able to designate the political future for a people whose sovereignty has been usurped by what is deemed to be an unrepresentative and tyrannical regime. I shall return to this aspect of the imperial encounter, but at this point in the argument I want to consider the issue of the drive to expand, and its relation to the envisioning of other societies and peoples.

Invasive imaginations

Penetrating other spaces

It could be argued that spatial diffusionism or geographical expansionism are natural expressions of the colonizer's model of the world. But is it inevitable that diffusionism must be associated with a colonizing imperative? Diffusion and expansion could surely also be linked to the possibilities of dialogue and symbiotic exchange. The will to exert and exercise power over other cultures and peoples does not necessarily, immanently, have to flow out of the desire to expand. It is when that will is intimately rooted in discourses of presumed superiority, mission and negative essentializations of the other that there is a coalescence of expansionism and subordinating power. Further, when evaluating such coalescences, to what extent can we hold to the view that the desire to exclude and dominate provides us with the key pivot of explanation? And moreover, in assessing the intimate associations between modes of representation and the forms of power over, the power to penetrate and structure the other, how do we include the influence of resistance, refusal and the refiguration of a power relation through counter forms of representation and interaction? It is here that the complex webs of inside and outside are so crucial, since in some analyses of the power *over*, for example, in discussions of North–South relations, there can be a depiction of 'others' or the 'subalterns' of the South in ways that imply a passive, receptive, almost inert world that has little if any power *to* modify, subvert, relocate or contest.[5]

The significance of 'reverse discourses', of the capacity to refuse, subvert, destabilize or divert, relates not only to the overall nature of penetration and resistance in the context of the varying forms or sources of the power over – economic, military, technological, cultural and so on – but also to the moment of reflection and interpretation. The ability to theorize back, the willingness and capacity to develop alternative understandings and explanations of international relations which do not simply derive from or copy the hegemonic readings of historical change, constitute a vital ingredient in any conceptualization of the inside/outside nexus. In other words, the politics of representation is itself a terrain of contestation, within which what is remembered and forgotten will be moulded by counterposed imaginations and visions emanating from different sites of experience and subjectivity. This is not to insinuate that, for example, the nationality of an author will automatically determine the way in which certain events are interpreted, but nevertheless, nationalism is a salient vector in the construction of an interpretative position. For example, the way Mexican or Cuban writers will tend to analyse the relations of their respective countries with the United States will usually contain a greater degree of nationalist opposition to American power than would be customarily present in the interpretations of US scholars (Aguilar, 1968).

One of the most persistent themes of the discussion so far relates to the emergence of ensembles of meaning and practice which include a desire to penetrate other cultures and polities. Some discourses incorporate the propensity to legitimize invasiveness. The transgression of frontiers and the subversion of sovereignty may be partly justified according to a desire to expand. But a belief in geopolitical predestination, as mentioned earlier, and expressed in the concept of 'Manifest Destiny', contains not only the will to expand but also the passion to possess. The drive to possess is intimately interwoven into visions of the other as inferior, but the forms of representation which may, as obviously was the case with colonialism, enframe these portrayals and designs are not uniform. It is valid to point out, as Grovogui (1996) has done, in his analysis of the transgression of African sovereignties, that the norms of international politics have been strongly conditioned by the capacity of the West to dominate non-Europeans in a hierarchical fashion. For Grovogui, the erasure of the fact of conquest from the discourses of law and international relations enabled the imperialist powers to claim rights and privileges within exclusively Western institutional practices, so that the interpretation and effectiveness of sovereignty and territorial integrity were already conditioned by ethnocentric privilege. This is an important point which in a sense follows on from one of the main motifs of Said's (1978) *Orientalism*, in which he stresses the long and slow process of appropriation by which the European awareness of the Orient transformed itself from being textual and contemplative into being administrative, economic and military, and that this change was a spatial and geographical one. Said (1978: 211) writes, for instance: 'in the precisely actual form in which the modern Orient was lived in, studied, or imagined, the *geographical space* of the Orient was penetrated, worked over, taken hold of' (emphasis in the original).

Connecting Grovogui with Said can help us to associate the issue of appropriation with the question of the modes of representation of other non-Western societies. Basic to all such modes is the exercise of monitoring and codification or surveillance and classification. Here different kinds of essentialization have been a symptomatic feature of colonial discourses, and these forms of portrayal and enframing of subject peoples have been a crucial part of the governmental project. The construction of a set of uniform images and meanings has been marked by an historical tension between the conflicting tendencies of segregation and assimilation, but in both cases the security of the stereotype still dominates. This does not mean that power only represses or censors according to simplified representations. Power under colonialism or imperialism produces reality and regimes of truth. For Bhabha (1994: 70), analysing discrimination and stereotype, 'the objective of colonial discourse is to construe the colonized as a population of degenerate types on the basis of racial origin, in order to justify conquest and to establish systems of administration and instruction'. Bhabha goes on to add that, 'despite the play of power within colonial discourse and the shifting positionalities of its subjects . . . I am referring to a form of governmentality that in marking out a "subject nation", appropriates, directs and dominates its various spheres of activity.' The influence of Foucault is clear, and the emphasis on the marking out of a subject nation corresponds to one of Said's main lines of interpretation, as indicated previously. However, it is also worthwhile observing that there is some dissonance between this particular view and the position outlined in some of Bhabha's other essays, where there is an emphasis on a specific duality within colonial authority, that duality arising from the contrasting demands for stable identity and historical reform. Moreover, in an important essay on the ambivalence of colonial discourse, Bhabha persuasively suggests that colonial authority is continually disrupted by the phenomenon of 'mimicry'. Hence, the reforming, civilizing mission can be threatened by 'the displacing gaze of its disciplinary double', since, for example, in the attempt to normalize the colonial state or subject, 'post-Enlightenment civility alienates its own language of liberty', and incites another knowledge of its norms which mocks its original authority (Bhabha, 1994: 86). Consequently partial visions of liberty or ethics are diffused within a colonial domain, so that there will be less danger that the colonialized subjects will become turbulent for liberty or ethical equality, but that very partiality undermines the authority of the diffusing discourse. Concomitantly, the modes of adoption of a colonial discourse by the 'subject nation' can involve forms of mockery and imitation that destabilize the effectiveness of colonial discourse, without engaging in open defiance.

In comparing the approaches of Said and Bhabha, it can be suggested that whilst Bhabha's critical comments on Said's presumed overstatement of colonial hegemony, or the view that power and discourse only take on significance in relation to the colonizer, are helpful points of intervention, equally it can be contended that Bhabha does not elaborate or theorize plurality or heterogeneity in the construction of colonial modes of representation and subjection. As Thomas (1994: 48), for example, observes, there is surely a difference between a project which positions the indigenous, colonized subject in a distinct and separate domain that is to be dominated and ordered and a project which seeks to convert or assimilate the colonized subject within a civilizing mission. In the history of European colonialisms, divergences were very real, as for example the distinctions between Portuguese and British rule in Africa clearly demonstrate. In South Africa the specificities of apartheid and the logics of separation posed another set of issues, whilst in the United States of the nineteenth century, the politics of segregation and racialized differentiation were confronted by a more universalist and liberal, albeit ethnocentric, strategy of societal integration. Inevitably this clash left its mark on the ways in which imperial modes of representation emerged, and this was especially evident in the case of United States foreign policy towards Cuba and Haiti (see Weston, 1972). Overall, what I am pointing to here is the relevance of seeing colonial or imperial discourses as plural and divided at their source, rather than only in their effects.

Governing visions

Above, I made reference to essentialization and mentioned, as an illustration, the significance of stereotypes. Toni Morrison (1992: 66–9), in her incisive writing on racial divisions in American literature, talks of the 'economy of stereotype', which allows the author a quick and easy image, thereby dispensing with the need for specificity and accuracy. One may encounter many examples of such stereotyping in a very broad range of literatures.[6] However, the process of essentialization entails more than a pejorative stereotyping, as Spurr (1993) has imaginatively shown in his study of the rhetoric of empire; juxtaposed to negation, one can encounter affirmation, and together with the tropes of idealization (strangers in paradise) there are the representations of the natural (the wilderness in human form) and the erotic (the Harems of the West). These kinds of rhetorical device or linguistic strategy have been explored by Pike (1992) in his enquiry into the history of United States–Latin American relations, and his study of myth and stereotype in the narratives of civilization and nature provide a pertinent contrast to Henry Commager's (1978) thesis of American empire as 'The Empire of Reason', or 'how Europe imagined and America realized the Enlightenment'.

As is well known, the adherence to Enlightenment virtue did not preclude the expression of racist sentiment. Benjamin Franklin, a paragon of eighteenth-century Enlightenment optimism, was a slave owner and he divided humanity according to skin colour, allocating to each colour characteristic traits, so that blacks, as one example, were designated as sullen, malicious, revengeful and cruel. But the tenets of virtue have always required the specification of vice. In the case of the territorial expansion of the United States, and specifically with regard to the Latin other, the war with Mexico (1846–8) brought to the surface a variety of images and definitions that set off posited virtue against unmistakable vice. Mexicans were caricatured as lazy, ignorant, dishonest and vicious, and, as Horsman (1981) shows in his survey of the American press at the time, these views were widespread. The characterization of the Mexican as belonging to an inferior race also carried a gender distinction. The war, as Takaki (1993: 176–7) puts it, seemed to express a masculine destiny; American men, for instance, claimed that their sexual attractiveness to Mexican women was God-given. The Anglo-Saxon conquest of the Mexican *señoritas* was deemed to be foreordained, as they awaited the males of a superior and expanding nation.

Towards the end of the 1890s, the United States, as an emerging global power, annexed the nominally independent Hawaiian Islands, and in the same year, 1898, Spain and the United States signed the Treaty of Paris, through which Spain ceded Cuba, Puerto Rico, Guam and the Philippine archipelago. In the cases of Hawaii and the Philippines, annexation had been strongly influenced by the perceived danger of another Pacific power, Japan, securing control of these island territories. In the case of Cuba, with its proximity to the United States and the absence of rival geopolitical powers, there was a deeply rooted belief that the island belonged naturally within the orbit of American power.[7] Furthermore, in contrast to the Philippines, Cuba, as a result of a protracted independence struggle, had run up large debts which under annexation would have become a direct US responsibility. In this overall context, anti-annexation tendencies within the United States argued that the deployment of a colonizing power would violate the founding ethos of the Republic, reminding us of Bhabha's contention that colonial discourse had the tendency to mimic and undermine the dream of 'post-Enlightenment civility' on which it was paradoxically based. Opposition to annexation, however, did not mean that other forms of control were not feasible, and in the Cuban case the establishment of a semi-protectorate constituted one such form.

Although territorial expansion was an intrinsic part of United States development before 1898, the Spanish-American War brought in its wake a qualitatively different form of expansion that entailed the acquisition or control of sizeable dependencies not contiguous to the home land, as had been the case with Mexico, and inhabited by other peoples with their own histories, ideologies and political institutions. American leaders had to determine how these new territories should be governed; whether for instance they should be permanent colonies in an American empire, or rather more loosely tied dependencies, with the possibility of some degree of self-government under American tutelage. In an important sense, the answers to these questions were gradually worked out in the 'twin laboratories' of Cuba and the Philippines, where two different approaches were applied. In the Philippines, formal annexation and direct colonial government brought insurrection by the Filipinos and discord in the United States.[8] The material and moral costs of the war and the internal divisions that it provoked in the United States acted as a powerful brake on the development of any future strategy of territorial annexation. At the same time, it needs to be remembered, as I intimated above, that opposition to annexation and imperialist power was not necessarily anchored in any anti-racist conviction, as Lasch (1973) has indicated. In fact, annexation was frequently opposed on the grounds that it entailed the incorporation of inferior races into the American Republic,[9] although it is also true, *contra* Lasch, that there were non-racialist orientations within the anti-imperialist movement (Healy, 1970: 218–19).

In the Cuban case, the United States developed a strategy that had a number of implications for the future of geopolitical interventions in Central America and the Caribbean. The strategy rested on five inter-woven policies. The first of these, which was basic to the others, con-sisted in the establishment of informal protectorates which provided a viable political space for internal self-government. When it was deemed necessary, as in cases of internal revolts and acute political instability, military occupation by United States forces became an option, but never the assumption of formal sovereignty. Second, through trade, treaties or financial arrangements, a series of strong economic ties was woven between the United States and the dependent country. Third, by means of investment and a variety of projects of improvement – the diffusion of progress – new forms of economic and social involvement were put into place, including improvements in health care, the reform of public education and a modernizing programme of public works (see Ben-jamin, 1990: 52–91; Healy, 1963: 179–88). Fourth, there was a reter-ritorialization of administrative power, including the introduction of an American version of local self-government, and the central problem here, as one commentator noted for the Cuban case, lay 'in the attempt to engraft the Anglo-Saxon principle of local self-government on an Iberian system to which it was wholly foreign' (quoted in Healy, 1963: 184).[10] Finally, through the disbandment or reorganization of certain indigenous institutions, such as those that had been developed by the Cuban independence movement – the Liberation Army, the provisional government and the Revolutionary Party – and the initiation of processes of cultural penetration and subordination, attempts were made to Americanize the 'subject peoples'.

The vitality of counter-representations

The refusal to recognize full sovereignty for Cuba provoked a recurrent series of protests from the beginning of the century. Opposition to the passing of the Platt Amendment was expressed within the Cuban Constitutional Convention, and in addition, through popular pamphlets and newspaper cartoons of the time, counter-representations of Cuban–US relations came to be expressed. These representations, which revealed a growing sense of nationalism and anti-imperialist sentiment (Foner, 1972: 593–612), played a crucial role in the eventual abrogation of the Platt Amendment in the 1930s and the end of the indirect protectorate.[11]

These counter-representations, alternative visions to the power of already established discourses of governability, often possess a depth and a breadth that goes well beyond concepts of mimicry or mockery, touched on above. Remaining for a moment with the Cuban example, it is important to remember that the currents of opposition to American interventionism in Cuba came out of a rich and heterogeneous body of indigenous ideas and philosophies (Zea, 1963). In particular, José Martí, in a wide-ranging series of writings, developed a view of US–Latin American relations that continually stressed the need for autonomy when faced by the 'colossus of the North'. Writing in 1891 he argued that although Spanish America had almost entirely freed itself from its first metropolis, a new and much more powerful metropolis was overtaking it under the guise of economic penetration, and by diplomatic, political and, where necessary, military means. In the context of economic penetration, Martí (1961: 19–29), in a stance not without contemporary relevance, was antagonistic towards proposals for a trade agreement between Mexico and the United States, whose only beneficiary, in his view, would be the United States. Furthermore, Martí, who for a part of his life had resided and worked in the United States, was in no doubt about the relation between geopolitical power and modes of subordinating representation. For instance, when writing of the ruling classes in the United States, he noted that they believed in necessity – 'this will be ours because we need it' – and in the invincible superiority of 'the Anglo-Saxon race over the Latin', as well as the 'inferiority of the black race, . . . and of the Indians' (quoted in Fernández Retamar, 1986: 10). Under the influence of Bolívar, it was crucial that Spanish America, and specifically Martí's own Cuba, should not commit the error of regarding Europe or North America as the foreign model to which it should adjust.[12]

The desire to design autochthonous solutions to Hispanic American and Caribbean problems emanates from Bolívar and moves through Martí into the twentieth century, being expressed across a range of interpretative and political domains. The Cuban writer Fernández Retamar (1989: 5), in his discussion of culture in 'our America', criticizes the way Latin American culture is taken as an 'apprenticeship, a rough draft or a copy of European bourgeois culture'. This sense of being subordinated by an outside culture or regime of truth has fuelled the fires of nationalism and has stimulated a wide range of counter-discourses, some of which have provided intellectual sustenance to projects of resistance and revolutionary change.[13] Frequently in the West, it is the actual eruption of political conflict and the practical impulse of rebellion that have captured the imagination, whereas the less visible, reflective, philosophical currents of opposition and refusal have received far less analytical oxygen (Slater, 1994a). Despite the clear presence of heterogeneity and conceptual hybridity, a pivotal feature of critical writing emanating from Latin America, as well as from Africa and Asia, has been the continual preoccupation with questions of autonomy and self-determination, a theme to which I shall return in the final section of the chapter. What is now needed is a further commentary on the changing contexts in which particular kinds of geopolitical interventions have taken place.

Contexts of containment

When considering a number of problems relating to identity politics, Alker (1996: xi) argues that it is necessary to have a view which is not only concerned with the current spaces within which identity operates, 'but also of the historical legacies lending persistence to some forms of global subjectivity and fragmentation to others'. This is an important point, since it raises the issue of the ways such historical legacies are grounded and reproduced. The sedimentation of persistent meanings and practices is a reflection of the effectiveness of power, which cannot be deciphered outside the context of those social and political discourses that construct the spatial frames of national and international politics. As suggested in earlier passages concerning the projection of American power, the interactive invocation of cultural representations and geopolitical practices has a history that cuts into the present and invests future visions with a significant continuity. However, although the presence of projects of mission and the deployment of invasive discourses into societies considered to be in need of incorporation and transformation have their own meaning and dynamic, they are not sufficient to account for the contemporary dispositions of geopolitical power. In contrast to the method of some studies of American interventionism in the Third World, the dominant enframing of other non-Western societies, and the relation of that enframing to power as penetration and incorporation, certainly have to be situated in an historical setting that takes us back to the nineteenth century, and the origins of the imperial gaze. But such a retracing can only provide one component of our analysis, since the representation of geopolitical encounters across the North–South divide is also rooted in the perceived emergence of a vital threat to those earlier constructions of civilization and progress.

The perceived threat of Communist power and subversion called for a concerted strategy of containment, and the key architect of this far-reaching strategy was George F. Kennan.[14] In two pivotal papers he outlined an argument which came to form a basis for future foreign policy. From his Moscow embassy telegram of 1946, an 8,000-word document that came to be known as 'The Long Telegram', and his anonymous 'Mr. X' paper of 1947 which discussed 'The Sources of Soviet Conduct', a number of relevant points can be highlighted. First, it is clear that in a cultural sense there was an Orientalist reading of Russian society – for example, he writes of 'the lessons of Russian history: of centuries of obscure battles between nomadic forces over the stretches of a vast unfortified plain ... here caution, circumspection, flexibility and deception are the valuable qualities', which are appreciated 'in the Russian or the oriental mind'.[15] Second, the American necessity of understanding and apprehending the new Soviet reality is likened to the way a 'doctor studies an unruly and unreasonable individual', although crucially this 'individual' is now possessed by a new creed – 'Communism'. For Kennan this new politics – the belief in 'World Communism' – is like a 'malignant parasite which feeds only on diseased tissue'. It is here that Kennan stressed the significance of the need to maintain the health and vigour of American society, and the combined reality of domestic and foreign policies. Kennan went on to argue that 'every courageous and incisive measure to solve internal problems of our own society, to improve self-confidence, discipline, morale and community spirit ... is a diplomatic victory over Moscow'. Third, Kennan's call for a strategy of containment was linked not only to a strong notion of the need for American moral and intellectual leadership, but to a specific geopolitical 'counter-force' – it was stated that 'the Soviet pressure against the free institutions of the western world is something that can be contained by the adroit and vigilant application of counter-force at a series of constantly shifting geographical and political points'.[16] This sense of a shifting threat was rooted in the idea that Soviet political action was like a 'fluid stream that moves constantly', and that attempts to fill 'every nook and cranny available to it in the basin of world power' (see Etzold and Gaddis, 1978: 86).

Kennan's vision of Soviet expansionism and his argument for containment were closely linked to US foreign policy towards the Third World, within which poverty and underdevelopment were seen as new threats to security.[17] The key difference with previous periods was that in the case of Soviet Communism the notion of 'threat' was envisaged in relation to the emergence of what was perceived to be an expansionist, mobile, fluid force that could invade and potentially transform the body politic of every society. In previous periods geopolitical interventions were more associated with the perceived need to restore order and the conditions for progress in societies of the periphery, and although movements of resistance were part of this general landscape,[18] they were not associated with the ostensibly expansionist ideology of an emerging global power. This point needs to be further specified. For example, I am not arguing that the invocation of a Soviet or Bolshevik threat was not deployed in earlier times. In the late 1920s, for instance, when US marines had been landed in Nicaragua to intervene in that country's political crisis, Mexico was accused of promoting anarchy in Nicaragua, and the secretary of state to President Coolidge associated the Mexican government with Soviet influences in an effort to provide greater justification for US interventionism (Salisbury, 1986). Equally, it can be pointed out that the Monroe Doctrine was also predicated on a concept of containment – the protection of United States influence within the Americas by the curtailment and eventual rolling back of European colonial power. What was specific to the post-war era was the depiction of the Soviet Union as a global threat to the *internal* functioning of peripheral societies; containment was necessary, since the new creed of 'World Communism' aimed to penetrate the body politic of vulnerable non-Western societies and transform them into malignant new orders that would be a mortal danger to America and the 'free world'. Post-war concepts of 'development' and 'modernization' were designed not only to bring progress, order and civilization in the older terms of the modality of encounter, but to act as key barriers to the threatening, expansive fluids of Communist ideology. It was the fear of the global danger of a fluid expansionist ideology, which would be able to penetrate the vulnerable Third World society and transform it through malignant mutation, that lent continuing vitality to projects of development and modernization. This was especially the case in the 1960s during a time of widespread political turbulence, both internationally and internally within the United States. Poverty and inequality were seen as fertile 'breeding grounds' for Communist subversion, which was once likened, in the spirit of Kennan, to a 'disease' of the transition from tradition to modernity.

Moreover, in one highly significant aspect the American strategy of containment was joined with the earlier discourses of imperial power and authority. I am referring here to the fact that the deeply embedded belief in Occidental superiority over the non-West nurtured a view that came to take resistances to the impact of Westernization and modernization as being generated by external agents, rather than being the authentic expressions of indigenous thought and organization. In other words, it was frequently assumed that a Third World radical government or movement would be manipulated or directed by Soviet elements.[19] Old prejudices concerning 'childlike peoples' and 'inferior cultures' continued to exert their influence. In contrast, what was perceived to be the external menace of Communist ideology may well have been insidious and demonic, but equally it was clever, well organized and certainly not infantile.

With the end of the Cold War, the events of 1989 and the dissolution of the Soviet Union, the strategy of containing Communism lost its driving foundation, but new constructions of containment have since emerged. New threats have been rapidly identified, and they include the spread of nuclear weapons, virulent and unpredictable, or what Laqueur (1996) refers to as 'postmodern' forms of terrorism: drug traffickers, recalcitrant Third World dictators, Japanese economic power, the expansion of 'Islamic fundamentalism', disease, migration and population issues, 'the environment' as a key national security question (Dalby, 1996), global mafias, and a general disquiet about the seemingly pervasive nature of uncertainty, risk and turbulence. Concern over cultural conflicts, and in particular the idea that Western civilization is under threat from other cultures and religions (Huntington, 1993) have led to a renewed focus on the 'Third World' or 'less-developed regions' as a potent source of new dangers and destabilizations.

One of the characteristically new dangers of the period has been identified as 'narco-terrorism'. By the mid-1980s in the United States the 'war on drugs' came to receive primary attention, and in the US invasion of Panama in 1989 President Bush used the issue of 'narco-terrorism' as one of the central arguments in his justification of US military action; in this case, and for the first time in the post-war period, the United States had intervened in a Latin American country without invoking the strategy of containing Communism. During the 1980s, the theme of containment resurfaced in the context of the 'war on drugs' and in some instances led to quite militant proposals, including, as Der Derian (1992: 108–9) reminds us, the call for an air attack on Medellín, or on another occasion an outright invasion of Colombia.

The overall development of a US strategy on drugs has created a concentration on what has been referred to as the 'supply side' of the problem. What has emerged has been an attempt to destroy or at least curtail the cultivation of coca leaves from which cocaine has been produced and distributed throughout the United States and beyond. To contain the problem at source, thus legitimizing a new round of interventions, has been a guiding priority of US policy, and in a number of cases, especially with regard to Bolivia, a US military presence has raised important questions of territorial sovereignty and national autonomy (Gamarra, 1994). In the context of representation and geopolitics, the way this particular issue has been conventionally enframed in the United States and elsewhere has tended to reinforce previously extant stereotypes of unruly, chaotic and chronically disturbed societies. The need for order seen as an externally induced solution has fuelled the desire for intervention. Further, the customary lack of attention to indigenous voices has gone together with the designation of policies that largely ignore the social and economic contexts in which the phenomenon of narco-power emerges, whilst concentrating instead on issues of law and order. At the same time the 'enemy' is seen as more diffuse, more unpredictable, lacking an overarching philosophy of expansion, whilst the grounds for effective intervention and solution are seen as more tenuous and more fragile. This ethos of uncertainty is closely related to the erosion of state legitimacy and the diversification of internal sources of conflict in many societies of the South. In this sense, and in specific relation to the example of the connection between the 'war on drugs' and containment strategy, the matrix of cultural representation and geopolitical practices combines the more recognizable meanings of earlier discourses on the Third World other with newer elements of signification that flow from a time of deep anxiety, precariousness and turmoil.

Agents and arenas of interpretation

Finally, I want to return to the problem of the objects and subjects of knowledge in times marked by the politics of global change. In the work of Edward Said, perhaps the most influential of the scholars associated with the 'post-colonial turn', there is a deep awareness of the centrality of the relation between self-reflexivity and the agents of knowledge. Hence, he continually cites the academic works of non-Western 'others', and deploys their arguments to help disrupt and destabilize the apparent normalcy of Occidental narratives and theoretical priorities. I would suggest that whilst the Western academy has been marked by a recent series of thematic and conceptual shifts, the growth of interest in questions of subject-ivities and re-presentation, including more enabling analyses of power and politics, has frequently not been accompanied by a diversification or globalization of the *sources* of theoretical knowledge. In fact, the agents or subjects of knowledge, the designers of the new arenas of enquiry and interpretation, have predominantly remained of Western origin. Consequently, whilst it is necessary to emphasize the variability and heterogeneity of new forms of critical Western thought, and to argue against any essentialization of its content and disposition, none the less it can be strongly maintained that there is not as much diversity in the sources and politics of conceptual thought as there could be, and that this lack constitutes a serious handicap in our attempts to globalize the arenas of knowledge and understanding.

In considering the various ways in which we might think about alterity, and doing so in the context of conquest, Todorov (1984: 185–6) distinguished three axes on which the problematic of otherness can be located. Initially there is the value judgement – the other is good or bad, or she or he is my equal or inferior. Second, there is the action of distancing in relation to the other, which might involve embracing the other's values, or imposing my own image on him or her; and between submission to the other and the other's submission there is a third term, which is neutrality or indifference. Finally there is for Todorov the epistemic level – I know or am ignorant of the other's identity, where we have a continuum between the lower or higher states of knowledge. Todorov shows that the relation between self and other cannot be understood on one level alone, and he does this by comparing the relations of people like Cortés and Las Casas to 'the Indians'. On the one hand Las Casas loved the Indians more than Cortés did, whereas on the epistemic level Cortés had a knowledge of the Indians that was superior to that of Las Casas. On the level of 'distancing in relation to the other' both proposed a relationship of assimilation – the submission of the other. This classification is useful in a number of ways, and it helps to underline the importance of avoiding the kind of easy thinking which is based on the notion that if only human collectives came to know one another better, they would act less violently towards one another. Alternatively, a lack of knowledge or indifference to the other will obviously restrict the possibilities of mutually enriching dialogues.

In our own case, an increased Western knowledge of the contributions made by non-Western academics gives no guarantee that such contributions will be respected or recognized. It is here that we can see how the agents and arenas of interpretation come together, since one of the crucial dimensions of the analysis of representations and geopolitics concerns the lack of respect and recognition involved in the development of imperial interventions. Counter-discourses of nationalism and popular sovereignty are in large part a vibrant response to an intervening power that attempts to submit the other to its own vision of the world. In the arena of critical theory, the propensity to listen to the non-Western other as a philosophical or reflexive other remains somewhat undeveloped. In some instances authors may well remain within that Rorty-type circle whereby imperial violence and oppression may well be acknowledged, but only in the context of a Western enclosure, whereby it is the enlightened Western academic who alerts us to such phenomena, thus erasing the disruptive non-Western other who is also an intellectual other. The mirror opposite of such a position would be to prioritize other non-Western voices in a frame which posited some kind of 'authentic', 'uncontaminated' and essentially subversive intellectual other. What I am suggesting is that we could benefit from a far greater hybridization of the sources of our critical thinking, whilst always maintaining a sharp awareness of the pitfalls of 'going native' in whatever guise. Conversations and dialogues and processes of mutual learning which need to preserve the right to be critical and respectful can generate the possibility of more reciprocity and enhanced understanding across diverse terrains. However, the challenge that the politics of recognition offers is not an easy one, since we live in a world riven by histories of distrust, prejudices, disrespect and violent oppositions. To develop new kinds of geopolitical representation that attempt to go beyond the enclosures of supremacy and enmity we need to attach greater importance to the legacies of invasive imaginations. Furthermore, whilst accepting the idea that the less powerful can also be implicated in othering, and distancing ourselves from the proclivity to blame the powerful for everything, it can be argued that a closer attention to the effects of the geopolitical histories of subordinating power might well amplify our understanding of today's politics of global change. At the same time, and in these kinds of reflection, we have to think seriously, as Western authors and social scientists, of our own position, and perhaps, in the process of new kinds of analytical engagement, part of our own identity as agents of knowledge might be altered and made more open to different modes of interpretation.

Notes

1 For all citations from Jefferson's messages and addresses to the Senate and House of Representatives, see Richardson (1896: 352–4).
2 It is important to note here that the term 'American' is not of course free from dispute, since its usage conventionally refers to the United States, whilst Latin Americans also and rightly regard themselves as Americans (americanos). However, at the same time, the existence of specific nationalities from Mexican to Chilean has no equivalent north of the Rio Grande

and therefore in this case I shall sometimes use the term 'American' as being equivalent to 'of the United States'.

3 See the Cuban Liberty and Democratic Solidarity (LIBERTAD) Act of 1996, Public Law 104–114, 12 March 1996, 110 Stat. 785–824, Washington DC, United States General Printing Office: 786, 788.

4 Ibid., p. 805.

5 The distinction between the power over and the power to is developed in Foucault's writings, and an interesting, insightful treatment of this aspect of Foucault's work is to be found in Patton (1989). I have also dealt with this theme in relation to social movements and political change in Latin America – see Slater (1994b).

6 In the geographical domain, one may recall a phrase from Dudley Stamp (1960: 177), who described some kinds of underdeveloped countries as 'slum nations', and of course Western literature is permeated by notions of 'savage', 'barbaric' or 'childlike' peoples.

7 My use of the word 'naturally' is not accidental, since in 1859 US Secretary of State Seward, who told the Spanish minister that Cuba must ultimately come to us 'by means of constant gravitation', also commented that Cuba had been formed by the Mississippi in washing American sand into the Gulf – see Weinberg (1963: 234).

8 Ten thousand well-armed insurgents backed Aguinaldo's republic, and they were prepared to fight. American troops and the Filipino insurgents waged war for nearly three years, and when in 1902 the War Department declared the insurgency at an end, an estimated 20,000 Filipino insurgents had been killed in battle, and as many as 200,000 civilians were dead of hunger, disease or other indirect result of the insurrection. For an analysis of US imperialism in the Philippines see, for example, Karnow (1989).

9 For some examples of racist prejudices towards the Filipinos at the time of annexation see Hunt (1987: 81). In 1904, at the Louisiana Purchase Exposition held in St Louis, juxtaposed to the usual array of goods on display was found a special Philippines Reservation, an exhibit of 1,200 Filipinos. The Philippines Reservation, organized by the United States government, marked the arrival of the United States as a world imperial power; one of the exhibit's organizers called it 'the largest and finest colonial exhibit ever made by any Government' – see Rydell's (1989) study of the 'culture of imperial abundance'.

10 The restructuring of municipal government in Cuba during the early years of the twentieth century, with the attempt to introduce American concepts of local government and decentralized financing, is not so far removed from today's fiscal decentralization policies of the World Bank and the United States Agency for International Development. As far as I am aware this potential connection has not been studied.

11 However, although the United States gave up its right to intervene in Cuba, and rescinded previous restrictions on the Cuban government to contract foreign loans or enter into alliances with other countries, nevertheless the US retained its rights over the naval base at Guantánamo, which it has kept until today.

12 The inclusion of this example is not made to underline some partisan posi-
    tion but to indicate the levels of forgetfulness and institutionalized indiffer-
    ence that make such a voice seem so disruptive of today's established
    traditions of international political analysis.
13 Fredric Jameson in his foreword to Fernández Retamar's text (1989: vii),
    stresses the important connection between language and politics, comment-
    ing that in the world outside the West, and certainly in Cuba, 'the political
    is a destiny, where human beings are from the outset condemned to politics,
    as a result of material want, and of life on the very edge of physical cata-
    strophe, a life that almost always includes human violence as well'. For
    Jameson, then, the peculiarity of First World life is the possibility of forget-
    ting the political altogether, at least for a time; 'of stepping out of the
    "nightmare of history" into the sealed spaces of a private life', which is
    strangely regarded as 'sheerly natural'. Although there are problems with
    the way Jameson depicts 'politics' as being somehow outside the private
    realm, his distinction between West and non-West is pertinent.
14 In 1947, after many years in the Foreign Service, George F. Kennan was
    given responsibility for organizing and directing a Policy Planning Staff for
    United States foreign relations. His various papers were highly influential in
    the early post-war years. For an imaginative discussion of key aspects of his
    geopolitical influence see Ó Tuathail and Agnew (1992).
15 From 'The Sources of Soviet Conduct', reprinted in Etzold and Gaddis
    (1978: 86).
16 Quotations taken from Etzold and Gaddis (1978: 62–3, 87).
17 For an interesting discussion of aspects of these connections see Escobar
    (1995: ch. 2).
18 For example, in the case of the Dominican Republic, United States inter-
    vention during the 1916–24 period was met with stiff internal resistance in
    the eastern part of the country, where a guerrilla insurgency continued for
    several years despite the presence of US marines – for a detailed survey see
    Calder (1978).
19 Niess (1990) touches on this theme in relation to Latin America.

References

Aguilar A. (1968) *Pan-Americanism – from Monroe to the Present*. New York
    and London, Monthly Review Press.
Alker, H.W. (1996) 'Preface' and 'Acknowledgements'. In M.J. Shapiro and
    H.W. Alker (eds), *Challenging Boundaries*. Borderlines, vol. 2. Minneapolis
    and London, University of Minnesota Press, ix–xiii.
Benjamin, J.R. (1990) *The United States and the Origins of the Cuban Revolu-
    tion*. Princeton NJ, Princeton University Press.
Bhabha, H. (1994) *The Location of Culture*. London and New York, Rout-
    ledge.
Blaut, J.M. (1993) *The Colonizer's Model of the World*. New York and
    London, Guilford Press.

Calder, B.J. (1978) 'Caudillos and *gavilleros* versus the United States Marines: guerrilla insurgency during the Dominican intervention, 1916–1924'. *Hispanic American Historical Review*, 58/4: 649–75.

Commager, H.S. (1978) *The Empire of Reason.* London, Weidenfeld and Nicolson.

Dalby, S. (1996) 'The environment as geopolitical threat: reading Robert Kaplan's "Coming Anarchy" '. *Ecumene*, 3/4: 472–96.

Deleuze, G. and Guattari, F. (1984) *Anti-Oedipus.* London, Athlone Press.

Der Derian, J. (1992) *Antidiplomacy.* Oxford, Blackwell.

Driver, F. (1992) 'Geography's empire: histories of geographical knowledge'. *Environment and Planning D: Society and Space*, 10: 23–40.

Escobar, A. (1995) *Encountering Development.* Princeton NJ, Princeton University Press.

Etzold, T.H. and J.L. Gaddis (eds) (1978) *Containment: Documents on American Policy and Strategy, 1945–1950.* New York, Columbia University Press.

Fernández Retamar, R. (1986) 'The modernity of Martí'. In C. Abel and N. Torrents (eds), *José Martí.* Durham NC, Duke University Press, 1–15.

Fernández Retamar, R. (1989) *Caliban and Other Essays.* Minneapolis, University of Minnesota Press.

Foner, P.S. (1972) *The Spanish-Cuban-American War and the Birth of American Imperialism. Vol. II: 1898–1902.* New York and London, Monthly Review Press.

Gamarra, E.A. (1994) *Entre la Droga y la Democracia.* La Paz, ILDIS.

Gregory, D. (1995) 'Imaginative geographies'. *Progress in Human Geography*, 19/4: 447–85.

Grovogui, S.N. (1996) *Sovereigns, Quasi Sovereigns and Africans.* Borderlines, vol. 3. Minneapolis and London, University of Minnesota Press.

Healy, D.F. (1963) *The United States in Cuba 1898–1902.* Madison, University of Wisconsin Press.

Healy, D.F. (1970) *US Expansionism.* Madison and London, University of Wisconsin Press.

Horsman, R. (1981) *Race and Manifest Destiny.* Cambridge MA, Harvard University Press.

Hunt, M.H. (1987) *Ideology and U.S. Foreign Policy.* New Haven and London, Yale University Press.

Huntington, S.P. (1993) 'The clash of civilisations?'. *Foreign Affairs*, 72/3: 22–49.

Karnow, S. (1989) *In Our Image.* New York, Random House.

Lafeber, W. (1963) *The New Empire.* Ithaca NY and London, Cornell University Press.

Laqueur, W. (1996) 'Postmodern terrorism'. *Foreign Affairs*, 75/5: 24–36.

Lasch, C. (1973) 'The anti-imperialist as racist'. In T.G. Paterson (ed.), *American Imperialism and Anti-Imperialism.* New York, Thomas Y. Crowell, 110–17.

Martí, J. (1961) *Obras Completas. XIX: Estados Unidos y América Latina.* Havana, Patronato del Libro Popular.

Morrison, T. (1992) *Playing in the Dark*. Cambridge MA and London, Harvard University Press.

Niess, F. (1990) *A Hemisphere to Itself*. London, Zed Books.

Norton, A. (1993) 'Engendering another American identity'. In F.M. Dolan and T.L. Dumm (eds), *Rhetorical Republic*. Amherst, University of Massachusetts Press, 125–42.

Ó Tuathail, G. and J. Agnew (1992) 'Geopolitics and discourse: practical geopolitical reasoning in American foreign policy'. *Political Geography*, 11: 190–204.

Patton, P. (1989) 'Taylor and Foucault on power and freedom'. *Political Studies*, XXXVII/2: 260–76.

Pike, F.B. (1992) *The United States and Latin America*. Austin TX, University of Texas Press.

Richardson, J.D. (1896) *A Compilation of the Messages and Papers of the Presidents. Vol. 1*. Washington DC, Government Printing Office.

Rydell, R.W. (1989) 'The culture of imperial abundance: world's fairs in the making of American culture'. In S.J. Bronner (ed.), *Consuming Visions*. New York and London, W.W. Norton, 191–216.

Said, E.W. (1978) *Orientalism*. Harmondsworth, Penguin.

Said, E.W. (1989) 'Representing the colonized: anthropology's interlocutors'. *Critical Inquiry*, 15: 205–25.

Salisbury, R.V. (1986) 'Mexico, the United States, and the 1926–1927 Nicaraguan crisis'. *Hispanic American Historical Review*, 66/2: 319–39.

Slater, D. (1994a) 'Exploring other zones of the postmodern: problems of ethnocentrism and difference across the North–South divide'. In A. Rattansi and S. Westwood (eds), *Racism, Modernity and Identity*. Cambridge, Polity Press, 87–125.

Slater, D. (1994b) 'Power and social movements in the other occident: Latin America in an international context'. *Latin American Perspectives*, 21/2: 11–37.

Spurr, D. (1993) *The Rhetoric of Empire*. Durham NC and London, Duke University Press.

Stamp, D. (1960) *Our Developing World*. London, Faber and Faber.

Takaki, R. (1993) *A Different Mirror*. Boston, Toronto and London, Back Bay Books and Little, Brown.

Thomas, N. (1994) *Colonialism's Culture*. Cambridge, Polity Press.

Todorov, T. (1984) *The Conquest of America*. New York, Harper Perennial.

Ulmen, G.L. (1987) 'American imperialism and international law: Carl Schmitt on the US in world affairs'. *Telos*, 72: 43–71.

Weinberg, A. (1963) *Manifest Destiny*. Chicago, Quadrangle Books.

Weston, R. (1972) *Racism in U.S. Imperialism*. Columbia SC, University of South Carolina Press.

Zea, L. (1963) *The Latin American Mind*. Norman, University of Oklahoma Press.

5

Collective Wish Images: Geographical Imaginaries and the Crisis of National Development

Michael John Watts

Introduction

I was once told an African fable by a Zairean friend – it went roughly as follows. Once upon a time, a number of North Atlantic research teams were hired by the United Nations to examine the intricate life of the African elephant. In the days prior to Kofi Annan and Jesse Helms, money and resources were almost limitless. Phalanxes of researchers were customarily despatched to the African savannas to study the intricacies of elephant diet, mobility, life cycles, reproductive habits and such like. After years of what we may assume was painstaking research, the time came for each national team to file its final report. The American volume was short, slick and colourful, chock-full of exuberant pictures and the latest in high-tech visuality – all form and no content. The British conversely produced a large, painfully detailed ethnography; modest in scope, careful not to overstep the demands of the evidence, understated in prose, and spectacularly boring – all content and no form. The French produced a slim and extremely elegant report on elephant recipes while the Germans produced the first of a projected eighty-five volumes on the elephant turd. And the Italians, embroiled in a small civil war among team members over the colour and design of the cover, were unable to submit any report at all.

From the vantage point of the West – as my friend was at pains to point out – Africa is always a space of projection: of race, darkness, sexuality, disorder, barbarism, and typically of cultural backwardness, as Hegel put it. Africa is, as jazz critic Stanley Crouch properly says in *Notes of a Hanging Judge* (1990: 201), one of the greatest fantasies of our time.

Almost two decades ago, Edward Said (1979) laid the foundation for an understanding of such fantastic geohistorical categories in his book *Orientalism* – though one might comfortably include 'Africanism' within its circumference (cf. Said, 1993: 67). He offered the West's representations of the Orient as a three-fold form of mapping: as a realm of study, as an epistemological and ontological rendering of the West and the Other, and as a nexus of institutions of power and knowledge. A number of scholars, among them Fernando Coronil (1996), have prodded and extended Said's account to include what Coronil calls Orientalism's 'dark side', the conditions for Orientalism's possibility; that is to say, to display the contours of the West's 'Occidentalism', by which Coronil means the forms of classification, hierarchy, exclusion, naturalization and spatiality rooted in the deployment of global power, in 'the constitution of international asymmetries underwritten by global capitalism' (Coronil, 1996: 57). If Coronil wishes to unmask the essentialist renderings of the West by Westerners, I seek to address another facet of this complex geohistorical mapping by which otherness is constructed, namely the rendering of non-Western alien societies by those societies themselves – what Carrier (1992) calls 'ethno-Orientalism' – and its particular geography. As such, I am pursuing what Said (1993: 7) himself has called a geographical enquiry into a particular experience, recognizing that, like all societies, the fabrication of African others by Africans themselves is necessarily a 'struggle over geography ... [which is] not only about soldiers and cannons but about ideas, about forms, about images and imaginings' (Said, 1993: 7).

My entry point is the much publicized struggle by the Ogoni people – a small ethnic society occupying a Lilliputian territory in the oil-rich Niger delta in southeast Nigeria – and their one-time leader Ken Saro-Wiwa to create a space of autonomy and self-determination enshrined in an Ogoni Bill of Rights and in a mass political movement (MOSOP, the Movement for the Survival of the Ogoni People). Running through this narrative is an effort by a non-Western ethnic minority – an 'indigenous people' – to construct simultaneously representations, first, of other Nigerians as 'ethnic majorities' and of themselves as minorities and indigenous people; and second, of political rights and entitlements, an Ogoni imaginary of a sort, on which alternative histories and geographies are constructed. In my view the Ogoni struggle for recognition is part of an incomplete decolonization of Africa, an effort to redeem something from the carapace of reformist nationalism and to maintain the imaginative liberation of an African people, what Aimée Cesaire in another time called the 'invention of new souls' (cited in Said, 1994: 39). The Ogoni discourse of otherness turns in large measure, as I shall argue, on articulations of history and geography. Articulation is employed here in the double sense endorsed by Stuart Hall (1996), namely as a way of rendering an identity (discursive coherence) and of linking that identity to a political subject and project (interpellation). The unity between these two sorts of articulation, in Hall's view, encompasses the process by which an ideology finds its subject – rather than how a subject locates and articulates an essentialized set of ideas or thoughts – a task which always entails the positing of boundaries and edges in an always provisional and contingent way (see Li, 1997, 1996). In exploring the case of Ogoniland I wish to emphasize the geographical content of such articulations: how geography is empirically developed, normatively construed and epistemologically constructed. My general concern is to explore how a particular geographical imaginary is contained within the Ogoni search for identity and development.

Of course this question of containment is enormously complex, and made more so by the irreducible fact that the case of the Ogoni is in no sense a simple rendition of what I previously called ethno-Orientalism. While MOSOP is indeed an instance of an African other constructing African – and, as we shall see, European – others, the boundary between Occidental and Oriental is profoundly blurred. The essentially local character of the claims over development and the Ogoni Bill of Rights was in practice part of a conversation with national discourses over such modernist sentiments as federalism, sovereignty, citizenship and nationalism, with multinational Occidental discourses of indigeneity, and with transnational oppositional discourses of environmental and human rights. Saro-Wiwa himself embodied this irreducibly hybrid, fluid and messy ethno-Orientalism. A visible and powerful member of the 'traditional' Ogoni elite, he was also, and simultaneously, an influential former politician and bureaucrat (serving in state and federal governments), a university-educated author of local soap operas, poetry and novels, and not least a global public intellectual living in the space of a transnational civil society.

I want to address this complexity by using Hall's notion of articulation in two geographical ways. The first draws upon Walter Benjamin and his notion of the collective wish image,[1] and the second upon Poulantzas's (1978: 81) observation that 'national unity or modern unity becomes a historicity of a territory and a territorialization of a history'. Specifically, I want to argue that Benjamin's notion of the fantastic mingling of the old and new at the beginning of the new era of industrialization, and the image fantasy from the ur-past, captures much of the Ogoni concern with nature and territory in their own vision of another development. As Susan Buck-Morss (1989: 116) puts it:

> In nature, the new is mythic, because its potential is not yet realized; in consciousness, the old is mythic because its desires were never fulfilled. Paradoxically, collective imagination mobilizes its powers for a revolutionary break from the recent past by evoking a cultural memory reservoir of myths and utopian symbols from a more distant ur-past. The collective wish images are nothing else but this. Sparked by the new from which they 'maintain their impulse', they envision its revolutionary potential by conjuring up archaic images of the collective 'wish' for social utopia.

Collective images stand at the intersection of a mythic nature with a mythic consciousness as a way of positing a utopian alternative. These images, in Benjamin's language, 'innervate' the collective. Saro-Wiwa worked Ogoni ur-history and its repository of images as a way of creating an identity and a utopia. Wish images, while derived from the local and from tradition – they are archaic meanings which can be awakened dialectically, like the fetishes of the new nature in which human potential is frozen – are, however, always confronted by the dangers of oppression and co-optation:

> [D]anger affects both the content of tradition and its receivers. The same threat hangs over both: that of becoming a tool of the ruling classes. In every era the attempt must be made anew to wrest tradition away from a conformism that is about to overpower it ... [E]ven the dead will not be safe from the enemy if he wins. (Benjamin, 1969: 255)

This brings me to my second point, namely the danger, as Poulantzas suggests, represented by the ways in which geography and history are fetishized. Markers of identity may become themselves commodities in a way that the histories of interrelated peoples become spatialized into bounded territories, and 'since these spaces appear as being produced naturally, not historically, they serve to root the histories of connected peoples in separate territories and to sever the links between them' (Coronil, 1996: 77). There is a double occlusion as histories of space are obscured and as social relations between societies are eviscerated. In my view, Saro-Wiwa's and his movement's vision of alternative development stood at the meeting ground of the collective wish image (geographical and dialectical) with the commodification and fetishism of history and space. At stake was the content of tradition and its receivers.

Post-development imaginaries

Against a backdrop of deepening global inequality and intractable Southern poverty – according to the United Nations Development Program (UNDP, 1996) the polarization of global wealth *doubled* between 1960 and 1989 – it is perhaps inevitable that development as theory and practice is once more mired in debate and controversy. Many intellectuals and activists from the South have come to see development as a cruel hoax – a 'blunder of planetary proportions' (Sachs, 1992: 3) – which is now coming to an unceremonious end. 'You must be either very dumb or very rich if you fail to notice', notes Mexican activist Esteva (1992: 7), 'that "development" stinks.' It is precisely the groundswell of anti-development thinking – oppositional discourses that have as their starting point the rejection of development, the end of Enlightenment and the failure of development as a modernist project – which posits the likes of the Ogoni movement as a site not simply of alterity but of a radical reimagining of development itself.[2]

Standing at the centre of a broad and heterogeneous field of so-called alternatives to development (Pieterse, 1996) is, broadly speaking, a philosophical sympathy towards poststructuralism, and correspondingly a strenuously enforced antipathy to the metanarratives of both neoliberal orthodoxy and Marxism. Anti-development efforts to imagine a 'post-development era' start from the capacity of the development imaginary to shape identity and produce particular sorts of 'normalized subject' in the South. Development here threatens diversity, homogenizing local traditions through the apparatuses of the state (investment, measurement and planning). The local is eclipsed by the use of general conceptual categories and Western assumptions. A post-development alternative, then, depends fundamentally on local spaces of self-determination and autonomy (Sachs, 1993; Escobar 1992a, 1992b). Both articulations are draped in the presumptions of anti-foundationalism and of a resistance to what are seen as universalizing discourses of the West. Escobar's work (1995) is central to imaging post-development because it links both of these lines of thinking and provides an explicitly theoretical framework for the study of development and environmental sustainability. Specifically, he finds modern development discourse to be an invention – more properly a 'historically produced discourse' (1995: 6) – of the post-1945 era, the latest insidious chapter of the larger history of the expansion of Western reason. This discourse is governed by the 'same principles' as colonial discourse but has its own 'regimes of truth' and 'forms of representation' (1995: 9–10). Development is about forms of knowledge, the power that regulates its practices, and the forms of subjectivity fostered by its impulses. Hegemonic development discourse appropriates societal practices and meanings into the modern realm of explicit calculation, thereby subjecting them to Western forms of power/knowledge. It ensures the conformity of peoples to First World economic and cultural practices. Development has in short penetrated, integrated, managed and controlled countries and populations in increasingly pernicious and intractable ways. It has produced underdevelopment, a condition politically and economically manageable through 'normalization', the regulation of knowledges and the moralization and technification of poverty and exploitation. The Third World came to believe what the First World promulgated: development as a technical project, as rational decision making, as specialized knowledge, and as normalization (1995: 52–3). What was and is missing from development, according to Escobar, is *people*.

People re-enter the post-development story in so far as there has been 'the resurrection, reemergence and rebirth of . . . civil society' (J. Cohen and Arato, 1992: 29), and it is within these attempts to thicken civil society that any alternative to development actually resides. Partly in response to the collapse of state resources, and partly as an outcome of an uneven democratization process, various forms of local and community movement have emerged in the interstices of the state— market nexus. These new multidimensional social movements (NSM) are taken to be new in so far as they represent a sort of postmodern politics outside of and in many respects antithetical to class or social democratic party politics (Rajnema, 1996; Escobar, 1992b). This multi-dimensionality is, according to Escobar (1992a), indicative of a new mode of doing politics, so-called 'autopoietic' (that is to say, self-producing and self-organizing) movements which exercise power outside the state arena and which seek to create 'decentred autonomous spaces'. The 'local community' and 'grassroots initiatives' loom very large in poststructural approaches to development. What they represent is certainly a form of collective action, but more specifically and profoundly a 'resistance to development' (Escobar, 1995: 216; also Routledge, 1994) which attempts to build new identities. The implication is, of course, that these identities fall outside of the panoptic gaze of the hegemonic development discourse as new forms of subjectivity which stand opposed to modernity itself.[3]

What then is the new content of such movements and what are their relations to post-development imaginaries? There are, in my reading, at least five fundamental and overlapping aspects attributed to grassroots movements as vehicles of counter-modernity. First, they purportedly contain new sorts of politics and new sorts of political subjectivity.

They are typically local, outside of the organized state sphere and 'without one particular ideology or political party' (Escobar, 1992b: 422). They are 'self-organizing and self-producing', exercising non-state forms of power. Second, 'cultural difference is at the root of postdevelopment' (Escobar, 1995: 225) and hence the movements are, above all, examples of popular cultural discourse. Minority cultural communities[4] figure centrally in both green and anti-development movements; indeed, the 'indigenous' becomes the lodestar for the 'unmaking of the Third World'. Indian confederations in Latin America, or 'ethnic' green movements in Africa, often turn on the ways in which cultural identity is mobilized as 'a transformative engagement with modernity' (Escobar, 1995: 219). Third, the movements employ, in creative ways, local or subaltern reservoirs of knowledge. Paul Richards's (1985) invocation of 'inventive self-reliance' rooted in local African peasant knowledge is an influential case in point of this line of thinking. The proliferation of the field of 'indigenous technical knowledge' (ITK) and so-called actor-oriented interface analysis is another. In singing the praises of this subaltern science position, women's knowledge and nature are often central. In Shiva's words: 'women as victims of violence of patriarchal forms of development have risen against it to protect nature' (1989: xvii), and by virtue of their organic relationships to things natural have a 'special relationship with nature' (1989: 43). Indeed for Shiva, feminine/ecological ways of knowing are 'necessarily participatory'. Fourth, local community and 'tradition' are neither erased nor preserved as the basis for alternative development but are refashioned as a hybrid: hybridity entails 'a cultural (re)creation that may or may not be (re)inscribed into hegemonic constellations' (Escobar, 1995: 220). This is the heart of the new political subjectivity which speaks to a 'transcultural in-between world reality' (Escobar, 1995: 220). And finally, these movements produce a defence of the local: such a defence is a 'prerequisite to engaging with the global ... [and represents] the principal elements for the collective construction of alternatives' (Escobar, 1995: 226).

A central weakness of the social movements as post-development approach is precisely how culture and popular discourse from below are privileged in quite uncritical ways: it is, in short, the centrality of geography and the simplicity of its deployment which are so striking in much of what passes for discourses on alternatives and their imaginaries. Identity politics is championed by Escobar, for example, because it represents part of an alternative reservoir of knowledge and because such ideas stand against the 'axiomatics of capitalism'. But there is surely nothing necessarily anti-capitalist or particularly progressive about cultural identity: calls to localism can produce Hindu fascism as easily as Andean Indian co-operatives. Running through much of the social movements as alternative to development literature is an uncritical appeal to the 'people' – that is to say, populist rhetoric – without a sensitivity to the potentially deeply conservative, and occasionally reactionary, aspects of such local particularisms. A striking feature of so much of the alternatives school is the constant uncritical appeal to the local, to place and to the cultural (where cultural is synonymous with a self-consciously local sense of community). Yet as Pierre Bourdieu has noted, in discussion of 'the people' and 'popular' discourse, what is at stake is the struggle between intellectuals (1990: 150). These debates among intellectuals celebrate, typically in an often romantic, reactionary and quasi-mystical way, the efficacy of all action/knowledge from below; they contain a rejection of, or profound ambivalence towards, *fin de siècle* modernity rooted in the losses and reaffirmations of local particularisms, which are and always have been the accompaniment of capitalism (Cowen and Shenton, 1996). Moreover, they often forget that the 'local' is never purely local, but is created in part by extra-local influences and practices over time.

It is the uncritical and sometimes unreflective ways in which the local is invoked in populist discourses of development imaginaries and the capacities of the subaltern that make the contribution of geography so fundamental. The Ogoni and MOSOP stand in this regard as a paradigmatic case, both because they are so typically held up – with others such as Chipko, the Amazonian rubber tappers – as exemplary cases of subaltern resistance and post-development, and also because they reveal so much of the ways in which custom, community and ethnicity need to be spatialized (Massey, 1995). In so doing, however, I wish to show something of the geographical content of the Ogoni imaginary (as an engagement with petrolic development), and of the limited and contradictory horizons of this geographical imaginary, which pays too much attention to authenticity and culture at the expense of what Gramsci (1972: 55) called the episodic, fragmentary and contradictory qualities of subalternity. Ogoniland may in some respects be a 'heterotopia' (Foucault, 1986) – a real space which seizes and activates the imagination through the density of its representation and inversion of the culture of which it is part – but one in which the subversive potential is itself compromised by geography – what I shall refer to as the fetishization of geography.[5]

Ogoni and the shock of petrolic modernity

If the recent history of Nigeria has been the tale of petroleum (Watts, 1994; Khan, 1994), then Ogoniland has simultaneously been at its centre and at its periphery.[6] Indeed, the paradox of Ogoniland is that an accident of geological history – the location of more than ten major oil-fields within its historic territory – ushered in not petrolic moderniza-tion but economic underdevelopment and an ecological catastrophe. Ken Saro-Wiwa and the Ogoni hated modernity because *they could not get enough of it*: the Ogoni were angry because they could neither afford the cars nor use the roads which were the icons of petrolic success. In this sense, the Ogoni story is deeply Benjaminian. Through-out his Parisian production cycle (M. Cohen, 1993) Benjamin employed two alternative vocabularies as a way of investigating base–superstruc-ture relations through the language of dreams: one was the vocabulary of *phantasmagoria*, the other that of *shock*. In Ogoniland it was the phantasmagoria of petrolic commodification (of wealth without effort) and the shock of modernity which framed the rise of MOSOP and what Benjamin himself (1969), in his concern with utopias, called 'the moment of awakening'.

The Ogoni are typically seen as a distinct ethnic group, consisting of three sub-groups and six clans.[7] Their population of roughly 500,000 people is distributed among 111 villages dotted over 1,050 square kilometres of creeks, waterways and tropical forest in the northeast fringes of the Niger Delta. Located administratively in Rivers State, a Louisiana-like territory of some 50,000 square kilometres, Ogoniland is one of the most heavily populated zones in all of Africa. Indeed the most densely settled areas of Ogoniland – over 1,500 persons per square kilometre – are the sites of the largest wells. Its customary pro-ductive base was provided by fishing and agricultural pursuits until the discovery of petroleum, including the huge Bomu field, immediately prior to independence. Traces of Ogoni 'nationalism' long predate the oil boom but they were deepened as a result of it. Ogoni fears of what Saro-Wiwa called 'monstrous domestic colonialism' (1992: 86) were exacerbated further by federal resistance to dealing with minority issues[8] in the wake of the civil war and by the new politics of post-oil-boom revenue allocation. Rivers State saw its federal allocation fall dramatically in absolute and relative terms. At the height of the oil boom, 60 per cent of oil production came from Rivers State but it received only 5 per cent of the statutory allocation (roughly half of that received by Kano, Northeastern States and the Ibo heartland, East Central State). Between 1970 and 1980 it received in revenues one-fiftieth of the value of the oil it produced. In what was seen by the Rivers minorities as a particularly egregious case of ethnic treachery, the civilian Shagari regime reduced the derivation component to only 2 per cent of revenues in 1982, after Rivers State had voted overwhelmingly for Shagari's northern-dominated National Party of Nigeria. The subsequent military government of General Buhari cut the derivation component even further at a time when the state accounted for 44.3 per cent of Nigeria's oil production.

Standing at the margin of the margin, Ogoniland appears (like Chiapas in Mexico) as a socio-economic paradox. Home to six oilfields, half of Nigeria's oil refineries, the country's only fertilizer plant and a large petrochemical plant, Ogoniland is wracked by unthinkable misery and deprivation. During the first oil boom Ogoniland's fifty-six wells accounted for almost 15 per cent of Nigerian oil production[9] and in the past three decades an estimated $30 billion in petroleum revenues have flowed from this Lilliputian territory; it was, as local opinion had it, Nigeria's Kuwait. Yet according to a government commission, Oloibiri, where the first oil was pumped in 1958, has no single kilometre of all-season road and remains 'one of the most backward areas in the country' (cited in Furro, 1992: 282). Few Ogoni households have electricity, there is one doctor per 100,000 people, child mortality rates are the highest in the nation, unemployment is 85 per cent, 80 per cent of the population is illiterate, and close to half of Ogoni youth have left the region in search of work. Life expectancy is barely fifty years, substantially below the national average. In Furro's survey of two minority oil-producing communities, over 80 per cent of respondents felt that economic conditions had deteriorated since the onset of oil production, and over two-thirds believed that there had been no progress in local development since 1960. No wonder that the systematic reduction of federal allocations and the lack of concern by the Rivers government was, for Ogoniland, part of a long history of 'the politics of minority suffocation' (Ikporukpo, 1996: 171).

If Ogoniland failed to see the material benefits from oil, what it did experience was an ecological disaster – what the European Parliament has called 'an environmental nightmare' (cited in *Village Voice*, 21 November 1995). The heart of the ecological harms stems from oil spills – either from the pipelines which criss-cross Ogoniland (often passing directly through villages) or from blow-outs at the wellheads – and gas flaring. As regards the latter, a staggering 76 per cent of natural gas in the oil-producing areas is flared (compared to 0.6 per cent in the US). As a visiting environmentalist noted in 1993 in the delta, 'some children have never known a dark night even though they have no electricity' (*Village Voice*, 21 November 1995: 21). Burning twenty-four hours per day at temperatures of 13,000–14,000°C, Nigerian natural gas produces 35 million tons of CO_2 and 12 million tons of methane, more than the rest of the world (and rendering Nigeria probably the biggest single cause of global warming). The oil spillage record is even worse. There are roughly 300 spills per year in the delta and in the 1970s alone the spillage was four times the much publicized *Exxon Valdez* spill in

Alaska. In one year alone almost 700,000 barrels were soiled according to a government commission. Ogoniland itself suffered 111 spills between 1985 and 1994 (Hammer, 1996: 61). Figures provided by the Nigerian National Petroleum Company (NNPC) document 2,676 spills between 1976 and 1990, 59 per cent of which occurred in Rivers State (Ikein, 1990: 171), 38 per cent of which were due to equipment malfunction.[10] Between 1982 and 1992 Shell alone accounted for 1.6 million gallons of spilled oil – 37 per cent of the company's spills worldwide. The consequences of flaring, spillage and waste for Ogoni fisheries and farming have been devastating.[11] Two independent studies completed in 1997 reveal total petroleum hydrocarbons in Ogoni streams at 360 and 680 times the European Community permissible levels (Rainforest Action Network, 1997).

In almost four decades of oil drilling, then, the experience of petrolic modernization in Ogoniland has been a tale of terror and tears. It has brought home the worst fears of ethnic marginalization and minority neglect: of northern hegemony, of Ibo neglect, and of Ijaw local dominance. The euphoria of oil wealth after the civil war has brought ecological catastrophe, social deprivation, political marginalization, and a rapacious company capitalism in which unaccountable foreign transnationals are granted a sort of immunity by the state.

Articulating Ogoni: geography and collective wish images

The hanging in November 1995 of Ken Saro-Wiwa and the other members of the Ogoni nine – accused of murdering four prominent Ogoni leaders who professed opposition to MOSOP tactics – and the subsequent arrest of nineteen others on treason charges, represented the summit of a process of mass mobilization and radical militancy which had commenced in 1989. The civil war had, as I have previously suggested, hardened the sense of external dominance among the Ogoni. A 'supreme cultural organization' called Kagote, which consisted largely of traditional rulers and high-ranking functionaries, was established at the war's end and in turn gave birth in 1990 to MOSOP. A new strategic phase began in 1989, with a programme of mass action and passive resistance, on the one hand, and a renewed effort to focus on the environmental consequences of oil (and Shell's role in particular) and on group rights within the federal structure, on the other. Animating the entire struggle was, in former MOSOP leader Garrick Leton's words, the 'genocide being committed in the dying years of the twentieth century by multinational companies under the supervision of the Government' (cited in Naanen, 1995: 66).

A watershed moment in MOSOP's history was the drafting in 1990 of an Ogoni Bill of Rights (Saro-Wiwa, 1992). Documenting a history of neglect and local misery, the Ogoni Bill took head-on the question of Nigerian federalism and minority rights. Calling for Ogoni participation in the affairs of the republic as 'a distinct and separate entity', the Bill outlined a plan for autonomy and self-determination in which there would be guaranteed 'political control of Ogoni affairs by Ogoni people ... the right to control and use a fair proportion of Ogoni economic resources ... [and] adequate representation as of right in all Nigerian national institutions' (Saro-Wiwa, 1989: 11). The Bill addressed the question of the spatial and political *unit* to which revenues should be allocated – and derivatively the rights of minorities. Largely under Saro-Wiwa's direction, the Bill was employed as part of an international mobilization campaign. Presented at the UN Sub-Committee on Human Rights, at the Working Group on Indigenous Populations in Geneva in 1992 and at UNPO in The Hague in 1993, the Ogoni became – with the help of Rainforest Action Network and Greenpeace – a *cause célèbre*.

Ken Saro-Wiwa played a central role in the tactical and organizational transformations of MOSOP during the 1990s. Under Saro-Wiwa, MOSOP focused in 1991 on links to pro-democracy groups in Nigeria (the transition to civilian rule had begun under heavy-handed military direction) and on direct action around Shell and Chevron installations. It was precisely because of the absence of state commitment and the deterioration of the environment that local Ogoni communities, perhaps understandably, had great expectations of Shell (the largest producer in the region) and directed their activity against the oil companies after three decades of betrayal. There was a sense in which Shell *was* the local government[12] (*Guardian*, 14 July 1996: 11) but the company's record had, in practice, been appalling.[13] Shell, which was deemed the world's most profitable corporation in 1996 by *Business Week* (8 July 1996: 46) and which nets roughly $200 million profit from Nigeria each year, by its own admission has only provided $2 million to Ogoniland in forty years of pumping. Ogoni historian Loolo (1981) points out that Shell has built one road and awarded ninety-six school scholarships in thirty years; according to the *Wall Street Journal*, Shell employs eighty-eight Ogoni (less than 2 per cent) in a workforce of over 5,000 Nigerian employees. Furthermore, the oft-cited community development schemes of the oil companies only began in earnest in the 1980s and have met with minimal success (Ikporukpo, 1993). In some communities, Shell only began community efforts in 1992 after twenty-five years of pumping, and then provided a waterproject of 5,000 gallons' capacity for a constituency of *100,000* (*Newswatch*, 18 December 1995: 13).

In an atmosphere of growing violence and insecurity, MOSOP wrote to the three oil companies operating in Ogoniland in December 1992 demanding $6.2 billion in back rents and royalties, $4 billion for damages, the immediate stoppage of degradation, flaring and exposed pipelines, and negotiations with the Ogoni to establish conditions for further exploration (Osaghae, 1995: 336; Greenpeace, 1994). The companies responded with tightened security while the military government sent in troops to the oil installations, banned all public gatherings, and declared as treasonable any claims for self-determination. Strengthening Ogoni resolve, these responses prompted MOSOP to organize a massive rally – an estimated 300,000 participated – in January 1993. As harassment of MOSOP leadership and Ogoni communities by state forces escalated, the highpoint of the struggle came with the decision to boycott the Nigerian presidential election on 12 June 1993.

In the wake of the annulment of the presidential elections, the arrest of democratically elected Mashood Abiola and the subsequent military coup by General Abacha, state security forces vastly expanded their activities in Ogoniland. Military units were moved into the area in June 1993 and Saro-Wiwa was charged with, among other things, sedition.[14] More critically, inter-ethnic conflicts exploded between Ogoni and other groups in late 1993, amidst accusations of military involvement and ethnic warmongering by Rivers State leadership. A new and aggressively anti-Ogoni military governor took over Rivers State in 1994 and a ferocious assault by the Rivers State Internal Security Task Force commenced. Saro-Wiwa was placed under house arrest, and subsequently fifteen Ogoni leaders were detained in April 1994. A series of brutal attacks left 750 Ogoni dead and 30,000 homeless; in total, almost 2,000 Ogoni perished between 1990 and 1998 at the hands of police and security forces. Ogoniland was in effect sealed off by the military. Amidst growing chaos, Saro-Wiwa was arrested on 22 May 1994, and several months later he and eight others were charged with the deaths of four Ogoni leaders with whom there had been increasingly rancorous and conflictual relations.

In spite of the remarkable history of MOSOP between 1990 and 1996, its ability to represent itself as a unified pan-Ogoni organization remained an open question, particularly for Saro-Wiwa. There is no pan-Ogoni myth of origin (characteristic of many delta minorities), and a number of the Ogoni sub-groups engender stronger local loyalties than any affiliation to Ogoni nationalism. The Eleme sub-group has even argued, on occasion, that they are not Ogoni. Furthermore, the MOSOP leaders were actively opposed by elements of the traditional clan leadership, by prominent leaders and civil servants in state government, and by some critics who felt Saro-Wiwa was out to gain 'cheap popularity' (Osaghae, 1995: 334). And, not least, the youth wing of MOSOP, which Saro-Wiwa had made use of, had a radical vigilante constituency which the leadership were incapable of controlling. What Saro-Wiwa did was to build upon over fifty years of Ogoni organizing and upon three decades of resentment against the oil companies, to provide a mass base and a youth-driven radicalism – and it must be said an international visibility – capable of challenging state power.[15]

What sort of articulation of Ogoni identity and political subjectivity did Saro-Wiwa pose? It was clearly one in which geography figured centrally: territory and Nature were the building blocks upon which ethnic difference and indigenous rights were constructed. And yet it was an unstable and contradictory sort of articulation – to return to Stuart Hall's lexicon. First, there was no simple Ogoni 'we', no unproblematic unity, and no singular form of political subject (despite Saro-Wiwa's ridiculous claim that 98 per cent of the Ogoni supported him). MOSOP had five independent units – an object of bitter dispute in itself – embracing youth, women, traditional rulers, teachers and churches. It represented a fractious and increasingly divided 'we', as the open splits and conflicts between Saro-Wiwa and other elite Ogoni confirm (Ogoni Crisis, 1996).[16] Second, Saro-Wiwa constantly invoked Ogoni culture and tradition, yet he also argued that war and internecine conflict had virtually destroyed the fabric of Ogoni society by 1900 (Saro-Wiwa, 1992: 14). His own utopia then rested on the re-creation of Ogoni culture – in so far as Africa's tribes are 'ancient and enduring social organizations' (1995: 191) – and suffered like all ur-histories from a mythic invocation of the past. Third, ethnicity was the central problem of postcolonial Nigeria – the corruption of ethnic majorities – and its panacea (the multiplication of ethnic minority power). To invoke the history of exclusion and the need not simply for ethnic minority inclusion, but for it as the basis for federalism, led Saro-Wiwa to ignore totally the histories and geographies of conflict and struggle among and between ethnic minorities. And not least, the narrative of Ogoni exclusion and internal colonialism proved also to be partial (and exclusionary). Compared to many delta minorities the Ogoni have fared well. The Ogoni produced roughly 4 per cent of Rivers State oil in 1998; two other small minorities with no political representation at all accounted for 68 per cent.

Coursing through the Ogoni story is, in short, a much more complex sort of social movement than the post-development literature might admit. Ogoni struggles represented a sort of hybrid political identity which was the continuation of a colonial hybridity. In both cases the articulation of a sense of community, of a singular and authentic identity and of a boundedness proved to be unstable, provisional and often contradictory. This internal instability was embodied in the leader's own central claim – for an autonomy in which Ogoni culture might flourish, when by his own admission that traditional culture was all but dead by 1900.

The Ogoni, post-development and the geographical imaginaries

Rather than starting with the ambitious claims of new social movements as alternative politics, or alternative knowledges and/or alternatives to modernity, I have started from a much more conventionally Marxist position, namely, of base and superstructure. In what sense then can the likes of the Ogoni movement and its development vision be grasped as 'products of the superstructure belonging to the inception of industrial production' (Benjamin, cited in M. Cohen, 1993: 42)? The reference point is Walter Benjamin's assault on conventional – that is, functional – base/superstructure thinking and his psychoanalytic recognition (like Althusser's somewhat later) that ideas and practices can take on the distorted form of dreams because they are doubly formed by material forces and the collective unconscious. Benjamin's great insight was to recognize that the collective unconscious – the need to give the new imagistic form – can shape the material reality because of the collective symbolic need to 'shape the new and unknown forces with the help of elements from prehistory' (M. Cohen, 1993: 43):

> In addition, these wish images manifest an emphatic striving for disassociation with the outmoded – which means, however, the most recent past. These tendencies direct the imagistic imagination which has been activated by the new, back to the primeval past ... These images are wish images and in them the collective seeks both to sublate and to transfigure the incompleteness of the social product and the deficiencies in the social order of production. (Benjamin, cited in M. Cohen, 1993: 43–4)

The rejection of the most recent past for the Ogoni was that of the monstrous marginalization and wreckage wrought by the arrival of the petroleum industry and transnational capital. The imagistic imagination activated by the shock of the (petrolic) new harkened back to an Ogoni tradition to transfigure a social product (a corrupt and venal form of ethnic federalism) and the deficiencies of the social order of production (the slick alliance between oil companies and the Nigerian state).

In my rendering, the ur-history of Ogoni tradition and its attachment to the Ogoni Bill of Rights (the Ogoni 'post-development imaginary') demanded an act of geographical imagination. First, in an *empirical* sense, the very idea of Ogoni tradition and culture was explicitly spatial – an Ogoni territory (Saro-Wiwa, 1992: 11) consisting of six territorially rooted claims and three local government areas. Indeed, the term 'tradition' (*doonu kuneke*), as Saro-Wiwa emphasized, meant honouring the land (1992: 12). The fact that the heart of the new was a land-based resource – petroleum – pumped from within the territory and with immediate consequences for it (environmental contamination), made these empirical geographies all the more compelling. Geography as place mattered. Second, geography was central in an *epistemological and ontological* sense in that MOSOP argued that rights and entitlements stemmed from this territory (Saro-Wiwa, 1992: 92–3). Land and identity conferred inalienable rights – states of being – in other words. Third, geography was *normatively* implicated in the sense of the 'autonomy' posited in the Ogoni Bill of Rights: autonomy within an ethnically (and hence geographically) reconfigured federation ('in a true federation, each ethnic group no matter how small is entitled to the same treatment', as the Ogoni Bill of Rights put it). Here geography confers equality and autonomy, normatively speaking.

In a curious way I am suggesting that Saro-Wiwa, a dialectical figure if ever there was one, seemed to express something of what Benjamin called the 'dialectical optics' of modernity (the ancient and the new) and the fundamental co-ordinates of the modern world. In the same way as Buck-Morss (1989: 210–12) has expressed Benjamin's dialectical image in the Parisian production cycle as a sort of matrix generated by two co-ordinates – dream-waking, and petrified and transitory nature – in which the fossil, the ruin, the fetish and the wish image are the constituent parts, so much of what Saro-Wiwa articulated can be understood in almost identical terms. The fossil is represented in the relics of Ogoni historical culture which leave a trace in the present – the palaces of the elites and their artefacts of power. The fetish as the arrested form of history – the reified form of the new nature in which future potential lies – was embodied in the phantasmagoria of modern industrial planning and construction: the oil refineries and petrochemical plants. The wish image is the dream form of that potential embodied in the fetish, namely the oil revenues – control over 'at least 50% of Ogoni resources', as specified in the Ogoni Bill of Rights – and the 'full development of Ogoni culture' (Bill of Rights). And the ruin in which wish images of the past appear as rubble is the semantic and material parts of tradition. As Benjamin saw it, *in toto* the ruin, the wish image, the fetish and the fossil represent a dialectical image – a utopia at a standstill. And this is contained in Saro-Wiwa's invocation of a return to something already lost:

I can confidently say that it is still possible to return to 'the local culture'
... in short to re-create societies that have been destroyed by European
colonialism ... or by even more destructive 'black colonialism'. And that
what we need to do is examine each society critically, identify the motive
spirit of its being. (Saro-Wiwa, 1995: 191)

For all dialectical images, however, the potential contained within
them – the moment of awakening – is always in danger. I have tried to
emphasize how the articulations – of discourse and political identity –
deployed by Saro-Wiwa compromised his utopian imagery. The first
danger is taken from Benjamin himself when he says that tradition itself
is never safe. Tradition will always be interpreted and read in a variety
of ways. Indeed at the heart of the struggles within MOSOP and the
Ogoni community was the very content of this tradition itself. Ogoni
'traditional' elites employed tradition to gain access to the state; Ogoni
elders sought to protect gerontocratic rule; Ogoni youth built a tradition (dating back to the 1970s) of militancy and of radical separatism.
And, not least, the Nigerian state sought to employ tradition to convert
ethnic difference – the narcissism of minor difference, as Freud called it
– into genocidal conflict. In other words, Saro-Wiwa's efforts to reconstruct an Ogoni tradition – as a singular experience from a multiplicity
of kingdoms, lineages, languages and histories – were replete with
dangers, contradictions and subversions. And the second danger builds
upon Poulantzas's insight and the ways in which tradition – the ur-
history which runs through the dialectical image – is geographically
fetishized, which compromises the moment of awakening and endan-
gers the utopia itself. Here, I have tried to highlight the Janus-faced
character of invoking culture as ethnicity and ethnicity as identity politics. In this regard there is a paradox: namely, that the retelling of
Ogoni history and indeed of Nigerian history by Saro-Wiwa actually
obscures history, or more properly the social relations between historical groups. Territory – as the repository of identity – is assumed to be
fixed, the natural ground for local histories, as Coronil (1996: 77) says.
History is territorialized at the same time as the histories of various
spaces are hidden. In Saro-Wiwa's articulation, ethnicity is both the
cause of Ogoni internal colonialism (the 'ethnic majorities') and the
means to the Ogoni utopia (ethnic autonomy). As a result, in Saro-
Wiwa's account, some of the historical relations between and within the
problematic entity called the Ogoni are actually occluded (in the name
of a purported Ogoni territoriality and ethnic unity) and various spaces
– for example, of kingdoms which stand ambivalently towards any
sense of pan-Ogoniness – are hidden. Space is naturalized and history
territorialized. The result is an account in which exclusion, boundedness

– rather than what Said calls 'contrapuntal perspectivism' (1993) – tends to prevail.

Running through the Ogoni story is the danger of a territorial essentialism and a fetishism of geography which is never adequately resolved. Indeed I would suggest, following Laurent Berlant (1991), that geography is embedded within the Ogoni cause, as it is within nationalisms of many sorts, as a part of what she calls the 'National Symbolic'. That is to say, it (geography) becomes part of the order of discursive practices 'whose reign within a national space produces ... the "law" in which the accident of birth within a geographical political boundary transforms individuals into subjects of a collectively held history' (Berlant, 1991: 60). As Berlant notes, the national symbolic aims to create what she calls a 'national fantasy' in which a national culture becomes local – typically in images, narratives, monuments and so on which circulate within the personal and collective consciousness. Nigeria as a national fantasy failed in fact to localize this fiction of citizenship and subjectivity among the Ogoni (and many other minorities); Saro-Wiwa and MOSOP attempted to create an alternative 'national' fantasy by localizing the national symbolic within the boundaries of a fragmented Ogoniland. Whether national or local fantasies, these symbolic domains are shot through with geography and the wish images of place and territory.

Every society constructs a self-identity in part in relation to the construction and representation of others. Running through such identity formation are, necessarily, quite specific culture traditions, histories and geographies. I have tried to show how in this case of Africans representing themselves in part through other Africans, there is an ethnocentric style – the language is Coronil's (1996: 78) – which is linked not (like Orientalism or Occidentalism) to the Western global power, but to the history of post-colonial Africa. Mbembe's (1992) notion of the post-colony as a plurality of spheres and arenas, in which the post-colonial subject has to bargain, improvise and adopt fluid identities, is helpful because it suggests a more hybrid way of thinking about geopolitical categories outside of the circumference of Orientalism or Occidentalism. I part company, however, quite radically with Mbembe's suggestion that this hybridity only produces connivance and a popular toying or playing with power. Nine Ogoni were hanged not for connivance or play but for confronting state legitimacy on the most sensitive of terrains: the *geographical* terrain on which, as one of the first post-colonial leaders of Nigeria, Obafemi Awolowo, put it, 'Nigeria is not a Nation ... [but] a mere geographical expression.'

Acknowledgements

The author wishes to thank Jan Nederveen Pieterse of the Institute of Social Studies, The Hague, for his Global Futures Conference, at which the ideas in this chapter were aired and discussed not least by Gustavo Esteva. Other versions benefited from the critical advice of Neil Smith, Rick Schroeder and Cindi Katz at Rutgers University, and faculty and students at the University of Arizona and the University of British Columbia. John Allen provided especially critical commentary.

Notes

1 The starting point for Benjamin's notion of wish images is of course Susan Buck-Morss's brilliant account in *The Dialectics of Seeing* (1989); see also Wolin (1992) and M. Cohen (1993).

2 Another line of critical thinking on development which meets up with the alternatives to development approach starts from the purported '*impasse*' of *Marxian political economy* (Booth, 1994; Schurmann, 1993). Geographers have been quite central to this impasse debate, which represents an effort to extend the postmodern project to development (see Brass, 1995, for a review). In Booth's view, the heart of the development theory impasse is the reductionist, economistic and epistemologically flawed nature of Marxism itself, which ignores complexity, diversity and non-class movements from below. Encompassed in this failure is another, namely the failure of radical development theory to engage with development practice, since 'we still do not know how to solve the problems of poverty by means of "applied" development' (Booth, 1994: 7). Marxism has failed, in other words, to provide practical assistance to those on the frontlines of development. See also Schurmann (1993).

3 As Escobar puts it (1995: 216), these movements are not cases of 'essentialized identity construction' but are 'flexible, modest, mobile, relying on tactical articulations arising out of the conditions and practices of daily life'. To the extent that these movements are 'environmental' or 'green', vast claims have been made on their behalf: they are a 'revolt against development', 'a new economics for a new civilization', 'learning to be human in a posthuman landscape'.

4 The greatest political promise for minority cultures is their potential for resisting and subverting the axiomatics of capitalism and modernity in their hegemonic forms' (Escobar, 1995: 224). Escobar, however, has little to say about what constitutes minority (Hindu nationalism? the Islamic Salvation Front in Algeria?) or what indeed is non-hegemonic modernity or capitalism.

5 I have been deeply influenced in my thinking about heterotopias by the brilliant work of photographer and critic Allan Sekula, and his astonishing trilogy of works on what he calls 'materialistic geographies' (1996, 1997, 1986).

6 For a more detailed account of Ogoniland and its relation to oil see Watts (1997); for the fullest accounts of oil and Nigerian political economy see Khan (1994), Ikein (1990), Lewis (1996) and Forrest (1995). I have written at length on the relations between the petro-boom in Nigeria and the shock of modernity which it precipitated (see Watts, 1994).

7 Ogoniland consists of three local government areas and six clans which speak different dialects of the Ogoni language. MOSOP is in this sense a pan-Ogoni organization.

8 What Rivers State felt in regard to federal neglect, the Ogoni experienced in regard to Ijaw domination. While several Ogoni were influential federal and state politicians, they were incapable politically of exacting resources for the Ogoni community. In the 1980s only six out of forty-two representatives in the state assembly were Ogoni (Naanen, 1995: 77). It needs to be said, however – and it is relevant for an understanding of state violence against the Ogoni – that the Ogoni have fared *better* than many other minorities in terms of political appointments: in 1993, 30 per cent of the Commissioners in the Rivers State cabinet were Ogoni (the Ogoni represent 12 per cent of the state population) and every clan has produced at least one federal or state minister (Osaghae, 1995: 331) since the civil war. In this sense, it is precisely because the Ogoni had produced since 1967 a cadre of influential and well-placed politicians (including Saro-Wiwa himself) that their decision to move aggressively towards self-determination and minority rights was so threatening to the Abacha regime (Whelch, 1995).

9 According to the Nigerian government, Ogoniland currently (1998) produces about 2 per cent of Nigerian oil output and is the fifth-largest oil-producing community in Rivers State. Shell maintains that total Ogoni oil output is valued at $5.2 billion before costs.

10 The oil companies claim that sabotage accounts for a large proportion (60 per cent) of the spills, since communities gain from corporate compensation. Shell claims that 77 of 111 spills in Ogoniland between 1985 and 1994 were due to sabotage (Hammer, 1996). According to the Nigerian Government commission (1996), however, sabotage accounts for 30 per cent of the incidents but only 3 per cent of the quantity spilled. Furthermore, all oil-producing communities claim that compensation from the companies for spills has been almost non-existent.

11 A spill in 1993 flowed for forty days without repair, contaminating large areas of Ogoni farmland. Petroleum residues appear in the rivers at levels of 60 p.p.m. and in the sediments around the Bonny terminal reach lethal levels of 12,000 p.p.m. In the ecologically delicate mangrove and estuarine regions of the delta, oil pollution has produced large-scale eutrophication, depletion of aquatic resources and loss of traditional fishing grounds (see NNEST, 1991: 44; Benka-Cocker and Ekundayo, 1995), which now threaten customary livelihoods.

12 Prior to the cessation of operations in 1993, Shell was the principal oil company operating in Ogoniland, pumping from five major oilfields at Bomu/Dere, Yorla, Bodo West, Korokoro and Ebubu.

13 In 1970, Ogoni representatives had already approached Rivers State

government to approach Shell – what they then called 'a Shylock of a company' – for compensation and direct assistance (a plea which elicited a shockingly irresponsible response documented in Saro-Wiwa, 1992). Compensation by the companies for land appropriation and for spillage has been minimal, creating constant tension between company and community.

14 The history of events since June 1993 is detailed in Human Rights Watch (1995), UNPO (1995) and UN (1996).

15 Following the MOSOP precedent, a number of southeastern minorities pressured local and state authorities for expanded resources and political autonomy: the Movement for the Survival of Izon/Ijaw Ethnic Nationality was established in 1994 and the Council for Ekwerre Nationality in 1993, and the southern Minorities Movement (twenty-eight ethnic groups from five delta states) has been active since 1992. The Movement for Reparation to Ogbia (MORETO) produced a charter explicitly modelled on the Ogoni Bill of Rights in 1992. These groups directly confronted Shell and Chevron installations (Human Rights Watch, 1995; Greenpeace, 1994) and in turn have felt the press of military violence over the last four years. The point is simply that MOSOP was a flagship movement for a vast number of oil-producing communities and threatened to ignite a blaze throughout the oil-producing delta.

16 Saro-Wiwa was often chastised by the Gokana (he himself was Bane) since most of the Ogoni oil was in fact located below Gokana soil. In other words, on occasion the key territorial unit became the *clan* rather than the pan-Ogoni territory.

References

Benjamin, W. (1969) *Illuminations*. New York, Vintage.

Benka-Cocker, M. and J. Ekundayo (1995) 'Effects of an oil spill on soil physico-chemical properties of a spill site in the Niger Delta'. *Environmental Monitoring and Assessment*, 30: 93–104.

Berlant, L. (1991) *The Anatomy of National Fantasy: Hawthorne, Utopia and Everyday Life*. Chicago, University of Chicago Press.

Booth, D. (ed.) (1994) *Rethinking Social Development*. London, Methuen.

Bourdieu, P. (1990) *In Other Words*. Cambridge, Polity Press.

Brass, T. (1995) 'Old conservatism in new clothes'. *Journal of Peasant Studies*, 22/3: 516–40.

Buck-Morss, S. (1989) *The Dialectics of Seeing*. Boston, MIT Press.

Carrier, J. (1992) 'Occidentalism'. *American Ethnologist*, 19/2: 195–212.

Cohen, J. and A. Arato (1992) *Civil Society and Political Theory*. Cambridge MA, MIT Press.

Cohen, M. (1993) *Profane Illumination: Walter Benjamin and the Paris of Surrealist Revolution*. Berkeley CA, University of California Press.

Coronil, F. (1996) 'Beyond Occidentalism: toward nonimperial geohistorical categories'. *Cultural Anthropology* 11/1: 51–87.

Cowen, M. and R. Shenton (1996) *Doctrines of Development*. London, Routledge.

Crouch, S. (1990) *Notes of a Hanging Judge*. London and New York, Oxford University Press.

Escobar, A. (1992a) 'Imagining a post-development era? Critical thought, development and social movements'. *Social Text*, 31/32: 20–56.

Escobar, A. (1992b) 'Culture, economics, and politics in Latin American social movements theory and research'. In A. Escobar and S.E. Alvarez (eds), *The Making of Social Movements in Latin America*. Boulder, CO, Westview Press, 62–85.

Escobar, A. (1995) *Encountering Development*. Princeton, NJ, Princeton University Press.

Esteva, G. (1992) 'Development'. In Wolfgang Sachs (ed.), *The Development Dictionary: A Guide to Knowledge as Power*. London, Zed Books, 6–25.

Forrest, T. (1995) *Politics and Economic Development in Nigeria*. Boulder, CO, Westview Press.

Foucault, M. (1986) 'Of other spaces'. *Diacritics*, 16/1: 1–24.

Furro, T. (1992) 'Federalism and the politics of revenue allocation in Nigeria'. PhD dissertation, Clark Atlanta University.

Gramsci, A. (1972) *Selections from the Prison Notebooks* (eds Q. Hoare and G. Nowell-Smith). New York, International Publishers.

Greenpeace (1994) *Shell Shocked*. Amsterdam, Greenpeace International.

Hall, S. (1996) 'On postmodernism and articulation'. In D. Morley and K.-H. Chen (eds), *Stuart Hall: Dialogues in Cultural Studies*. London, Routledge, 131–50.

Hammer, J. (1996) 'Nigerian crude'. *Harpers Magazine*, June: 58–68.

Human Rights Watch (1995) *The Ogoni Crisis*. Report no. 7/5. New York, Human Rights Watch.

Ikein, A. (1990) *The Impact of Oil on a Developing Country*. New York, Praeger.

Ikporukpo, C. (1993) 'Oil companies and village development in Nigeria'. *OPEC Review*: 83–97.

Ikporukpo, C. (1996) 'Federalism, political power and the economic power game: control over access to petroleum resources in Nigeria'. *Environment and Planning C*, 14: 159–77.

Khan, S.A. (1994) *Nigeria: The Political Economy of Oil*. London, Oxford University Press.

Lewis, P. (1996) 'From prebendalism to predation: the political economy of decline in Nigeria'. *Journal of Modern African Studies*, 24/1: 79–104.

Li, T. (1996) 'Images of community'. *Development and Change*, 27: 501–27.

Li, T. (1997) 'Constituting tribal space'. Paper presented to the Environmental Politics Workshop, University of California, Berkeley, 17 October.

Loolo, G. (1981) *A History of the Ogoni*. Port Harcourt, Saros.

Massey, D. (1995) 'Rethinking radical democracy spatially'. *Society and Space*, 13/3: 283–8.

Mbembe, A. (1992) 'Provisional notes on the postcolony'. *Africa*, 62/1: 3–37.

Naanen, B. (1995) 'Oil producing minorities and the restructuring of Nigerian federalism'. *Journal of Commonwealth and Comparative Politics*, 33/1: 46–58.

Nigerian Government (1996) 'Ogoni Crisis'. Lagos, Ministry of Information, Nigerian Federal Government.

NNEST (1991) *Nigeria's Threatened Environment*. Ibadan, Nigerian Environmental Study Action Team.

Osaghae, E. (1995) 'The Ogoni uprising'. *African Affairs*, 94: 325–44.

Pieterse, J. Nederveen (1996) 'My paradigm or yours?'. Working Paper no. 229. The Hague, Institute of Social Studies.

Poulantzas, N. (1978) *State, Power, Socialism*. London, New Left Books.

Rainforest Action Network (1997) *Human Rights and Environmental Operations Information on the Royal Dutch/Shell Group of Companies*. San Francisco, RAN.

Rajnema, R. (ed.) (1996) *The Post Development Reader*. London, Zed Press.

Richards, P. (1985) *Indigenous Agricultural Revolution*. London, Hutchinson.

Routledge, P. (1994) *Resisting and Shaping the Modern*. London, Routledge.

Sachs, W. (ed.) (1992) *The Development Dictionary*. London, Zed Books.

Sachs, W. (1993) 'Global ecology and the shadow of development'. In W. Sachs (ed.), *Global Ecology: A New Arena of Political Conflict*. London, Zed Books, 3–21.

Said, E. (1979) *Orientalism*. New York, Vintage.

Said, E. (1993) *Culture and Imperialism*. New York, Knopf.

Said, E. (1994) *Representations of the Intellectual*. New York, Pantheon.

Saro-Wiwa, K. (1989) *On a Darkling Plain*. Port Harcourt, Saros.

Saro-Wiwa, K. (1992) *Genocide in Nigeria*. Port Harcourt, Saros.

Saro-Wiwa, K. (1995) *A Month and a Day*. London: Penguin.

Schurmann, F. (ed.) (1993) *Beyond the Impasse: New Directions in Development Theory*. London, Zed Books.

Sekula, A. (1996) *Fish Story*. Dusseldorf, Richter Verlag.

Sekula, A. (1997) *Geography Lesson*. Boston, MIT Press.

Sekula, A. (1986) *Canadian Notes*. Halifax, Nova Scotia, Press of Novia Scotia College of Art and Design.

Shiva, V. (1989) *Staying Alive*. London, Zed Books.

UN (1996) *Report of the Fact-Finding Mission of the Secretary-General to Nigeria: Summary of Information and Views Received*. New York, United Nations.

UNDP (1996) *The Human Development Report*. Geneva, UNDP.

UNPO (1995) *Ogoni: Report of the UNPO Mission to Investigate the Situation of the Ogoni*. The Hague, Unrepresented Nations and Peoples Organization.

Watts, M. (1994) 'The devil's excrement'. In S. Corbridge, R. Martin and N. Thrift (eds), *Money, Power and Space*. Oxford, Blackwell, 406–45.

Watts, M. (1997) 'Black gold, white heat'. In S. Pile and M. Keith (eds), *Geographies of Resistance*. London, Routledge, 33–67.

Whelch, C. (1995) 'The Ogoni and self determination'. *Journal of Modern African Studies*, 33/4: 635–50.

Wolin, R. (1992) *Walter Benjamin*. New York, Columbia University Press.

Part III
Geography and Difference

Introduction

Recently, the issue of 'difference' has gained some prominence in geographical debates. Why might this be so? What is striking about the emergence of the term 'difference' is that it marks *not only* an engagement with cultural politics within geography *but also* the use of spatial metaphors within cultural politics. The spatial turn within cultural politics and the cultural turn within geography have, however, more often seen them cross each other at right angles, than permitted a sustained dialogue between them. In part, this is because the term 'difference' to describe people's 'positions' within social relations of power has not meant the same thing to everybody. The chapters in this section seek to move beyond these misunderstandings, both by treating spatial metaphors sceptically and by thinking about 'difference' *spatially* and *relationally*.

So, what exactly is difference and how might thinking about differentiation spatially and relationally add to our understanding? Surely, everyone is different from everyone else. Isn't it obvious that no two people are alike? Similarly, no two places are exactly the same (even if they look like it on the surface). Surely, everywhere is different? However, there are some ways of imagining difference that tend to undermine the presumption that everyone and everything is unique. Usually difference is seen as a corollary of identity – and identity is seen as produced out of binaries. Identity is a form of subject position in which the individual is thinking along these lines: 'I am white, but not black; I am male, but not female; I am masculine, but not feminine; I am middle class, but not working class; I am ... but not ...; and so on'. From this perspective, identity is constructed out of social 'positions', forming subjects who are (in this example) clearly, unambiguously and unproblematically white, male, masculine, middle class, and so on. Using spatial metaphors to ground this argument, it is believed that every person has a *place* in the social order and that in order to become a social subject they have to occupy that *place*, fully and without hesitation.

A major feature of this book is the way authors have attempted to 'escape' binary understandings of identity/difference. But what is a binary? At its simplest, a binary is an opposition between two terms, where this opposition is an internal relation between the two terms. Thus, Nature and Culture are binaries – defined in opposition to each other – because neither is imagined, or definable, without the other. The paradox, then, is that they are presumed to be unrelated, yet they each necessitate the existence of the other. If we think about this paradox, the real problem with binary thinking is not that it assumes a relationship between the two terms, but that it doesn't. One way in which this relationship between the two terms is denied or ignored is by installing a gap or closed border between the two terms in the binary. Thus, rather than thinking that masculine and feminine are related and attempting to think through this relationship, it is assumed that masculine and feminine are absolutely separate and that clear distinctions can be drawn between them. Such thinking does not stand up to critical scrutiny, as we will see in this section.

However, we should attend to another aspect of the paradox inherent in binary thinking. Remember, the two sides of the binary are simultaneously brought into relation *and* kept apart: this is a specifically spatial relationship – it is about distance, separation and closeness. It is here that geographers have taken up the challenge of thinking difference spatially and relationally. They have noted that differences between people can lead to a social exclusion that is spatially enforced. From this perspective, it can be understood that people who are seen as unacceptably different are locked up, moved on, shunned, marginalized, ridiculed, and/or even murdered.

Unavoidably, geographers have had to consider the ways in which differences are both socially produced and also lived and practised by embodied subjects *in situ*. These issues are universal, but they cannot be universalized. Instead, geographers have had to struggle with the ambiguities and ambivalences inherent in social positions that are not quite 'positions' (because people continually evade or exceed them), in 'mobilities' that aren't quite as free and easy as some might wish, and in 'identities' that are never as fixed nor as sovereign as they might at first seem. In their own way, each of the authors in this section struggles both with the relationship between difference and space, and also with the consequences of not being able to adopt easy or trite political resolutions.

6
Creating Geographies of Difference

David Sibley

The problem with sameness

'We moved to be nearer to people like us. It's big things that keep us together. Aspirations, ambitions and mortgages.'

'Here, your house will appreciate faster and, when you walk up to the school for the parent-teachers' evening, everyone knows you. It's "Hello Jean, hello Barry". There are barn dances, a children's disco, and lots of family occasions like the school fete. Young people have grown up with proper respect for family values, even the teenagers are concerned about the elderly. The local policeman says the people in his patch took to the introduction of Neighbourhood Watch like ducks to water.'

D. Meadows, *Nattering in Paradise*

Familiarity and predictability are important for many people. There is a common desire to live in a place which is stable and orderly, where social interaction entails what George Herbert Mead called 'a conversation of gestures', gestures which are mutually understood. This desire for order reflects anxiety about not being understood, anxiety about unpredictable encounters, and concern about changes to the local environment which reduce aesthetic satisfaction. Such a life is not available to all who want it, however. Attaining control over the social and material conditions of everyday living, real or illusory, requires power and creditworthiness. This desire for a stable and predictable residential environment also fuels the engine of accumulation, so the ideal of the stable, ordered community is promoted by property developers and financial institutions. The ordered community of responsible citizens and nice families also has a political cachet in developed societies at the end of the twentieth century, when polarization and the social exclusion of sections of the population are perceived to threaten the social well-being of 'middle England', 'middle America', and so on. There is political capital to be made from advocating increasing control of the dispossessed, the underclass, in what Neil Smith (1996: 94) has called 'the revanchist city', and in other exclusionary spaces. In Britain this is manifest in such things as new penal sanctions against Travelling People and a 'hot-line' to shop social security cheats. This is the other side of a political programme that focuses on the family and moral education.

Constructing psycho-social geographies

In this chapter, I will explore representations of sameness and difference primarily through the writings of psychoanalytical theorists, some of whom provide clues to the construction of rich and intriguing geographies which embrace the self, society and the material environment. Psychoanalysis can help in the elucidation of meanings – it provides a way into a world of distorted understanding and communication, including the distortions which contribute to the bounding of territories separating 'us' and 'them'. Fragmented social space is marked by stereotyped images of places and of others, and these stereotypes are rooted in the unconscious. Theories of the self which I review in this chapter connect the unconscious and the social and material world. Thus, what I am suggesting is that the self can be *placed* and that psychoanalysis provides not just another layer of understanding but a means of unravelling the complex connections between people and place.

Psychoanalysis has an additional attraction for humanistic geography. In mapping the topography of the mind, the psychoanalyst is necessarily concerned with feelings. Feelings of repulsion and desire, of nervousness, elation and so on, contribute to distanciation, the avoidance of certain places and people, or conversely, attraction to place and to particular social milieux. Thus, it might be argued that a psychoanalytical treatment of emotions has an important role in understanding the production of social space. However, human geography, still affected by a legacy of scientific detachment, has been largely silent about sensations and emotions. As the psychoanalyst Karl Figlio (1996: 75) has argued: 'Every mapping into geometrical space – every act of picturing – leaves a gap between what is present in emotional space . . . and what appears in mapped space: and the finitude of geometrical space cannot encompass the infinitude of emotion.'

Emotions do have an important role in the construction of geographies, for example, in decision making in regard to residential location, in the mapping of risk by financial institutions, and in other mundane aspects of the organization of space which are affected by distorted images or stereotypes that themselves reflect fear and anxieties. Such anxieties are embedded in the material world. This was well illustrated by Alain Corbin (1986), who wrote convincingly about the spatial separation of social groups through smell, as a dimension of the history of French culture. According to Corbin, the pure, bourgeois 'I' was separated from the defiled and smelly working-class 'other', not just in terms of the social hierarchy but also in space, a tendency which was furthered by grand schemes of urban design such as the insertion of boulevards and squares into the fabric of nineteenth-century Paris. Studies like Corbin's, inspired by psychoanalytical argument, bring us closer to people's experience of space as well as providing a commentary on power relations.

My own use of psychoanalytical theory is quite selective. I draw primarily on British object relations theory as it has been developed by Melanie Klein (1960) because it provides a convincing argument about the connections between the self and the social and material world which are implied in studies such as Corbin's. As Kahane (1992: 284) puts it: 'Object relations theory assumes that from birth the infant engages in formative relations with "objects" – entities perceived as separate from the self, either whole persons or parts of the body, either existing in the external world or internalized as mental representations.' It is clear from Klein's arguments that the self is socially positioned, that what is internalized is representations of others as 'good' or 'bad' objects. Klein refers to this as the process of *introjection*. But at the same time as the good and the bad are internalized, anxieties and pleasures are *projected* onto others. The effect of introjection and projection is to create a sense of border, the boundaries of the self defined in terms of good and bad objects. However, I have argued that the objects of objects relations theory can be construed also as places (Sibley, 1995). People and places in their social and material relationships can constitute good or bad objects; they can be depositories for feelings of pain and anxiety, pleasure and excitement. Thus, the denial of difference is not just an indicator of anxiety about people who are 'not like us' but also an expression of negative feelings about places which are 'not like our place'. Drawing on Julia Kristeva's writing on abjection (Kristeva, 1982), I similarly argue that 'other' places can also be abject – people try to distance themselves from 'abject places' but they are always there as a source of anxiety.

Object relations theory provides one means of thinking about the ways in which people relate to 'the good' and 'the bad', how they construct geographies of difference. At the same time, I would suggest that geography has a contribution to make to object relations theory. Beyond rather naive conceptions of attachment to, or anxieties about, 'things' (Csikszentmihalyi and Rochberg-Halton, 1981) we can think about complex relationships between the material and the social world as they enter the unconscious. Perceptions and recollections of place are an important part of the bounding of the self. The myriad elements of place, as they combine with 'others', either present or absent, can be usefully described and analysed in order to deepen our understanding of good and bad objects. Repressed emotions may be intimately associated with the received images of place or the experience of place – with neat lawns, weed-strewn wastelands, wet pavements, and so on. Thus, psycho-social geographies may become part of a larger, spatialized psychoanalysis. Geography can articulate feelings about space and place which have only been hinted at in the psychoanalytical literature. Some of these ideas are explored in the following account of social and spatial difference, where I make connections between object relations theory and the more familiar terrain of social geography.

Conformity and the built environment

We can usefully assume that the values of residents and the values expressed in the material environment are mutually reinforcing. In this connection, Mead made one useful contribution when he suggested that objects to which people relate in the process of self-identification need not be only people, as is assumed in much of the literature on object relations theory, but could also be 'things'. As Mead puts it: 'Any thing – any object or set of objects, whether animate or inanimate, human or animal, or merely physical – towards which he acts, or to which he responds socially, is an element of what for him is the generalized other' (1934: 154, fn 7). Thus, the material environment of the suburb – gardens, verges, streets, houses, trees and shrubs – may convey a desirable sense of order, reflecting the domestic order of the home and feelings about cleanliness, tidiness and firm boundaries which contribute to an individual's sense of well-being. Drawing on Erik Erikson rather than Mead, Richard Sennett developed a critical view of this conception of the good life in his early writing, particularly in *The Uses of Disorder* (1970).

As Sennett recognized, this kind of order and harmony is potentially exclusionary. Within the home, for example, a parent's desire for order may lead him or her into conflict with a child who has a different conception of the organization of domestic space. Such a conflict is often resolved by limiting a child's freedom in the use of time and space in the home (Sibley and Lowe, 1992). In the locality, as Sennett later observed (1991), the sameness and neutrality of the grid and the curving street of the suburb were marks of power, a power to dominate through the imposition of rules and power to exclude. The archetypal case is the 'gated suburb' which excludes through the erection of a strong physical boundary and a system of surveillance and control (with armed guards at the gates of some suburban developments, in Rio de Janeiro and Johannesburg, for example). As Mike Davis (1990: 206) described the construction of exclusionary spaces in the Los Angeles region:

> Residential areas with enough clout are ... able to privatize local public space, partitioning themselves from the rest of the metropolis, even imposing a variant of 'passport control' on outsiders. The next step, of course, is to ape incorporated enclaves like Palos Verdes or Hidden Hills by building literal walls ... In the once wide-open tract land of the San Fernando valley, where there were virtually no walled-off communities a decade ago, the 'trend' has assumed the frenzied dimensions of a residential arms race as ordinary suburbanites demand the kind of social insulation enjoyed only by the rich.

Gates are not necessary, however, to make people feel out of place or to make residents feel anxious about discrepant others. The internal order of the home and the suburb are usually enough to signal conformity. Constance Perin (1988: 71) describes the concern of one Minneapolis resident about the arrangement of mailboxes in her suburban street: 'they're strung out all over the place on this side of the street' – an anxiety about a small detail of the built environment which probably extends to signs of spatial and social disorder in general.

This urge to bound and homogenize urban space is not a new problem, although it may be the case that more residential communities now have the power to keep others out than was the case, say, in the nineteenth-century Western city. The way in which the exclusionary tendency heightened feelings of difference in the past is illustrated by Sennett's study of a panic in late nineteenth-century Chicago, one which was triggered by a perceived crime wave attributed to recently arrived Italian immigrants (Sennett, 1971: 28–9). He concluded that one solid, middle-class community 'felt its own existence to be so threatened that only a state of rigid barriers, enforced by a semi-military state of curfew and surveillance, would permit it to continue to function'. Where and whenever the problem surfaces, the power to control space, to produce a homogeneous community and a general sense of sameness, seems to combine with a *feeling* of powerlessness, so that some outsider group constitutes a real threat to the integrity of the rejecting community. This threat, in turn, requires the negative representation of the other, drawing on some deep-seated feelings about the boundaries of the self. In this regard, Julia Kristeva's writing on abjection (Kristeva, 1982) is particularly illuminating.

Abject others, abject spaces

> The abject is an impossible object, still part of the subject; an object the subject strives to expel but which is ineliminable. In ingesting objects into itself or expelling objects from itself, the 'subject' can never be distinct from these 'objects'. These ingested/expelled 'objects' are neither part of the body nor separate from it. (Grosz, 1992: 198)

In Western societies, most children become aware at an early age that bodily wastes are defiling and polluting. Socialization induces anxieties about the defiled outer body, about the residues which are an inevitable product of existence. The body has to be kept clean, sanitized and purified, but the constant production of residues frustrates the individual's efforts to achieve a separation, to maintain a boundary between a purified, socially acceptable body and the sweat and dead skin which have been socially constructed as polluting. Additionally, the elimination of bodily wastes, defecation and urination, is hidden away because these functions are also abject in most Western societies. As Julia Kristeva has argued, abject things 'hover' on the boundary; that is, the body is always threatened by the abject, things we want to distance ourselves from but cannot. They are always there.

The importance of the abject in the construction of difference and the fashioning of social space is that other people and groups and the spaces they occupy are rendered abject through the process of elision. They are represented as residues, they *become* residues. This may involve the merging and substitution of several images. For example, the rat, as a member of the more general category 'vermin', is abject because of its association with bodily wastes and other residues, through its presence in sewers and on refuse tips, and because it is transgressive. It enters people's homes, it carries the threat of disease, and so it threatens social and personal boundaries. Certain groups of people are then described as rats or vermin because they are also associated with residues and because their assumed migratory behaviour makes them transgressive. The European Roma or Gypsies, for example, are represented in this way.

In 1993 in the Transylvanian village of Hadareni, three Gypsies were murdered and thirteen Gypsy houses were destroyed by Romanian villagers in retaliation for the killing of a Romanian by a Gypsy during a fight. Commenting on the deaths of the Gypsies, one resident said: 'We did not commit murder – how could you call killing Gypsies murder? Gypsies are not really people, you see. They are always killing each other. They are criminals, sub-human vermin' (*Independent*, 19 October 1993). Gypsy culture in Europe is generally represented as defiled or abject in relation to the culture of the majority because of the association between Gypsies and residual matter, like scrap metal, and because many of their separations reverse those required by the larger society. Defecation, for example, should be done at a distance from the home rather than being a private, domestic act. Their abject status is reinforced by their occupation of residual spaces, because they have been pushed to the margins by state agencies and/or because they find such locations a convenient base for their economic activities.

The incident in Hadareni was an extreme example of a response to difference, but the problem is much more general than this case might suggest. Feelings of abjection are projected onto populations whose stereotyped images do not accord with idealizations of certain bodies. In northern Europe, in particular, at least since the early nineteenth century, the ideal body has been white, athletic, between twenty and thirty and of sound mind, and more often male than female. This has left many abject others, people who are dark-skinned, mentally ill, with learning disabilities, physically disabled or old. The stereotype is more potent when several marks of discrepancy are combined, as in the case cited by Sander Gilman (1985) of the 'mad black woman'.

Precisely the same images as those used to construct negative stereotypes of people have been deployed in the characterization of spaces as pure or defiled (abject). Thus, the imagery of purity, with allusions to the body, runs through writing on the city by Le Corbusier, who was a major influence on modernist design. He was positively ecstatic about simple geometries:

> [settlements] are evidence of a spirit working right up to the limits of its own force and grandeur and expressing itself in the right angle which is obviously, geometrically, a perfect thing ... a marvellously perfect figure, unique, constant and pure; capable of being applied to ideas of glory and victory or to the idea of complete purity.

This idea is then used in a critical comment on cities, which Le Corbusier apparently saw as rather messy conglomerations of people. For example, 'Paris is a dangerous magma of human beings gathered from every quarter by conquest, growth and immigration; she is the eternal gipsy encampment from all the world's great roads', but '[Paris] digs and hacks through her undergrowth and out of these evils she is tending towards an ordered system of straight lines and right angles; this reorganization is necessary to her vitality, health and permanence; this clearing process is indispensable to the expression of her spirit, which is fundamentally limpid and beautiful' (Le Corbusier, 1929 (1978): 31). These sentiments are remarkably similar to the views of Le Corbusier's friend Pierre Winter, who remarked that 'A truly new mind can only exist in a "new body" ... The human body is going to reappear naked in the sunlight, showered, muscular and supple ... and it will be beautiful' (Saunders, 1995: 15). Winter was a French fascist. Le Corbusier's ordered environment and Winter's perfect body both consign disordered and abject people and cultures to residual spaces or death. Modern (and postmodern) living spaces, consumption styles and images of consumption promoted by the advertising media echo this quest for purity. This then confirms the abject status of certain 'imperfect people', to use Constance Perin's phrase, who are dirty, mad or otherwise marked and geographically defined by their absence in pure spaces (the homeless in indoor shopping centres, for example) or by their presence in defiled spaces (like the homeless in pedestrian underpasses).

Other spaces of difference

I have considered space and difference primarily as a local issue but the question of difference is also important at other territorial levels, notably in relation to nationalism, a feeling of collective identity which may be associated with the nation state but one which could also be manifest at the regional level or in connection with groups of states. This is not a problem which can be considered entirely apart from socio-spatial relations at the local level. For example, a racist immigration policy which denies access to a state or determines repatriation primarily on the basis of colour may encourage racist behaviour in localities, although the opposite case has been made by the British government, namely, that a more restrictive immigration policy and stronger rules for repatriation are a condition of good race relations. I think the former connection is more likely, however, and I will try to demonstrate this with reference to post-Communist east European states in a moment.

A second point that I would make about difference and national identity is that ideas about belonging and not belonging have particular histories and the kinds of differences that are represented as discrepant are manifest in episodes of expulsion or exclusion. The exclusion of 'Communists' in the United States during the 1950s, for example, was fuelled by the Cold War. Anxieties about the Soviet Union, portrayed stereotypically by government and the media as inherently untrustworthy and expansionary, a regime bent on world conquest, were amplified by propaganda designed to make people suspicious of their neighbours, any one of whom could be 'the Communist next door'. Senator Joe McCarthy's House Un-American Activities Committee exploited these fears in a vain attempt to purify national space, to draw a clear line between the righteous, God-fearing United States and the satanic, godless Soviet Union. The crude stereotypes employed during this period had less power after the Cuban missile crisis, when the superpowers acknowledged that they had some common interests, although they were briefly revived by Ronald Reagan as president, possibly fondly remembering his earlier participation in Communist witch-hunts in Hollywood. The essential point is that American–Soviet tensions during the 1950s prompted an American redefinition of itself and the process of finding a national identity assumed the form of a moral panic. This swirling, homogenizing process, involving the identification of unacceptable forms of difference, could not last long because it depended on sustaining crude stereotypes and an unsupportable form of global division. Real politics eventually demanded a more moderate view of both international relations and internal social relations.

The way in which nationalism produces alien others is nicely demonstrated by eastern European states which are striving for a new identity in the post-Communist period, although the differences between Communist and post-Communist periods could be exaggerated. When Romania, for example, was a people's republic it rendered its Roma (Gypsy) population invisible by the simple device of leaving them out of the census. Since World War II, the Roma population has probably been about 5 per cent of the total population, one of the largest Roma populations in post-war Europe, with a high rate of natural increase compensating for outmigration. The 1956 census, however, recorded no Roma. Eleven nationalities were identified (although Serbs, Croats and Slovenes were lumped together) and there was an 'others' category, which may have included some Gypsies, comprising 1.2 per cent of the population. The disregard of Gypsies was consistent with the state's view of them as an 'anti-social element'. They did not warrant official recognition as a nationality and this has legitimated their persecution, both by the Communist state and, in the post-Communist period, by the state and local Romanian populations. In Romania, and in Bulgaria and Slovakia, the Roma are not a part of the vision of national identity. It is not surprising, therefore, that attacks on them, like the killings in Hadareni described earlier, have not been taken seriously by the law enforcement agencies. An official purification of national space, based on a deeply rooted negative stereotype of a minority, lends tacit support to an attempted purification of localities.

More generally, it might be argued that uncertainty about national identity leads to increased concern with borders and the attempted removal of abject others. This simplifies the question of identity, and the rejection or exclusion of others is assumed to give greater security. In western Europe and North America, for example, the increased articulation of the global economy and accelerated capital movements towards lower cost locations and expanding markets have heightened feelings of economic insecurity. Labour from the South, from the Caribbean, central America, the Middle East, India and Pakistan, and so on, which made an important contribution to wealth creation during the late-Fordist period, has in some places been cast in the role of a threatening other as economic growth has flattened out or gone into reverse. Moves against illegal immigrants from Central America in California and racist attacks on Turkish workers in Germany seem to demonstrate heightened anxiety about alien others in a world where perceived economic certainties have evaporated. Certainty and order at the national level are achieved by the rejection of difference. Maybe, but certain representations of other cultures as bad objects are enduring and cannot be related in a simple fashion to economic upturns and downturns. Prejudices are more deeply engrained.

In white northern European cultures, associations with dirt, blackness and nature have created negative stereotypes of Africans, Afro-Caribbeans, people from the Indian subcontinent and Gypsies which have informed constructions of national identity that omit these groups and represent them as threatening. Their abjection is related to colonial histories but also to those things which threaten the boundaries of the (white) body and with which colonial minorities have been elided in the process of dehumanizing them. White signifies both purity and order and black signifies defilement and disorder in racist discourse, so representations of blackness create anxieties about borders – of the body, the neighbourhood and the nation – which are deeply rooted in states with colonial experience. As Richard Dyer observed in relation to a selection of films portraying the colonial experience, produced in Britain and the United States from the 1930s to the 1960s, 'they all [associated] whiteness with order, rationality, rigidity, qualities brought out by contrast with black disorder, irrationality and looseness' (Dyer, 1993: 145). These ideas have been reinforced by centuries of negative representations of colonial others, but the images are intimately associated with anxieties about the integrity of the white self.

Landscapes of desire

So far, I have discussed only the abject and threatening aspects of social difference. However, the urge to keep others at a distance, to expel or exclude them, is never a simple case of rejection. Repulsion is mixed with desire. As Zygmunt Bauman (1971: 279) commented on the process of stereotyping, it manifests 'an intricate mixture of interest and fear, reverence and abhorrence, impulsion and repulsion'. The feelings engendered by stereotypes are often connected with feelings about place, so we can talk about (imaginary) geographies of desire, where romanticized representations of others are complemented by similar constructions of landscape. Imagining others in this way has important practical consequences.

To illustrate this problem, I will first refer to an obscure article by the Toronto-based writer Deborah Root, in which she reviews a novel based on the French colonial experience in Algeria – Paul Bowles's *The Sheltering Sky* (1949). This concerned a journey by two French people and an American into the Sahara. Root argues that a 'pure outside', an empty, untouched wilderness, constitutes an important space in the imagination of the Western city dweller. Under the colonial regime, French citizens had access to such an imagined space in the Sahara desert, where 'in colonial eyes, the desert is a landscape without culture, wild, uncultivated land that remains out of control' (Root, n.d.: 30). To fit people into this landscape without spoiling the picture, it is necessary to represent them as unaffected by civilization, existing in a harmonious relationship with nature, effectively as a part of nature. People and the place represent something that has been lost by civilization through its separations of culture and nature. In *The Sheltering Sky*, however, the desired image of the 'desert Arab', at one with nature, is shattered by an encounter with two actual Arabs, one of whom is shaving his pubic hairs in public. This sight disturbs the French colonial travellers because it conflicts with their beliefs about what belongs in the public and private spheres. The Arab is degraded in their eyes, not just because of this discordant cultural practice but also because the encounter is so much at variance with the romanticized good stereotype. Their expectations about 'desert Arabs' are conditioned by their romanticized view of the desert. What is for them authentic, then, is 'not real', it is an imagined other, living in harmony with an imagined nature.

Ironically, the identity of romanticized indigenous peoples commonly requires the prefix 'real' – real Eskimos, real Aborigines, real (non-indigenous) Gypsies – which connects them with nature, but this idealization only serves to emphasize the negative qualities of those actually encountered. So, Gypsies living in or around cities in Britain, as most of them do, are often described in terms which suggest that they are not real. This is the connotation of 'itinerant' and 'tinker', for example. These ascriptions are often coupled with epithets suggesting that the minority is dirty, degraded and dangerously nomadic, dole-scrounging and criminal, because their presence in cities contradicts the romantic image of self-reliant Romanies living in harmony with nature in some imagined countryside. They are discrepant because they do not conform to their imagined geography.

Desire, for a more sensuous and natural existence, for a remerging with residues, is displaced onto romanticized others, mythical 'good objects' who inhabit 'other' places – deserts, the tundra, rain forests, the English countryside as it never was – which all have the qualities of a purified nature. Ultimately, these imagined geographies only serve to confirm negative stereotypes, those bad objects which threaten the borders of self, community (as a homogenized, purified construction), or nation.

Conclusion

> Our Manichean perception of the world as 'good' or 'bad' is triggered by the recurrence of the type of insecurity which induced our initial division of the world into 'good' and 'bad'. For the pathological individual, every confrontation sets up this echo ... for the non-pathological individual, the stereotype is a momentary coping mechanism, one that can be used and then discarded once anxiety is overcome. (Gilman, 1985: 18)

In this chapter, I have focused on the 'good' and the 'bad' in suggesting ways in which geographies of difference are constructed, but the dichotomies of object relations theory need some qualification. It is important to emphasize that life for most is rather messier and boundaries are more ambiguous, fuzzier, than my argument implies. The good and the bad may be tempered through engagement with others and the experience of other places. In the quotation above, Gilman distinguishes between pathological individuals whose life is dominated by bad stereotypes, the kind of people who consistently draw a sharp line between themselves or their community and some negatively stereotyped other, and those who feel strongly about distancing themselves from others only in times of crisis, when they may be swept up in a moral panic. We could identify a third self, who most of the time embraces and enjoys difference, who sees the ethnic and racial diversity of a neighbourhood, for example, as a positive and desirable characteristic of urban life.

Similarly, associations between otherness and place or community are unlikely to be always as predictable as my case studies suggest. Ultimately, object relations theory provides means of identifying a range of selves, variously constituted by good and bad objects, but objects rendered less absolute through engagement with others and with places which might otherwise have been seen in stereotyped terms. *Gajes* (non-Gypsies) who drink with Gypsies in the local pub, for example, may be less inclined to subscribe to a negative stereotype of the latter but a Gypsy encampment may still engender feelings of nervousness, reflecting the introjection of the Gypsy as a bad object.

Having said that, it is undeniable that social space, in certain places and at certain times, has been constructed in such a way that it has been complicit in producing others who are threateningly different, and examples of progressive, weakly bounded and heterogeneous places are less easy to find than excluding ones. The latter are most readily recognizable – as strongly bounded and homogenized spaces – when they try to defend themselves against some transient threat. Such communities may emerge and define themselves when, for example, there is a proposal to build a residential home for people with learning difficulties in proximity to a residential area where the majority are disposed to reject difference. We should not expect everyone to join in, however. Some people refuse to sign petitions or police the borders because they recognize the injustice of exclusion or because they are indifferent. Except in cases such as gated communities in the affluent suburbs of Los Angeles or Johannesburg or Moscow, reactions to difference are not entirely predictable. Some places are just more likely than others to reject or to embrace difference.

References

Bauman, Z. (1971) 'Semiotics and the function of culture'. In Julia Kristeva, J. Rey-Dubove and D. Umiker-Seboek (eds), *Essays in Semiotics*. The Hague, Mouton, 279–95.

Bowles, P. (1949) *The Sheltering Sky*. Harmondsworth, Penguin.

Corbin, A. (1986) *The Fragrant and the Foul: Odor and the French Social Imagination*. Cambridge, MA, Harvard University Press.

Csikszentmihalyi, M. and E. Rochberg-Halton (1981) *The Meaning of Things: Domestic Symbols and the Self*. Cambridge, Cambridge University Press.

Davis, M. (1990) *City of Quartz*. London, Verso Press.

Dyer, R. (1993) *The Matter of Images: Essays on Representation*. London, Routledge.

Figlio, K. (1996) 'Knowing, loving and hating nature: a psychoanalytical view'. In G. Robertson, M. Mash, L. Tickner, J. Bird, B. Curtis and T. Putnam (eds), *FutureNatural: Nature, Science, Culture*. London, Routledge, 72–85.

Gilman, S. (1985) *Difference and Pathology: Stereotypes of Sexuality, Race and Madness*. Ithaca NY, Cornell University Press.

Grosz, E. (1992) 'Julia Kristeva'. In E. Wright (ed.), *Feminism and Psychoanalysis: A Critical Dictionary*. Oxford, Blackwell, 194–200.

Kahane, C. (1992) 'Object relations theory'. In E. Wright (ed.), *Feminism and Psychoanalysis: A Critical Dictionary*. Oxford, Blackwell, 284–90.

Klein, M. (1960) *Our Adult World and its Roots in Infancy*. Tavistock Pamphlet 2. London, Tavistock.

Kristeva, J. (1982) *Powers of Horror*. New York, Columbia University Press.

Le Corbusier (1929 (1978)) *The City of Tomorrow and its Planning*. London, Architectural Press.

Mead, G.H. (1934) *Mind, Self and Society*. Chicago, University of Chicago Press.

Meadows, D. (1988) *Nattering in Paradise: A Word from the Suburbs*. London, Simon and Schuster.

Perin, C. (1988) *Belonging in America*. Madison, University of Wisconsin Press.

Root, D. (n.d.) 'Sacred landscapes/colonial dreams'. *Lusitania*, 1/4: 25–33.

Saunders, F. (1995) *Hidden Hands*. London, Channel 4 Television.

Sennett, R. (1970) *The Uses of Disorder*. Harmondsworth, Penguin.

Sennett, R. (1971) 'Middle-class families and urban violence: the experience of a Chicago community in the nineteenth century'. In T. Haravan (ed.), *Anonymous Americans*. Englewood Cliffs NJ, Prentice Hall, 280–305.

Sennett, R. (1991) *The Conscience of the Eye: The Design and Social Life of Cities*. New York, Alfred Knopf.

Sibley, D. (1995) *Geographies of Exclusion: Society and Difference in the West*. London, Routledge.

Sibley, D. and G. Lowe (1992) 'Domestic space, modes of control and problem behaviour'. *Geografiska Annaler*, 74B/3: 189–97.

Smith, N. (1996) 'After Tompkins Square Park: degentrification and the revanchist city'. In A. King (ed.), *Re-Presenting the City: Ethnicity, Capital and Culture in the 21st-Century Metropolis*. London, Macmillan, 93–110.

7
The Cultural Politics of Difference

Susan J. Smith

The politics of difference

The idea of social difference immediately implies processes of categorization and identification based on group characteristics. This means that the concept of difference is inherently political and politicized. People define themselves and label others partly as a means to an end – an end which is often about access to, and control over, material, symbolic and territorial resources.

History shows that the politics of difference does not have to be explicit or acknowledged in order to carry weight. For example, key modern projects – notably imperialism, colonialism and nationalism – have required difference to be taken for granted and routinely reproduced. It would have been impossible for the European colonial powers to exploit slave labour in order to expand their own economies and control the world map if the difference between European 'selves' and colonized 'others' had not been firmly established in the public mind. This modern idea of difference casts social and spatial categories, divisions between places and peoples, as a natural and therefore unproblematic fact of life. So successful was this construction that it has only been through recent critiques of modernism that the political content of the process of social differentiation has become fully apparent.

Whatever we call these critiques – postmodernism, post-traditionalism, post-colonialism – they have played a significant role in rethinking the concept of difference. Social difference is now more readily recognized as a political construction, rather than a natural condition. The result is that difference is no longer regarded as an ascribed characteristic, fixed by one's time and place of birth. It is acknowledged rather to be a property which varies through time and over space and which acts as a marker of diverse struggles over power. What we need to know now is more about where, why, how and by whom social difference is made (and unmade).

If the construction of difference is about the exercise of power – veiled or overt, conscious or unconscious, routine or sporadic, subdued or aggressive – it follows that by exploring difference it should be possible to cast light on the political process; on how people seek to influence the course of events to serve particular sets of interests. This means that by grasping the difference that difference makes, we can begin to understand why and how people do or do not participate in social and economic life, how inequalities in access to entitlements and in the exercise of obligations impinge on the social order, and how people act to make things change or to keep them the same. The conduct of politics is embedded in, and articulated through, the negotiation, articulation and mobilization of sameness and difference. And if one side of the political coin is the process of creating or sustaining categories of similarity or difference, the other side is the process of identification. Categorizing others and positioning ourselves is what the struggle for power and resources is all about. In sum, therefore, and as Harvey puts it, 'It is hard to discuss the politics of identity, multiculturalism, "otherness" and "difference" in abstraction from material circumstances and from political project' (Harvey, 1993: 41).

Perhaps the most obvious, and certainly the most widely explored, way to approach the link between politics, difference and identity is to study the formal political arena – party affiliations, voting behaviour, and so on. In the end, however, this provides only a partial and rather narrow interpretation of politics, as well as of the identities and allegiances that mobilize political engagement. A broader perspective recognizes that the bulk of politics is conducted outside the formal arena; that politics is about social participation in the widest sense; and that there is no clear dividing line between politics and life, economy and culture.

One important area of social scientific work on political participation outside electoral and party politics has focused on local social movements. Social movements are concerned primarily with political engagement around a specific cause or mix of causes. Such movements are important precisely because they challenge the established means of regulating and distributing political power. But in the flood of studies which followed their 'discovery' by Manuel Castells, researchers often seemed more inspired by the political efficacy of such movements than did participants. Thus, although social movements have made a significant mark on the intellectual landscape, their practical effects have often been blunted by apathy and ineffectiveness (explanations which are also invoked to account for low voter turnout in elections). There are notable and well-documented exceptions, but on the whole, social movements organized around single issues or causes rarely seem to sustain the public imagination for any extended period of time, and few have direct spin-off into other areas of political engagement (in the broadest sense). In my view, therefore, while social movements push at the boundaries of formal politics, and turn our attention to political life beyond the ballot box, they have not really transformed our understanding of politics, participation, identity or difference.

It might be helpful, in the light of this, to think about other ways in which political activity is incorporated into social and cultural life (and vice versa) in order to engage in the negotiation of sameness and the production of difference. I shall approach this by examining the politics of difference in contexts where the majority of people do not mobilize around 'causes' – they do not put their heads above the parapet of daily life in response to this or that issue, certainly not routinely, and for the most part rarely at all. However, as we shall see, this does not mean that such people are not political actors, that they do not use geography to link history with destiny, or that they have no role in the regulation of difference. Indeed, it may be that the really enduring politics of everyday life – the negotiations that keep things going, that balance out the forces for stability and the impetus to change – is only partly organized around voting patterns, social movements and worthy one-off causes. It may be organized, too, around the diverse events and performances that punctuate, and are an integral part of, local routines. Perhaps politics is as much about 'being' as about 'doing', as much about interconnected events as about individual campaigns; and if so, by exploring these more routine affairs it may be possible to come to a rounder appreciation of the links between politics, difference and identity.

The point I am making, then, is that politics can be found in all areas of life, even where we least expect it. As Abner Cohen (1993) has suggested, politics masquerades as everyday life, concealed within a variety of ostensibly non-political, social, cultural and economic forms. If we accept this view, then we also accept that what encourages people to participate in society, what captures their imagination, what propels them into action, what makes them want to influence the course of life (to be 'political'), is not just charismatic leaders, heady elections, or morally compelling one-off causes, but also people's stake in a range of routine events played out on the local stage. In the world of masquerade politics, it is not the exception – the unprecedented worthy cause or the emotive moral panic – but rather an enthusiasm for the day-to-day, and for localized representations and enactments of this, that invites political involvement.

As an aside it is worth noting that the result of this kind of politics is as likely to be a quest for stability as an impetus for change. Indeed, by focusing on what we might think of as 'localized event sequences', we are better able to acknowledge that participating in local affairs, celebrating commonalities and recognizing difference can simply be about having fun and enjoying life in its present form. It might be as much about changing that life in subtle understated ways as about engaging in high-profile campaigns designed to promote rapid and radical alterations to the local political order. And in an age where the idea of progress is viewed sceptically, and 'change' does not necessarily mean 'get better', being able to explore the politics of maintenance or inertia is as important a challenge for the social scientist as having insight into social change.

The implication of the ideas outlined above is that to explore the politics of difference fully, it is necessary to appreciate the happenings that are a regular part of local life. It is my contention that these regularities are often framed by anniversary events – symbolic statements about the local social order which are repeated every year at certain times and places, and which draw people of all ages and from all walks of life into collective experiences with political consequences. (These consequences may arise both through the enactment of the event itself and through its extension into other strategic and decision-making arenas which affect the locality.) It is no coincidence, in my view, that anniversary events are both widespread and increasing, and that they play a key part in the way that people handle their conditions of existence, reflect on history, and influence destiny (Johnston, 1991). This kind of event provides an appealing starting point for exploring the cultural politics of difference. The annual festivity is, furthermore, the crucible from which Cohen's idea of masquerade politics emerged. The conduct and consequences of such events testify still further, in Cohen's view, to the fact that the politics of difference is only partly about elections and parliaments; it is quintessentially a cultural affair: 'the cultural is continuously interpenetrated by the political ... [and] the political is constantly expressed, articulated and objectified in terms of cultural forms and performances. There is no pure culture. There is no pure politics' (Cohen, 1993: 8).

Masquerade politics is played out in anniversary celebrations, carnivals, processions and other popular festive forms and public displays in which the cultural and the political combine. For reasons I have laid out more fully elsewhere (S.J. Smith, 1996) these festive forms may offer a more promising route into the politics of difference in a postmodern world than either party politics or local social movements. There is, moreover, a growing literature within social geography which testifies to their political salience (for example, Jackson, 1992; Lewis and Pile, 1996; Marston, 1989; Spooner, 1996). As Bakhtin points out, popular festive forms are always linked with the projects of domination or empowerment and with the assertion or subversion of identity. Yet such masquerade politics are centred on routine and recurrent events rather than single politicized causes. These events are an enduring part of local life, whereas causes come and go. Causes are 'just' about politics; events are about the elaboration of social life, with political engagement as one of its facets. By adopting an approach to social research which argues that aesthetic questions relating to taste, style and performance cannot be divorced from political questions about power, inequality and oppression, popular festive forms might be seen to be as central as voting behaviour to an understanding of how people make history, geography and difference.

The difference that space makes

By interrogating some key works in historical and sociological thought it is possible to make a number of generalizations about the political significance of festive forms; about the kinds of event in which politics masquerades, about the nature of the political engagement this implies, and about the social bases of the political actions concerned. Likewise, by exploring a new-found interest in the spatiality of social life it is also possible, in a similar vein, to make some generalizations about the relevance of place and position to the conduct of these masquerade politics. In this section, I will take these two sets of generalizations in turn.

Most social scientists write about the politics of popular festive forms with (implicit or explicit) reference to their location along the types of continuum summarized in figure 7.1. The extremes of these continua may be thought of as two axes of power: formal authority on the right and usurpationary struggles on the left. Mikhail Bakhtin (1965), for example, distinguishes two 'ideal' types at each end of a continuum of festive forms. *Ritual ceremonies* are serious, formalized, official occasions designed to be observed rather than engaged with and used to persuade society to meet certain (political and moral) ideals. Politically, these festive events are a form of social control. *Carnival*, on the other hand, is an all-embracing public spectacle based on laughter,

Usurpationary struggles		Formal authority

Festive form

Carnival <--> Ceremony
Civil unrest < ---> Formal celebration

Political content

Confrontational < --> Compliant
Contentious < ---> Conforming
Charismatic < --> Institutionalized
Disruptive <--> Hierarchical
Subversive < --> Patriotic

Character of society

Authentic < --> Invented
Meaningful < ----------------------------------> Bureaucratized/Commodified
Experienced < --> Imagined

Figure 7.1   The politics of everyday life

consecrated by tradition and performed by the people. These events are generally more about confrontation than compliance. Harrison's (1988) discussion of crowd behaviour in nineteenth-century England pushes a little further along Bakhtin's continuum, distinguishing formal celebration (mass mobilization around patriotic events) at one extreme from radical mass meetings or major riots (civil unrest) at the other.

This broad distinction between the ceremonial and the carnivalesque is carried over into writings on the political content of collective behaviours. Here the distinction between the left-hand and right-hand side columns of figure 7.1 is formalized by Charles Tilley (1995), who differentiates between confrontation and compliance, contention and conformity – axes which distinguish between what he calls continuous and discontinuous claims for rights, resources, space and attention. The former, which we might label 'conforming' claims, are enacted through the routine of parliamentary politics and institutionalized collective bargaining (a politics of hierarchy and patriotism). The latter, which he describes as contentious claims, are exacted through various more spontaneous, symbolic forms of collective behaviour (a politics of disruption and subversion).

In practice, of course, most festive forms fall somewhere between Bakhtin's, Harrison's and Tilley's ideal types – between formal authority and usurpationary struggle – so that each one can be thought of as a contest between the forces for stability and the impulse for change. This contest in turn might indeed be the key that specialists on collective action have looked for when attempting to specify the connections between larger-scale socio-economic processes and the character of popular struggle. These connections are made through the exercise of what Tilley calls repertoires of action and interaction, which are developed by, and available to, people at different times and places:

> By analogy with the various improvisations known to a jazz band or a troupe of strolling players ... people in a given place and time know how to carry out a limited number of alternative collective action routines, adapting each one to the immediate circumstances ... In the manner of jazz musicians, the players embed their known routines in shared understandings, including references to well-known themes and previous performances. (Tilley, 1995: 42)

By drawing on these repertoires, festive forms play out a cultural politics of difference through which society reflects on itself, dramatizes its collective myths, interprets the past and leans towards the future. In reflecting on the social bases of such public performances, and on the character of the societies in which they are located, Chaney (1993) draws one further distinction between what he calls 'spectacular societies' and what Debord (1967) dubbed 'society of the spectacle'. If we think of this as a continuum, we might label the ends 'authentic' and 'invented' (even 'depthless'), 'traditional' and 'ahistoric', 'meaningful' and 'commodified', or 'experienced' and 'imagined'. Whatever the label, the wider point is that festive forms are spectacular, yet routinized, events whose political content expresses and shapes the character of the society in which they are embedded. They are sites where the political is articulated through the cultural to inform the samenesses and differences that make up local life.

So far, I have discussed an historical and sociological literature which contains some important clues on where to look for the politics of difference in the events of everyday life. These are summarized in figure 7.1, which gives a clear steer on the distinctions between a politics which has been constructed around notions of formality, order, hierarchy and stability (on the right-hand side of the figure), and a politics of disruption, displacement, instability and change (on the left). Reflecting on these writings, we might, nevertheless, be forgiven for thinking that they take place on the head of a pin; that *where* things happen has no bearing on why things happen or what they mean. Yet, as the postmodern turn has made us acutely aware, nothing could be further from the truth. Neither politics, nor sociology, nor the construction of difference, nor the festivities that provide a window on this can happen without 'taking place'. Geography matters.

It is worth turning our attention, then, to a growing interest in the importance of space for the construction of difference. I am thinking here of the work of Homi Bhabha, bell hooks, Fredric Jameson, Henri Lefebvre, Edward Said and others who make the point that spatial concepts – core, periphery, border, boundary and margin – whether used symbolically or encountered in a material sense, can help us understand the way that difference is produced and reproduced. The message these authors deliver is that the ideas about difference embedded in local life are not simply nurtured through time but are also primed by position. Identities are shaped by geography as well as by history. This means that the political forms outlined above are positioned. It is not, then, surprising to learn that a distinctive feature of the recent reconfiguration of space in social thought is its preoccupation with politics. On the one hand, Kirby (1996: 3) observes that the construction of difference is a fundamentally spatial process: 'Contemporary political thought is much concerned with "difference," with *refiguring* difference, with *transfiguring* difference. To do so it often goes through space. How could it do otherwise? Difference itself seems a spatial concept, unimaginable or just barely imaginable. outside the register of space.' On the other hand, N. Smith and Katz (1993) point out that a distinctive feature of the reassertion of space in social theory is its preoccupation with politics. The appropriation and use of space are political acts.

So, every fair, festival, spectacle or masquerade is positioned; it has a location within international, regional and community space; it has a setting relative to the other symbolic and practical activities that make up local life. Masquerade politics are positioned, physically and metaphorically, in relation to other parts of the life and culture of the wider society. Even the naming of festivals reflects this, distinguishing between, for instance, mainstream and fringe events. Fairs and festivals make and transform space, and by exploring this we can gain insight into the identities they express and constitute. Festive forms are about the exercise of politics through the establishment and bounding (or disestablishment and unbounding) of territory, and as such, they may be seen as an exercise through which people use space to think themselves into similarity and difference. Thus, just as Bakhtin identifies the two poles of a socio-political continuum of popular festive forms (ritual ceremony and the carnivalesque), so I would argue for two extremes or 'ideal types' of positioning which we might term *heartland* and *border*.

Spaces of resistance		Centres of power
Border <	-- >	Heartland
Periphery <	-- >	Core
Contested territory <	-- >	Undisputed realm
Margin <	-- >	Mainstream
Displaced <	--- >	Placed
Dislocated <	--- >	Located
In-between <	-- >	Positioned
Mobile <	-- >	Fixed
Unbounded <	--- >	Bounded

Figure 7.2 Politics in its place

Politically we might expect heartlands and borders to be poles apart, as indicated in figure 7.2. The two extremes of the figure may again be thought of as an axis (on the right) of centred, stable, conforming and consolidated power, and an axis (on the left) of marginalized, resistant, disruptive spaces whose openness may contain an impulse for change. These contested axes are most readily contrasted in discussion comparing colonial and post-colonial thinking, though in principle they have relevance to any spatialized struggle. Crush (1995), for example, talks of the importance of 'decentring' a colonial discourse (which is therefore implicitly 'centred'), whose core is fixed and whose periphery is marginalized.

Heartlands or cores are centres of power which may be thought of as taken-for-granted spaces, positioned well inside an unambiguous boundary, strategically located at the centre of an undisputed, though tightly controlled, territory. Interestingly, in the explosion of writings on spatial metaphor, such centres have received relatively little attention, except as the symbol of a politically questionable status quo around which alternative spaces are organized. Borders and margins have proved much more popular, as the radical standpoint from which (what is constructed as) the comfortable integrity of the core is challenged. Part of the 'decentring' of social thought has indeed been a recognition that spaces on the margin have an authority of their own.

Borders, peripheries and margins are those unbounded spaces wrapped around, or sandwiched in between, cores; and despite a history of being silenced, they are no longer on the edge of social affairs. Spatial metaphor generally is in vogue (see Silber, 1995), but in practice most theoretical attention in this spatial turn (and for politically sound reasons) has been devoted to the margins, or at least to the complex set of ideas that make up the left-hand axis of figure 7.2. The reasons for this are laid out in Shields (1991) in what is still one of the best introductions to 'places on the margin'. This signals growing interest in an exciting 'new politics' of the margins, whose complexities have been reviewed more recently by Soja (1996). The key message from this literature is that the left-hand pole of figure 7.2 represents spaces which are no longer to be defined only in terms of the oppressive structures of the right-hand pole. Borderlands and margins are being transformed (albeit, as we shall see, rather unevenly) from spaces to which marginalized groups are relegated, into places which are chosen, as a speaking position and a site of resistance (hooks, 1991). Likewise, displacement is no longer a process by which more powerful groups remove less powerful ones from the mainstream; rather, it has become a strategy invoked to challenge and unsettle the spatial categories mapped out by the centre (Trinh, 1989). And dislocation is no longer simply an imposition; it can also be made into a bid for freedom (Laclau, 1990).

I shall return to heartlands and borders shortly. To summarize the argument so far, I have suggested first (based on figure 7.1) that by looking at the political content of fairs and festivals we can understand something about local histories and destinies. Second (drawing from figure 7.2), by considering how the cultural politics of festive forms are positioned, we can cast light on local geographies and identities. Given this neat distinction, it is tempting to think that by putting figures 7.1 and 7.2 together it might be possible to map them onto one another, so producing a sense of how society, history and geography intersect with politics to illuminate the (corresponding) axes of differentiation and identification which form figure 7.3.

If this mapping were to work, the axes on the right-hand side of figures 7.1 and 7.2 would need to be seen as an expression of the political sociology and geography of modernism. Here, ritual ceremony helps reproduce an institutionalized social hierarchy and a literal spatial hierarchy (what Soja (1996) refers to as 'Firstspace') by invoking the essentialized and dichotomized notions of identity which form the corresponding right-hand axis of figure 7.3. The axes on the left of figures 7.1 and 7.2, in contrast, would be interpreted in terms of the cultural politics of postmodernism. Here, carnivalesque festive forms would provide a speaking position for those moving within in-between or marginal spaces to live out (through a medium Soja might term 'Thirdspace') the more radical, open and hybrid identities associated with the left-hand axis of figure 7.3.

Postmodern identities	Modern identities
Constructed, resisted, remodelled	*Given, not made*
Polyvocal < ---> Dichotomized	
Hybrid < --> Essential	
Contested < ---> Taken-for-granted	
Individualized < ---------------------------------> Grouped, ranked, ordered	

Figure 7.3 The politics of identity

Now, it is possible – and I believe likely – that the masquerade politics of the margin do encapsulate identity in ways that differ from festivities in the mainstream. As figures 7.1, 7.2 and 7.3 together imply,
being on the edge requires and draws on different resources for identification to those required for being in a more central position. It is quite
reasonable to imagine that festive forms rely on spatial strategies to
establish cultural difference, and that in doing so they engage in a struggle for space which symbolizes a range of wider social and political con-
tests. Therefore, I think that Pratt (1992) is right when she argues that it
may only be meaningful to consider identity, and therefore also difference, with reference to particular places at particular times. Place
matters if we want to understand the way social identities are formed,
reproduced and marked off from one another. *Where* identities are
made is likely to have a bearing on which markers of difference – class,
gender, 'race' and so on – are salient, and which are veiled. However,
what I want to go on to suggest is that the difference that space makes
is rather more complex than simply adding (figures) one and two
together to get to (figure) three. As Slater (1992) has pointed out,
spatial relations are no less complex and contradictory than historical
processes, and the empirical challenge for the spatial turn in social
science is to explore this complexity.

To begin to address this challenge, I shall sketch the findings of two
case studies: the Palio of Siena, and the Common Ridings of the Scottish
borders. These are annual events which also preoccupy local people all
the year round. They are an integral part of local routine, and therefore
part of the production, reproduction and elaboration of local life. They
are the kind of event which I have argued may, in the end, have a political salience which is complementary to, and possibly more widely
embracing than, that of one-off causes or single-issue social movements.

Geography matters

Both case studies refer to festivities which are steeped in history and tradition, and which are associated with the celebration of geography and the expression of identity. But they are performed from what, for the purposes of this chapter, may be regarded as rather different positionings. Their locations may be thought of in spatial terms as a heartland and a borderland – a core and a periphery. Siena is in Tuscany, at the heart of Italy, whereas the Scottish borders are on the edge of the country and on the boundary with England.

Now, it is important to recognize that these positionings are only different for a given scale and context. From the perspective of post-colonial international politics, for example, these two places might be seen as sharing a core position, at the centre of the 'old Western world'. From the perspective of an urban geography concerned with global cities, these case studies might be seen as sharing a space on the rural periphery. But from the perspective of their respective nation states (which continue to manage the kind of political participation which has a bearing on most people's lives) their positions are very different.

My suggestion below is that these contrasting positionings have a bearing on the production and reproduction of difference, though not always in the way that the currently dominant discourse around cores and peripheries, mainstreams and margins, might lead us to believe. It could perhaps fairly be said that geographies of difference are currently over-theorized and under-specified. I want to use these empirical examples – albeit in the briefest and most preliminary of ways – to explore empirically some of the difference that geography can make to different relations of difference.

The heart of the matter

The Sienese Palio is a horse race (literally, the *palio* is the banner awarded to the winner). It belongs to a long, politicized tradition of public horse racing in Renaissance Italy (Mallett, 1996) and it is one of several 'games' which became common in Italian cities, especially in Tuscany, from at least the thirteenth century. The significance of the Palio today is that it is the only such game to survive, and (barring one or two recently instituted tourism-inspired revivals) Siena is the only city to retain its Palio. The Sienese Palio – which is normally run twice a year, in July and August – is a great annual spectacle, a symbol of the life and times of the town, and the pivot of the Sienese calendar.

The Palio is played out in what (within the framework outline above) we might think of as a heartland location. It focuses on the centre of the city, and is run on a (roughly) circular 'track' improvised by covering the Piazza del Campo in layers of local red earth. There is no ambiguity about the fact that this festivity is Italian, and more especially Tuscan, to the core. Likewise, there is no ambiguity about the fact that it symbolizes the magnificence of Siena (which stems from its historical status as an independent republic). The Palio is a spectacular event which displays the history, geography and social life of the city in full glory. It is even a key element of local 'place promotion' (attracting, as it does, a huge tourist following). At first glance, therefore, the Sienese Palio appears to be an archetypal expression of the stability, solidarity, fixity and continuity that we have come to associate with those processes of identification which are played 'in the mainstream', at the real and symbolic centre of things.

However, probing more closely (and here I draw on works by Cecchini and Neri (1958), Dundes and Falassi (1975), Cesarini and Merisio (1988) and Magi (1996), as well as on my own preliminary research), it is apparent that the Palio is only marginally about expressing what it is to be Italian generally or even Sienese in particular. Once the tourist trade is catered for, this festivity is primarily about membership of, and rivalries among, the seventeen *contrade* (neighbourhoods) that make up the town. Local people belong first to a *contrada* and second to the city. Celebrating the Palio is traditionally a means of bestowing honour and acquiring magnificence, but today such celebrations are the ritualized focus for a range of internal confrontations, aggressions and emotions that make up Sienese social geography.

I refer to social geography deliberately, because these confrontations are so explicitly territorial in nature. A visitor to the city will find clues to this territoriality at any time of the year. Every *contrada* has a name based on a specific symbol or group of symbols, and these lend each neighbourhood its specific iconography – a clubhouse with heraldic symbols over the door, graphically designed and publicly positioned baptismal fonts, a local church, and even a range of 'street furniture' bearing local references. The only spaces in Siena where more than one *contrada*'s symbol is found in the same place at the same time are in the ceramics shops, on the souvenir stands, and in the Piazza del Campo during the Palio itself. During the days of the Palio, territorial signage is even more evident, with elaborate street-light fittings, flags and other paraphernalia all marking out the spatial structure of social life in Siena. Long tables appear in the streets for the traditional *contrada* feasting, and the wearing of scarves, colours and costumes restates local claims to specific places and identities within the city.

Probing beyond '*the* Sienese' Palio, then, we find that an ostensibly 'heartland' display is in fact testimony not to territorial solidarity but rather to a spatial process of social fragmentation. Not only do these spatializations subsume gender differences (the roles of men and women are taken for granted in the spaces of the Palio, but this requires a paper of its own), they even take precedence over local differences in income, wealth and prestige. In the run-up to the Palio, for example, it is the wealth of the *contrade* as a whole, not of individuals within them, which is put at risk; and the risk comes not from losing (which is comparatively cheap) but from winning (which is expensive) or preventing a rival *contrada* from winning (which might be more costly still). The emphasis throughout is on *contrada* solidarity irrespective of an individual's politics, finances or social standing.

Allegiance to a *contrada* is a fact of life secured by ancestry and birthplace. *Contrada* membership is bestowed at birth; it cannot be earned, won or paid for. It is one's 'natural' affiliation; a local loyalty that is inevitable rather than chosen. It may, therefore, be no coincidence that most *contrada* symbols are rooted in nature, for example giraffe, snail, panda, porcupine and caterpillar. These 'natural' symbols mark off the various neighbourhoods because of the way they are physically embedded in the landscape; but they are also drawn into the *social* landscape, as apparently 'natural' signs of distinction are linked with a range of cultural characteristics which are routinely drawn on to help people identify themselves and label others. As Dundes and Falassi observe:

> Whether the alleged characteristics of the inhabitants of a given contrada are mere stereotypes or whether they correspond in some way to reality is moot. What is certain is that all the contradioli insist that there are definite personality differences between the various contrade, and that they go to some lengths to reinforce and perpetuate such would-be distinctions. (1975: 26)

This extends even to thinking about others in terms of subtle differences in physical traits. Given the extent of intermarriage over a long history within each *contrada* it is just about conceivable that locals might be able to identify subtle physical similarities among residents (though, if they exist, they have certainly eluded me). What gives pause for thought, however, is the way that these differences appear to be linked to the behavioural and personality-type labels that members of the *contrade* use to position themselves within Sienese space. For example, Dundes and Falassi report that the population of the Shell *contrada* are labelled as smelly, Wolf residents are thought of as childish, Unicorns are labelled blockheads, and Giraffes are typified as long-necked. Supposed physical traits and behavioural characteristics, it seems, are being generalized and linked to the social and personality characteristics of people who occupy particular spaces. If we stop to think about what the implications of such a process on a global scale have been, we can see how short a step it is to observations like 'sangue d'ebrai e'Torraioli' (a phrase claiming that the residents of the Tower *contrada* are of Jewish ancestry, but which is more often used as a ritual insult than as an historical referent).

These and other categorizing devices mark out some of the most salient axes of social difference in the town. It is, of course, easy to dismiss them as a local quirk – a whimsification of the Italian social landscape. However, examined more closely, they draw our attention to wider and more problematic processes of social categorization. Using appearance to index a wide range of assumptions about the relationship between birthplace, character, personality and behaviour may (in this instance) be a generally frivolous undertaking on the local level, yet if we set the process into a national and international, post-colonial context, it becomes immediately analogous to politically questionable processes of racial differentiation. Such markers bear more investigation, therefore, because they show how powerful the alliance between culture and politics can be when it comes to marking out and legitimizing the difference that place makes to identity.

Quite apart from opening a window onto the detail of Sienese social geography, this case study is already beginning to suggest the importance of being cautious when thinking of centres, cores and heartlands as shot through with homogeneity, stability, conformity and fixity. On the contrary, it might be suggested that a core location provides the space required for internal conflict to thrive, for internal fragmentation to proceed, and for the localization of difference to become extremely finely tuned. At the very least, this example suggests that centres do not all conform to the presuppositions of similarity and solidarity which are built into the current vogue for spatial metaphor.

There are, nevertheless, at least two further, perhaps more predictable, corollaries of the heartland positioning of the Palio. First, from this centred location, wherein so many facets of life can be taken for granted, uncertainty is not a threat to the integrity or continuity of identity. Indeed uncertainty is deliberately built into the Palio, and it is viewed as a prospect to be engaged with rather than resisted. For example, the horses which run in the Palio are chosen to be roughly equal to one another in speed and ability – very good horses are excluded, and so are those with little prospect of staying the course. Which horse runs for which *contrada* is determined by drawing lots, and even which neighbourhoods get to compete in each race (only ten of the seventeen) is partly a matter of chance. The real skill of the Palio is in the secret deals needed to stack these random odds in favour of some *contrade* and against the interests of others. Uncertainty appears to be part of the vitality of the Palio; it is what makes life challenging and exciting; it is what shapes and makes the social fabric. Siena would not be the same without it.

The second corollary of the security built into heartland identities is that outsiders are not a threat. The commercialization of the Palio is taken for granted, but the tourist's experience bears little resemblance to that engaged in by locals. Nothing that outsiders might contribute can substantially affect the substance of the Palio or the identities of its participants. Outsiders can enjoy the event, but they will not shift the focus of a cultural politics which is primarily about what it is to belong to one, or another, fragment of the local landscape.

To summarize, the Palio is a heartland celebration. It takes being Italian, Tuscan and Sienese for granted, and so concentrates attention on the difference that space makes within the city. Outsiders – tourists, commerce, even participants in the Palio – are welcome in the spaces of the city, because they cannot impinge on the identity bestowed by birth into a *contrada*. The salience of identities conferred through territorial allegiance subsumes class differences and veils gender difference (both of which require further investigation), but they do help us begin to understand how ideas about the naturalization of spatial difference might be reproduced. Crucially, however, this example provides insights into how empirical investigation may begin to disrupt some hitherto appealing ideas about how a particular spatial metaphor is incorporated into the processes of social categorization and identification. What happens in 'the mainstream' cannot be taken for granted any more than what happens on the margin. Which brings me to my second case study.

Bounding the borders

The Scottish borders are, at the scale and in the context that we are considering, in an altogether different position. They are part of a rural borderland on the very edge of Scotland. On the one hand, this is a position which must signify all that is Scottish, marking out a real and much contested point of differentiation with England. On the other hand, these are border towns which are marginal to the Scottish political economy and to the Scottish cultural order. As I noted above, places on the margin are currently rather attractive to social scientists.

bell hooks (1995) regards them as a source of radical ideas and as a catalyst for radical politics. 'Within a certain postmodern current', observes Slater (1992: 320), it appears to be 'trendy to be marginal, "in" to be different and peripheral.' 'The border' has, in short, become 'the appropriate metaphor for the postmodern subject' (Watts, 1991: 11).

Since the Scottish borders are experiencing the winds of change, they appear to fit quite well into this postmodern framework. Global economic restructuring has undermined the woollen textile industries, the commuting population has grown, the population is ageing, and there is a significant retirement population (including English immigrants). Against this backdrop, the annual Common Ridings provide perhaps the best window on the cultural politics of difference and position. The Ridings are a celebration of history, geography and difference and they provide an important cultural resource for defining and preserving local identity in the face of changing times and outside influences.

The Common Ridings are by definition a geography of the margins. Their very rationale is the protection of marginal territory. Today's rituals re-enact yesterday's necessity, and they derive from a time when local men rode out to protect the common lands from both local lairds and English intruders. Most large border towns have some kind of Common Riding, and these are usually linked to a more general festival designed to depict and celebrate local life. I have discussed these events in more detail elsewhere (S.J. Smith, 1993, 1995, 1996). In this section, I shall relate just two observations to make the point that margins, like mainstreams, that peripheries, like cores, are differentiated spaces whose content has been quite fully theorized but perhaps too little scrutinized. Geography matters, even when places share a position on the edge; and just how it matters is an empirical question.

My first observation is explored in detail in S.J. Smith (1993). This is a story of the Peebles Beltane and Common Riding festival of 1991 – the year in which a supposed outsider requested the Beltane Committee to withdraw the golliwog costumes from a children's parade which precedes the crowning of the Beltane Queen. The request was in line with local guidelines on multicultural education, and (because so much of the ceremony relies on input from local schools) it was (eventually) complied with. However, because the initiative was perceived to have stemmed from outside interference (though ironically the person concerned was a Peeblean who had moved to Edinburgh), it was constructed by 'insiders' as a symbolic challenge to local history and identity. Once couched in these terms, the event prompted an astonishing outburst of local resistance. Golliwogs may have been banned from the Court of the Beltane Queen, but they put in an appearance in virtually every informal space available during the festival week. The annual fancy dress parade was awash with golliwogs, as local people rejected charges of political insensitivity and 'commonsense' racism, and expressed their determination to preserve (what they saw as) a deeply ingrained tradition as well as the ways of life from which it stems.

While the racism embedded in this event should not be downplayed, a full interpretation of the incident is, in my view, rather more complex than it first appears. However, even from this brief sketch, it is apparent that borders are not necessarily places from which something new 'begins its presencing' (Bhabha, 1994). There clearly are margins where mobile and multiple identities speak of a new stability, self-assurance and self-determination amongst once-oppressed peoples; but equally there is space on the margin to resist political correctness along with anything else that seems new and threatening in the wake of an enforced (even if timely) movement for change. As Young (1995) has pointed out, these latter spaces, open and marginal though they may be, might engender a marked and not always welcome fixity of identity, as well as an unreservedly conservative local politics.

These 'marginal identities of the second kind' are equally apparent in my second observation, which is based on events of the past few years in the borders town of Hawick. I have noted before how any appeal to tradition in the context of the Common Ridings invokes particular ideas about gender roles and about the nature of masculinity and femininity (S.J. Smith, 1995). Hawick, however, has the dubious distinction of holding the only Common Riding which is exclusively an all-male event. In 1995, three local women challenged this, and so embarked on a long, often bitter and always uphill struggle to join the Ridings. The controversy this stirred up was to divide the town (as well as many families, and many groups of men and women, within it) and culminate in a sexual discrimination action supported by the 'outside' forces of the Equal Opportunities Commission.

Again the problem was, and continues to be, constructed not in terms of the politically questionable reproduction of longstanding and outdated gender inequalities, but rather in terms of the threat to local life posed by any change to a longstanding local tradition. 'Here in Hawick', observed one (female) local resident to a reporter on the *Sunday Post*, 'we are loyal to our ancient traditions. If you start tampering with them and changing them, it will spoil everything' (16 February 1997). And the very worst scenario is when the impetus for change comes from outside the burgh. As one (traditionalist) member of the Common Riding Committee explained: 'It's quite ridiculous that Hawick's name has been dragged through the mud by those who want to interfere with local customs. Outsiders simply don't understand what we are fighting for' (*Hawick News*, 28 September 1996).

As in Peebles, the debacle attracted national and even international media attention, and Hawick (as an editorial in the *Scotsman* put it) 'has been pilloried as a town mired in the dark ages, populated by male chauvinists and pigheaded bigots' (3 April 1997). Once again a full interpretation of the events is, I think, quite complex and reaches well beyond issues of gender. However, the key point is that just as in Peebles sticking to tradition invoked a crisis over representations of 'race', in Hawick it resulted in a bitter dispute over constructions of gender and over the position and role of women. This example is therefore again unsettling to the prevailing common sense. Not all borders and margins are radical and open 'thirdspaces'. Even the fact that local women are finding a voice and claiming a place in the Ridings is not quite as radical as it seems. For despite the opposition their claims have attracted, the women's project is in fact quite modest and limited in ways that would surprise many feminists.

The irony thrown up in both these case studies is that it may well be their place on the margin that underpins their rampant, as well as their more tempered, conservatism. Because the Common Ridings are mounted from a marginal location, they cannot take being Scottish, a borderer, a Peeblean or a Teri (a person from Hawick) for granted. As a consequence, they point local people's attention directly towards the spatial and social boundaries that divide themselves from others. In this context, difference is made by drawing uncritically on the certainties of the past in order to set the parameters of local identity in the present. Any challenge to the integrity of the past thus becomes a threat to the integrity of the present. An appeal to tradition, a fear of uncertainty, and a wariness of the influence of others all contribute to the way in which the spatialized festivals and Ridings are also very explicitly gendered and racialized (in ways that often exclude those who believe they have a right to belong). The festivities are thus simultaneously about promoting a local status quo and about resisting the imposition of alternative world views either from England to the south, or from the Scottish mainstream to the north, or from the apparent vagaries of socio-economic change in the world at large. Once again, even though the fact that gender and race have come onto the agenda means that the winds of change are blowing (S.J. Smith, 1996), these empirical case studies do disrupt what is fast becoming an orthodoxy about the radical new ideas and identities associated with spaces on the margin.

The right to difference

This chapter began by considering why the idea of difference is inherently political. Most of the text, however, concentrates on the difference that space makes to our understanding of difference, using examples which disrupt our expectations about what 'cores' and 'peripheries' contain.

Revisiting figures 7.1–7.3, it is easy to see how recent work in critical human geography has challenged the ideas about politics, place and identity which are associated with a positioning towards the core locations on the right-hand sides of the continua, by exploring and exploiting the alternative geographies of the margin, on the left. It is also easy to understand why these alternative places and spaces are so enticing. It is surely time to recognize the potency of the ostensibly powerless and to explore the flexible, radical spaces of the periphery rather than preoccupying ourselves exclusively with the fixed, conservative realms of the centre. It is certainly time to make space for the experience and expression of identities that turn the old social order on its head.

What the case studies I have sketched suggest, however, is that there is still some way to go before we have grasped the full significance of the spatial turn in the politics of difference and identity. Slater (1992: 320) has already pointed out that while the literature on peripheries is engaging and persuasive, 'there is at the same time a tendency here to fail to specify the types of marginality' and thus to over-romanticize the position. Likewise, it might be argued that while it is decidedly unfashionable to be mainstream, by failing to recognize the diversity associated with this position, its place in the production of difference will be worryingly misrepresented.

So I would like to redraw figures 7.1–7.3 into something much more complex, as the various continua cross-cut and interact to produce spaces, politics, identities and difference in many different dimensions. Place does matter for the politics of difference but in ways that remain to be specified for particular circumstances. At the moment we might argue that geographies of difference are over-theorized and under-specified. I suspect that when theory and practice are more fully brought together we will be moving towards a geography of what Lefebvre has called the right to difference. This will be a geography concerned not just with what difference does look like, but also with what it ought (or, more practically, what it ought not) to look like in a socially just society. It will be about the code of ethics that informs the politics that masquerades as culture in the differentiation of local life.

Acknowledgements

Thanks to Doreen Massey and the editorial team for patience and helpful suggestions; and to Jan Penrose for inspiration and advice.

References

Bakhtin, M. (1965) *Rabelais and his World*. Cambridge MA and London, MIT Press.

Bhabha, H. (1994) *The Location of Culture*. London and New York, Routledge.

Cecchini, G. and D. Neri (1958) *Il Palio di Siena*. Milan, Electra Editrice.

Cesarini, P. and P. Merisio (1988) *Il Palio*. Siena, Lombardi.

Chaney, D. (1993) *Fictions of Collective Life*. London, Routledge.

Cohen, A. (1993) *Masquerade Politics: Explorations in the Structure of Urban Cultural Movements*. Oxford, Berg.

Crush, J. (1995) 'Post-colonialism, de-colonization and geography'. In A. Godlweska and N. Smith (eds), *Geography and Empire*. Oxford and Cambridge MA, Blackwell, 333–50.

Debord, G. (1967) *Society of the Spectacle*. London, Rebel Press.

Dundes, A. and A. Falassi (1975) *La terra in piazza: An Interpretation of the Palio of Siena*. Berkeley CA and Los Angeles, University of California Press.

Harrison, M. (1988) *Crowds and History*. Cambridge, Cambridge University Press.

Harvey, D. (1993) 'Class relations, social justice and the politics of difference'. In M. Keith and S. Pile (eds), *Place and the Politics of Identity*. London, Routledge, 41–66.

hooks, b. (1991) *Yearning: Race, Gender and Cultural Politics*. London, Turnaround.

hooks, b. (1995) *Art Matters*. New York, New Press.

Jackson, P. (1992) 'The politics of the streets: a geography of Caribana'. *Political Geography*, 11: 130–51.

Johnston, W.M. (1991) *Celebrations: The Cult of Anniversaries in Europe and the United States Today*. New Brunswick NJ, Transaction.

Kirby, K.M. (1996) *Indifferent Boundaries. Spatial Concepts of Human Subjectivity*. New York and London, Guilford Press.

Laclau, E. (1990) *New Reflections on the Revolution of Our Time*. London, Verso.

Lewis, C. and S. Pile (1996) 'Woman, body, space: Rio Carnival and the politics of performance'. *Gender, Place and Culture*, 3: 23–41.

Magi, P. (1996) *Il Palio dentro e fiori*. Florence, Bonechi.

Mallett, M. (1996) 'Horse racing and politics'. In *Culture, Politics and Society in the Age of Lorenzo di Medici*. Warburgh Institute.

Marston, S. (1989) 'Public rituals and community power: St Patrick's Day parades in Lowell, Massachusetts, 1841–1874'. *Political Geography Quarterly*, 8: 255–69.

Pratt, G. (1992) 'Commentary: spatial metaphors and speaking positions'. *Environment and Planning D: Society and Space*, 10: 241–4.

Shields, R. (1991) *Places on the Margin: Alternative Geographies of Modernity*. London and New York, Routledge.

Silber, I.F. (1995) 'Space, fields, boundaries: the rise of spatial metaphors in contemporary sociological theory'. *Social Research*, 62: 323–55.

Slater, D. (1992) 'On the borders of social theory: learning from other regions'. *Environment and Planning D: Society and Space*, 10: 307–27.

Smith, N. and C. Katz (1993) 'Grounding metaphor: towards a spatialized politics'. In M. Keith and S. Pile (eds), *Place and the Politics of Identity*. London, Routledge, 67–83.

Smith, S.J. (1993) 'Bounding the borders: claiming space and making place in rural Scotland'. *Transactions of the Institute of British Geographers* (n.s.) 18: 291–308.

Smith, S.J. (1995) 'Where to draw the line?'. In A. Rogers and S. Vertovec (eds), *The Urban Context*. Oxford, Berg, 141–63.

Smith, S.J. (1996) 'Bordering on identity'. *Scotlands*, 3/1: 18–31.

Soja, E.W. (1996) *Thirdspace: Journeys to Los Angeles and Other Real-and-Imagined Places*. Oxford and Cambridge MA, Blackwell.

Spooner, R. (1996) 'Contested representations: black women and the St Paul's Carnival'. *Gender, Place and Culture*, 3: 187–203.

Tilley, C. (1995) *Popular Contention in Great Britain, 1758–1834*. Cambridge MA, Harvard University Press.

Trinh, T.M.-H. (1989) *Women, Native, Other*. Bloomington, Indiana University Press.

Watts, M.J. (1991) 'Mapping meaning, denoting difference, imagining identity: dialectical images and postmodern geographies'. *Geografiska Annaler*, 13/B: 7–16.

Young, R.J.C. (1995) *Colonial Desire: Hybridity in Theory, Culture and Race*. London and New York, Routledge.

8
Geographies of Identity and Difference: Marking Boundaries

Geraldine Pratt

Introduction

I want to begin with three fragments from my own research.

1 In 1992 I published an essay with two colleagues on the social geography of Vancouver (Ley et al., 1992); my responsibility was to cover gender, Dan Hiebert handled race and immigration. Writing about the ways that suburban mothers juggle their identities and responsibilities as mothers and paid employees, I generalized Isabel Dyck's (1989) qualitative research among a small number of suburban women in Vancouver to argue that middle-class women use their networks among other mothers to create safe spaces within their neighbourhoods for their children, to compensate for their own absence during the day. By extending the safety of 'the home' into the neighbourhood and broader community, these women can be read as destabilizing conventional geographies and geographical distinctions (for example, home/neighbourhood, private/public) in order to stabilize their identities as mothers and employees.

2 In 1994 a very different geography of childcare and identity became visible to me as I began a research project on domestic workers in Vancouver (G. Pratt, 1997; G. Pratt in collaboration with the Philippine Women Centre, 1997). Thousands of women come to Canada annually through the Live-in Caregiver Program, roughly 60 per cent from the Philippines. In the following quotation, taken from a transcribed focus group with Filipina domestic workers, Mhay describes her efforts to make herself visible within the micro-geography of her (and her employers') home:

I bought a picture with a frame and put it up on the wall [of my bedroom]. Prior to this, all four walls were bare. I did this without telling them because I thought that since I paid for this room, I should be allowed to do something about it. So I arranged the room, put furniture and TV [the way I wanted them]. I would leave the door open so that they [my employers] could see what's in my room, that it's not dull anymore.

3 Filipina domestic workers nevertheless negotiate visibility and invisibility. Mhay, for example, states that: 'Sometimes my employer will open up to me about her family as I am open to them about my family in the Philippines. But when it comes to boyfriends and other private matters, I don't share this with them.' Some domestic workers expressed resentment towards their employers' interest in their family circumstances in the Philippines, partially because they suspected that disclosure was unlikely to work to their advantage. They were certain, as well, that Vancouver employers' interest in their lives as domestic workers in Singapore and Hong Kong was self-concerned, and hinged on their desire to import the labour conditions that the domestic workers experienced there (longer hours and the requirement to work at a wider range of tasks, such as washing the employer's car) into the Canadian context.

These three fragments illustrate many themes that emerge in contemporary theorizing about identities and geographies. The narratives that we construct about geography and identity are situated (Haraway, 1991); as a white middle-class academic I simply did not see the geographies of Filipina identity at one point in time. The first fragment none the less illustrates the multiplicity of identities inhabited by middle-class suburban women, and the way that they renegotiate geography as one way of smoothing the tensions and contradictions between their identities as mothers and as employees. The case of Filipina domestic workers introduces current preoccupations with transnational migration, and the ways that 'differences are constituted at the multiple hinges of the local and the global' (Barnes and Gregory, 1997: 443). It disrupts a simple conjunction of identity and place, and makes obvious the point that multiple identities can inhabit a space (in this case, the space of a single Canadian home: see Gupta and Ferguson (1992) for a cogent critique of assumptions of isomorphism between identity and place). The selective negotiation of visibility and invisibility on the part of Filipina domestic workers also suggests the constructed nature of identity; rather than an essential identity, we see the partial disclosure of identifications (for example, identity as daughter to family in the Philippines but not a heterosexual identity). Stuart Hall has likened this process of identification to the practice of taking a bus: 'you just have to get from here to there, the whole of you can never be represented in the ticket you carry but you have to buy a ticket in order to get from here to there' (quoted in Watts, 1997: 494). Drawing out this metaphor, Watts writes: 'Accounting for the processes by which we acquire our bus ticket(s) – not least in a world in which the routes are many and global – is a worthy and rather important project ... [M]apping the spectrum of cultural forms onto spatial, class and social identities in the context of global interconnectedness might constitute an important frontier for geographic inspection' (1997: 494, 493).

Over-valuing mobility and hybridity

This 'frontier' has now attracted a good deal of attention, and bold attempts have been made to chart its topography. Attempting to conceptualize these new cultural geographies, 'as configurations of people, place, and heritage lose all semblance of isomorphism', Appadurai (1996: 46) proposes that 'we begin to think of the configuration of cultural forms in today's world as fundamentally fractal, that is, as possessing no Euclidean boundaries, structures, or regularities.' But why, we may ask, search for one correct geometry to articulate contemporary configurations of identity, difference and geography? What nomothetic desire underlies such an effort? This tendency towards simplification through generalization has been noted by Grewal and Kaplan: 'We mean to address precisely this construction of inert, ahistorical generalisations. The relationship between "transnational," "postcolonial," "center–periphery," and "diaspora" in contemporary usage can be found in the way modernity masks particularities in favor of the appearance of universal categories' (1994: 16).

Efforts to resist the normalization of one correct geometry of identity and place certainly exist; they have emerged especially around what seems to be an over-valuing of mobility and hybridity. Stuart Hall's metaphor of identity as a bus ticket nicely illustrates the way in which mobility has come to define identity. Mobility articulates a non-essentialist identity that emerges out of identifications rather than an essence. One is not born a woman, for example, but one can come to identify as one, and these identifications (of gender, sexuality, class, race, nation, etc.) can shift in time and place. The geographical literature is now rich in empirical examples of historical geographies of identification (Blunt and Rose, 1994; G. Pratt and Hanson, 1994; Rose, 1993). But relatively early on, it was also seen that metaphors of mobility and travel have to be held in tension with the recognition that identities do become stabilized. There were suspicions that the unambiguous pleasures of mobility and travel were more easily viewed from masculine rather than feminine subject positions (Wolff, 1993; Morris, 1988, 1996), from middle-class rather than working-class perspectives (Kaplan, 1987; Lavie and Swedenburg, 1996), and as a white as opposed to African American (hooks, 1992). These correctives reminded us that non-essential identities are nevertheless boundary projects; identities are constructed through identifying who one is not. Identities emerge from historical geographies of conflict and difference, and these geographies themselves work to stabilize identities. In short, some identities are more mobile than others, but all involve exclusion.

The concept of hybridity has a similar history. The term 'hybridity' has been attractive to cultural theorists because it articulates a non-essentialist view of cultures, one in which cultures are continually produced in relation to others. As a theory of culture, it suggests radical heterogeneity that disrupts notions of purity and stasis: 'wherever it emerges it suggests the impossibility of essentialism' (R. Young, 1995: 27). As Katharyne Mitchell (1997a: 535) notes: 'The identification of peoples who have multiple loyalties, move between regions, do not occupy a singular cultural space, and who often operate in some sense exterior to state boundaries and cultural effects, has proven attractive for theorists who have sought to disrupt normative narratives and understandings of nation and culture.'

There has been a productive layering of notions of hybridity onto our understanding of geographies. Massey (1992) has argued that local places have long been open to global influences. This has the effect of destabilizing claims to the purity of local cultures and places, claims that can be used in attempts to preserve a place and 'people' from 'outside' influences, such as immigration. By tracing the influence of British colonialism in nineteenth-century London, Driver and Gilbert (1998) unsettle the 'purity' of English culture. Colonialism is not something that happened elsewhere; British colonialism shaped the architecture, street names and gardens of London, and not simply those of the towns and cities of 'the colonies'. The especial 'leakiness' of contemporary 'habitats' (Chambers, 1994: 245) is nicely distilled by Clifford (1988: 14) when he states: 'Difference is encountered in the adjoining neighborhoods; the familiar turns up at the ends of the earth', and is a theme that is explored by Jacobs (1996) and Appadurai (1996), among others (for a review of recent scholarship, see Lavie and Swedenburg, 1996). There is also considerable interest in 'thirdspace', as an in-between space that unfixes cultural solidarity and boundaries across difference. Within geography, Rose (1993) and Soja (1996) explore the emancipatory potential of such a space, as a way of dis-ordering binaries: thirdspace is 'a product of a "thirding" of the spatial imagination, the creation of another mode of thinking about space that draws upon material and mental spaces of the traditional dualism but extends well beyond them in scope, substance and meaning' (Soja, 1996: 11).

Critics have been wary, however, of over-generalizing a particular experience and politics of hybridity, of positing hybridity as naturally good (Grewal and Kaplan, 1994; Mitchell, 1997a, 1997b). Rey Chow (Discipline and Place Collective, 1997: 530) argues that the critical potential of the concept of hybridity depends on the context in which it is deployed. She judges it to be of use in 'dealing with a very centrist regime, like the People's Republic of China, where you still have a notion that culture is one thing and where you have a very clear bound-ary between "us" and "them". There is where you can use hybridity with good political results.' But then:

> I wouldn't say that in the context of the US, hybridity is totally not useful. I would not say that because the US also has many, many pockets of monoculturalism, monolingualism and so forth, where hybridity can be a useful kind of intervention. For me it's very much a matter of when some-thing like hybridity can be a useful tactic.

Mitchell also draws our attention to the complexities and contradic-tions of specific contexts. She attributes tendencies towards homogeniz-ing, simplifying narratives (of both hybridity and globalization) to 'a frequent disregard for grounded empirical work' (1997b: 109). Morris has argued that relating 'concepts to circumstances' is one way of main-taining an open system of thinking. It offers a way of dislodging moral-istic stances towards distinctions, both the act of making them and the categories that emerge through them, by forcing us to pay closer atten-tion to how categories operate in specific spatial and historical contexts: 'good and bad are in the middle of things, in the processes and conflicts of social life' (Morris, 1996: 393).

Along with a continual movement between concepts and circum-stances, we need to remind ourselves of the inherent contradictions and boundary projects that lie within all of our concepts. Robert Young traces the genealogy of the term hybrid to suggest that if it is held against a notion of a dominant, pure culture it will repeat its nineteenth-century origins in theories of cultural/racial degeneration (that is, it will have the effect of reinscribing boundaries). But the rele-vant point would seem to be that boundaries and conflict are inherent in any identification and that it is politically unproductive to search for 'good' or 'bad' identities.

This is precisely the point of recent theorizing of radical democracy: identities are always defined through difference, through the construction of a 'constitutive outside' (Mouffe, 1992). A 'we' is inevitably defined through the identification of a 'them'. The democratic imaginary is tied, then, not to founding a 'good' identity of citizen, but to maintaining an arena of conflict by keeping the process of boundary construction alive and open to contestation (Deutsche, 1996; Mouffe, 1995). By extension, we can see our role as critics, not as one of valorizing one resting place of identity over another (whether it be static or framed in terms of mobility and hybridity), but as one of keeping the process of boundary construction in view, as well as tracing the interdependencies of what lies on either side of the boundary. Romanticizing mobility and hybridity could make us rather complacent in carrying out this task.

My argument, then, is that a focus on border maintenance is as politically productive as attending to movement across boundaries and difference; the two complement each other, though one may be more strategic than the other in particular contexts. I would like to particularize this call for contextualized theorizing and the necessity of tracing boundaries through two geographical narratives: one around the home, another involving boundary construction in transnational spaces. I ground both in the circumstances of Filipina domestic workers in Vancouver, as well as examples from the literature.

Feminist geographies of home

Feminist debates about the home can be used to exemplify the strategic nature of theory construction, the limits of over-valuing mobility, and the contextuality of meaning. Materialist feminists have long been critical of the home as a site of oppression for women: they reframed the home as a place of battery and exploitative labour relations (Barrett and McIntosh, 1982). This has been an important and strategic means for disrupting the public/private divide, and opening to critical scrutiny power relations in the home. In the 1980s, this criticism of the home merged with a scepticism about the 'home' of feminism, as a movement that concealed difference and inequalities among women (for reviews of this literature, see I.M. Young, 1997). Young cites the interlinked essays of Martin and Mohanty (1986), Minnie Bruce Pratt (1984), de Lauretis (1990) and Honig (1994) as seminal; they all 'express a deep distrust of the idea of home for feminist politics and conclude that we should give up a longing for home' (1997: 156). Just as materialist feminists revealed the portrayal of the home as a peaceful refuge as a masculinist one, 'women of colour', working-class women and lesbian women, among others, criticized the home of feminism as a fantasy of white, middle-class, heterosexual feminists, one that veiled power relations among women.

There has been an interesting exchange between these two critiques of the home, as criticism of a feminism that concealed differences between women works its way into actual residential choices. This occurs, for example, in the concluding sections of Minnie Bruce Pratt's (1984) narrative of travel and self-discovery. At the end of the narrative, Pratt is living as a solitary, white, lesbian woman in an African American neighbourhood in Washington DC, choosing this residential location, in part, as a vehicle for continuously destabilizing her sense of identity. Stanley and Wise (1990: 33) take up Pratt's residential choice as a feminist model: 'Pratt is located in an immediate social context in which the origin and oppressed "other" becomes in a sense the norm . . . her account is a suggestive one.' Blending the two critiques of home, Massey (1994: 11) has ventured that: 'One gender-disturbing message might be – in terms of both identity and space – keep moving!'

There have, none the less, been two productive reactions to a purely negative rendering of home. First, the simple point has been made that it is easier to criticize home from the position of having a secure one. The meaning and value of home depends on circumstances. To return to the introductory fragments, Mhay's efforts at home-making must be set against the fact that, as a domestic worker admitted into Canada by means of a special work visa, she has a fragile claim to home. The paradoxical situation of mobility and confinement experienced by Mhay is captured by Tolentino's (1996: 58) characterization of the geography inhabited by Filipina overseas contract workers: 'It is precisely in these domestic spheres that Filipinas are allocated to transnational space.' Many Canadian employers are negligent about providing the barest minimum of control over this domestic space. For example a lock on the domestic worker's bedroom door, required by the Canadian State, is often missing (G. Pratt in collaboration with the Philippine Women Centre, 1997). It is within this context that Mhay's invitation to look into her room must be understood. Her resistant efforts to stake this place as her home can be read against her sense of vulnerability and stigmatization in other spaces of the home. She recounts her attempts to control the boundaries (visual and olfactory) of her identity in the shared spaces of her (employers') home:

Once, I really wanted to cook my own food, which they do not eat. I
opened the windows so they could not smell it in the house. Then I ate in
the living room so that I could see them coming. Once I saw them, I
would go the kitchen and fix everything so that they would not find out
that I cooked my own dinner or food. It's quite tough. (Laughs.)

I am moved by this passage because it conveys Mhay's feeling that she
must control not only her bodily and visual presence, but the scent of
food that is her 'own'; her culture/home has no place within this house.

It is perhaps not surprising that two of the strongest evocations of
home in recent feminist writing come from personal knowledge of the
difficulties, as well as the potentials, of home-making. bell hooks writes
about the importance of home for African Americans as a space at least
partially apart from the oppressive structures of white, racist society, as
a space in which positive identifications and powerful political resistance can be nurtured and sustained. 'Historically,' she writes, 'African
American people believed ˙ that the construction of a homeplace,
however fragile and tenuous (the slave hut, the wooden shack), had a
radical political dimension. Despite the brutal reality of racial
apartheid, of domination, one's homeplace was the one site where one
could freely confront the issue of humanization, where one could resist'
(1990: 42). In her evocation of the meaning of home for African Americans, hooks has chosen, perhaps strategically, to foreground race and
sideline gender relations within the home.

Iris Marion Young tells of her nonconformist mother's efforts to
maintain a home. As a recently bereaved widow, newly arrived in a
New Jersey suburban development, who drank too much and failed to
keep a clean house, her children were removed by the state on two
occasions. 'Neglect. The primary evidence of neglect was drinking and a
messy house. We ate well enough, had clean enough clothes, and a
mother's steady love' (1997: 146). When reunited after the second
arrest and separation, 'my mother wasted no time packing up and
moving us all back to the safe indifference of New York City' (1997:
147). Against this experience of both the oppressive conformity
required of women by middle-class ideals of home, and her own
family's, at times desperate, efforts to maintain one, Young outlines
four normative values of home that she believes should be accessible to
all people: rights to safety, individuation, privacy, and the preservation
of individual and collective memories through 'rituals of remembrance'
embodied in the home. Young recognizes the 'depoliticising, essentialist,
and exploitative implications that the idea of home often carries' but is
attempting to balance this against the recognition that 'home carries a

core positive meaning as the material anchor for a sense of agency and a shifting and fluid identity' (1997: 159).

Young recognizes that the home can materially anchor a shifting and fluid identity. This points to a second feminist reaction to purely negative representations of the home: we need to consider how binaries run through these representations in ways that flatten and homogenize the meaning of home. There is a growing literature that explores the interdependence between home and 'away' so as to destabilize the meaning of each term (Blunt, 1997; Taylor, 1992). Morris also subverts the equation between nomadism and adventure, and home and stasis, by retelling the stories of Ulysses and Penelope: 'When Ulysses fails to return home after the fall of Troy, Penelope is pestered by suitors. She promises to choose one as soon as she has finished weaving a shroud for her father-in-law: but at night, she unravels what she has accomplished during the day and indefinitely defers the ending of her labours. Ulysses travels from place to place, but Penelope, "model of all the domestic virtues" . . . , is the quick one' (1996: 388). Morris reinterprets home as a moment in a three-point process, both as a way of drawing a boundary around an uncertain identity, and as a place from which to venture: 'home is in the middle of things, like "place" in the work of Doreen Massey (1994); neither origin nor destination, "home" is an effort to organize a "limited space" that is never sealed in, and so it is not an enclosure but a way of going outside' (1996: 386). Massey notes that this unbounded conception of home is, in any case, a more accurate representation: 'a large component of the identity of that place called home derived precisely from the fact that it had always in one way or another been open; constructed out of movement, communication, social relations that always stretched beyond it' (1992: 14). But along with emphasizing the movement inherent in dwelling, we need also examine the process of boundary construction, the efforts to 'organize' this 'limited space'.

The importance of this rearticulation of home as a place is that it suggests that the possibilities and politics of home are also open ones. Moralizing about home in the abstract is likely to be unproductive: 'good and bad are in the middle of things', and the politics of home is a situated one. Mhay's efforts to construct a home as a Filipina living in a white Canadian home on a temporary work visa, Minnie Bruce Pratt's residential choice as a privileged white woman, Iris Young's mother's decision to flee suburbia for the indifference of the city: these are actions that can only be assessed in relation to the identities and geographies in question. This is simply to restate that assessments about identities and places cannot be made in the abstract, and that suspicion about essentialized identities does not flow unproblematically into assessments of place. As feminist debates about the home have developed, we have come to recognize that it is unhelpful to designate homes in general as 'good' or 'bad'.

Considering the trajectory of feminist theorizing about 'home' also gives us ground for thinking about the movement between spatial metaphors and material practices. One of the attractions of spatial metaphors has been the ability to move across genres; Kathleen Kirby (1996: 9) speaks of the capacity for spatial language to mediate a divide between materiality and metaphor: 'the theoretical turn to space stems from the delicate reference that category [space] promises with concrete reality'. As noted above, Soja portrays thirdspace as existing beyond a dualism between metaphor and materiality. But as we attempt to sort out the complex linkages between proliferating identities and new geographies, it may be problematic to let arguments that develop in relation to identities as 'homes' seep uncritically into our understandings of other homes (as places). The seepage has undoubtedly been creative and suggestive; we must also consider whether critical distinctions have been lost. Home as an identity really is somewhat different from home as a place, though the two are interconnected. It has, without a doubt, been productive to elide this distinction temporarily and consider how theories of identities can be brought into our readings of geographies. But we should also consider that we may be simultaneously simplifying our narratives as we seek to enrich them.

Border crossings/boundary constructions

In a second attempt to relate concepts to circumstances, I want to consider the multiplicity of boundaries and naturalized identities that are constructed as Filipina women cross national borders to come to Canada as live-in caregivers. I pursue this to make the simple points that the effects of mobility and hybridity are multiple (and by no means necessarily beneficial), that new boundaries are constructed even as borders are crossed, and that these boundaries are multiple and complex. We need to map out these boundaries with care in order to think through political strategy in relation to the Candian government's policy towards and regulation of domestic workers.

The domestic workers with whom I have worked have told numerous stories about the reinscription of essentialized identities and boundaries within transnational geographies. They told the most explicit stories of stereotyping and stigmatization in relation to other Filipinos in Vancouver. Mhay, for example, tells of some boundary maintenance that took place in an ideally inclusive public space: a city park:

> I encountered someone once. My driving lessons were over, and we were in the park to eat, because we were hungry. There were many Filipinos in the park, and near the car were some Filipino men and women talking. My companion asked me: 'Why are they smiling at you? Do you know them?' I said 'No, and I didn't know why they were smiling.' They must have heard me, so they said something ... bad. They said, 'Oh, those are nannies. And they're trying to look like something else.' They were criticising some other women, and perhaps they were including me. So I said, 'Oh, I don't know' but I was feeling uncomfortable. So we left. It was okay with me, because I really am a nanny, but it was my companion who was hurt. (Laughs.) So I asked my friend why he was going into this dark mood, when it was me who was a nanny, not him! [He said,] 'No, it's because those people look down on nannies. Where are their roots, anyway?' I said, 'Well, from nannies.' I was also curious [about his reactions] so I said, 'And what about you? If your girlfriend was a nanny, what will you tell your parents about her? Will you say she's a nanny?' 'Well, yes' he said. 'What if your family looks down on her?' 'Well, many people here are like that. If they do that, then they're denying where they came from.' It turns out that his family was able to come here because his sister was a nanny. So it was funny that he was reacting like that. But it's really hurting here, that people look down on nannies.

This is an instance of boundary maintenance at the line between immigrant and domestic worker, two distinct points of entry into Canada. The line also marks class and gender differences: entry into Canada as an independent immigrant is possible through either the point system (in which technical, typically masculinized occupations tend to be more favourably weighted) or the business class of programmes (which require substantial capital). A woman who initiates immigration for herself and her family is more likely to enter via the Live-in Caregiver Program, a temporary work programme that allows the possibility of applying for landed immigrant status after two years of working as a live-in domestic worker.

The line between immigrant and live-in caregiver works away at what Rafael (1997) has identified as an identity crisis for Filipinos, one that he ties to massive state-encouraged movements of Filipino workers and immigrants over the last twenty-five years. The middle-class press in the Philippines features anecdotes about:

Europeans equating the word 'Filipino' with domestic helpers, or Filipino tourists being asked by OCWs [Overseas Contract Workers] in Singapore shopping malls or Madrid parks if they, too, were on their day off. In these stories, Filipino elites as well as nationalists feel themselves incapable of maintaining the boundaries of class differences as they are associated with an ethnically marked group of service workers. Embarrassment arises from their inability to keep social lines from blurring (thereby rendering problematic their position as privileged representatives of the nation) and maintaining a distinction between 'Filipino' as the name of a sovereign people and 'Filipino' as the generic term for designating a subservient class dependent on foreign economies. (Rafael, 1997: 276–7)

But just as the massive international movement of workers and immigrants has altered the meaning of Filipino in uncontrollable ways, Rafael argues that the pity felt for overseas contract workers has, in recent years, generated a sense of national community. In a 1988 speech to a group of domestic workers in Hong Kong, President Cory Aquino first referred to OCWs as heroes: 'You are the new heroes' (Rafael, 1997: 274). The execution of the domestic worker Flor Contemplacion in Singapore in 1995 then ignited a further surge of nationalist identification. President Ramos saw in Flor Contemplacion's death the beginning 'of our own soul searching ... We have been reborn as a national family' (quoted in Rafael, 1997: 279). In Rafael's view, the politicization of the situation of OCWs foundered on the commercialization of the Flor Contemplacion 'story', but the fact remains that the identity of Filipina domestic workers is interwoven with other identities and geographies in complex ways: though it confuses key class boundaries in ways that embarrass elites, it is simultaneously taken up by key political elites to reconstruct national boundaries.

As Vancouver Filipino immigrants strive to reinstate the class boundary between themselves and domestic workers, they supplement other boundary projects that produce Filipinas as inferior to European nannies in a hierarchy of live-in caregivers. This hierarchy is produced through a complex set of processes, but the globalization of information is by no means irrelevant. Two domestic workers discuss how their employment conditions in Singapore are brought to Vancouver by agents and Vancouver employers:

ANA: These employers here in Canada, they just ask you about
            your previous employer because maybe they will learn the
            fact of what you are doing in Singapore. Like, oh, [you were]
            washing the car, then they will think that they can ask you to
            do this here.
ENDROLYN: They are asking me. [They think:] Oh, I like this girl. She
            washes the car. But they [her employers] wash the car. I said

she should do that. It is not my job. That's why I came here
to Canada: to work less. That's why I spend my money (more
than two thousand dollars) to come here to Canada. Because
I want to escape my job in Singapore.

ANA: They are thinking, maybe, just like, 'Oh, maybe she will do it
here, because she did it in Singapore. Why can she not do it
here?'[1]

Personal and collective histories, as with domestic workers in Hong
Kong and Singapore, are dragged into the Vancouver labour market by
agents and employers, who expect Filipina domestic workers to work
longer hours and at a wider range of (non-childcare-related) tasks than
would be asked of European women.[2] They solidify a hierarchy of difference among live-in caregivers, in which Filipinas inhabit the identity
of 'housekeeper' and European women are thought of as 'nannies'.

Boundaries that are blurred in one place may be reinvented elsewhere: sensitivities about the blurring of class distinctions may add to
their vigorous re-establishment within the Filipino community in Vancouver. A remarkable mobility as part of a transnational labour process
may have no necessary relation to non-essentialized identities. In the
Philippines, OCWs are taken up in the creation of an essentialized
national identity, sutured around an ethos of familialism, care and suffering: 'the figure of Flor Contemplacion appeared to furnish a benign
basis for reconsolidating the imaginative borders of the Philippines'
(Rafael, 1997: 278). (This parallels an example cited by Mitchell
(1997b) of the creation of a new essentialist discourse of 'Mexican'
identity, built around the transnational movement of people and
capital.) In Vancouver, knowledge of labour experiences elsewhere
helps to define Filipinas as exploitable servants, distinct from European
nannies.

At the same time, one can see the emancipatory potential of travel.
Filipinas are well aware of the different labour standards in Vancouver
and Singapore; their knowledge of this is what has driven a second
round of migration, and they defend this difference against their
employers. Creative acts of translation also emerged in workshops with
domestic workers, as, for example, when Mhay defended herself from
stereotypes within the Filipino community in Vancouver by a subtle act
of translation. Mhay is resisting the stereotype of husband stealer:

I don't get entangled with that issue, because I don't steal husbands.
That's a dangerous situation. I'm not ashamed of myself, and think very
low of myself because I'm a nanny, since I'm not doing anything wrong. I
cook, clean, take care of children. I'm not just a nanny. I'm also a nanay
[Tagalog for mother]. (Laughs.)

Mhay resists one identity by calling up her identity as nanny, but she simultaneously reworks the meaning of that term through a readily available but imaginative translation. In the end, and through a striking play of cultural hybridity, she has metamorphosed herself within the terms of the classical representational dualism of 'Woman', from whore to mother. But the point is that precisely at the moment that boundaries are blurred, they are reconstructed. There is no end of conflict in thirdspace, and new boundaries are created even as we move through space.

Mhay's invitation

By decorating her room, Mhay stakes a territory. When she leaves her door ajar, she is redefining the boundaries between her and her employer: she is both defining her identity (a border) and opening a space for exchange. The opening is situational and strategic: Mhay tells her employer about her family in the Philippines but not about her boyfriends. Mhay's invitation suggests to me the necessity and possibilities of working across borders, of seeing into each other's worlds and working across differences, without erasing histories of conflict and difference, without identification.

I have argued that our commitment should be one of opening doors for communication and that this can be done not only by documenting the hybridity of all cultures (that is, the fragility of borders and the interdependence of differences) and the creative potential for new critical identities to emerge at the border, in thirdspace, but by remembering the exclusions that found every identity. I see our job as one of creating trouble, even in thirdspace, by making visible boundary constructions and the production of difference, and by keeping alive the question of who, inevitably, is being excluded as identities are defined. My current research involves an effort to make visible the boundary that prevented me from seeing domestic workers living in Vancouver in 1992. This involves unsettling the complacency that many Canadians feel about admitting live-in caregivers into Canada without granting citizenship rights or guaranteeing live-in domestic workers the same regulative protection expected by other classes of workers. It seems to me that it is by starkly outlining the boundaries that separate my life from that of Mhay, by unravelling the layers of social-material borders that both produce and hem in our movements and identities, that a basis for communication and collaboration can be established. Marking boundaries, insisting on the materiality and persistence of differences, may be as politically productive as blurring them in notions of mobility, hybridity and thirdspace.

Acknowledgements

I would like to thank Derek Gregory and Tohmm Cobban for their help in focusing my argument, and the editorial team for encouragement and good editorial advice. As ever, I am indebted to Mhay, and others at the Philippine Women Centre, for opening their doors to me.

Notes

1 Employers often come to know about practices in Singapore and Hong Kong because descriptions have been put into domestic workers' profiles by their nanny agent.
2 Agents commonly complained of European nannies' unwillingness to do housework, or to cook for the entire family (as opposed to the children only). For details see G. Pratt (1997).

References

Appadurai, A. (1996) *Modernity at Large: Cultural Dimensions of Globalization*. Minneapolis and London, University of Minnesota Press.
Barnes, T. and D. Gregory (eds) (1997) *Reading Human Geography: The Poetics and Politics of Inquiry*. London and New York, Arnold.
Barrett, M. and M. McIntosh (1982) *The Antisocial Family*. London, Verso.
Blunt, A. (1997) 'Travelling home and empire: British women in India 1857–1939'. Unpublished PhD Dissertation, Department of Geography, University of British Columbia.
Blunt, A. and G. Rose (eds) (1994) *Writing Women and Space: Colonial and Postcolonial Geographies*. New York, Guilford Press.
Chambers, I. (1994) 'Leaky habitats and broken grammar'. In G. Robertson, M. Mash, L. Tickner, J. Bird, B. Curtis and T. Putnam (eds), *Travellers' Tales: Narratives of Home and Displacement*. London and New York, Routledge, 245–9.
Clifford, J. (1988) *The Predicament of Culture*. Cambridge MA and London, Harvard University Press.
de Lauretis, T. (1990) 'Eccentric subjects: feminist theory and historical consciousness'. *Feminist Studies*, 16: 115–50.
Deutsche, R. (1996) *Evictions: Art and Spatial Politics*. Cambridge MA, MIT Press.
Discipline and Place Collective (1997) 'Moving spaces/firm groundings: an interview with Rey Chow'. *Environment and Planning D: Society and Space*, 15: 509–32.
Driver, F. and D. Gilbert (1998) 'Heart of empire? Landscape, space and performance in imperial London'. *Environment and Planning D: Society and Space*, 16/1: 11–28.
Dyck, I. (1989) 'Integrating home and wage workplace: women's daily lives in a Canadian suburb'. *Canadian Geographer*, 33: 329–41.

Grewal, I. and C. Kaplan (1994) 'Introduction: transnational feminist practices and questions of postmodernity'. In *Scattered Hegemonies*. Minneapolis and London, University of Minnesota Press, 1–33.

Gupta, A. and J. Ferguson (1992) 'Beyond "culture": space, identity and the politics of difference'. *Cultural Anthropology*, 7/1: 6–23.

Haraway, D. (1991) *Simians, Cyborgs, and Women: The Reinvention of Nature*. New York and London, Routledge.

Honig, B. (1994) 'Difference, dilemmas, and the politics of home'. *Social Research*, 61/3: 563–97.

hooks, b. (1990) *Yearning: Race, Gender, and Cultural Politics*. Toronto, Between the Lines.

hooks, b. (1992) 'Representing whiteness in the black imagination'. In L. Grossberg, C. Nelson and P. Treichler (eds), *Cultural Studies*. New York and London, Routledge, 338–46.

Jacobs, J.M. (1996) *Edge of Empire: Postcolonialism and the City*. London and New York, Routledge.

Kaplan, C. (1987) 'Deterritorializations: the rewriting of home and exile in Western feminist discourse'. *Cultural Critique*, 6: 187–98.

Kirby, K. (1996) *Indifferent Boundaries: Spatial Concepts of Human Subjectivity*. New York, Guilford Press.

Lavie, S. and T. Swedenburg (eds) (1996) *Displacement, Diaspora, and Geographies of Identity*. Durham NC and London, Duke University Press.

Ley, D., D. Hiebert and G. Pratt (1992) 'Time to grow up? From urban village to world city, 1966–1991'. In G. Wynn and T. Oke (eds), *Vancouver and its Region*. Vancouver, University of British Columbia Press, 234–66.

Martin, B. and C.T. Mohanty (1986) 'Feminist politics: what's home got to do with it?'. In Teresa de Lauretis (ed.), *Feminist Studies/Cultural Studies*. Bloomington, Indiana University Press, 191–212.

Massey, D. (1992) 'A place called home?'. *New Formations*, 3: 3–15.

Massey. D. (1994) *Space, Place and Gender*. Cambridge, Polity Press.

Mitchell, K. (1997a) 'Different diasporas and the hype of hybridity'. *Environment and Planning D: Society and Space*, 15: 533–53.

Mitchell, K. (1997b) 'Transnational discourse: bringing geography back in'. *Antipode*, 29/2: 101–14.

Morris, M. (1988) 'A Henry Parkes motel'. *Cultural Studies*, 2/1: 1–47.

Morris, M. (1996) 'Crazy talk is not enough'. *Environment and Planning D: Society and Space*, 14: 384–94.

Mouffe, C. (1992) 'Feminism, citizenship, and radical democratic politics'. In Judith Butler and Joan Scott (eds), *Feminists Theorize the Political*. New York and London, Routledge, 369–84.

Mouffe, C. (1995) 'Post-Marxism: democracy and identity'. *Environment and Planning D: Society and Space*, 13: 259–65.

Pratt, G. (1997) 'Stereotypes and ambivalence: nanny agent's stereotypes of domestic workers in Vancouver, B.C.'. *Gender, Place and Culture*, 4/2: 159–77.

Pratt, G. and S. Hanson (1994) 'Geography and the construction of difference'. *Gender, Place and Culture*, 1: 5–29.

Pratt, G. in collaboration with the Philippine Women Centre (1997) 'Is this really Canada? Domestic workers' experiences in Vancouver, B.C.'. Occasional Paper of the Centre for Women's Studies and Gender Relations at the University of British Columbia.

Pratt, M.B. (1984) 'Identity: skin blood heart'. In E. Burkin, M.B. Pratt and B. Smith (eds), *Yours in Struggle: Three Feminist Perspectives on Anti-semitism and Racism*. New York, Long Haul Press, 10–63.

Rafael, V. (1997) ' "Your grief is our gossip": overseas Filipinos and other spectral presences'. *Public Culture*, 9: 267–91.

Rose, G. (1993) *Feminism and Geography: The Limits of Geographical Knowledge*. Minneapolis, University of Minnesota Press.

Soja, E. (1996) *Thirdspace: Journeys to Los Angeles and Other Real-and-Imagined Places*. Oxford and Cambridge, MA, Blackwell.

Stanley, L. and S. Wise (1990) 'Method, methodology and epistemology in feminist research'. In L. Stanley (ed.), *Feminist Praxis: Research Theory, and Epistemology in Feminist Sociology*. London, Routledge, 20–60.

Taylor, J.B. (1992) 'Re: locations – from Bradford to Brighton'. *New Formations*, 17: 86–94.

Tolentino, R. (1996) 'Bodies, letters, catalogs: Filipinas in transnational space'. *Social Text*, 14: 49–76.

Watts, M. (1997) 'Mapping meaning, denoting difference, imagining identity: dialectical images and postmodern geographies'. In T. Barnes and D. Gregory (eds), *Reading Human Geography: The Poetics and Politics of Inquiry*. London and New York, Arnold, 489–502.

Wolff, J. (1993) 'On the road again: metaphors of travel in cultural criticism'. *Cultural Studies*, 7: 224–39.

Young, I.M. (1997) *Intersecting Voices: Dilemmas of Gender, Political Philosophy and Policy*. Princeton, Princeton University Press.

Young, R. (1995) *Colonial Desire: Hybridity in Theory, Culture and Race*. New York, Routledge.

Part IV
Spatialities of Power

Introduction

Over the past few years there seems to have been a resurgence of interest in power and power relations; only this time rethinking power has put spatiality at the centre of the task. Orthodox approaches to the workings of power are being asked: 'How might thinking spatially both disrupt and add to our understanding of how power works?' In many ways the chapters in this part address this question directly. Each chapter is focused on the issues that arise when power is spatialized, hence the title of this part. The point here is that what is being addressed is not simply the increasing use by geographers and others of a spatial vocabulary of power, but instead a wish to interrogate the ways in which space affects the operation and realization of power. To say that a form of power rests in a particular institution, for example, says little about how space – the space of nations, of borders, for instance – makes a difference to and interrupts the operation of that institution's power and influence. Equally it is less and less helpful to think about power as resting in particular territories and being held unproblematically by nation states. The fragmentation of space, developments in communications technology and so on, all make feasible sub-national access to supposedly empowering global flows.

How we think about power too is unsettled once space is foregrounded. This is particularly relevant in a world where the outcomes of power can be seen far more clearly than the workings of power. In today's space of flows, for example, private finance and international institutions such as the International Monetary Fund are said to have a certain sort of economic power, one that clearly has a spatial reach. But as to how that power actually works across space to have particular, presumably desired effects, one can be less sure. For while it is reasonable to say that such power works across space, it is less easy to say how a certain power is transferred and reconstituted in a distant space to achieve those desired results. In part that is what lies at the heart of spatializing power. It is about unpacking the operation of power – how it works through key practices and discourses, arranging space and time in ways that help constitute particular effects.

There is an accompanying danger here, however, in the way in which we address the question of power and its workings. This is the risk of slipping into an idea of power which is about domination on the one hand and resistance on the other. Here power is a 'thing' wielded over the less powerful. Power is either held or it is not. Space is present in this conception of power, but it is in the background. For sure, such an approach would acknowledge that the exercise of power in order to dominate is always spatial, but a truly spatialized power pushes for more than this. Spatializing power through a geographical imagination, as we have begun to suggest, reveals that such power is not always the same across space-time, and its exercise is not a continual process. Power in the singular breaks into various modalities of power, as one of the authors in this part argues. What this suggests is that power should not be viewed as separate from what it can do but as emerging out of what is done. Indeed, as another author writes, the assembling of power is part and parcel of social reproduction; it is a spatially active, discursive and representational process.

The attempt to orchestrate distant spaces and times involves ongoing discursive and representational practices, the defining of others and their spaces, to give regularity and legitimation to a particular power. Whether this is successful or not depends largely upon limiting alternative discourses and representations across a range of spatial scales from the body through to the region and beyond.

Spatializing power in this way and seeing other forms of power as potentially emergent serves two further purposes, both of which are pursued here. First, it offers a reminder that 'power' is not always bad; it is not always and everywhere a power *over* people. As power comes from doing, different discourses, different arrangements and representations may emerge tangentially from supposedly dominant powers. Second, whilst power may be viewed as the ability of certain groups to define others, by spatializing power, by becoming aware of its various modalities and its workings, it becomes clearer how these same others can challenge collaboratively in just as powerful ways. The gaps in the exercise of 'dominant power' thus provide the space for thinking imaginatively and geographically about an emancipatory politics.

9

The New Geopolitics of Power

John Agnew

Introduction

The purpose of this chapter is, first, to examine how and why political power has been closely associated with territorial states and, second, to show how the spatiality or geographical organization of power is not necessarily tied for all time and all places to the territoriality of states. The 'state-centred' account of spatiality, what I have termed the 'territorial trap' (Agnew, 1994), is the historical projection of a world in which political power is envisioned as 'pooled up' in equivalent units of territorial sovereignty (at least for the so-called Great Powers). Most explicit in the case of international relations theory, but common throughout the contemporary social sciences, the conventional understanding of the geopolitics of power is underpinned by three geographical assumptions: (1) that states have an exclusive power within their territories as represented by the concept of sovereignty; (2) that 'domestic' and 'foreign' affairs are essentially separate realms in which different rules obtain; and (3) that the boundaries of the state define the boundaries of society so that the latter is 'contained' by the former. These assumptions reinforce one another to produce a state-centred view of power in which the space occupied by states is seen as fixed, as if for all time. Thinking about the spatiality of power is thus put beyond history by assuming an essential state-territoriality to the workings of power.

This perspective did work reasonably well for the state-centred world that began to develop in the late nineteenth century. It made sense in the context of that time to see trajectories of economic and social change as increasingly characterized in terms of the experiences of the bits of space delimited by the geographical boundaries of states. Both businesses and trade unions, representative politics and social life were increasingly organized on a state-by-state basis. But there was also a normative element to thinking about power largely in terms of states. As a reflection of the burgeoning nationalism in Europe (and elsewhere) in the late nineteenth century, politics was seen as *best* thought of in terms of national states. Ideas of distinctive 'national characters' and their reflection in military, sporting, technological, artistic and educational prowess came to prominence. At the same time, the new social sciences (economics, sociology, political science) used the territories of modern statehood to serve as a fixed and reliable template for their investigations into a wide range of phenomena. The 'modern' (European) world was seen as one in which local communities were in eclipse to the rising sun of nation-state-based 'societies'. *Gesellschaft* (society) was replacing *Gemeinschaft* (community) as the dominant cultural-geographical ordering principle. In this way a largely implicit 'methodological nationalism' came to prevail in political and social thought. Currents of thought allowing for explicitly localized or international-ized understandings of the geographical scales at which social, economic and political processes could take place were effectively marginalized (Agnew, 1989).

The territorial state was underpinned, therefore, by the claim that it was the people's 'mentor' in the cult of the nation. At its extreme, for the French revolutionary disciples of Rousseau, the nation state provided the basis for re-establishing a religious foundation to political authority; only now, instead of the person of the emperor-god or divinely appointed monarch, the *educating state* would give citizens a feeling of moral unity and identification with the father (or mother) land (Mosse, 1975). This 'sacralization' of the nation gave the territorial state a competitive advantage over other possible types of spatial-political organization such as confederations, loose empires and city states simply because it was by means of occupying a common territory that state and nation were conjoined.

The drawbacks of a state-centred perspective on power have only recently become obvious. This owes much to perceived changes in the ways in which states relate to one another and to the emergence of a global society in which states must share power with other types of actor. We live in an epoch in which the declining military viability of even the largest states, growing global markets, expanding transnational capitalism, and modes of governance alternative to that of the territorial state (such as the European Union, the various UN agencies, the World Bank and the International Monetary Fund) have begun to undermine the possibility of seeing power as solely a spatial monopoly exercised by states.

The problem is, however, more profound than one of a mere 'goodness of fit' to the changing economic and social conditions of the contemporary world. 'State centredness' is a key manifestation of the 'fixing' of space into timeless blocks (as state territories) that has been the main strategy of modern intellectuals of all political persuasions in limiting 'politics' to the domestic realm of *the* state (a way of thinking that has its roots in the works of Aristotle as well as those of Machiavelli). Representing space as state territoriality also serves to put statehood outside of time, because of the strong tendency to associate space with stasis (see, for instance, Massey, 1993), and thus to impose an intellectual stability on the world that would otherwise be difficult. As a result, state-centred thinking has continuing normative attractions for both intellectuals and political activists even as its empirical reach recedes. It provides a grounded set of social-geographical units for both longitudinal and cross-sectional analyses. It offers a set of concrete institutional opportunities (however weakened or compromised in effective performance) for political action.

The territorial trap

Three analytically distinct but invariably related assumptions underpin the territorial trap: thinking and acting as if the world were made up entirely of states governing blocks of space which between them constitute the politico-geographical form of world politics (Agnew, 1994). The first, and most deeply rooted, is that modern state sovereignty requires clearly bounded territorial spaces. The modern state differs from all other types of organization by its claim to total sovereignty over its territory. Defending the security of its particular spatial sovereignty and the political life associated with it is the primary goal of the territorial state. Vested at one time in the person of the monarch, or other leader within a hierarchy of 'orders' from the lowest peasant to the warriors, priests and nobles, sovereignty is now vested in territory.

The second crucial assumption is that there is a fundamental opposition between 'domestic' and 'foreign' affairs in the modern world. This rests on the view common to Western political theory that states are akin to individual persons struggling for wealth and power in a hostile world. One state's economic and political gains always come at the expense of others. Only inside the boundaries of the state, therefore, are civic culture and political debate possible. Outside, *raison d'état* rules supreme. This fixes processes of political and economic competition at the level of the system of states.

Third, and finally, the territorial state acts as the geographical 'container' of modern society. Social and political organization are defined in terms of this or that state. Thus, we speak and write unselfconsciously of 'American' or 'Italian' society, as if the boundaries of the state are also the boundaries of whatever social or political process we might be interested in. Other geographical scales of thinking or analysis are thereby precluded. Often this is because (as, most obviously, in Durkheimian accounts) the state is seen as the guarantor of social order in modern societies. The state substitutes for the self-reproducing cultural order that can be found in other (pre-modern) societies.

Together these three assumptions underpin a timeless conception of statehood as the font of power in the modern world. The first one dates from the period in European history when sovereignty shifted from the person of the monarch to the state and its citizens. In Europe, this did not happen overnight. It lasted from the fifteenth to the nineteenth centuries. The second two date from the past one hundred years, although the domestic/foreign opposition has roots in the mercantilist economic doctrines of the seventeenth century. Together they serve to put the modern territorial state beyond history in general and the history of specific states in particular. They define a world made up exclusively of territorial actors achieving their goals through control over blocks of space.

Power and territoriality

Power over blocks of space

Three drawbacks to the conventional view have been crucial in limiting understanding of the spatiality of power to the territoriality of states. These made the 'territorial' perspective on power problematic long before recent changes in the workings of the international political economy called it more fully into question. The first has been the widely accepted definition of power as the capacity to coerce others legitimately into doing your will (or power *over*). This leads to a notion of power as a monopoly of control exercised equally over all places within a given territory by a dominant social group ('despotic power') and thus misses both the contingency and the fragility of the 'infrastructural power' (state provision of public goods and services, etc.) upon which state legitimacy largely rests. Michael Mann (1984) has pointed out in

Infrastructural power

		Low	High
	Low	Feudal	Bureaucratic
Despotic power			
	High	Imperial	Authoritarian

Figure 9.1 Two dimensions of state power and the four ideal types of state they define. *Source:* Mann (1984: 188)

some detail the critical role of infrastructural power in distinguishing modern territorial states (both bureaucratic and authoritarian) from both feudal and classic-imperial types of rule (figure 9.1). With the ability to provide centrally and territorially organized services that other organizations cannot, the territorial state is no longer entirely the creature of state elites (and their 'despotic' power). It has an autonomous source of power in its co-ordinating and directing roles. But this relative autonomy depends upon the state delivering a set of services that cannot be provided in some other way. This, of course, opens up to challenge both the regime (current institutions) and the state if the state cannot be depended on to deliver the goods.

A related problem is that this definition completely ignores the degree to which power is inherent in all human agency (for example, Lukes, 1975; Bourdieu, 1977; Giddens, 1979). All social practices involve the application of power; the ability to engage in actions towards the completion of socially sanctioned goals (or power *to*). From this point of view, power is not some thing or potential vested solely in states (or associated political institutions) but the application of agency inherent in all social action to achieve chosen ends. Territorial states are one type of concentration of social power that emerged in specific historical conditions in which state territoriality was practically useful in fulfilling the objectives of both dominant and subordinated social groups. Today, we see the emergence of local/regional governments and supraregional communities in the application of infrastructural power for such ends as economic development and political identity, usually without the coercive power traditionally associated with territorial states (see, for instance, on Italy, Trigilia, 1991; Agnew, 1995). Of course, such alternative spatial configurations of power to that of the modern territorial state of international relations theory are not entirely new. Deudney

(1996: 191) mentions, for example, the Hanseatic League, the Swiss Confederation, the Holy Roman Empire, the Iroquois Confederation, the Concert of Europe and the early United States as potentially familiar examples of alternative systems of power and authority to that of the 'Westphalian' system of territorial states. The actual existence of these kinds of institutional arrangement points to the range of possible ways in which power can be organized spatially. They suggest that forms of power are generated, sustained and reproduced by historically and geographically specific social practices, rather than given for all time in one mode of spatial organization: that of state territoriality. Indeed, there was nothing inevitable about the emergence of the modern system of territorial states. Up until the nineteenth century even their monopoly over coercive power was easily challenged and alternative arrangements for the geographical organization of centralized power were widespread (see Spruyt, 1994).

More radically, the power of states ('sovereign power') can be understood as resting on power 'from below'. In other words, the territorial state draws its power in capillary fashion from social groups and institutions rather than simply imposing itself upon them. From this point of view, power is present in all relationships among people and animals and the power of the state relies on the wide range of sources it can tap into. Foucault terms this a non-sovereign conception of power, in contradistinction from that view which sees power as flowing from a single (sovereign) source, such as the state. In this construction, power is best thought of as equivalent to the energy moving a circulatory system rather than as a mechanical opposition between a source of power, on the one hand, and an obedient (or truculent) subject, on the other. There are multiple points at which consent and resistance come into play in expanding and restricting the interplay between states and subjects and, hence, in defining the state's effective territoriality: how well it dominates its claimed block of space. The spatial monopoly of power exercised by a state is not and cannot be total when its power derives from that given up and potentially retaken by others.

Power as coercion in international relations

A second drawback is that coercive relations between states have usually been seen as the basic way in which power is exercised beyond state territorial boundaries. Even co-operation between states is interpreted as 'getting your way' in disguise. Indeed, the practices of politics, group divisions and struggles over 'the good society' and who gets what, when, how and where within state boundaries have been contrasted with *raison d'état* and *realpolitik* beyond them (Walker, 1993). Democratic theory, for example, has been largely limited to the possibilities of political representation and participation within states and not their prospects among, between or beyond them. At the level of the state system the concept of 'hegemony' is used to indicate the domination exercised by a particular state over others during a specific historical epoch. This definition is indicative of the central position given to despotic or coercive power in international relations, irrespective of the specific 'relation' in question.

Yet the concept of hegemony can be given a different meaning, close to one originally suggested by the Sardinian Marxist Antonio Gramsci, that refers to the power implicit in dominant practices that govern society, both within and beyond state territorial boundaries. In this construction, therefore, international relations involve a variety of social practices that require the deployment of power, not simply military coercion by states. The identities and interests of states (and other actors) are formed in interaction with one another and in the nexus between global and local social practices. Hegemony refers to the nature of the dominant social practices in a given historical epoch and how they bind together the various actors into a global society. The dominant practices may benefit one state disproportionately (such as Britain in the mid-nineteenth century and the United States since World War II), but the costs and benefits (both economic and cultural) can be more diffusely distributed among all of the actors (both state affiliated and otherwise) subscribing to the contemporary 'principles' of international life, irrespective of their geographical location. This is one of the insights emanating from so-called post-colonial studies, drawing attention to the world-wide penetration of dominant practices and understandings (such as those labelled 'nationalism') and their naturalization into the routines of everyday life as 'common sense' and 'facts of life' (see, for example, Krishna, 1994; more generally on nationalism, see Billig, 1995). In a world of social practices rather than reified institutional forms, therefore, not only must states play by 'rules' established by dominant social groups that are active in all of them, but the nature of rule making presupposes that states (and other actors) are not simply coercive agents in a world of anarchy (Cox, 1987; Agnew and Corbridge, 1995).

Two examples serve to illustrate why this argument matters. The first concerns the changing social and technological conditions for the military viability of states and their impact on the possibility of war serving *raison d'état*. The advent of nuclear weapons has meant that security now 'derives from the paralysis of states rather than from the exercise of state power, and from the acceptance of the impossibility of territorial violence monopolization rather than its pursuit' (Deudney, 1995: 219). At the same time, the spread of easy-to-use conventional weapons (Kalashnikov machine guns and Stinger surface-to-air missiles, for example) has made it much easier for local populations to resist the designs of apparently more powerful adversaries. As Deudney (1995: 217) puts it in summarizing the point about contemporary military practices: 'It is nearly impossible to protect territory from annihilation; but it is easier than ever to prevent conquest.'

The second involves the contemporary decentring and deterritorialization (at a state level) of the means of production and communication. This reflects the opening up of the world economy for increased cross-border flows of trade and investment under American auspices during the Cold War. Recent developments in financial markets and information technologies, however, have accelerated changes in the ways people, places and states interact and how economic and political actors perceive these interactions. States (and others) must now *manage* these interactions. Though external coercion is a real possibility for the most powerful states, it is of limited use now state policies must be concerned with attracting 'foreign' capital and gaining access to global flows of information. Contemporary economic practices, therefore, point towards the incipient creation of a transnational liberal hegemony (see the next section) in which territorial states are no longer the basic building blocks; they are being rapidly challenged by new spaces of networks and flows (Rosecrance, 1996; Castells, 1996). Even in contemporary France, often pointed to as a zone of changelessness by those sceptical of claims about an emerging world of flows challenging that of territories, a recent neo-Gaullist government support a new European currency and a withdrawal of that state from many areas of life. It was General de Gaulle who said that France only exists because of the state, the army and the franc. His disciples now stand watch over their dismantling.

Statehood and the protection of property rights

When states are situated in the context of a world of evolving social practices they lose their exclusivity. But one historic role of states is thereby re-emphasized. This is that of the definition and regulation of property rights. The modern territorial state system has been associated from its origins in Europe in the seventeenth and eighteenth centuries with the framework for definitions of property rights (legal rights of ownership and use) without which global capitalism would not have been possible. States are never so 'sovereign', in the conventional sense of singular entities endowed with power monopolies within their territories, as when they are seen as definers and enforcers of property rights.

The third drawback of state-centred accounts of the spatiality of power, therefore, is that they miss the role that states have played in the growth of certain basic social practices of capitalism – defining and protecting private property rights – that have inexorably led beyond state boundaries in pursuit of wealth from the deployment of 'mobile property' (capital: Burch, 1994). The term 'property' implies a fixity or permanence in place that modern territorial states have given a high priority to protecting. Consequently, much of the law in most Western states is devoted to establishing rights of ownership and access. But a home territory also provides a base from which to launch attempts at acquiring property elsewhere. This requires that assets be reasonably liquid and transferable over space and across state boundaries. At a certain point, however, states endure a tension, what Ruggie (1993: 164) calls the problem of 'absolute individuation', which can give rise to an 'unbundling' of territoriality when states effectively exchange control over economic flows emanating from their territories for increased access to flows coming from elsewhere. As a result, when increasing proportions of property are mobile beyond any one state's boundaries, individual states provide only a partial and tenuous protection for absolute property rights. Other geographical levels of governance and regulation become attractive, as was the case with the Bretton Woods system regulating international finance from 1944 to 1972 and is now (if signally more ineffectively so) with the annual G8 summits between the leaders of the Big Seven industrial countries and Russia. But uncertainty as to future political actions and macroeconomic changes (tariffs, interest rates, etc.) also gives an incentive to property-holders to spread assets around further rather than leave them pooled up in one state.

This process is not new. Its origins go back to the merchant capitalism of the sixteenth century. What is new is the increased quantitative scale and the enlarged geographical scope of the mobile property now moving to and fro across the boundaries of the world's trading and investing states. In this context states and firms have changed their orientation from free trade to what has been called 'market access' (Cowhey and Aronson, 1993). The underpinnings of the world trade regime that prevailed in the aftermath of World War II are being replaced by those of a regime in which a premium is placed on the openness of borders. 'Leakiness' in cross-border flows of goods and investment and in firm multinationality has become a torrent of capital, trade and corporate alliances. Cowhey and Aronson (1993: 237) contrast the nature of the old regime with that of the new one by identifying the six 'pillars' that they claim have underpinned each and the policy instruments associated with the new regime (table 9.1). The policy instruments reflect an abandonment of classical state sovereignty in return for guaranteed rights of access to other states' territories. The world has moved away from the strict association of property rights with state territoriality. A range of non-territorial factors now determines the competitiveness of firms in many industries: access to technology, marketing strategies, responsiveness to consumers, flexible management techniques (Julius, 1990: 82). All of these are now the assets of firms, not territories. Firms grow through deploying their internal assets as successfully as possible. States now compete with one another to attract these mobile assets (property) to their territories.

Three features of the market access regime are particularly notable with respect to the changing geopolitics of power. One is the internationalization of a range of domestic policies to conform to global norms of performance. Thus, not only trade policy but also industrial, product liability and social welfare policies are subject to definition and oversight in terms of their impacts on market access between countries. Another is the increased trade in services, once produced and consumed largely within state boundaries. Partly this reflects the fact that many manufactured goods now contain a large share of service inputs – from R&D to marketing and advertising. But it is also because the revolution in telecommunications means that many services, from banking to design to packaging, can now be provided to global markets. This represents a significant material challenge to the domestic/international distinction upon which the 'realism' of strictly territorial accounts of the spatiality of power rely. Finally, the spreading reach of transnational firms and the emergence of international corporate alliances have had profound influences on the nature of trade and investment flows, undermining the identity between territory and economy. Symptomatic of the integration of trade and investment are such frequently heard concerns as rules on international investment and unitary taxation, rules governing local content and place of origin to assess where value was added in the commodity chains of globalized production, and rules involving unfair competition and anti-trust or monopoly trading practices.

Transnational liberalism and the new geopolitics of power

Outlining the three main drawbacks of conventional accounts of the geopolitics of power brings into focus their central deficiency: taking the territoriality of states for granted as a fixed feature of the modern world

Table 9.1 Pillars of the emerging 'market access' world economy

Pillars of the free trade regime	Pillars of the market access regime	Policy instruments
Governance		
1 US model of industrial organization	Hybrid model of industrial organization	More reliance on bilateral and multilateral negotiating forums
2 Separate systems of governance	Internationalization of domestic policies	Transparency, specialized rights of appeal, and self-binding behaviour
3 Goods traded and services produced and consumed domestically	Globalization of services; eroding boundaries between goods and services	National treatment and tiered reciprocity for services
4 Universal rules the norm	Sector-specific codes are common	Reforms of voluntary restraint agreements, anti-dumping and subsidy codes
Rules		
5 Free movement of goods; investment conditional	Investment as integrated coequal with trade	Rules of origin and new investment rules to ensure market access, global anti-trust policies
6 National comparative advantage	Regional and global advantage	Fair trade rules for procurement, standards and R&D

Source: Cowhey and Aronson (1993: 237)

rather than seeing it as the outcome of a number of historical contingencies. The contemporary 'unbundling' of state territoriality provides the most direct evidence for the reshaping of hegemony away from the state-centred practices of the previous epoch (Agnew and Corbridge, 1995: ch. 7). This does not mean to say that territorial states are (finally) 'withering away', only that they must now operate in a global context in which their interactions with one another must take into account a changed military and economic environment. Indeed, in the absence of higher-level units for the enforcement of property rights and the delivery of public goods, states have a continuing and vital role to perform within the evolving world of networks and flows (Castells, 1996). For example, the deregulation of financial markets requires the deliberate action of governmental authorities (Cerny, 1993; Dodd, 1995). It does not simply 'happen'. During the 'Cold War' between 1947 and 1990, the United States, in competing militarily and ideologically with the Soviet Union, sponsored an unprecedented opening of the world economy, partly to spread its political-economic 'message' and partly to take advantage of opportunities for its businesses. The net effect has been that markets have acquired powers heretofore vested in leading states. As this process has intensified and expanded, some localities and regions within states have been privileged within global networks of finance, manufacturing and cultural production to the disadvantage of others. The 'market access regime' ties local areas directly into global markets. Successful ones are those which can enhance their position by increasing their attractiveness to multinational and global firms. A patchwork of places within a global node and network system therefore co-exists with but is slowly eroding the territorial spatiality with which we are all so familiar. Two consequences of this trend are illustrated in the rest of this chapter to give some empirical substance to the claim that a new geopolitics of power based on global networks and flows is in the offing: the explosion of non-territorial state political identities associated with global and local political movements (illustrated, respectively, by new post-national and local literary productions) and the increasingly decentralized world financial system, illustrated by the 'deterritorialization' of currencies.

From Literature to literatures

One of the common assumptions of literary study is that of the historical conjunction between the creation of the novel as a literary form and the origins of the modern territorial state. Literary theorists from Lukács (1971) to Watt (1957) have claimed that the novel 'rises'

(Watt's term) alongside the new state, tying the idea of nation to that of state. Daniel Defoe's *Robinson Crusoe* (published in 1719) is sometimes credited with being the first novel, identifying the self-sufficient Englishman who is the hero of the story with a particular national space. His various traits also define the ideal typical Englishman who is thereafter the subject of English novelistic discourse. The appeal to certain landscape images and historic forms of sociality (consider, for example, the novels of Jane Austen or Anthony Trollope) also served to confuse nation with state, the former involving the identity of a social group, the latter a patterned exercise of power. The conflation (particularly strong in the English-speaking world) effectively underwrote the 'naturalization' of existing and prospective states as the right and proper representatives of the nations into which the world's population was seemingly divided.

The 'rise of the novel' also involved, however, the creation of a new category of literary production: Literature. The new works demanded, in contradistinction from older forms which were often oral in delivery, 'literacy, privatized, silent reading practices, and an elite to determine what constituted it. It depended on market capitalism for printed books, social practices that both permitted and limited literacy according to class and gender, and the invention and adjudication of taste by the individuals who constituted the elite' (Allen, 1995: 99). The study of Literature is still largely compartmentalized for reasons of linguistic specialization and competence into genres identified with specific state territories: Italian Literature, Irish Literature, etc. But two trends signal the extent to which the historic association of the novel with the modern territorial state is undergoing a significant stress. The first is the increased importance on best-seller lists around the world of so-called post-national novels. Examples include Umberto Eco's *The Name of the Rose*, Salman Rushdie's *The Satanic Verses*, Milan Kundera's *The Unbearable Lightness of Being*, Gabriel García Márquez's *One Hundred Years of Solitude* and Margaret Atwood's *Lady Oracle*. These novels are deeply infused with particular national identities or readily associated with specific states but they are not limited to an audience that shares the identity of the main protagonists or has experienced the places to which the novels refer. At publication they appear almost simultaneously in many languages and are distributed on a global scale. Publishing is now one of the most globalized of activities. Place of publication has ceased to have much meaning for the publication of many works of 'fiction'. Some of the post-national novels have been made into films (another globalized industry) which reach an audience around the world that cannot or does not read novels at all.

The appeal these novels and films have is that they usually show that the identities with which they are concerned are deeply problematic. In other words, they call into question the stability of the very identities older novels were intent on both representing and building. They hold before people from elsewhere a mirror to their own identity in the exposure of someone else's national identity. As the literary scholar Beverly Allen (1995: 103) expresses this, using a particularly evocative example:

> Consider the possibility, for example, that a non-print-literate person in Norway or the Philippines or the United States might see the film made from Kundera's novel. Each viewer's distance from the characters' negotiations of their own Czech national identity contains the possibility that the viewer's own national identity might take on a relative value, a sense of arbitrariness, even perhaps a tinge of virtual exchangeability in a world of floating rates of national identity exchange.

The world-wide circulation of the 'identity codes' contained within post-national novels, therefore, involves a shift away from the territorial nation state as the total organizer of identity and towards a transnational space of engagement in which social identities are contingent and partial.

The second trend in literary production is the revival of local literature. In focus and content this literature predates Literature and has existed in the shadow of national genres ever since the territorial nation state took hold in Europe and the Americas. Its very existence has weakened the monopolistic claims of national literary canons, particularly when the local literature is expressed in a dialect or local language distinct from the national one. Cultural identities have always had class, ethnic, gender and other dimensions that often intersected differentially in different places within the boundaries of putative nation states to produce alternatives to or variants of dominant national identities. In the literatures representative of the complex mosaic of such cultural identities, characters are drawn from local rather than national 'types' and a world view is located in the thoughts and behaviour of people living localized lives that are manifestly not 'typical' of national or other 'larger' contexts. Local novels and poetry obviously appeal to audiences who are part of the worlds they portray. But they also, as with post-national novels from 'above', call into question from 'below', as it were, established social identities associated with particular nation states when read by both insiders and outsiders. Allen (1995) uses the examples of contemporary Italian dialect poetry and the Glasgow novels of James Kelman and Alasdair Gray to show how local literature in its positive appraisal of regional, local and municipal identities exposes all identities as constructs rather than 'natural' categories. The very existence of local poetry and novels challenges the monopolistic claims of national genres. When local novels enter into global circulation, as with the recent world-wide success of the Edinburgh novel *Trainspotting*, they feed into the rising tide of literature viewing space, like the lives of that novel's protagonists, as profoundly shaken and fragmented. The flexing of local identities, based on historic claims to distinctiveness, works alongside the circulation of post-national novels, therefore, to call into question the fixity of the territorial spaces on which literary production has long been based.

Money and states

The control and maintenance of a territorially uniform and exclusive currency is often regarded as one of the main attributes of state sovereignty. If a state cannot issue and control its own currency then it is not much of a state. Cohen (1977: 3) offers a concise statement of this view:

> the creation of money is widely acknowledged as one of the fundamental attributes of political sovereignty. Virtually every state issues its own currency; within national frontiers, no currency but the local currency is generally accepted to serve the three traditional functions of money – medium of exchange, unit of account, and store of value.

Currency has a further and vital symbolic role in underwriting statehood. 'As Keynes [the famous economist] understood, the creditworthiness of a nation's money is perhaps the primary evidence to the faithful (the citizens) that the ultimate object of their faith, the nation-state, is real, powerful and legitimate; it is the ultimate "guarantor of value" ' (Brantlinger, 1996: 241). The paper money that began in the late eighteenth century in France, the United States and England to replace currency backed by the promise of immediate conversion into gold or silver coinage is based on the promise of the state to pay the face value of its bills. It is the ultimate 'sign' exchanged for things. Its use depends on trust in the promise of the issuers to redeem its value. As a result, 'The emission and acceptance of paper money brings into being an imagined community, internally dependent on itself' (Barry, 1997: 15), in which political virtue attaches to participation in a territorial sharing of the costs of public credit. Uneasiness over the decoupling of the value of money from that of precious metals gave way to an association between trust and the state that issued the money for your nation, even if, in the final instance, as in the United States, God was the ultimate guarantor. It has been money as much as literacy in a vernacular (or other means of communication) that has bonded state to nation in a process of mutual reinforcement.

Yet since the late 1960s a number of trends challenge the notion that every state must have its own 'territorial currency' (currencies that are homogeneous and exclusive within the boundaries of a given state: Helleiner, 1996: 1). This portends not necessarily a crisis for the state system as such so much as a challenge to that legitimacy of states which rests on claims to represent particular nations and associated national interests by means of control over singular currencies. Territorial currencies developed on a large scale only in the nineteenth century, after the 'Westphalian system' of states was already in place (Helleiner, 1996). Symbolically, however, currencies (including the symbols found on coinage and bank notes) were important elements in establishing central state legitimacy long before then (see, for instance, on late medieval France, Piron, 1996). As emphasized previously, modern statehood was not achieved independently of processes of nation building, even though 'state' and 'nation' can be distinguished analytically, the former referring to a set of institutions ruling over a discrete territory and the latter signifying a group of people who share a sense of common destiny and occupy a common space. The fact that the construction of territorial currencies was largely a nineteenth-century phenomenon, therefore, should not detract from the persisting linkage over many centuries between currency and statehood, however ineffective in practice that linkage often was.

Three monetary developments have begun to delink currencies from states in the way they were once largely mutually defining. The first is the growing use of foreign currencies for a range of transactions within national currency territories. The best-known of these is the growth of the so-called Eurodollar markets in London and other European financial centres (see, for example, Helleiner, 1994: ch. 4). Others include the development of off-shore financial centres such as the Bahamas and the Cayman Islands largely devoted to exchanging and sheltering foreign currencies (Hudson, 1996). This trend is one part of that set of processes leading to global financial integration (at least among the world's richest economies) that O'Brien (1992) has referred to as 'the end of geography' (thus provocatively confusing geography *tout court* with state territory).

The second is the emergence of projects such as that in the European Union to restrict or abolish national currencies in favour of supranational or world-regional currencies. In practice the US dollar, the ECU (or European Currency Unit), the German mark and the Japanese yen have served as transnational currencies for some years. Much of world trade is denominated in one or other of these currencies, irrespective of its particular origins or destinations. Currencies such as the US dollar and the French franc have also come to dominate large regions beyond their borders, the dollar in Latin America and the French franc in parts of West Africa formerly part of the French empire. Some of this is the result of internationally mandated economic reform (Melvin, 1988), while some is more the result of local political elites keeping their funds in 'harder' (more stable and reliable) currencies. The prospect of a 'Euro' or other European currency eliminating at least some of the existing European territorial currencies suggests that the process of transnationalization of currencies will intensify in years to come (Sandholtz, 1993).

Third, and finally, a number of uses have appeared in recent years for 'local currencies' – forms of scrip and token money – that substitute for regular national currency (Rotstein and Duncan, 1991). Such uses are often the result of experiments in local communities and consumer co-operatives or tokens issued by firms for their products or services. As yet, they cannot really be seen as posing a major threat to territorial currencies. But they are often symptomatic of the lack of trust that territorial currencies now elicit in some quarters, perhaps as a result of the uses of monetary policies which have disadvantaged some groups (and localities) when currencies are rapidly revalued, or persisting high inflation which pushes people out of the official monetary economy and into a 'black' or underground economy, where barter, trusted foreign currencies (such as the German mark in many parts of eastern Europe) or local currencies prevail.

The deterritorialization of currencies, therefore, has three aspects to it: the explosion of foreign currency transactions within the territories of hitherto 'territorial currencies'; the rapid increase in the number of economic transactions involving supranational currencies; and the growing use of local currencies. None of these should be read as totally undermining existing territorial currencies. The continued erosion of territorial currencies will take place only if states continue to allow it. That there is still advantage in it for the most 'powerful' currencies means, however, that it will probably continue. As it deepens it could well gain a momentum that even the most powerful of states will find difficult to counteract.

Conclusion

At one time it made some sense to see the path of history or social change as a series of 'stages' (as in Rostow's (1960) famous account of 'the stages of economic growth') inscribed upon the fixed territories of state spatiality. Today, however, development is increasingly a process determined by the relative ability of localities and regions *within states* to organize access to global networks. In this context, understanding power as if it is attached singularly and permanently to state territories makes little or no sense. Many regions and localities now tie directly into global networks which privilege some of them (the City in London or parts of west Los Angeles, for example) relative to others that are increasingly either disadvantaged by their lack of connectivity (parts of sub-Saharan Africa, for example) or subordinated within the spatial division of labour implicit in the hierarchy of nodes within global networks (chicken-processing plants in Arkansas or export-processing zones in northern Mexico, for example). This is not to say that it is a planetary economy in which everything that happens anywhere is determined solely by links to global networks. There are still important local and state-level sources of both economic and political activities. But the emerging world of fragmented spaces is one in which political power is vested in those organizations and people who control access to global networks of information and finance: the critical medium of the market access regime. Political power itself is now more about control over information, finance and cultural production than about military coercion, control over raw materials or even trading capacity. It still rests, of course, on the collaboration, sufferance or indifference of the multitudes. But the points of maximum connection and potential resistance to political power are decreasingly coincidental with those of state territoriality. To maintain the possibility of popular regulation of increasingly fragmented spaces, repertoires of political action will have to engage simultaneously at the regional geographical scale (within states) and in coalition building at wider scales (such as the continental and global), so as both to set limits to the competitive pressures on places from the market access regime and to offer avenues 'from below' to challenge the global advance of transnational liberalism.

The commitment to an unchanged geopolitics of power, however, retains considerable appeal. Not only does it allow for the intellectual restriction of politics to an unproblematic and neatly bounded 'domestic' space, it also provides an attractive intellectual and political stability by equating space with the fixed territories of modern statehood, which can then serve as a template for the investigation of other phenomena or as the basis for organizing political action. Putting state territoriality in question undermines the 'methodological nationalism' that has lain behind the ontologies and methodologies of both mainstream and much radical social science. The major social sciences in the contemporary Western university – economics, sociology and political science – were all founded to provide intellectual services to modern states in, respectively, wealth creation, social control and state management. It is little surprise, therefore, that they find difficulty in moving beyond a world unproblematically divided up into discrete units of sovereign space. Yet to do so is precisely the major challenge facing social science at the close of the twentieth century.

References

Agnew, J.A. (1989) 'The devaluation of place in social science'. In J.A. Agnew and J.S. Duncan (eds), *The Power of Place: Bringing Together Geographical and Sociological Imaginations*. Boston, Unwin Hyman, 11–35.

Agnew, J.A. (1994) 'The territorial trap: the geographical assumptions of international relations theory'. *Review of International Political Economy*, 1: 53–80.

Agnew, J.A. (1995) 'The rhetoric of regionalism: the Northern League in Italian politics, 1983–1994'. *Transactions of the Institute of British Geographers*, 20: 156–72.

Agnew, J.A. and S. Corbridge (1995) *Mastering Space: Hegemony, Territory, and International Political Economy*. London, Routledge.

Allen, B. (1995) 'From multiplicity to multitude: universal systems of deformation'. *Symposium*, 49: 93–113.

Barry, K. (1997) 'Paper money and English Romanticism: literary side-effects of the last invasion of Britain'. *Times Literary Supplement*, 21 February: 14–16.

Billig, M. (1995) *Banal Nationalism*. London, Sage.

Bourdieu, P. (1977) *Outline of a Theory of Practice*. Cambridge, Cambridge University Press.

Brantlinger, P. (1996) *Fictions of State: Culture and Credit in Britain, 1694–1994*. Ithaca NY, Cornell University Press.

Burch, K. (1994) 'The "properties" of the state system and global capitalism'. In S. Rosow, N. Inayatullah and M. Rupert (eds), *The Global Economy as Political Space*. Boulder CO, Lynne Rienner, 37–59.

Castells, M. (1996) *The Rise of the Network Society*. Oxford, Blackwell.

Cerny, P.G. (1993) 'The deregulation and re-regulation of financial markets in a more open world. In P.G. Cerny (ed.), *Finance and World Politics: Markets, Regimes and States in the Post-Hegemonic Era*. Aldershot, Elgar, 45–82.

Cohen, B. (1977) *Organizing the World's Money*. New York, Basic Books.

Cowhey, P.F. and J.D. Aronson (1993) *Managing the World Economy: The Consequences of Corporate Alliances*. New York, Council on Foreign Relations Press.

Cox, R. (1987) *Power, Production, and World Order: Social Forces in the Making of History*. New York, Columbia University Press.

Deudney, D. (1995) 'Nuclear weapons and the waning of the *real*-state'. *Daedalus*, 124: 209–31.

Deudney, D. (1996) 'Binding sovereigns: authorities, structures, and the geopolitics of the Philadelphian system'. In T. Biersteker and C. Weber (eds), *State*

Sovereignty as Social Construct. Cambridge, Cambridge University Press, 190–239.

Dodd, N. (1995) 'Money and the nation-state: contested boundaries of monetary sovereignty in geopolitics'. *International Sociology*, 10: 139–54.

Giddens, A. (1979) *Central Problems in Social Theory: Action, Structure and Contradiction in Social Analysis*. London, Macmillan.

Helleiner, E. (1994) *States and the Reemergence of Global Finance: From Bretton Woods to the 1990s*. Ithaca NY, Cornell University Press.

Helleiner, E. (1996) 'Historicizing territorial currencies: monetary structures, sovereignty and the nation-state'. Paper presented at the International Studies Association, Annual Meeting, San Diego, 17–20 April.

Hudson, A.C. (1996) 'Globalization, regulation and geography: the development of the Bahamas and the Cayman Islands as offshore financial centres'. Unpublished PhD dissertation, University of Cambridge.

Julius, D. (1990) *Global Companies and Public Policy: The Growing Challenge of Foreign Direct Investment*. New York, Council on Foreign Relations.

Krishna, S. (1994) 'Cartographic anxiety: mapping the body politic in India'. *Alternatives*, 19: 507–21.

Lukács, G. (1971) *The Theory of the Novel*. Cambridge MA, MIT Press.

Lukes, S. (1975) *Power: A Radical View*. London, Macmillan.

Mann, M. (1984) 'The autonomous power of the state: its origins, mechanisms and results'. *European Journal of Sociology*, 25: 185–213.

Massey, D. (1993) 'Politics and space/time'. *New Left Review*, April: 65–84.

Melvin, M. (1988) 'The dollarization of Latin America as a market-enforced monetary reform: evidence and implications'. *Economic Development and Cultural Change*, 36: 543–58.

Mosse, G. (1975) *The Nationalization of the Masses*. New York, Howard Fertig.

O'Brien, R. (1992) *Global Financial Integration: The End of Geography*. New York, Council on Foreign Relations Press.

Piron, S. (1996) 'Monnaie et majesté royale dans la France du 14è siècle'. *Annales (Histoires, Sciences Sociales)*, 51/2: 325–54.

Rosecrance, R. (1996) 'The virtual state'. *Foreign Affairs*, 75: 118–42.

Rostow, W. (1960) *The Stages of Economic Growth: A Non-Communist Manifesto*, New York, Cambridge University Press.

Rotstein, A. and C. Duncan (1991) 'For a second economy'. In D. Drache and M. Gertler (eds), *The New Era of Global Competition*. Montreal, McGill-Queen's University Press, 415–34.

Ruggie, J.G. (1993) 'Territoriality and beyond: problematizing modernity in international relations'. *International Organization*, 47: 139–74.

Sandholtz, W. (1993) 'Choosing union: monetary politics and Maastricht'. *International Organization*, 47: 1–39.

Spruyt, H. (1994) *The Sovereign State and its Competitors: An Analysis of Systems Change*. Princeton NJ, Princeton University Press.

Trigilia, C. (1991) 'The paradox of the region: economic regulation and the representation of interests'. *Economy and Society*, 20: 306–27.

Walker, R.B.J. (1993) *Inside/Outside: International Relations as Political Theory*. Cambridge, Cambridge University Press.

Watt, I. (1957) *The Rise of the Novel*. Berkeley CA and Los Angeles, University of California Press.

10
Spatial Assemblages of Power: From Domination to Empowerment

John Allen

Introduction

In many recent studies of power and power relations, space and spatiality have become increasingly central to an understanding of the workings of power. Such an understanding is clearly apparent in the work of Michel Foucault, it is evident in the writings of Gilles Deleuze, especially the later essays, and it is present in the thinking of Bruno Latour.[1] And in case such an understanding should be casually attributed to the influence of so-called poststructuralist writings, space is also integral to the thoughtful analyses of power produced by both Anthony Giddens and Michael Mann.[2] Whilst such writers often represent spatiality in rather stilted ways, they do none the less share a sense of the significance of spatiality to the workings of power. In direct contrast, many traditional Weberian and Marxist conceptions of power and domination are noteworthy for their limited grasp of any such appreciation.

In this chapter, the intention is to build upon this more recent understanding of spatiality and power, although in a manner which may strike some as particularly ironic given the above statement. The central line of argument is that despite advances in our spatial *vocabularies* of power, a spatialized *theory* of power requires that we rethink the different modalities of power deployed in traditional accounts, especially those presented by Max Weber and Hannah Arendt. What such theorists lacked in terms of spatial imagination, they made up for in their grasp of the subtle distinctions and modalities of power. It is perhaps an appropriate moment, therefore, to see if it is possible to blend the two and, indeed, to go beyond them in terms of our understanding of the spatiality of power relations.

The chapter is divided into two parts. In the first, attention is drawn to the different spatial vocabularies of power, from the more central-ized, linear forms of power inspired by Weber's writings on organiza-tion and bureaucracy, where space appears as little more than a complication to its distribution, to the more mobile and diffuse dia-grams of power drawn by Deleuze and Foucault, and less explicitly by Latour. In the second part of the chapter, the focus switches to the dif-ferent modes of power which, it is contended here, come into play in various combinations whenever and wherever power relationships are constituted through space. Starting with Weber's useful distinction between domination and authority, the account moves from instrumen-tal modes of power based on constraint and control to consider the less familiar, but equally important, associational modes of power based on integration and empowerment.

Spatial vocabularies of power

By drawing attention to the spatial vocabularies of power employed by different writers, the intention here it to show that all such accounts of power more or less include spatial characteristics in their frameworks of meaning. Although often restrictive in form, such characteristics none the less have a useful significance. Weber, for instance, talks about the powers of command and their distribution, Giddens refers to 'contain-ers' of power and their leverage over tracts of space and time, Foucault speaks about institutional spaces of power and their organization, and Deleuze is vocal about the different segments, flows and lines of power, and so forth. In all such accounts, space in one way or another is impli-cated in relationships of power; it is significant to their realization or actualization. The way this significance is represented diagrammatically, however, has taken a variety of forms and is richer in some accounts than in others.

Centred powers, distributed capabilities

When power is said to be in the 'hands' of a particular individual or social group, such as the middle classes, or 'held' by institutions of the state or commerce, an implicit spatial vocabulary of power is invoked.

For once power is conceived as a possession, as something which can be held – regardless of whether or not it is used – its location is relatively easy to trace. Certain social groups are said to possess power and others are deemed to have little or none, as a superficial reading of Mike Davis's (1992) remapping of Los Angeles as an ecology of fear would tell us. The ability of affluent, middle-class groups to construct, in Davis's terms, 'social control districts' which effectively exclude 'dangerous' others can easily be read as a script of the powerful versus the powerless. Likewise, it is not hard to believe that certain institutions, such as the large US finance houses, possess sufficient power and influence to shape, as well as constrain, contemporary economic events. The crucial point about this understanding is that once power is conceived as something separate from what it can do, or rather the capacity to influence and control the actions of others is conceived as distinct from the exercise of that capability, it is possible to pinpoint its location. Put another way, once the location of that power is revealed, it is as if the person, group or institution in some sense 'contains' that power, which is then either extended, distributed or resisted across the surrounding social space.

Broadly speaking, this 'centred' view of power is similar to that criticized by Latour (1986) for its reified projection of power across space; a critique which, interestingly, would encompass most Weberian and Marxist understandings of power. A common feature of such accounts, according to Latour, is that a 'store' of centralized power – located in, say, the apparatus of the state or an economic body – is marshalled and transmitted through time and space and, allowing for an element of distortion or resistance, used to secure organizational or institutional goals. On this understanding, the transmission of powers from the centre is relatively straightforward and the outcome of power plays relatively easy to discern: either the actions of the centre are successful in achieving their identifiable goals, in which case success is attributed to the powers of the centre and its distribution, or the goals are not achieved, in which case failure is attributed to the degree of resistance met. And aside from the possibility that the chain of command may encounter distortion through misunderstanding or a slackening in the pace of distribution, little else other than the force of the central power or the extent of resistance may influence the eventual outcome.

Although somewhat sparse as a diagram of power, this binary model is none the less quite commonplace. It underpins, for example, much of the literature on 'global cities', where places like New York, Tokyo and London are considered to act as either centres of command and control in the world economy or as production sites for the services and financial inputs which constitute a capability for global control. In the former case, the financial and decision-making powers of multinational headquarters based in the global centres appear to be able to trigger an effective capacity for control across a world-wide system of markets and production locations.[3] In the latter case, the capability for global control is assumed to be effective in a rather unmediated fashion.[4]

Perhaps the clearest illustration of how a centralized power is actually thought to be transmitted in a uniform manner is the realist account of the nation state, which has recently been subject to criticism by John Agnew (1994) and others such as Rob Walker (1993). Starting out from the position that nation states are fixed units of sovereign space, the political realist conceives the state as a unitary actor capable of controlling and commanding a particular territorial space through the distribution of its powers to select elites and bureaucratic organizations. Distinguishing between an internal, domestic space in which governments exercise power in a rational, orderly fashion over a defined territory and an external, international domain defined by the absence of order, the 'territorial state' is represented as a homogeneous political community maintained and controlled from an identifiable centre. On this view, the state as the central actor guarantees social order through the distribution of its powers and thus effectively 'contains' society with its territorial boundaries. Thus in what appears to be an almost effortless transmission of power from the centre to authoritative locations in the political community, the solid capabilities of the state seem to be realized in full.[5]

What is particularly illuminating about this example, however, is the manner in which the whole centralized force comes into play through its distributed parts. The state as a whole is represented as a dynamic force which is able to bind the ensemble of its parts. Read in this way, the centre and its extended powers are equivalent to a *whole–part relationship*, where the powers of the centre are transmitted intact through a hierarchy of commands from one official to the next. An equivalent diagram of power is to be found in Weber's influential writings on bureaucracy, where the supervisory and regulatory powers of the centre are distributed through a variety of organizational spaces and realized in the form of administration. According to Weber:

> The individual bureaucrat cannot squirm out of the apparatus into which he has been harnessed ... In the great majority of cases he is only a small cog in a ceaselessly moving mechanism which prescribes to him an essentially fixed route of march. The official is entrusted with specialized tasks, and normally the mechanism cannot be put into motion or arrested by him, but only from the very top. The individual bureaucrat is, above all, forged to the common interest of all functionaries in the perpetuation of the apparatus and the persistence of its rationally organized domination. (1978: 988)

Of course, not all forms of centralized power are transmitted in such a rigid fashion, a point which Weber well understood. In many accounts of the state, however, whether the simple unitary version noted above or the more complex institutional version elaborated by Bob Jessop (1990), the state's powers often appear to be passed relatively intact through the political apparatus. Even in Jessop's account, far removed from any essentialist notion of power, the plurality of powers inscribed in the contradictory institutional ensemble that is said to be the state may be activated by officials in one part of the state's territorial apparatus and transmitted to another, with what appears to be little significant change or effect. Whilst the conditionality of outcomes is fully recognized in this account, the conditionality of the mediating links is not.[6] As such the extension of powers across space barely seems to problematize their establishment or effectiveness, apart that is from possible forms of distortion or resistance.

In Latour's terms, such accounts of the state's political apparatus (and much more besides) fail to consider how power and its commands are translated rather than transmitted across space. In any chain of actors, power is modified and transformed as it passes from hand to hand, so to speak.[7] It is not necessary to endorse Latour's model of continuous transformation, however, to argue that power may be actively constituted through space, rather than conceived as something which merely radiates out from a central location, or indeed locations.

The key issue to note, then, is that by slipping into the assumption that power is an attribute, a property, a possession – in short, is something separate from what it can do – it becomes a matter of relative ease to talk about centralized powers and distributed capabilities. In adopting such a spatial vocabulary, however, it is less well understood that much of what happens *in between* and why it happens tends to fall out of the frame of enquiry.

Mobilized powers, stretched resources

A rather more elaborate spatial vocabulary of power is evident in the writings of both Giddens and Mann.[8] For both authors, power is generated through the actions of individuals, groups or organizations, networked or otherwise. In other words, it is a medium which is brought into being through the mobilization of collective or individual resources, not a centralized property which is always already present and awaiting distribution. Rather than thinking of power as a property or possession, therefore, it is possible to conceive of it as an effect produced through the actions of people or institutions pooling their resources to secure certain outcomes. On this view, then, it makes little sense to talk of power as something held 'in reserve'. For once power is conceived as something which is *produced* it becomes relatively difficult to locate, especially in comparison with power which is said to be 'centred' in social bodies.

Having said that, the manifest production of power does not imply that its location is impossible to fix, especially since it is understood that power is produced through networks of social action, and may in fact expand or decrease in such networks. Powers generated through collective association, through the resources that are brought to bear in a situation, may be manifest, for instance, in middle-class actions which lead to the 'purification' of social space.[9] Short-term goals achieved through practices of spatial closure and based upon the collective mobilization of resources may, for example, lead to the evaporation of a group's power once the process of mobilization is over. Or, to make the point firmly, power may be conceived in this manner, in contrast, that is, to something which the middle classes are said to possess. In this way, it is possible to see how collectivities, such as the middle classes or indeed rather different forms of social solidarity such as transnational social movements (in relation to the environment, for example), can pool resources of money, contacts and information, as well as other skills and competencies, to generate an effect called power.

A related aspect of this broad understanding of power, however, and one developed by Giddens, is that power is produced through social interaction, which itself may stem from and in turn promote the 'stretching' of social relations over space. The line of thought runs something like this. As control over longer spans of time and space is achieved, so the means of power available is directly enhanced. In this much-vaunted global age, a number of disembedded relations and institutions, from the money markets and transnational firms to expert systems and communications technologies, are said to have the ability to 'lift' social relations out of nation state involvement. So, in a world of rapid, intensive information flows, the mobilization and retrieval of resources over space are likely to be in the control of those disembedded institutions which are capable of linking local practices to global relations. In this way, a more distanciated form of power involving interaction with those physically absent may be seen to represent a modern, facilitative means of securing outcomes.[10]

On this understanding, then, power is clearly not some preformed entity with latent abilities. Rather, distanciated forms of power may be considered to manifest their abilities through a series of often routinized and repetitive practices 'stretched' over space. Administrative power, in transnational institutions for example, can be seen to work through an ability to regulate the timing and spacing of social activities. Those 'locales' in which resources tend to concentrate, from cities, nation states and beyond, are said to 'contain' sufficient powers to control events 'at a distance'.[11] What may also be understood from this, however, is that power generated in one part of a distanciated network is transmitted intact across it. As a diagram of power, therefore, it is possible to read such distanciated networks merely as *conduits* for the transmission of all kinds of organizational and institutional ability. And, somewhat surprisingly, these networks seem to undergo little in the way of displacement or transformation.

In part, this may be because Giddens conceives of power as facilitative, as enabling in the first instance rather than constraining. Although the effectiveness of power as a means of getting things done 'at a distance' does entail institutional mediation, this appears to be of a regularized rather than a redefined nature. In those cases where the actions of others are controlled or directed against their will, power may be deflected by counter-strategies and sanctions, but – as in centred accounts – there appears to be little else happening between the initiation of control and resistance to it.[12]

Not all networked diagrams of power possess such a lack, however. Mann's selective mapping of the logistics of power, for instance, displays a sensitivity to their spatial mediation in the way that information, ideas, people and materials are seen to flow across historical borders and territories.[13] To condense his broad argument, the 'stretching' of power relations and their consolidation are assumed to take their shape from a series of networks organized over space which cross-cut and overlap one another; the most important of which are given to stabilize around four types of (re)sources – broadly defined as economic, ideological, political and military. A wide variety of institutions and practices, from the broad, sweeping alliances of geopolitical bodies and their equally international economic counterparts, transnational firms, to the more regional associations of culture, religion or political practice, are seen to connect people and places together over short and long distances in the pursuit of defined ends. More to the point, the organizational reach of different institutions and associations is assumed to vary, with the most effective organizations in terms of power 'stretching' their resources through extensive and intensive networks, and combining authoritative and diffused techniques of organization to achieve far-flung goals. In short, different types of resource, their organization and mobilization, are distinguished by their *spatial reach and scope*.[14]

Whilst this is a thoughtful conception of networked power, not least for its spatial sensitivity, we are none the less left with the view that networked social relations merely act as the carriers of power through their ability to transmit resources mobilized elsewhere. Whilst it is no doubt the case that the organizational means available to different sources of power are important to register, if only because they alert us to the limitations and consequences of 'stretching' power over space, Mann's analysis frequently stops at just the point where the more pressing questions occur; in particular, the question of how distance and mobility affect not just the extent of power, but also its mode and constitution.[15]

To be fair, Mann is not alone in this respect. Even in relatively complex accounts of networked interactions, such as Castells (1996) – where different kinds of network are seen to involve different resources and each network is said to construct its own geography of control, with specific sites on the network producing, switching, directing and co-ordinating resources – little attention is paid to the constitution of power. The power of the networked flows, the manner in which they enable cultural and economic elites to interact in real time, is clearly considered by Castells, and yet their revisable and redefinable nature is not. It is as if the space of power is somehow projected across societies with little or no apparent distortion, when it should be readily apparent that this is not the case.[16]

In thinking about power as something which is produced through networks of social interaction, it thus appears to be relatively easy to assume that it is transmitted uniformly across tracts of space and time. The crucial limitation of this view, however, is that with power conceived as an effect of 'stretched' interaction, networks may appear as little more than *carriers* of resources mobilized at different sites and locations on the network. Although in spatial terms this representation may be considered as more sophisticated than a centred diagram of power, as a spatial vocabulary it is remarkably limited.

Immanent powers, constitutive practices

In comparison with the two previous accounts, the idea that power may be actively constituted through space produces a rather different spatial vocabulary of power. The writings of Foucault and Deleuze in particular provide an obvious reference point here and indeed a direct contrast to the two earlier diagrammatic representations of power.[17] A key aspect of their understanding of power is that it is something practised before it is possessed or brought into being through the mobilization of resources. More to the point, the practices of power are judged more by the effectiveness with which subjects internalize their effects than by the extent to which they conform or comply with them. In that sense, on this account the thing called power is not so much above us, as around and among us. It is an immanent not an external force; or put another way, it is conceived as inseparable from its effects. This appreciation is perhaps clearest in Foucault's writings, where power is said to work through indirect techniques of self-regulation which make it difficult to constitute oneself in ways other than those directed. Whilst something that touches us all in this way is naturally quite hard to pinpoint, the capillary quality of power, the mass of lines which constitute us, to draw upon Deleuze's terminology, provide a way forward.

If, for Foucault, power is concerned with the techniques which govern the possible limits of action, then the organization of space – the zoning, partitioning, enclosing and serialization of activities – is critical to such a practice. The arrangement of space, the particular assemblages of space which make up institutional complexes, are understood as integral to the ways in which particular forms of conduct are secured. In this line of thinking, different spatial arrangements reflect the possible ways of acting inscribed in different schemas and serve to regulate, as well as enable, mobility through them. So, with power working on subjects, rather than over them, and through an open set of possibilities composed in space and time, the multiple arrangements of power can be conceived as just so many diagrams of power.[18] Indeed, for Deleuze such diagrams map the practices of power, in particular the points and distributions through which they are effective.[19] Above all, the practices which are embedded within institutional spaces are understood as constitutive of social action.

Perhaps the best known of Foucault's diagrammatic representations of power is Bentham's Panopticon. It is commonplace to emphasize the spatial arrangements which characterize its penal technology; namely, the distribution of prisoners who are seen yet are themselves unable to see and the guards who see all yet remain unseen. It is less well understood, however, that it was not so much the Benthamite technology which induced certain forms of conduct as the ways in which the schema took hold in the official imagination and served to influence the timing and spacing of activity. On this view, what happened in prisons, their actual functioning on a day-to-day basis, was in Foucault's words 'a witches' brew compared to the beautiful Benthamite machine' (1991: 81), yet the schema, once installed, worked as a 'grid' shaping individuals' perceptions and practices. Because people believed it to be 'true', it had real consequences for all those involved, providing a guide to which kinds of behaviour were deemed acceptable and where. Power, as such, can be seen to work indirectly upon the self, not as a by-product of some 'inert' technology or diagram, but as a series of regulatory effects induced by a whole range of embedded practices and convergent discourses across sites.

Characterized in this way, power for Foucault is not so much an exercise in confrontation as it is a series of provocations and incitements. It is best understood as a form of 'government' which works through a multiplicity of actions and reactions, rather than through a simple domination/resistance binary.[20] On this understanding, power reaches deep inside an institution in an immanent rather than a hierarchical fashion, composing and recomposing all manner of arrangements in space and time, although not to any particular tune orchestrated by a centralized power. Power, in this sense, may be loosely considered to be everywhere, but it is more accurately described as diffuse and embedded in particular institutionalized spaces.

This is clearly a thought-provoking analysis, but in many ways it represents a displacement of those concerns we have already encountered, rather than their resolution. Unlike the two previous accounts, power relationships are transformed *in* space, on site as it were, as opposed to being transmitted intact from one site to the next. Thus, although he distances himself from a notion of power as unmediated domination, the only mediations which actually come into play in Foucault's analysis are site-specific practices. This then makes it difficult to conceive of how power is transformed *through* rather than in space: how 'government' links together discrete technologies and practices across sites and aligns various forms of discipline so as to make self-regulation possible.[21] In other words, how are such dispersed powers effectively translated across different sites and institutional domains?

As if on cue, a rather elaborate answer to this question is provided by Nikolas Rose and Peter Miller, who, in attempting to splice Foucault with Latour, set out to show how 'governing at a distance' is possible.[22] In keeping with Latour's stress upon how others distant in space and time are enrolled, mobilized and 'fixed' or 'locked' into particular forms of conduct, Rose and Miller outline in formulaic fashion how individuals, organizations and objectives may be brought into alignment. In doing so, however, they give the rather disconcerting impression that the conditions necessary to secure such an alignment are quite straightforward and relatively unproblematic, as well as more or less effective. Through a complex of relays and interdependencies, governmental techniques and practices are considered to be able to shape social conduct 'at a distance' without, it seems, undue loss of freedom. Intriguingly, one set of techniques and practices appears to fold into another in a way that conveys little if any of the inventive 'witches' brew' of institutional life that we know characterizes open, mutating relationships.

For that inventiveness, we have to look to Deleuze's assessment of Foucault's treatment of power, where the dispersed arrangements of power which are co-extensive with a particular institutional field exhibit many more points of suppleness and mutation than are entertained in Rose and Miller's thinking.[23] For Deleuze and his co-writer Guattari, the exercise of power is something of a hit-and-miss affair, with attempts to fix a particular institutional coding limited in their ability to guide or constrain actions. Power, in this vitalistic sense, is conceived as internal to what it can do, and what it can do is the outcome of its immersion in organizational forms where all manner of inventive rein-terpretation, fluid negotiation and subtle translation hold sway. In this more uncertain script, the variety of institutions in which power is said to be 'centred' – the financial institutions, the state bureaucracies, the private corporations and the like – aim at best to adapt and convert the fluid lines of social activity into more stabilized institutional segments. Caught up in the entanglement of lines, however, such 'centres' of power are conceived as unstable combinations, open to mutation in altogether new and often unanticipated ways.[24]

One clear advantage of Deleuze and Guattari's interpretation of how diagrams of power may hold together, yet mutate through space and time, is the recognition that lines of power may be 'centred' in a way altogether different from that previously understood. In contrast to a whole–part diagram, where a centralized force exercises power through its distributed parts, for Deleuze and Guattari a 'centre' of power is always caught up in the intense flow of social activity, much of which eludes it, some of which transforms it, but without which the whole apparatus would not hold together.[25] In that sense, it is the microtex-ture of power relations which, for Foucault, Deleuze and Guattari, acts as the social cement that, on their view, never quite sets.

In considering power from this angle, however, where the multipli-city of effects generated by power remains the central focus, it is still difficult to avoid the conclusion that those effects can only be discerned at the microlevel, at the level where power is transparently constitutive: that is, on any number of *specific sites*. For if power is assumed to be an immanent force which does not admit an exterior, then it is difficult to see how it is possible to conduct an 'ascending analysis' of power.[26] As a spatial vocabulary of power, therefore, it would appear to be restricted to the embedded spatial arrangements of power rather than to power as a form of distanciated 'government'.

Power/space modalities

So far the analysis of the different theorizations has shown how the extension of power over space or its ability to be 'stretched' over more or less long distances problematizes its reach. It has also shown how adding space to the constitution of power can destabilize its effects. It is not enough, however, merely to point out the complex and continuous ways in which power may be modified, interpreted or practised as it moves across the networks or from one organizational point to the next. Such translations may offer a richer spatial vocabulary of power, but they do not deliver a spatialized theory of power. In one sense we need to spatialize such accounts even further, to rethink the theories spatially. What is missing from all three is an examined conceptualization of the modes that power takes when the spatiality of social relations forms an integral, rather than an additional, part of the picture. The argument advanced here is that we cannot usefully discuss the mediation of power over space and time without recognizing that distance, movement, mobility and containment entail the adoption of different *modes* of power (see also Allen, 1997). To be more precise: different modes of power – for example, domination, coercion, authority, inducement and seduction – are adopted as a matter of course by institutions and organizations, often in overlapping and co-existing spatial arrangements, whenever power relationships are constituted through space. In the remainder of this chapter, this line of argument will be developed, first in relation to instrumental modes of power, and then in terms of more collaborative, empowering modes.

Instrumental power, or power over others

In simple binary models of power, where the powerful and powerless face one another across the lines of resistance, it is commonplace to find the terms 'power' and 'domination' used as synonyms. The ability to impose one's will on the actions of others despite resistance is more or less thought about as just so many ways of achieving dominance. Given an asymmetrical distribution of power, in a situation of conflict or competition those with the greater power are frequently assumed to be in a position to dominate those with less. Once this situation of conflict is extended over space, then the outcome of this unequal power play is likely to result in one side being subject to the instrumental will of another over a defined space, be it an institutional space such as the workplace or a demarcated political territory. In short, domination over space is established by those with the greatest power, give or take an element of distortion or a degree of resistance.

Even allowing for an element of exaggeration in this scenario, it is not hard to see how it is flawed theoretically in at least two respects. In the first place, domination and power are not the same thing, as Weber was careful to point out. For Weber, *domination* was a 'special case of power' which, broadly defined, involves some degree of imposition and constraint.[27] At this general level, Weber stressed the free interplay of all parties involved and the absence of any formal lines of constraint, emphasizing instead the 'objective circumstances' which made it difficult for individuals or groups, realistically, to do anything other than submit to the interests of those in a dominant position. In particular, Weber had in mind those organizations or groupings which, by virtue of positions of monopoly, say, in relation to financial or commodity markets, were able to exercise a constraining influence, often on a far-reaching basis. As such, domination in general has little directly in common with notions of command, discipline or physical compliance.

Yet for Weber, the very absence of formal rules or regulatory practices associated with this broad mode of domination is thought to limit its effectiveness and reach over space. Domination, as a form of constraint, may be established close at hand or across vast distances, but the means to secure and maintain it on an ongoing basis requires something more. As is well known, the means, according to Weber, is the fashioning of a more structured, authoritarian form of organization, where the powers of supervision and control are distributed hierarchically across a series of institutional spaces. To be effective, such powers have to be clothed in legitimacy, and this is the role that Weber bequeathed to authority. In contrast to domination, *authority* is conceded, not imposed; it is something that is formally claimed and, once recognized, serves as a means to secure a willingness to comply. As such, authority is less a form of direct constraint and more a particular means of securing assent within 'structures of domination'.[28] Moreover, it is an instrumental mode of power which, it can be argued, is used selectively in combination with other modes, such as coercion, manipulation or seduction, to secure and maintain a structure of domination.

Left at this, the importance of distinguishing between power and domination, and also recognizing that there is more to power than domination, appears relatively straightforward. But – and this highlights a second weakness in the binary model – when concern goes beyond the distribution of powers to address issues of its extension and spatial reach, the analysis stops. Yet the extension of power over space-time not only involves modes of power other than domination, it also entails their *interaction* if power is to be at all effective. Rather than power being distributed intact from a central location, from a state body or corporate headquarters or such like, it is modified by institutions employing different modes of power to realize their defined goals. And because modes of power vary in terms of their spatial reach and intensity, the contention here is that specific modes of power will be employed in overlapping and co-existing spatial assemblages depending upon the ends sought.

Significantly, this analysis holds for distanciated forms of power, where networks act as a conduit for the transmission of resources, as much as it does for centralized diagrams of power. Despite the fact that Mann, for instance, distinguishes between diffuse and author-itative power (in much the same way as Weber distinguished between domination in general and authoritarian domination), it is the power (re)sources rather than the spatiality of power which, for Mann, appear to predispose a network to operate in a particular way.

In military networks, for example, power is regarded by Mann as essentially concentrated, coercive and highly mobilized relative to place. As the social organization of physical force, military power is seen as intensive, tightly controlled, and able to command a high level of commitment from all those mobilized. When 'stretched' over large expanses of territory or enacted at great distances, however, coercion is limited in what it is able to achieve.[29] In contrast, power in state polit-ical networks, although organized on a more centralized basis than that of military power, is assumed to be quite capable of extensive reach into the daily life of citizens. Through the generation and concentration of 'infrastructural' resources – customary taxation, property administra-tion, market regulation and the like – the state is able to 'penetrate society and to implement logistically political decisions' (Mann, 1986: 170; see also Mann, 1984).

Whilst the contrast drawn between the two types of network high-lights the episodic nature of coercion, the direct tie-up of the latter to one source of power none the less makes it harder to demonstrate how powerful institutions – of whatever type – employ different modes of power in various combinations, which, significantly, alter the nature of power relationships established across the networks. *Coercion*, for example, should be understood as limited by its intensity and acute visi-bility, which makes the short duration of its effectiveness an issue, unless there is some form of productive interaction between it and other modes of power across the networks. Power, as we have seen, may be mobilized at different sites and locations on a network, but it is not transmitted intact: it mutates and is arguably constituted through the combination of different modes employed and their interaction.

Interestingly, it may be the ease with which we think of power rela-tionships as extended or 'stretched' over space which makes it more dif-ficult to conceive of them as actively constituted through space-time. With Foucault, this appreciation is possible largely because of the embedded nature of site-specific practices, and because of the notion of power as a normalizing rather than a subjugating force which works on, not over, subjects. How far this sort of analysis can go beyond the reconstitution of individuals through sets of open-ended practices, or indeed explore this alignment across sites, is as noted earlier not entirely clear, however. What is evident is that a singular focus upon the plethora of techniques and practices which may influence social conduct 'at a distance' tends to obscure the modes of power which underpin them.

Lois McNay (1994), in particular, has drawn attention to certain modes of power which underpin normalizing practices – such as those of manipulation and persuasion – which remain unstated. Where *manipulation* involves the concealment of intent so that power may be exercised unknown to those subject to it, *persuasion* by comparison works on the basis of open communication and therefore the possibility of indifference. In complete contrast to domination, persuasion operates at the level where choices are part of the schema. Thus, in many respects, it is more in keeping with Foucault's stress upon the indirect nature of power relationships than it is with the idea that power is about the production of 'programmed' bodies. In fact, as McNay points out, both 'takes' on power, as intersubjective communication and as states of domination, are present in Foucault's work, and the inability to differentiate further only serves to gloss over a range of intermediate issues.[30] One of these, as indicated, is the different and combined ways in which modes of power and their related practices 'make up' people in and through space.

It is for this reason, among others, that Lipovetsky (1994) has distanced himself from techniques of disciplinary constraint in favour of *seduction* as a dilute mode of power. Seduction, in many ways, is the perfect example of an indirect mode of power, yet it is both extensive and effective in its reach. In part, this is because its limited effects – suggestion rather than prescription – are an integral rather than a residual feature of how it is practised. In the political arena or in the economic domain, in relation to, say, the activities of multinational cultural industries, seduction works on choices, on curiosity, seeking to take advantage of 'embryonic tendencies that are already present by making them more attractive to people' (Lipovetsky, 1994: 165). It is a modest form of power which intentionally acts upon those who have the possibility to opt out. And although Lipovetsky does not make the claim, its indeterminacy is precisely what enables it to be effective 'at a distance'. If it were the orchestration of tastes along monopolistic lines which was sought or the ability to influence conduct directly through the threat of negative sanctions, then different modes of power would be called into play, perhaps in combination, perhaps not, depending upon the desired outcomes and the spatial assemblages involved. There is no spatial template to power, only a series of modal effects through which power is known.

The key point about knowing the meaning and use of these instrumental modes of power, however, is not simply that they are often lost beneath a nominalistic blanket of technologies, practices or programmes. Rather, it is that once the spatiality of power relations is acknowledged as constitutive of how the different modalities operate and is seen to frame the different space-times through which they are effective, it is then possible to think through their specific institutional uses.

Associational power, or power with others

So far, we have considered power almost exclusively as an instrumental force, as a means of achieving 'leverage' over others, rather than as a means to get things done or as a form of empowerment. The difference between the two is perhaps best understood by contrasting the 'power over' dimension with the 'power to' side of things. Whereas the former broadly refers to an instrumental ability to shape the will of others or to gain at their expense, the latter term rests upon enablement and the possibility of collective, integrative action. Where one sees the potential for domination, the other sees the possibility of collaboration. Weber's name is closely associated with an instrumental view of power, but others – Giddens, Mann and Foucault in particular – are sufficiently pliant in their vocabularies also to entertain notions of facilitative, collective or productive power. Significantly, however, each fails to explore fully what role associational modes of power may take when they are exercised *with* rather than over others across space.

If we consider Mann's work on the collective mobilization of resources, for example, power, although integrative in spirit, may be used to further the sectional interests of like-minded groups or institutions to the detriment of other, less collectively organized individuals and bodies. There is no legitimate common endeavour, only joint powers acting to the disadvantage of others. This, then, is an instance of 'power over', but one organized through collective association. Such practices are evident, for example, in the networks of east Asian businesses that Castells (1996) and others have highlighted, where family connections and ethnic ties in overseas Chinese networks, for instance, serve not only to overcome the barriers of distance, but also to enable particularistic trust relations to be established over tracts of space and time.[31] In pooling their resources across extended networks, however, the power of such networks rests upon an ability to, in Mann's terms, 'organizationally outflank' those less networked than themselves. The distanciated character of these economic networks, based upon the resources of loyalty, duty and obedient trust, give the overseas Chinese a specific cultural advantage over their economic competitors. As with the earlier example of the collective powers of the middle classes being used to exclude the less organized from their neighbourhood preserves, collaboration once again spills over into competition and we are back with division and constraint. The circle is closed in an almost predictable fashion.

None the less, what is illuminating about such forms of collective association is that they can throw light upon modes of power other than those deployed in hierarchical, instrumental relationships. In thinking through the nature of these networks, in particular what it is that holds them together over space, it is possible to identify *lateral* as well as *vertical* modes of power being used to fix a collective orientation. *Negotiation* and *inducement*, for example, can sit alongside authority and, if necessary, coercion in such networks, and although less familiar as a language of power, such lateral modes are indispensable to the effective spatial reach of organizations and institutions. In so far as what happens in one part of a network is affected by those absent as well as those present, a combination of modes is likely to be drawn upon to stabilize relationships across the networks and thus enable collaboration 'at a distance' to be effective. Having said that, the 'power to' mobilized in such networked assemblages may still ultimately be made to serve instrumental ends.

Not all accounts of the powers of association lead to such instrumental ends, however. The work of Arendt is a case in point, where the collaborative, enabling side to power is valued in its own right, as both a resource to be cultivated and an end in itself. Power for Arendt, as for Foucault, is a benign rather than a repressive force, but unlike Foucault's understanding it is something which is produced by people coming together to pursue a common purpose. It is rooted in *mutual action*.[32] It is not something which can be practised like a mode of conduct or measured like military strength; it is always of the moment. When it is not sustained by mutual action, it passes away. On this basis, Arendt is able to argue that power is largely independent of material factors, such as the size and volume of resources in play. The ability of smaller players to mobilize effectively against the demands of those greater in size is possible precisely because of the collaborative, integrative resources mobilized. Moreover, the mobilization of such qualities is viewed as a positive gesture, as empowering of those taking part, rather than simply as an act of resistance directed towards more powerful forces.

Association, in this context, is thus conceived neither as a form of resistance by the powerless, nor as a collective endeavour of the powerful to bend another's will. Rather, the aim for Arendt is the formation of a common will which enriches public life, and in so doing reaps benefits for all involved, especially in the way people relate to one another. At the root of this conception is a concern for the quality of *public space*, in particular the moral, ethical and political concerns which raise rather than diminish civic communities. Seyla Benhabib (1992), among others, has sought to interpret Arendt's views on public space in a manner that clearly reveals the positive powers of association.[33] For Benhabib:

> public space ... emerges whenever and wherever, in Arendt's words, 'men act together in concert'. On this model, public space is the space 'where freedom can appear'. It is not a space in any topographical or institutional sense: a town hall or a city square where people do not 'act in concert' is not a public space in this Arendtian sense. But a private dining room in which people gather to hear a *Samizdat* or in which dissidents meet with foreigners become public spaces; just as a field or a forest can also become public space if they are the object and the location of an 'action in concert', of a demonstration to stop the construction of a highway or a military airbase, for example. These diverse topographical locations become public spaces in that they become the 'sites' of power, of common action coordinated through speech and persuasion. (1992: 93)

'Sites' of collective mobilization which draw upon expressive resources to make their voices heard are, on this interpretation at least, not directed towards the pursuit of sectional interests. Rather such forms of social solidarity are intended to transcend particular interests by mobilizing around issues faced in common. Public spaces may encompass the local (as in the Newbury by-pass or Manchester airport protests) yet reach out to a much wider arena of associational politics. Or they may directly involve the mobilization of moral and political energies 'at a distance' across distanciated networks of association (as in many environmental and feminist campaigns).[34] In such collective endeavours, the ideal of public space as an arena for action and informal debate has less in common with the notion of winners and losers and rather more with positive-sum scenarios in which all may benefit.

Perhaps the sharpest way of illustrating the associational modes of power which Arendt appears to promote can be gauged by the utter contempt in which she holds bureaucracy as a form of domination, or 'rule by nobody' as she terms it (Arendt, 1970: 38). If we consider Benhabib's observation that a town hall falls short of becoming a public space because people do not 'act in concert', then Weber's authoritarian official operating a rule-bound system of control is the antithesis of

Arendt's conception of power. Public officials and private managers who operate on the basis of impersonal, bureaucratic reason define a form of governance as control over others, which Arendt refuses to recognize as power. Instead, she invokes a language of power which, broadly speaking, is concerned with *transverse* relationships of power; that is, those which cut across conventional organizational lines and practices. What matters for Arendt is not so much the substantive issues which give rise to different kinds of public space as the manner in which associations are conducted. As Benhabib rightly stresses, what is important 'is not so much *what* public discourse is about as the *way* in which discourse takes place' (1992: 95–105). This is a difficult set of relationships to pin down, but to exercise power with others in this context would, for Arendt, be very likely to involve the openness of public negotiation and persuasion, as well as recognition of these relationships as modes of *empowerment*. Authority, too, as a mode of power takes on a different meaning from that understood by Weber and is interpreted by Arendt as more advice than commmand or control. Those who are recognized 'authorities' have authority *among* rather than over people.[35] It is with this frame of mind that perhaps we should be looking to recast the meaning of certain conventional modes of power and their instrumental contexts, as well as thinking about which modes enhance rather than diminish the plurality of public spaces. In so doing we may also come to understand how the spatiality of such relationships influences their use and combination as well.

Conclusion

As stated at the outset, the aim of this chapter is to build upon our understanding of the relationships between spatiality and power. The ability to go beyond a vocabulary of centralized powers and their distributed capabilities to encompass more distanciated networks of power relations or their embedded spatial arrangements is a significant advance in understanding, but it is possible to go further. Here, it has been argued that spatiality is constitutive of power relations not only in general, but also in the particular ways in which different modes of power are called into play. It is this recognition that leads towards a spatialized theory of power. Power is always already spatial, but it is neither uniform, nor continuous over space. It is actualized in different and combined modes *precisely because spatiality makes a difference to the effects that power can have.*

Moreover, as a series of effects, power is not just reducible, as Arendt points out, to the 'business of domination' (1970: 44), even though that remains one of its significant expressions. There are many possibilities for exercising power with rather than over others, not all of which entail different sets of relations from those routinely described in terms of instrumental power. As yet, however, the language of power over others has a stronger hold on our spatial imaginations than that of empowerment and enablement or the entanglement of its many different forms.

Notes

1 Among the most important writings which engage with issues of spatiality and power are Foucault (1977, 1980, 1982, 1986, 1988, 1991), Deleuze (1988), Deleuze and Parnet (1987), Deleuze and Guattari (1988), and Latour (1986, 1987, 1991, 1993) and Latour and Callon (1981).
2 See especially Giddens (1977, 1979, 1981, 1984, 1985, 1990) and Mann (1984, 1986, 1993).
3 See Friedmann (1986) and Friedmann and Wolff (1982), for example.
4 See Sassen (1991).
5 See Waltz (1979) and Keohane (1984), for example.
6 In defence of Jessop's (1990) arguments, there is far more to them than is possible to convey here and, of course, he does not go so far as to suggest that the transmission of powers is entirely unmediated. But neither does he address directly their potential transformation as they move through and beyond the state apparatus.
7 'According to the [model of translation], the spread in time and space of anything – claims, orders, artefacts, goods – is in the hands of people; each of these people may act in many different ways, letting the token drop, or modifying it, or deflecting it, or betraying it, or adding to it, or appropriating it . . . Each of the people in the chain is not simply resisting a force or transmitting it in the way they would in the diffusion model; rather they are doing something essential for the existence and maintenance of the token. In other words, the chain is made of *actors* – not patients – and since the token is in everyone's hands in turn, everyone shapes it according to their different projects . . . Instead of the *transmission* of the same token – simply deflected or slowed down by friction – you get . . . the continuous *transformation* of the token' (Latour, 1986: 267–8).
8 See n. 2 above.
9 See Sennett (1971) and, relatedly, Sibley (1995).
10 See Giddens (1984, 1990).
11 See Giddens (1984, 1985).
12 See Giddens (1984, 1985).
13 The mapping is selective in so far as it only considers those locations and states which in some sense represent what Mann refers to as the 'leading edge of power'; namely those that exhibited new, extensive and concentrated organizational means. From Mesopotamia in the sixth century BC, through Phoenicia, classical Greece and imperial Rome, up to the emergence in

Europe of the nation state and classes as the major actors of modern times, he seeks to trace the developed 'infrastructures' of power related to each historical moment. Third and fourth volumes are planned which bring the analysis into the twentieth century and provide a broader set of theoretical conclusions.

14   See Mann (1986, 1993).

15   In fact, it would be misleading to say that Mann does not consider issues of coercion, persuasion and such like, but he does so in relation to power sources rather than the spatiality of power.

16   Castells (1996) argues that inclusion and exclusion from networks, and the dynamics between networks, are the critical sources of domination which mark the beginning of an information age. More significantly, however, there is only a limited sense in which Castells's version of networks may actually be constitutive of the power held by various elite groupings.

17   See n. 1 above.

18   '[T]he Panopticon must not be understood as a dream building: it is the diagram of a mechanism of power reduced to its ideal form; its functioning, abstracted from any obstacle, resistance or friction, must be represented as a pure architectural and optical system: it is in fact a figure of political technology that may and must be detached from any specific use' (Foucault, 1977: 205).

19   See Deleuze (1988) on Foucault's account of power, which highlights the diagrammatic element in Foucault's understanding.

20   See Foucault (1986) on the subject and power, where he speaks of an 'agonistic' relationship involving reciprocal incitation and permanent provocation.

21   Moreover, such alignment and connections amount to more than an exercise in 'pastoral' care, in which self-directed development takes place on the basis of self-examination and confessional guidance. See, in particular, Donnelly (1992) and Driver (1985) on similar concerns over the coordination and perpetuation of different schemes and technologies.

22   See Rose and Miller (1992); Miller and Rose (1990).

23   See Deleuze (1988) and the more developed discussion on power, micropolitics and segmentarity in Deleuze and Guattari (1988).

24   'To continue the use of geographical terms: imagine that between *the West and the East* a certain segmentarity is introduced, opposed in a binary machine, arranged in the State apparatuses, overcoded by an abstract machine as the sketch of a World Order. It is then from *North to South* that the destabilization takes place, as Giscard d'Estaing said gloomily, and a stream erodes a path, even if it is a shallow stream, which brings everything into play and diverts the plane of organization. A Corsican here, elsewhere a Palestinian, a plane hijacker, a tribal upsurge, a feminist movement, a Green ecologist, a Russian dissident – there will always be someone to rise up to the south. Imagine the Greeks and the Trojans as two opposed segments, face to face: but look, the Amazons arrive, they begin by overthrowing the Trojans, so that the Greeks cry, "The Amazons are with us", but they turn against the Greeks, attacking them from behind

with the violence of a torrent. This is how Kleist's *Penthesilea* begins. The great ruptures, the great oppositions, are always negotiable; but not the little crack, the imperceptible ruptures which come from the south. We say "south" without attaching any importance to this. We talk of the south in order to mark a direction which is different from that of the line of segments. But everyone has his south – it doesn't matter where it is – that is, his line of slope or flight. Nations, classes, sexes have their south' (Deleuze and Parnet, 1987: 131–2).

25 See Deleuze and Guattari (1988) on power centres and the microtexture of relations in which they operate.

26 See McNay, who argues that it is only possible to discuss the microstrategies of power at their most precise points of operation (1994: 91).

27 See Weber (1978: 941–8).

28 Weber (1978: 212–16, 941–8).

29 See Mann (1986: 146–76).

30 See McNay (1994: 159).

31 See for example Redding (1990), Olds (1995), and Yeung (1996) on particularistic social relationships in the overseas Chinese network.

32 See Arendt (1975) especially, and also Habermas (1977) on Arendt's 'communications' concept of power.

33 Arendt's account of public space has been the subject of much critical debate, not least for its grounding in dubious ideals which reach back to classical Greek and Roman times. None the less, there are those such as Benhabib (1992), Hartsock (1985) and Disch (1994) who have sought to show how Arendt's views can be understood as an alternative to competitive, divisive accounts of power formation. Hartsock, in particular, is enthusiastic about the rejection of the notion of power as domination over others, and keen to show how power as mutual action is in line with much feminist thinking on power as competence and enablement rather than dominance. In a related sense, Disch wishes to argue how Arendt's notion of power rests upon plurality as a condition of public space and is in keeping with Iris Marion Young's recognition of a 'heterogeneous public' (Young, 1990).

34 Although Arendt appears to assume close proximity as a precondition of association, the mobilization of such energies at a distance, as a form of mediated interaction, is perfectly feasible across today's distanciated networks.

35 See Arendt's (1961) essay on 'What is authority?' and, more recently, Giddens (1994) on guardians and experts.

References

Agnew, J. (1994) 'The territorial trap: the geographical assumptions of international relations theory'. *Review of International Political Economy*, 1/1: 53–80.

Allen, J. (1997) 'Economies of power and space'. In R. Lee and J. Wills (eds), *Geographies of Economies*. London and New York, Arnold, 59–70.

Arendt, H. (1961) *Between Past and Future: Six Exercises in Political Thought*. London, Faber and Faber.

Arendt, H. (1970) *On Violence*. San Diego, Harvest.

Arendt, H. (1975) *The Human Condition*. Chicago and London, University of Chicago Press.

Benhabib, S. (1992) *Situating the Self: Gender, Community and Postmodernism in Contemporary Ethics*. Cambridge, Polity Press.

Castells, M. (1996) *The Rise of the Network Society*. Oxford, Blackwell.

Davis, M. (1992) 'Beyond *Blade Runner*: urban control, the ecology of fear'. Open Magazine pamphlet series, 23. Westfield NJ.

Deleuze, G. (1988) *Foucault* (trans. S. Head). London, Athlone Press.

Deleuze, G. and F. Guattari (1988) *A Thousand Plateaus: Capitalism and Schizophrenia*. London, Athlone Press.

Deleuze, G. and C. Parnet (1987) *Dialogues*. London, Athlone Press.

Disch, L.J. (1994) *Hannah Arendt and the Limits of Philosophy*. Ithaca NY and London, Cornell University Press.

Donnelly, M. (1992) 'On Foucault's uses of the notion of "biopower"'. In F. Ewald (ed.), *Michel Foucault: Philosopher*. Hemel Hempstead, Harvester Wheatsheaf, 199–203.

Driver, F. (1985) 'Power, space and the body: a critical assessment of Foucault's *Discipline and Punish*'. *Environment and Planning D: Society and Space*, 3: 425–46.

Foucault, M. (1977) *Discipline and Punish: The Birth of the Prison* (trans. A. Sheridan). London, Allen Lane.

Foucault, M. (1980) (ed. C. Gordon) *Power/Knowledge*. Brighton, Harvester.

Foucault, M. (1982) 'The subject and power'. In H.L. Dreyfus and P. Rabinow (eds), *Michel Foucault: Beyond Structuralism and Hermeneutics*. Brighton, Harvester, 208–26.

Foucault, M. (1986) *The History of Sexuality. Vol. 3: The Care of the Self*. Harmondsworth, Penguin.

Foucault, M. (1988) 'The ethic of care for the self as a practice of freedom'. In J. Bernauer and D. Rasmussen (eds), *The Final Foucault*. Boston MA, MIT Press.

Foucault, M. (1991) 'Governmentality'. In G. Burchell, C. Gordon and P. Miller (eds), *The Foucault Effect: Studies in Governmentality*. Hemel Hempstead, Harvester Wheatsheaf, 87–104.

Friedmann, J. (1986) 'The world city hypothesis'. *Development and Change*, 17/4: 69–84.

Friedmann, J. and G. Wolff (1982) 'World city formation: an agenda for research and action'. *International Journal of Urban and Regional Research*, 6: 309–43.

Giddens, A. (1977) *Studies in Social and Political Theory*. London, Hutchinson.

Giddens, A. (1979) *Central Problems in Social Theory: Action, Structure and Contradiction in Social Analysis*. Basingstoke, Macmillan.

Giddens, A. (1981) *A Contemporary Critique of Historical Materialism*. London and Basingstoke, Macmillan.

Giddens, A. (1984) *The Constitution of Society: Outline of a Theory of Structuration*. Cambridge, Polity Press.

Giddens, A. (1985) *The Nation-State and Violence*. Cambridge, Polity Press.

Giddens, A. (1990) *The Consequences of Modernity*. Cambridge, Polity Press.

Giddens, A. (1994) 'Living in a post-traditional society'. In U. Beck, A. Giddens and S. Lash (eds), *Reflexive Modernization: Politics, Tradition and Aesthetics in the Modern Social Order*. Cambridge, Polity Press, 56–109.

Habermas, J. (1977) 'Hannah Arendt's communications concept of power'. *Social Research*, Spring: 3–24.

Hartsock, N. (1985) *Money, Sex and Power*. Boston, Northeastern University Press.

Jessop, B. (1990) *State Theory: Putting Capitalist States in their Place*. Cambridge, Polity Press.

Keohane, R.O. (1984) *After Hegemony*. Princeton NJ, Princeton University Press.

Latour, B. (1986) 'The powers of association'. In J. Law (ed.), *Power, Action and Belief*. London, Boston and Henley, Routledge and Kegan Paul, 264–80.

Latour, B. (1987) *Science in Action*. Cambridge MA, Harvard University Press.

Latour, B. (1991) 'Technology is society made durable'. In J. Law (ed.), *A Sociology of Monsters: Essays on Power, Technology and Domination*. London and New York, Routledge.

Latour, B. (1993) *We Have Never Been Modern* (trans. C. Porter). Hemel Hempstead, Harvester Wheatsheaf, 103–31.

Latour, B. and M. Callon (1981) 'Unscrewing the big Leviathan: how actors macro-structure reality and how sociologists help them to do so'. In K. Knorr-Cetina and A.V. Cicourel (eds), *Advances in Social Theory and Methodology: Towards an Integration of Micro- and Macro-Sociologies*. London, Routledge and Kegan Paul, 277–303.

Lipovetsky, G. (1994) *The Empire of Fashion: Dressing Modern Democracy* (trans. C. Porter). Princeton NJ, Princeton University Press.

Mann, M. (1984) 'The autonomous power of the state: its origins, mechanisms and results'. *Archives Européennes de Sociologie*, 25: 185–213.

Mann, M. (1986) *The Sources of Social Power. Vol. I: A History of Power from the Beginning to* AD *1760*. Cambridge, Cambridge University Press.

Mann, M. (1993) *The Sources of Social Power. Vol. II: The Rise of Classes and Nation States, 1760–1914*. Cambridge, Cambridge University Press.

McNay, L. (1994) *Foucault: A Critical Introduction*. Cambridge, Polity Press.

Miller, P. and N. Rose (1990) 'Governing economic life'. *Economy and Society*, 19/1: 1–31.

Olds, K. (1995) 'Globalization and the production of new urban spaces: Pacific Rim megaprojects in the late twentieth century'. *Environment and Planning A*, 27: 1713–44.

Redding, S.G. (1990) *The Spirit of Chinese Capitalism*. New York, de Gruyter.

Rose, N. and P. Miller (1992) 'Political power beyond the state: problematics of government'. *British Journal of Sociology*, 43/2: 173–205.

Sassen, S. (1991) *The Global City: New York, London, Tokyo*. Princeton NJ, Princeton University Press.

Sennett, R. (1971) *The Uses of Disorder*. London, Allen Lane.

Sibley, D. (1995) *Geographies of Exclusion: Society and Difference in the West*. London and New York, Routledge.

Walker, R.B.J. (1993) *Inside/Outside: International Relations as Political Theory*. Cambridge, Cambridge University Press.

Waltz, J.F. (1979) *Theory of International Politics*. New York, Random House.

Weber, M. (1978) *Economy and Society* (eds G. Roth and C. Wittich). New York, Bedminster Press.

Yeung, H. (1997) 'The socio-spatial constitution of business organizations: a geographical perspective'. *Organizations*, 4: 101–28.

Young, I.M. (1990) *Justice and the Politics of Difference*. Princeton NJ, Princeton University Press.

11
Popular and State Discourses of Power

Sarah Radcliffe

Introduction

To think through the geographies of social relations, it has become crucial to think about power and its effects. While the nature of power effects and the mode of their organization is much debated, there is general agreement that power and space/place are deeply intertwined, acting jointly to shape social and geographical relations and processes. Embedded within the quotidian dynamic of socio-spatial interaction, power(s) are at work at a variety of spatial scales. For this reason, the unpacking of the workings of power in systems of social reproduction speaks to the spatialities of power.

Drawing on Foucault we can argue that power effects are about a will to order, an attempt at a (never complete) hegemony. Yet the will to order (*Social Research*, 1993) 'falls down', cannot dispose of objects, ideas, behaviours, practices in the regularities desired, foreseen and anticipated (cf. Gramsci, 1971). Displacing an abstraction of power as an 'invisible' force, 'chess-boarding' objects and relations over space, analysts have turned to the groundedness of power, in the interstices of society and space. The will to order then is only one dimension of socio-spatial life, it is not the final determinant, and yet it is continually called up by those claiming and reproducing their power. The will to order, however partial and cross-cut by other powers and the networks (Latour, 1996) upon which they are substantiated, come to rest upon and within social subjects, in locations and within institutionalized behaviours (cf. Giddens, 1990). Power and its effects comprise the instantiation of regularization and the regularities of the inventory (Anderson, 1991) of territorial disposition (Foucault, 1983; Driver, 1985).

The operationalized spatialities of power, given their origin and basis for reproduction in social relations, rest upon quotidian work – including its ideological, representational and material work (see, respectively, Poovey, 1989; Bhabha, 1994) – which is work carried out by social subjects, themselves reproduced within the inventories and power effects. The discursive work to power speaks to the constant processes of matching up representations, personal/subjective dispositions, and 'desired' regularities (projected into the interface between social identity and subjectivities). Representational work, then, engages to create (to have created) imagery and imaginations, in which this disposition across space (the will to order) is apprehended as 'true', real, desired. One related crucial aspect of the work to power is that of biopolitics, the ordering of social, embodied habitus, practices and visualizations (Bourdieu, 1977).

Given that such will to power and power effects are constituted in the workings of networks, and at the interstices of social reproduction, the notion of resistance becomes 'fuzzy', losing its capacity to define the edges of its project and its parameters. Yet the incompleteness and inequalities of power effects, not least the internal contradictions arising with cross-cutting wills to order, inevitably give rise to the visions and practices which resist and challenge the ordered dispositions of power(s). How to describe and analyse the practices of resistance without falling into the trap of romanticization; that is, of understanding resistance which encompasses armed rebellion on the one end of a continuum and the weapons of the weak (Scott, 1985) at the other?

Such a retheorization of power away from previous 'zero-sum' conceptualizations, towards a framework which highlights power's effects and reproduction, has various implications for geographers in their attempts to identify, analyse and in turn critique the nature of contemporary socio-spatial organization. Different powers operate and have their effects in varied social spaces – body, household, city, region, global spaces – in which spatialities of power cross-cut various sites and levels of operation. Moreover, a will to order on one scale often rests upon, and draws from, inventories and dispositions of order at one or more other spatial scales, thereby focusing attention on the nature of these interdependencies and the ideological-material work they do (cf. Jonas, 1994). The scale of the actions of power can be pinpointed momentarily, but slips to other levels and sites, in which its productive effects can reinforce the initial site of operation. In other words, the simultaneity of the will to order is inherently spatial and scaled.

The fuzziness of resistance is mirrored in the fuzziness of power, acting in a way unbounded by any one level of operation, although grounded in specific locations, practices and dispositions. The plurality of forces towards hegemony is contextualized by the project of resisting. In other words, as soon as the analysis of power, effects and counter-effects begins, there is a need to specify the practices, discourses, representations which operate to underpin a will to order and the will to resist. The terminology of power's networks and of subversions requires its own detailed, substantive context in which to substantiate and flesh out the material groundings of the process.

In geography the emphasis has been on how the will to order operates across a number of socio-spatial relations engaging with the productive social differences of, variously, gender, sexuality, class, race/ethnicity and location. Such overlapping social divisions in turn become the outcome and the raw material for the will to order, reiterating a template for geosocial organization and the forms that an order could take. The practices utilized by hegemonic powers engage with and regulate these relations, disposing of subjects and their subjectivities in ways which move towards (but never achieve) the spatialities of hegemony. In this regard, recent work in the discipline of geography has highlighted the role of surveillance, representation, narratives, racializations, (hetero)sexualizations and gendering as key practices through which power constitutes its social and spatial effects. Unfolding through space and time, such practices and discourses may intervene in the disposition of attitudes, objects, and spaces, creating orders or the attempt at hegemonic order.

In my discussion, I particularly utilize Latin American and American examples to illustrate some themes around power and their spatialities, in relation to the nation state. The entangled nature of power relations, the fuzziness of resistances and the incompleteness of power projects are all brought into play simultaneously, so as not to fall back into a dualistic view of power and its resistances. The uneven and incomplete 'spatial reach' of power (effects) – in its working through practices, discourses and representations – is also a constant theme, as I would suggest it is integral to the way power may be analysed. My focus is primarily on modernity and its power (effects), as the project of mapping out the spatialities of a late/post-modernity's powers has not, to my knowledge, been started (cf. Soja, 1996). Such a focus on the spatialities of modernity's powers applies to Latin America as to the 'West', in so far as modernity's contours have been shaped in the ground constructed between the two.

One could organize a discussion about power and its effects according to the type of order which is willed/desired, a typology which also integrates the sequence of spatial scales to which power effects are oriented and through which they can be understood. I start my discussion of the sequence of scaled/spatialized powers with a discussion of embodiments and subjects' constitution through power, then move on to questions of race and ethnicity, territories and nations, and finish with issues around narratives of national history and commemorations. The different operations of power – organized spatially through the disposition of subjects and objects – are highlighted in each section. The spatiality of power in different spaces or sites is illustrated by the mobilization of space and/or place to order people into certain geographies and dispositions, a cartographic grid through which order is to be organized. In other words, powers operate simultaneously at a sequence of scales in order to reinforce the disposition and discipline of social subjects in diverse dimensions of their social world, from the body through the racialization and gendering of groups, to the nation and the city.

Biopolitics and its powers

Individualization and medicalization of the body in the time-space of the Enlightenment have been traced extensively by Foucault and many others following his fruitful line of enquiry. In the light of the extensive material on these issues, the challenge for geography and geographers remains to analyse and critique the connections created through social-spatial relations which contextualize and situate such bodily constructions. In other words, contemporary work on the spatiality of powers has yet to connect fully with the literature on embodiments. The utilization of space – and its ordering – to discipline bodies and the process of embodiment remains to be fully analysed.

The colonial cartographies which overlay Foucault's own interpretations of these issues have recently been discussed by Stoler, whose book on the 'colonial order of things' (Stoler, 1995) prompts us to reconsider the connections across spaces between bodies and powers. As Stoler points out, the cultivation of a European embodied self rested upon bodily oriented discourses and practices through which the ordered, modern subject could be constituted, and differentiated in turn from the racialized, colonized and non-ordered embodiments represented by colonized people, children and women. Drawing upon and intertextually referring to discourses and practices of pedagogy, parenting, children's sexuality, servants and hygiene (particularly tropical hygiene), embodiments rested upon cross-cutting 'orders' of race, colonialism, gender and generation. The disciplining of certain bodies and their organization across space rested upon a complex of discursive, practical and representational work, in which the 'maps' to be followed were devised and operationalized by certain (thereby empowered) subjects. In this context, bodies were 'micro-sites where designations of racial membership were subject to gendered appraisals and where "character" and "good breeding" and proper rearing were implicitly raced' (Stoler, 1995: 11).

The embodied constructions of such orders not only engaged with the European bourgeois regularities of marriage and procreation, but were also taken up in the mid- to late nineteenth-century Latin American independent republics. Racked by concerns about racial degeneracy and 'failing to make the grade' *vis-à-vis* their European role models, certain republics proposed to institute 'matrimonial eugenics' (Stepan, 1991) to control the reproductive 'health' of their citizens by means of premarital health checks, and efforts to inventory and channel male and female sexualities into 'beneficial' reproduction. While many of these measures remained on the drawing board, they reflected a node of discourse among decision makers and intellectual circles in which embodiments were constructed as the route into modernity and nationhood. In this example, we see the attempt to align the discourses of progress with the disposition of reproductive habitus, mediated via the constitution of racialized and sexualized bodies. Yet the spatiality of power rested crucially on the internationality of comparison in which the European nations – themselves constituted as embodiments of particular virtues – provided a representational and comparative frame for 'national' politics.

Hygiene is another modernist power effect working most directly on the scale of the body, yet referring to and dependent upon the deployment of power effects in other spheres. The modernist emphasis on hygiene engages with wider powers to do with class difference, cultural notions of pollution (Douglas, 1966), and racialized colonial and gender difference (McClintock, 1995). As long as 'soap is civilization' (a slogan of the Unilever Company, quoted in McClintock, 1995: 207), the local/Western knowledge of hygiene serves to operate at a universalizing scale, practised on a daily basis on the body, yet a body positioned in the context of imperial rule and global advertising. The quotidian disciplining of bodily hygiene reflects the cartographics of power effects which came down to the scale of individual bodies. Both in the colonial context of the nineteenth century and in the contemporary context of 'development', bodies can be valued or disparaged, depending on their achievement of the standards of hygiene associated with modern state power. Combined with a constraint on women's physical mobility, such a power effect became gendered (Mills, 1996).

A couple of examples illustrate this process. In late nineteenth-century Ecuador, around the time of the liberal revolution which put into place the framework of a 'modern' nation state, commercial elites were attempting to shape the disposition of their emergent nation through the mobilization of particular embodiments, bodily spaces. The modernist era – so-called 'progressivism' – was marked by representational work to align the imagery of Ecuador with the imagination of 'global' (read European – not North American at this time) standards. The imagination of place ('local'/Ecuadorian) engendered its own agenda of the disciplining of indigenous groups, who were to 'stand in' (Bowman, 1994) for the space of the nation – but only if they reached certain standards. Participation in global exhibitions, such as the 1892 Madrid exhibition (organized to commemorate the four-hundredth anniversary of Columbus's arrival in the Americas), required the selective endorsement of state representations, which were bound up in notions of hygiene and modernity. Given these criteria (templates for spatial order), it is not surprising to note that Paris-trained Ecuadorian elites chose Otavaleño Indians to represent their country, who were – it was said – 'intelligent, hardworking, sober, had good customs, and were *used to cleaning, order and cleanliness*' (Muratorio, 1994b: 126, emphasis added). Amazon lowland indigenous groups, by contrast, could not suit these discursive agendas of key decision makers, who in turn were bound up in the spectacles of modern statehood, namely exhibitions, anthropology and the museum (Harvey, 1996). Here we have an example of the matching up of representations (in this case 'representative' embodiments) with the will to order, the bourgeois power-holders whose ambivalence towards Europe informed the syncretic symbol of the Otavaleño Indian – an Indian (not European) cleaned (European) – a hybrid which could speak to the agendas of newly emerging elites in the Southern republics.

That the notions of hygiene and the disciplinary practices around them are not just in the past is illustrated by the contemporary ideological, material and discursive work done by development agencies throughout Latin America to organize and order certain populations. The efforts to order the behaviours and practices of peasantries were integral to the food and nutrition programmes instituted in Colombia and elsewhere from the 1970s (Escobar, 1995). The habitus of small farmers was reconfigured through the requirement imposed on the peasantry of filling in on paper a detailed account of techniques, practices and action. The microspaces of subjects thus became disciplined in the space of the farm through the requirement to record the 'correct' practices for the gaze of the development institution. Health measures such as the spraying against fleas, shown in the illustration from Andean Peru (plate 11.1), provides further evidence that the types of body envisioned in national development are expected to reach certain

Plate 11.1   Modern hygiene in the Andes

state-endorsed standards. Relying upon discourses which dichotomize between backwardness/progress, 'other'/Western, modern/pre-modern, such practices of hygiene-as-power discipline the embodied subject, placing it within a frame whereby such practices become acceptable.

Resulting from the focus on embodied subjectivities under modernity, the body has become the 'primary physical site of personal identity' (N. Smith, 1993: 102). Therefore the will to psychic order rests upon the power to negotiate and manage social difference in the boundaries between subjects. Identity construction has now widely been acknowledged as an ongoing and contested process on which geographies and their associated powers impinge (Pile and Thrift, 1995). Thinking through the spatialities of power also implies that identity construction rests upon the disciplining of bodies within certain sites, which then resonate with meaning for the interpellated subjects. Yet in the terrain of resistance, there are other places and imaginative geographies which provide for other, distinctive, dispositions of their subjectivity and practices. For certain subjects marginalized by prevalent discourses, alternative subjectivities and habitus rest in turn upon the situating of the body in spaces which have been reconfigured/reimagined. For example, the emergence in the social spaces of the US–Mexico borders of a *mestiza* (mixed race, European and Indian) feminist identity rests in part on the excavation of interstices of autobiography (M.B. Pratt, 1984). It rests upon the placing of the raced, colonized, classed (and sometimes raped) body of the *mestiza* within a critical geopolitics (Anzaldúa, 1987). The constant ordering work of nation, race and gender nevertheless leaves interstices from which other orders, other geographies can be imagined and spoken. The hybridity which comes to rest upon the disciplined body does not, in other words, close off other avenues and other agendas for change; the power effects of marginalization leave – despite their attempts otherwise – spaces at the margin from which to create different visions (hooks, 1994).

The process of repositioning the body within the practices and discourses of power can result in personal (and inevitably political) engagement with other spaces and their subjects. In her discussion of black-descent American women raised in 'white' families, Twine (1996: 222) demonstrates how these women's white identities were not only 'enacted under specific demographic and social conditions' but also (something which is not drawn out) mapped out onto the white geographies of American suburbia. Suburban white identities were transformed when, as young adults, the women began university careers, and saw their comfort in the 'white' spaces of dominant US society contested by politicized African American colleagues. In this space, 'racial' identities were destabilized, in some cases resulting in a radical shift to a 'black' racial (and political) identity. Returning to the issue of biopolitics, Twine (1996: 221) interestingly points out how the 'construction of "white" identity [for these women] is an interpretative framework which privileges "individualism" and racial neutrality', an aspect with its own connotations for bodies in space. As their identities shifted away from individualistic privilege, so too did their body-space (Duncan, 1996) lose its sense of 'home' and comfort. Displaced from their white-bodily security, women became unable to recuperate a lost sense of bodily freedom taken for granted under a 'white' identity. In summary then, affiliations with empowered discourses appear to impact upon bodily dispositions in space, not only in terms of 'time-geographies' and spatial mobilities (see for instance Massey, 1993) but also in terms of self-identity and embodied securities.

Embodiments thus engage with – and are produced by – the co-ordination by power effects of subjects and their bodies. Embodiments are the outcome and the effect of the disciplining of people, a disciplining which results from the co-ordination of space, place and society by groups invested with power. The disposition, attitudes and practices of embodiments can be surveyed, organized and regularized; yet, as we have seen, such practices of power are constituted in the context of certain geographies – both imagined and material – around which discursive and practical alignment is constantly attempted.

Race/ethnicity

The making of races through which to order the colonial encounter is well documented by now (see, among others, Young, 1995; Stoler, 1995; Stepan, 1991), yet the changing spatialities of power to which it gave rise, and the corresponding patterns of resistances, have yet to be traced in detail. Segal and Handler (1994) have highlighted the simultaneous emergence during the late eighteenth century of racialized colonialism in the South and 'nations' in the North, thereby finally laying to rest the idea that the nation state form lies outside the power effects of 'race' as an ideological and political construct. In the post-colonial setting, the new twists given to racializations under the name of national unity and 'cohesion' demonstrate that the process of 'inventing' (dis)empowered racial categories is far from over, and can spill over into violent confrontations between groups so constituted. Overall, the racial projects (Winant, 1994) of states draw upon the power effects of categorizations and embodied boundaries between groups, through which disciplining orders can be organized. Yet the state's racial projects are countered by the racial projects of those subjected to these same racial fictions, in a dynamic of resistance, appropriation and reordering.

The forging of new racial categories, and the disciplining of bodies thereby constituted, were the aim of colonial administrations and categorical systems, from the early sixteenth-century colonial presence in

South America through to the nineteenth-century environmental racialisms. Whilst in the early years geography as a discipline did not have a professional stake in such racializations, by the nineteenth century modern geography and modern colonialism came together in the cartographics of racism (Godlewska and Smith, 1994; Livingstone, 1991).

While the local Western racializations via mapping are now well known among geographers, the ways in which these professionalizations and racializations came together in the South are perhaps less widely recognized. To give one illustrative example, we can look to events in Peru. Faced with defeat in a war with Chile in the 1880s, Peruvian geographers turned to a project of overcoming the 'racial and environmental factors which [they] saw as limiting the prosperity of the country' (Orlove, 1993: 308). Following a Humboldtian[1] agenda of measurement and ideas of environmental determinism, the topographies of the Andean mountains were constituted simultaneously as racialized societies: in other words, mountains meant Indians, which in turn meant blocks to progress and modernity (Orlove, 1993). The 'spatial incarceration of the native' (Appadurai, 1990: 10) through the academic discipline of geography subsequently shaped wider cultural debates around nation and development, generating their own spatialities of power that continue until today (for instance, Radcliffe, 1996b).

Yet the socially constituted and malleable boundaries around racial groups can be appropriated and reoriented by those subject to racialization by such practices. Whereas in pre-colonial Andean Latin America, social affinities nucleated around the communities or *ayllus* even under Inca conquest, the Spanish colonial state created two 'republics' – one of Spaniards, the other of Indians. In the to-and-fro of colonial violence and resistance, the invented category of 'Indian' gave seventeenth-century Andeans a means by which to forge alliances. Silverblatt (1995: 285) traces how Indianness became deeply oppositional to Hispanicization in this period and informed widespread rebellions, starting with *Taki Onqoy* ('dancing sickness') of 1565. Although at the very centre of the racially ordered colonial project, the racializations provided:

> a new way for Andeans to cast themselves and their social universe. Andeans put these classifications into nativism's service, as 'Indians' caught some of the spirit of the church militant and the modern state-categorical, spreading out beyond traditional *ayllu* [village] boundaries and forging alliances between *kurakas* [indigenous leaders] and peasants. (Silverblatt, 1995: 285)

In the contemporary period, states are attempting to reinvent racialized categories around ethnicized narratives of origin and worth (cf.

A. Smith, 1991). Constituted more and more through relations of globalization and the domestication of difference, states can increasingly be conceptualized as multi-ethnic, variably diasporic communities actively constituted through the practices of nation building (see below) into 'imagined communities' (Anderson, 1991). Yet even with the 'new indigenism' of Andean republics we still see the division between 'raced' others and the 'national' self. For example, in the main Ecuadorian ethnographic museum, diverse indigenous groups are labelled and (re)presented as cultural icons, yet the constitution of nationhood around whiteness and *mestizaje* (the creation of racial mixtures) goes unremarked. The disciplining of ethnicized people into the cartographics of the museum thereby reinforces the marginalization of such groups, by denying them the status (even the hybrid status) of fully authoritative citizenship. Although given the vote, people marked as 'indigenous' are not imagined as fully national.

The representational work done around racial difference has a long history in Latin America (Rabasa, 1993) and – given their disposition in space (the imaginative space of readers' minds, and the public spaces of cities and monuments) – racial differences have functioned to reinforce boundaries between subjects and the power effects to which subjects are exposed. Over time, texts and figures produced by various intellectuals, writers, travellers and missionaries have shaped the polyvalent images of indigenous populations in Latin America (Muratorio, 1994a: 10–13). While the iconographic and textual representations are transformed over time, revealing changing attitudes and disciplinary impulses towards indigenous populations, they become signs of power and demarcate the spatialities of power behind their production.

In summary, the power effect of racialization can be said to result from the disposition across space – material and representational – of certain disciplining projects, which include practices and legal provision for migration, citizenship and marriage, as well as the discursive and representational aspects of inculcating meaning and value. The practices of determining who can marry whom, or immigrate where, attempt to shape the flows through which diasporic populations are made and/or resisted. Yet the powers and incarcerating effects of such practices are only made meaningful through the creation, diffusion and reinterpretation associated with discursive, aesthetic and representational work. The constitution of 'races' is thus inherently spatial as well as being socially constructed.

Nations: creating territorial power effects

By means of power relations, the nation state attempts to provide closure and boundedness to its own project, the substantiation of territorial affiliations coincident with the borders of the state (cf. Radcliffe and Westwood, 1996). Geographical practices, resting on the territorial and socio-spatial inventories of bounded nations, are central to the state's techniques of power. The 'imagined geographies' upon which a social sense of identity rests (Said, 1978) can be manufactured and circulated by the state, through its institutions, orders and discourses, and can provide the basis for the 'collective internalization of a territorial identity' (Escolar et al., 1994: 352). Oriented towards such an end, state-led practices and discourses actively intervene to inculcate such an identity, utilizing representation, visualizations, poetics and disciplinary power to reinforce the state's power-filled spatialities. However, as with the other powers discussed above, such a project generally remains unfulfilled, challenged by distinct voices and practices of 'popular national identities' (Radcliffe and Westwood, 1996). Yet because of the relatively limited stock of national symbols and discourses, official and popular geographies of identities may be interconnected and mutually constituting. In Latin American countries, the centrality of territorial issues to the social representations of nationality is increasingly well documented, and provides evidence for the overlapping of geopolitical imaginations and popular imaginative geographies (Hepple, 1992). Again, the Ecuadorian case provides an interesting perspective on these issues, which leads on to a discussion of the Argentine case.

Various state institutions elaborate and refine ideas of sovereignty, the differing roles of regions in national development, as well as nationalist histories (often connected to territorial issues; see below). Within such representational and discursive orderings, geographical professionalism and geographical skills have often provided the knowledge/power with which to carry these forward (Hooson, 1994). Moreover, the state reinforces the 'obviousness' of the national territory through the creation of the palimpsest of the national map, which is 'logoized' into an immediately recognizable symbol (Anderson, 1991). In such practices, representations and discourses, there are literal maps of national sovereign territory, yet the crucial effect of state power is to create resonances around such texts which elicit certain responses and 'structures of feeling' among citizens. The surveillance offered by the map *tout court* is thereby complemented by the instantiation of its validity and 'thinginess' in the recipient population. Citizens are corralled into certain identities through the creation of discursive power effects around the lines on the map. These structures of feeling are shaped by spaces and practices such as state schooling and a national educational curriculum, as well as imageries diffused by the media to the general population. Such institutions, and the practices they oversee, thereby build up a national imaginative geography, an imagined space in which other practices in the name of the state (interventions in other imagined and material geographies) are justified and legitimated, in the name of the 'fatherland'.

In Ecuador, the armed forces – with their monopoly of cartographic and geographical knowledge – and the state educational system (with specific curricular content, and routines for children), as well as the broader textual and visual representations created by intellectuals, politicians and elites, all create particular resonances and behaviours concerning the territory with which people identify as citizens. Despite the ideological work put into such imagery, the geographical imagination of citizens remains cross-cut by other meaningful places; the geographies of identities of citizens thus remain partially informed by other spatialities of power. In the Ecuadorian case, the nationwide indigenous movement directly resists the state's notion of territorial sovereignty, going so far as to produce alternative cartographic representations – other lines on the map for Other spatialities of power (Radcliffe, 1996a).

In the curriculum for geography and history, taught in all Ecuadorian schools regardless of their religious or funding status, pupils are taught from a young age that they are Ecuadorian and that this identity has certain imaginative geographies. The claims to Amazonian territory by reference to colonial laws, and to discoveries by Ecuadorian citizens/colonial subjects, are further reinforced by the widespread diffusion of school maps showing the pre-1941 national borders, rather than the contemporary reality (Peruvian control over substantial Amazon areas). Such spatio-historical narratives are combined with explicit calls to contemporary young citizens to carry forward the sovereignty claims of the country; 'it is the duty of the present and future generations to demand our rights over the Amazon and its riverside territories' says one textbook (see Radcliffe, 1998: 281). The teaching of geography is explicitly associated by children and adults with the teaching of 'Ecuadorian-ness' or *ecuatorianidad*, in which pupils acquire a love for the landscapes and territory of the country, a sense of the borders' histories, in addition to knowledge about the roles of different subnational regions in economic development. In other words, people's horizons are brought into line with the cartographics (and emotions) of territorial sovereignty, through practices, discourses and representations.

Imagining national territories in pedagogic material originates with the professionalized geographers of the Ecuadorian armed forces, who constitutionally are awarded full control over cartographic and mapping practices. As in other Latin American countries, the twentieth century is characterized by the coming together of military interests, geopolitical concerns, and the professionalization of geography as a discipline. Starting in the 1920s with a mapping project to inventorize the country's natural resources, the Ecuadorian military has consolidated its position as the generator of visual imageries and knowledge of the nation state. The authority of such productions is endorsed by powers instantiated by representational (military buildings carry national maps) and judicial powers (penalties for the production, distribution and sale of non-official maps can reach sixteen years' imprisonment). Although the national map does not have the constitutional endorsement of being a national symbol (compared with the flag, anthem and shield), it is mass-reproduced and imbricates Ecuadorian citizens in discourses around the truncated and mutilated nature of the national territory (Radcliffe, 1998). Throughout (Latin) American countries, school children have long saluted the national flag at the start of the school day.

School teaching revolves around the memorization by children (future citizens) of the geography of the country, and the moments in its history when that sovereignty was threatened. Collective and individual dispositions are regulated and reiterated via institutions such as the state and the church (Cohen, 1993; cf. Billig, 1995). The centrality of territorial issues to state power and to popular imaginative geographies is also found in Argentina, where the inculcation of a nationalist territorial imaginary among citizens has a long (and apparently successful) history. In Argentine schools, children salute the national flag as it is raised each morning, replay key commemorative dates and heroes, and sing patriotic songs. History and geography lessons inculcate knowledges of pre-twentieth-century South American experiences, and draw upon structures of feeling which depict the Falklands/Malvinas islands as part of the 'heart'/*corazón* of Argentina (Cutts et al., 1992). Social psychological research on Argentine schoolboys[2] demonstrates that such disciplining associations of nation with territory result in certain interpretative schemas among young people. Around two-thirds of Argentine schoolboys surveyed believed that questions of territorial sovereignty were legitimate reasons for war. Moreover, their knowledge of national territorial geographies (including the Falklands/Malvinas islands) was extensive, significantly higher than that of English schoolboys of the same age and class (Cutts et al., 1992). In other words, nationalist Argentine structures of feeling are articulated on the basis of extensive politicized knowledge of national territory, the bringing into alignment of patriotic feelings with the knowledge of the territory.

In summary then, the instantiation of state power rests crucially on the creation and reproduction of imaginative geographies and their associated 'trajectories of affiliation' (Desmond, 1993: 104). The discursive and material practices of the state are inherently spatialized, at the level of agendas and in the objectives articulated through these power effects. The relation between such cognitive training and the geopolitical decisions by states has recently been explored by geographers (Dijkink, 1996), yet on a more quotidian level such practices and their connotations also shape popular imaginative geographies, as shown in the Argentine example (also Radcliffe and Westwood, 1996).

Yet such geographical dispositions of feeling and organization do not remain unchallenged, given the working through of multiple perspectives from which to view state power. Popular geographical imaginations may coincide with official spatialities, as the Argentine case above illustrates, yet among other social groups, alternative visions and spaces are created. Popular geographies may attempt to 'redraw the map' of state power, by generating alternative affiliations to territory/place or by challenging the discursive and representational grounds upon which state power is reproduced, while clearly in a hybridized setting – in which the boundaries between popular, official and resistant projects are blurred – new cross-cutting practices can emerge and be reproduced. In such popular constructions, place may act as a resource, anchoring social and political identities around which new socialities and new spatialities can emerge (Gupta and Ferguson, 1992; Fog Olwig and Hastrup, 1997).

In Latin America, new imaginative geographies are associated with such non-state groups as indigenous movements, new social movements and women's organizations. Indigenous confederations in Ecuador utilize cartographic practices and mapping not to reinforce state-instituted identities, but to articulate and establish a different vision of nation and citizenship. The primary activity in which the Ecuadorian indigenous movements articulate their perspective is in the negotiations over land rights and land use. Using the judicial system (at times with international lawyers and allies), indigenous federations present petitions and lobby government and oil companies to present their land-rights claims. Conducted in Spanish, this political process entails the production of maps, cartographic representations of their identity and place, for the state's legitimation and recognition of their demands. Topographic teams, trained by German non-governmental organizations, have surveyed and mapped the Amazon territory of indigenous populations, using the cartographic techniques and conventions of their military counterparts (Radcliffe, 1996a). In one case, the lands of nineteen indigenous communities covering a total of some 1.1 million ha were mapped, a project which was one of the most coherent proposals for restructuring geographies and power in the continent. The Ecuadorian state eventually granted the communities land title to the disputed area, although the sovereign rights to the subsoil remain with the state, an aspect which is greatly criticized by indigenous federations concerned with environmental degradation.

While there are certain continuities with colonial creole mappings of the state, the contemporary imaginative geographies of belonging to Ecuador are much more complex. The state has attempted to utilize a series of practices and discourses to create a regularized relationship between territory and identity, yet the interpretations of what this geography represents and entails remain diverse. In official versions of a national imaginative geography, the visualization of national belonging has taken a particular, and arguably central, role. The use of the map-as-logo and official spatialities – instantiated in representations, discourses and cartographic practices – illustrates this well.

As globalization and deterritorialization reorient and reconstitute relations in and through space, so too the nature of state spatialities of power is transformed. Demonstrations of the national uniqueness of place and 'trajectories of affiliation' to those places may call up more disciplinary and authoritarian responses from states, whose cultural authority rests upon particularly bounded spatialities. Yet the resistances of non-official and popular imaginative geographies to state powers continue, and articulate alternative spatialities and societies.

Narratives of history and commemorations

The writing of history in line with nationalist interpretations and identifications has been well covered by historians (for instance, Gillis, 1994; Hobsbawm and Ranger, 1983), yet the fact that these narratives rest upon and draw from spaces and places and their connotations has not been analysed to the same extent. In other words, the temporal narratives of power interface with spatialities of power. Class and racialized power relations are instantiated through these narratives, which in turn are endorsed by the implicit referencing to powerful groups.

The gendering of such historical narratives adds a further twist. Female subjects are represented ambiguously in the imaginative geographies of nationhood, acting in some commentators' eyes as the domesticated ground, a figure for nostalgia and 'home' within discourses around national progress (McClintock, 1995). In the analysis of newspaper articles and government policy documents in Ecuador, it is possible to see the reinforcement of certain notions of the nation state's

past by reference to gendered (as well as classed and racialized) spatialities (Radcliffe, 1996b; also Mills, 1996). Male and female figures
appear in the national Ecuadorian press to commemorate certain key
moments in national progressive history. Citizens, in their gendered
positions, are re-presented in these texts in particular ways, in certain
places and social relationships. The largest cities of the country, and
within them the bourgeois domestic and political spaces of family
homes, are highlighted, a discursive and representational spatiality
which reinscribes the racialized, class-bound and urban nature of state
power in Ecuador. White creole elite women are offered as contemporary role models to female citizens, through discourses which normatively construct an ideal image of national womanhood.

In the disciplining spaces of school, history curricula construct official histories as male narratives, whether these males are pre-Conquest
indigenous kings or the heroes of colonial and republican adventures.
While Manuela Saenz is popularly regarded as the most famous
Ecuadorian woman from history (Radcliffe and Westwood, 1996),
history is conveyed as a reflection of those currently in power, rather
than as a narrative of diverse struggles and interpretations. As mentioned above, the history of the national land is itself given a central
role, with the 'history of the borders' being a key element of classroom
history lessons. Providing an explanatory framework for constant
changes in territorial outline, such histories also instantiate structures of
feeling with regard to past injustices against the state, experienced as
grievances against the citizenship itself.

Monuments and plaques are another material outcome of discourses
around history and the state (Gillis, 1994). Playing on the additional
resonances around gender and race, such plaques are materializations of
state power and self-image, nodes around which power (effects) are
realized. Although in early post-independence Latin America indigenous
women could be represented in monuments (as well as on shields,
medals and money) in the first flush of post-independence liberalism,
the racialization of state power was increasingly mirrored in late
nineteenth-century monuments and statues of white, creole men. Where
women remain, they are cyphers of classical virtues or foils to the heroic
white masculinity of nationalist narratives, rather than reflections of
empowered female subjects (Muratorio, 1994a; cf. Radcliffe, 1997). By
the end of the nineteenth century, monuments in Ecuador were erected
to the male individual subjects, said to embody and re-represent progressive statehood – Bolívar ('The Liberator'), Sucre ('The true father of
the patria'). While such symbolism risked slipping away from nationalist claims to uniqueness (other South American republics erected statues
to Bolívar), the state's agenda of drawing parallels between Ecuador

and modernist Europe was more significant. The 'rampant statue-mania in Paris' of the nineteenth century highly impressed the commercial elites of Ecuador who lived and worked in that capital and cultured themselves there to modernity (Muratorio, 1994a: 10). In other words, the (post-) colonial ties and power effects filtered through to the disposition of national and urban spaces in Ecuador, yet drew on gendered and racialized embodiments to discipline and mirror back to citizens the state's powers. This mobilization of space – a mobilization which in turn depended upon the constitution of social groups – thus operated to 'discipline' subjects into particular dispositions into space. This example highlights the simultaneity of discursive, ideological and geographical work being carried out in the spatialities of power.

Conclusion

Power operates in the interstices of social reproduction, a reproduction which is channelled in certain orders and certain geographies, trailing in its wake (while simultaneously chasing) particular representational and discursive orders. The representational work of dominant groups attempts to co-ordinate their discursive construction of society-in-place with the patterns of socio-spatial organization, drawing the discursive/representational literally and metaphorically into line with the willed disposition of subjects. Such alignments rest upon political and ideological co-ordinates, a cartographic exercise in which constant energy is expended matching up representations, subjectivities and social organization. Whether at the scale of colonialism or of the practices of rural development, the disciplining of subjects around and through space is an integral component of the power exerted over people. The achievement of a common-sense co-ordination between discursive constructions and sociality is the goal. In other words, the constant repetition of practices and representations 'grounds' the daily, taken-for-granted habitus of power within certain locations (place). Moreover, the mobilization of flows and perceptions of connections (space) is laid down through the creation of discursive and representational dimensions, reinforcing the hegemony of certain dispositions of society and geography through the alignment of flows and their representation with the daily habitus of power. Power and its effects are thus very much about the arrangement and regularization of spaces – whether bodies, nations or 'rural areas' – while simultaneously about the creation of meaning around these spaces as places. In other words, space and place get called up in the discursive and representational aspects of power, the legitimating and meaning-ful dimensions which underpin power.

Nevertheless, the under*pinning* of power relations can shift subtly to the under*mining* of power's effects, in that the discursive and representational projects to order society are comprised of, and depend upon, ongoing practices, with all the messiness and incompleteness that practice entails. In the interstices of multiple social relations, contradictions can arise which begin to allow for a challenge to, an opposition to, the prevailing socio-spatial relations. But such challenges cannot be predicted, whether they are to be explicit resistances in the public political arena, or the often-hidden discursive, representational and/or daily practice which results in rerouting power effects. Power's geography of operation is thus mirrored by – overlain by – another geography of interactions and social relations which do not run along the grooves of established power, but create their own spaces and places. If the discursive and representational work of power is analogous to a cartographic exercise – with the claims to power gaining visual counterparts – then disruptions to the will to order may be analysed as deliberate and focused acts of reorientation of the 'map', or the outcome of taken-for-granted habitus which does not engage with the will to power but operates in those places 'unseen' by the cartographics of power.

That both of these trends can be called resistance reflects the current paucity of adequate terms available to geographers and other social scientists. But the main point is that the binary of domination and resistance is no longer useful in our analysis of power relations; the binary of power/not power has been replaced by an attempt to unpick the intricacies of interrelationships (even dependencies?) of certain wills to order with countervailing orders and dispositions, and the engagements of representational and discursive dimensions to power which end up creating new power (effects). For example, the appropriation (another less than adequate term for a range of interpretative and discursive projects) of representational and/or discursive elements indicates a constant power-play between different social subjects, which can be illustrated most succinctly by cases where a previously derogatory term (gay, queer, black) is used in resistances to power. Moreover, the practices of power – the quotidian operations to place objects and subjectivities in relation to each other – operate unevenly over space. Such uneven processes and results arise from the engagement of social relations with the spatial and located nature of power relations. Most crucially, this spatiality to power means that the disposition of subjects and relationships across space is exposed simultaneously to differing powers and effects, so that the achievement of an order remains always on the horizon.

Beyond the spatiality of power, geographers have also become increasingly aware of the complex and diverse social relations which substantiate power. Rather than viewing people as having or not having power, the analysis – following that developed above, concerning power's representation and resistance – has increasingly focused in on individuals' multiple positionings within power relations. This has two main implications for geographers' understanding of power. First, and most uncontroversially, individuals' positionality in the spatial habitus of social relations differs, and hence their perspective on the operations of power(s) varies: viewed from one angle, a relationship is power, from another it is resistance or indifference to that power. Subjects therefore can be differentially positioned regarding power's effects. A diversity of positionings *vis-à-vis* power relations is thus given in the relationships which make up society.

Second, the very positionalities of subjects – individuals' own relationship to power relations – rests in part on their insertion into the social landscape of power. In other words, the social markers of difference – whether gender, age, race or nation – around which people identify and live their lives are in themselves markers invested with power, reinforced through the representational and discursive construction of difference and opposition. Geographical analysis comes in at this point by arguing that these forms of difference are constituted through the layout and flows of social interactions, creating a social cartographics around which people take positions on the basis of 'difference'. The inscription of difference – social reproduction along power-saturated lines that attempt to deny hybridity and mutual constitution – is one dimension of the spatiality of power, in the sense that the mapping out of difference onto place and landscape through the spatially defined daily routines of social groups and individuals (and representational and ideological work done around it) means that social difference acquires its own spatiality and representational power.

To conclude, in discursive, practical and ideological work done by power, the spatialities of power are spatialities of resistance, each operating simultaneously at a number of different sites, and constituting subjects in the interstices of cross-cutting orders: 'domination' and 'resistance' are relational. Despite this advance in our conceptualization of power, however, there is no easy decoding of the spatialities of power. The rejection of the binary of domination/resistance leaves in place the more difficult analytical and methodological aspect of identifying and explaining the different geographies and dynamics of coexisting (and at times contradictory) powers. This will require detailed and substantial ethnographic analysis, in which the nature of the will to order can be examined at the same time as the diverse types of disruption ('resistance') to that will to order are elucidated.

None the less, the debates around the representational and discursive dimensions to power – objects of analysis which by definition engage centrally with issues around the 'fuzziness', sequencing by scale, and spatiality of power – are now firmly established in geography and promise exciting work in the future.

Notes

1 The projection of drama onto the Andean landscape by Alexander von Humboldt (1769–1859), traveller and writer – an authorizing deployment of his own power – in time entered into the power games of the local elites, whose ideological positioning as a nationalist vanguard worked by comparing themselves favourably to Europeans and the republic's subalterns (M.L. Pratt, 1992).
2 Cutts et al. (1992) recognize the methodological and analytical implications of such a gendered study.

References

Anderson, B. (1991) *Imagined Communities: Reflections on the Origin and Spread of Nationalism*. London, Verso.

Anzaldúa, G. (1987) *Borderlands/La Frontera*. San Francisco, Aunt Lute Press.

Appadurai, A. (1990) 'Disjuncture and difference in the global political economy'. *Public Culture*, 2/2: 1–24.

Bhabha, H. (ed.) (1994) *The Location of Culture*. London, Routledge.

Billig, M. (1995) *Banal Nationalism*. London, Routledge.

Bourdieu, P. (1977) *Outline of a Theory of Practice*. Cambridge, Cambridge University Press.

Bowman, G. (1994) ' "A country of words": conceiving the Palestinian nation from the position of exile'. In E. Laclau (ed.), *The Making of Political Identities*. London, Verso, 138–70.

Cohen, A. (1993) *Self-Consciousness: An Alternative Anthropology of Identity*. London, Routledge.

Cutts Dougherty, K., M. Eisenhart and P. Webley (1992) 'The role of social representations and national identities in the development of territorial knowledge: a study of political socialization in Argentina and England'. *American Educational Research Journal*, 29/4: 809–35.

Desmond, J. (1993) 'Where is the "nation"? Public discourse, the body and visual display'. *East–West Film Journal*, 7/2: 81–110.

Dijkink, G. (1996) *National Identity and Geopolitical Visions*. London, Routledge.

Douglas, M. (1966) *Purity and Danger: An Analysis of Concepts of Pollution and Taboo*. London, Routledge and Kegan Paul.

Driver, F. (1985) 'Power, space and the body: a critical assessment of Foucault's *Discipline and Punish*'. *Society and Space*, 3: 425–46.

Duncan, N. (ed.) (1996) *Bodyspace*. London, Routledge.

Escobar, A. (1995) *Encountering Development: The Making and Unmaking of the Third World*. Princeton NJ, Princeton University Press.

Escolar, M., S. Quintero and C. Reboratti (1994) 'Geographical identity and patriotic representation in Argentina'. In D. Hooson (ed.), *Geography and National Identity*. Oxford, Blackwell, 346–66.

Fog Olwig, K. and K. Hastrup (eds) (1997) *Siting Culture: The Shifting Anthropological Subject*. London, Routledge.

Foucault, M. (1983) 'The subject and power'. In H. Dreyfus and P. Rabinow (eds), *Michel Foucault: Beyond Structuralism and Hermeneutics*. Chicago, Chicago University Press.

Giddens, A. (1990) *The Consequences of Modernity*. Cambridge, Polity Press.

Gillis, J. (ed.) (1994) *Commemorations: The Politics of National Identity*. Princeton NJ, Princeton University Press.

Godlewska, A. and N. Smith (1994) *Geography and Empire*. Oxford, Blackwell.

Gramsci, A. (1971) *Selections from the Prison Notebooks*. London, Lawrence & Wishart.

Gupta, A. and J. Ferguson (1992) 'Beyond culture: space, identity and the politics of difference'. *Cultural Anthropology*, 7/1: 6–23.

Harvey, P. (1996) *Hybrids of Modernity: Anthropology, the Museum and the Nation-State*. London, Routledge.

Hepple, L. (1992) 'Metaphor, geopolitical discourse and the military in South America'. In J. Duncan and T. Barnes (eds), *Writing Worlds*. London, Routledge, 136–54.

Hobsbawm, E. and T. Ranger (1983) *The Invention of Tradition*. Cambridge, Cambridge University Press.

hooks, b. (1994) *Outlaw Culture: Resisting Representation*. New York, Routledge.

Hooson, D. (1994) *Geography and National Identity*. Oxford, Blackwell.

Jonas, A. (1994) 'The scale politics of spatiality'. *Environment and Planning D: Society and Space*, 12: 257–64.

Latour, B. (1996) *We Have Never Been Modern*. London, Verso.

Livingstone, D. (1991) *The Geographical Tradition*. Oxford, Blackwell.

Massey, D. (1993) 'Power geometry and a progressive sense of place'. In J. Bird, B. Curtis, T. Putnam, G. Robertson and L. Tickner (eds), *Mapping the Futures: Local Cultures, Global Change*. London, Routledge, 59–69.

McClintock, A. (1995) *Imperial Leather: Race, Gender and Sexuality in the Colonial Contest*. London, Routledge.

Mills, S. (1996) 'Gender and colonial space'. *Gender, Place and Culture*, 3/2: 125–47.

Muratorio, B. (ed.) (1994a) *Imágenes y imaginarios: Representaciones de los indígenas ecuatorianos, Siglos XIX y XX*. Quito, FLACSO.

Muratorio, B. (1994b) 'Nación, identidad y etnicidad: imágenes de los indios ecuatorianos y sus imaginarios a fines del siglo 19'. In B. Muratorio (ed.) *Imágenes y imaginarios*. Quito, FLACSO, 9–24.

Orlove, B. (1993) 'Putting race in its place: order in colonial and postcolonial Peruvian geography'. *Social Research*, 60/2: 301–36.

Pile, S. and N. Thrift (eds) (1995) *Mapping the Subject: Geographies of Cultural Transformation*. London, Routledge.

Poovey, M. (1989) *Uneven Developments: The Ideological Work of Gender in Mid-Victorian Britain*. London, Virago.

Pratt, M.B. (1984) 'Identity: skin blood heart'. In E. Bulkin, M. Bruce Pratt and B. Smith (eds), *Yours in Struggle: Three Feminist Perspectives on Anti-Semitism and Racism*. New York, Long Haul Press, 9–63.

Pratt, M.L. (1992) *Imperial Eyes: Travel Writing and Transculturation*. London, Routledge.

Rabasa, J. (1993) *Inventing America: Spanish Historiography and the Formation of Eurocentrism*. London, University of Oklahoma Press.

Radcliffe, S. (1996a) 'Imaginative geographies, postcolonialism, and national identities: contemporary discourses of the nation in Ecuador'. *Ecumene*, 3/1: 23–42.

Radcliffe, S. (1996b) 'Gendered nations: nostalgia, development and territory in Ecuador'. *Gender, Place and Culture*, 3/1: 5–21.

Radcliffe, S. (1997) 'The geographies of indigenous self-representation in Ecuador: hybridity, gender and resistance'. *European Review of Latin American and Caribbean Studies*, 63: 9–27.

Radcliffe, S. (1998) 'Frontiers and popular nationhood: geographies of identity in the 1995 Ecuador–Peru border dispute'. *Political Geography*, 17/3: 273–93.

Radcliffe, S. and S. Westwood (1996) *Remaking the Nation: Place, Politics and Identity in Latin America*. London, Routledge.

Said, E. (1978) *Orientalism*. Harmondsworth, Penguin.

Scott, J. (1985) *Weapons of the Weak: Everyday Forms of Peasant Resistance*. New Haven CT, Yale University Press.

Segal, D. and R. Handler (1994) 'Introduction'. In D. Segal and R. Handler (eds), 'Nations, colonies and metropoles', Special Issue of *Social Analysis*, 33.

Silverblatt, I. (1995) 'Becoming Indian in the Central Andes of 17th century Peru'. In G. Prakash (ed.), *After Colonialism: Imperial Histories and Postcolonial Displacements*. Princeton NJ, Princeton University Press, 279–98.

Smith, A. (1991) *National Identity*. Harmondsworth, Penguin.

Smith, N. (1993) 'Homeless/global: scaling places'. In J. Bird, B. Curtis, T. Putnam, G. Robertson and L. Tickner (eds), *Mapping the Futures: Local Cultures, Global Change*. London, Routledge, 87–119.

Social Research (1993) Special Issue on 'Order', 60/2.

Soja, E. (1996) *Thirdspace: Journeys to Los Angeles and Other Real-and-Imagined Places*. Oxford, Blackwell.

Stepan, N. (1991) *'The Hour of Eugenics': Race, Gender and Nation in Latin America*. London, Cornell University Press.

Stoler, A.L. (1995) *Race and the Education of Desire: Foucault's 'History of Sexuality' and the Colonial Order of Things*. Durham NC, Duke University Press.

Twine, F.W. (1996) 'Brown-skinned white girls: class, culture and the construction of white identity in suburban communities'. *Gender, Place and Culture*, 3/2: 205–24.

Winant, H. (1994) *Racial Conditions: Politics, Theory and Comparisons*. Minneapolis, University of Minnesota Press.

Young, R. (1995) *Colonial Desire: Hybridity in Theory, Culture and Race*. London, Routledge.

Part V
Rethinking Space and Place

Introduction

Space and place are two of the central organizing terms of geography. They are concepts to which we seem endlessly to return, and with good reason, for not only are they fundamental to our discourses but, as each of the chapters in this part demonstrates, they are crucial organizing frames for the more general way in which we understand the world and make our way about in it. Moreover, both terms have recently been prominent on a number of agendas. Within the social sciences and humanities we have been witness to what has been characterized as 'the spatial turn': a greater recognition of the significance of the spatial and an increasingly generalized use of a vocabulary which draws on terms that heretofore have had their most common use within geography. For human geography as a discipline, this is an opportunity. What we want to do in this book is to respond constructively to the challenge, to argue for taking place and space seriously at a conceptual level. If we are going to argue for a thorough spatialization of social theory then we had better do some thinking about what that might mean.

There is another reason, too, why attention to these concepts is warranted now. This is that in one way or another, the agenda of 'politics' today also frequently revolves around spatial, or apparently spatial, issues. The greater attention paid to questions of identity/ difference/locatedness is one element of this. There is also the range of conceptual issues posed by 'globalization', by the so-called retreat to the local, by the ambiguities inherent in the tension between the desire to appreciate the specific (difference, the particular place) on the one hand and the dangers of a defensive and exclusive parochialism on the other.

All in all, it was relatively easy, therefore, to decide that this book should include a part dealing with space and place.

Yet, when all the authors had gone away and thought about things, and had submitted their drafts, we were surprised by what lay before us. Here was a rethinking which was more challenging – wilder even – than what we had expected. This is reflected in the wide range of approaches taken to the subject, in the variety of authors drawn upon, and in the wider context – of the situatedness of 'the intellectual' and the limited nature of the claims that can be made from that position – in which the reflections are set. Thinking in these ways about space and place is clearly part and parcel of re-evaluating much wider issues.

What emerges from the part is, first of all, an understanding of both space and place as *made*: through materially embedded practices, or through the social production of lived space, or as the result of a particular version of interrelational performance. To take just one example, globalization is not so much, or not only, a distancing over space as it is the creation of new spaces (and places). We make spaces and places, from the geopolitical to the intimate, in the living of our lives. And all identities/entities, likewise, are co-constituted with the making of these (time-)spaces. This is easier to say than it is actually to practise in the thinking through of our research. Most simply it means that 'place' and 'space', and places and spaces, should no more be taken as given than should any other objects of enquiry. This has a number of implications. Clearly it renders actual spaces and places themselves more immediately 'political'. But further, it can be argued that the fact that space and place are in a constant process of *being made* retains in them that element of openness which is essential to the imagination of the democratic-political. Moreover, taking seriously this relationality and the constant process of practising/performing space/place means two things (at least) for us as intellectuals. First, we ourselves are embedded in the making and practising of those relations. Second, and following from that, the very act of understanding/describing will itself alter the configuration of those relations. Both of those things in turn imply a necessary caution about 'knowledge claims', and lead us perhaps to be critical of those approaches which centre on discourse and representation either as the totality of what is available or as a level somehow detached from something else called the 'real practice of life'.

12

Performing Space

Gillian Rose

This chapter thinks about space as the articulation of collisions between discourse, fantasy and córporeality. Thinking of space as discursive, fantasized and corporealized must make the spatial highly complex and possibly contradictory; but I am more interested in the way such a thinking can also produce a more radically unstable notion of spatiality. How might the imperatives of desire flout the logics of discourse, for example? And if the corporeal is inscribed as a site of representation, and certain corporeal sites are invested with desire, how none the less might a body's materiality abut the discursive and psychic in a fleshly refusal of their demands? I want to think of space as articulating, giving form to, the conquests, alliances, raids, inscriptions, investments, revolts and refusals among the discursive, the fantasized and the embodied. In particular, I want to think of these three terms – discourse, fantasy and the bodily – as each providing a disruptive surplus to the others. I am, then, most intrigued by the critical possibilities of thinking of space as the form of these disruptive excesses, as extraordinarily convoluted, multiply overlaid, paradoxical, pleated, folded, broken and, perhaps, sometimes absent.

Discourse, fantasy and the bodily are three critical elements in the thinking of space, I suggest, because each participates in the relation between self and other (and there are many possible forms this relation may take). I am thus arguing that space is relational, as many geographers have done before. This relationality is not given between two pre-existing actants, however. Rather, I prefer to think of such relationalities as performed, as constituted through iteration rather than through essence. Judith Butler elaborates this notion of performativity in her discussions of the gendered, sexed and sexualized subject. Arguing that gender is 'performative – that is, constituting the identity it is purported to be', she goes on to say that 'gender is always a doing, although not by a subject who might be said to pre-exist the deed' (Butler, 1990: 25). I want to argue that space is also a doing, that it does not pre-exist its doing, and that its doing is the articulation of relational performances. Butler spatializes her discussion of the performance of heterosexual male and female bodies, for example, by discussing what she describes as its other production, the abject body that is not heterosexualized. These abject bodies, she says, are 'an abjected outside':

> This exclusionary matrix by which subjects are formed thus requires the simultaneous production of a domain of abject beings, those who are not yet 'subjects', but who form the constitutive outside to the domain of the subject. The abject designates here precisely those 'unlivable' and 'uninhabitable' zones of social life which are nevertheless densely populated by those who do not enjoy the status of the subject, but whose living under the sign of the 'unlivable' is required to circumscribe the domain of the subject. This zone of uninhabitability will constitute the defining limit of the subject's domain. (Butler, 1993: 3)

This particular performance of difference thus produces, Butler suggests, a specific space. Other performances of other kinds of relationality will produce other spaces. Space then is not an anterior actant to be filled or spanned or constructed, and to claim it is runs the risk of making a contingent spatial articulation of relationality foundational. Instead, space is practised, a matrix of play, dynamic and iterative, its forms and shapes produced through the citational performance of self–other relations.

Which is not to say that space is infinitely plastic. Certain forms of space tend to recur, their repetition a sign of the power that saturates the spatial in its three modalities. The repetitive consignment of those bodies inscribed as abject to spaces of unlivability, for example, is, as Butler argues, never inevitable. It is, though, a heavy tendency, a regulative citation of certain zones and their boundaries. Indeed, the spatiality of performative relations is precisely a symptom of the power that saturates every self–other encounter. This was Foucault's understanding of space, I think: space as a strategy of power. Writing in *Discipline and Punish* about the 'disciplinary machinery' that through the eighteenth century constituted the institutionalized 'docile body', Foucault wrote that 'this machinery works space' (Foucault, 1977: 143). The persistence of certain forms of spaces points to the persistence of certain configurations of power, and so 'the spatialising description of discursive realities gives on to the analysis of related effects of power' (Foucault, 1980: 70–1). Space is the medium of the flux and labour of power that Foucault analysed; his sense of power as play indicated not frivolity but the repetitive dynamism that Butler's notion of regulatory performance also evokes.

If space is a performance of power and we are all its performers in our everyday relationalities, the project of interpreting space critically cannot claim to be an effort to escape power. Instead, it must work towards its realignment in particular contexts. And this is my reason for choosing the three key terms of this chapter and for my concern with their incompatibilities as well as their intersections; I am led to them by recent feminist critiques of the exclusions of contemporary academic geographic discourse. I want to use the terms 'fantasy' and 'corporeality' to disrupt the certainties of discursive interpretation in geography. The turn to 'discourse' in the discipline seems to be working as a strategy for rendering everything legible to critique, and thus for producing critics who can read anything. It is thus enacting yet again the phallocentric prerogative of interpretation, the masculinist mastery of knowledge; and the disruptions of the bodily and of fantasy both remain outside the discipline as its inadequate but necessary and feminized others. I therefore want to place limits to what discourse and its interpretation can do by insisting on the insurgency of unconscious fantasy and on the refusals of the corporeal. This is not a simple challenge to the centre by confronting it with its margins, however. I am not suggesting that geography should 'get in touch with its feminine (out)side'. I want to distort this gendering and heterosexualizing of geography's exclusions by focusing in this chapter on the spatial articulations of sexual difference across all three of these terms. I want to perform a different difference.

Moreover, I would like these three categories to be both as tactically important and as essentially insignificant as one of them already is in geographical discourses: the body. For some feminist geographers, the corporealization of geographical discourse is crucial, because it marks the false universalism of so many geographic traditions. Once embodied as, for example, white, male, straight or able-bodied, the intrepid explorer and his voice of reason lose their transparent cloak of neutrality, and their academic practices can be interpreted as performances of specific bodily practices; it can be argued that the body of their work bears the traces of their other, more fleshy corporealities. And then for some feminist geographers, it becomes important to practise other embodiments, textual or otherwise: to produce other bodies of work. Both these corporealizations aim then to mark difference, to make the body work as a marker of inclusion or exclusion. But other invocations of the bodily by feminist geographers (and this is not a contradiction) are efforts to deny the corporeal as a site that consistently signifies self or other, centre or margin. The body in this work is a performance which is never certain of reproducing the same thing. Performance, as an iterative act, assumes that no performance outlasts the moment of its acting; the act must be repeated in order to reassert its meaning and power again. The body then, for all its heavy signification, actually means nothing at all.

This is the double role the body should play in the work of Judith Butler. Her weighty analysis makes the body massy, but the body should also dissipate under her critical attention. As is well known now, Butler wants to denaturalize the sexed body of Western heterosexuality by insisting that its differentiation into male/masculine and female/feminine is not inherent but is a process of making intelligible: ' "intelligible" genders are those which in some sense institute and maintain relations of coherence and continuity among sex, gender, sexual practice, and desire' (Butler, 1990: 17). Bodies, gendered identities and sexualities, she argues, are produced by the regulatory norms and practices of discourse and power. Butler here is not rehearsing the perhaps overly simple argument that *genders* are discursively constructed, for she is not suggesting that there is a 'body' that awaits its cultural encoding as male or female, masculine or feminine. Instead, she is arguing that *bodies* are discursive. Sexed bodies are not therefore the 'foundation' or 'ground' of sexuality; indeed, Butler rejects all claims that there is an 'outside' of discourse or a 'before' the symbolic of any kind. Drawing on Foucault's arguments in the first volume of *The History of Sexuality* and in his introduction to *Herculine Barbin*, she claims that the 'body' itself, anatomized as sexed, is a consequence of a certain discourse of (hetero)sexuality which produces male and female bodies as its apparent foundation. Butler also argues, however, that the discursive performativity of the sexed body is erased by what she calls its 'substantializing effects'; 'the subject is not *determined* by the rules through which it is generated because signification is *not a founding act, but rather a regulated process of repetition* that both conceals itself and enforces its rules precisely through the production of substantializing effects' (Butler, 1990: 145). Substantialization materializes sexed difference: it '*stabilizes matter over time to produce the effects of boundary, fixity, and surface we call matter*' (Butler, 1993: 9). And that process of substantialization is thus a performance through a particular space: the straight sexed body is performed as a bounded surface containing an interior. Other, unintelligible bodies are constituted as lacking these qualities, as abject, and consigned to zones of apparent unlivability. A particular corporeality is thus articulated through a particular space. Yet, as this substantialized body's unacknowledged twin, abjected bodies can subvert its certainties: 'this disavowed abjection will threaten to expose the self-grounding presumptions of the sexed subject, grounded as that subject is in a repudiation whose consequences it cannot fully control' (Butler, 1993: 3). For Butler, then, discourse both produces and threatens heterosexed bodies through the instabilities of that particular substantializing corporeal space.

Yet in the anti-foundational course of this desubstantializing account, the body – or rather, a body – nevertheless starts to condense weightily and to mark Butler's text. The form of the body of her work has been criticized by some other feminists. In particular, there has been some discussion of the aloneness of Butler's theoretical body. Despite her crucial denaturalization of the bounded corporeality of the straight Western subject, Butler's own corpus seems strangely marked by that same corporeal topography. Her work appears to contain the very notion of the substantial sovereign subject (sovereign because an autonomous agent) and his body (sovereign over his own, bounded, corporeal territory) that she is at such pains to defy. Some critics make this complaint by arguing that Butler's discussion of drag as performance assumes performers who as active agents do indeed pre-exist the deed; but I think this underestimates Butler's emphasis on *regulative* practices. Other critics, however, have commented, more importantly for my purposes here, on the isolation of Butler's performing 'body'. Produced as bounded and able only to parody or multiply that boundedness, Butler's body is single, and this emphasis on its boundaries seems to negate any concern for its relations with other bodies. As Lynne Huffer points out, this body is thus entirely self-referential. 'Does the concept of response, and thus responsibility, even matter in theories of performativity?', she asks, and her answer is no: 'performativity denies the possibility of conversation between two people with different stories to tell' (Huffer, 1995: 27). Subversion is judged to have or have not taken place only by what Sagri Dhairyam (1994: 30) calls 'critic philosophers', like Butler herself. Butler's effort to make gender trouble thus seems, ironically, to be shadowed by its own twin: the active and, as Dhairyam points out, white sovereign subject.

This singular appropriation of critical judgement has been diagnosed by Joan Copjec (1994) as a symptom of Butler's refusal to acknowledge anything outside discourse. If all is discursive, all is also amenable to the critic who knows how discourse works; and if subjectivity is produced through discourse then all subjects can also be fully known. Copjec queries the ethics of this notion of the subject 'as calculable, as subject to laws already known, as manipulable', and suggests that, in its refusal to concede any radical alterity to the other, it is the foundation of many contemporary 'crimes against otherness' (Copjec, 1994: 21). Butler's reliance on 'discourse' has trapped her in its substantializing space in which all is made, and can be, intelligible; and in a stinging critique, Butler's theorized and fleshy discursive bodies become one, as Dhairyam (1994) argues that this performing body is none other than Butler's own masterly performance in the spotlight of academic superstardom.

Butler's corpus has been criticized for its imperviousness, then; it remains bounded by, formed through, the spatiality of the sovereign subject who masters himself and his others, even though rethinking relations between such sovereign body-subjects is one of the most pressing aims of contemporary Western feminisms. For Huffer, for example, bodies are never one but (at least) two because they should always be thought of in terms of relations between; as Teresa de Lauretis (1994) remarks, it takes two to make a lesbian, for example. These critics are sensitized to the intactness of Butler's borders, perhaps, by their own rather different understanding of corporeal geographies. Instead of Butler's space of boundaries and surfaces – bodily surfaces between the interior self and the 'exterior space' in which she performs (Butler, 1990: 140), boundaries between intelligible and abject – these feminists prefer to imagine a space of relation. How are bodies positioned in relation to each other? What kinds of connection do these positions make possible, thinkable, visible, tangible? And this again becomes a spatial question: what kinds of space articulate what kinds of corporealized relation? If a critical feminism should refuse to spatialize its practices through boundaries and zones, bodily or otherwise, for fear of enthroning the sovereign subject once more, what different kinds of space might be necessary?

The most sustained meditation on these questions is offered by Luce Irigaray. Irigaray rarely offers straight answers, nor does she place any faith in the straight answers of the sovereign subject's identity cards and autobiographies:

> The only response one can make to the question of the meaning of the text is: read, perceive, experience . . . *Who are you?* is probably the most relevant question to ask of a text, as long as one isn't requesting a kind of identity card or autobiographical anecdote. The answer would be: *how about you?* Can we find common ground? talk? love? create something together? What is there around us and between us that allows this? (Irigaray, 1993a: 178)

Irigaray imagines a space that might allow engagements between differences. As Huffer (1995) notes, for Irigaray this is an effort to construct an ethical space – which is also performed. For, like Butler, Irigaray is intensely interested in the regulatory fictions of phallocentrism and, like Butler, suggests that femininity is now the citation of phallocentric femininity but that this does permit subversion:

> To play with mimesis is, thus, for a woman, to try to recover the place of her exploitation by discourse, without allowing herself simply to be reduced to it. It means to submit herself – inasmuch as she is on the side of the 'perceptible', of 'matter' – to 'ideas', in particular to ideas about herself, that are elaborated in/by a masculinist logic, but so as to make 'visible', by an effect of playful repetition, what was supposed to remain invisible: the cover-up of a possible operation of the feminine in language. (Irigaray, 1985a: 76)

Unlike Butler, however (and Butler criticizes her for this), Irigaray is interested in attempting to constitute 'a possible operation of the feminine in language'. Irigaray works at the limits of discourse: 'I am going to make an effort – for one cannot simply leap outside that discourse – to situate myself at its borders and to move continuously from the inside to the outside' (1985a: 122). Her 'outside' discourse is what exceeds discourse (an 'outside' rejected by Butler) but which by reworking the symbolic can be made to signify.

Irigaray's reimagining of bodily morphology is one such effort, and it is made in conjunction with her analysis of the space through which phallocentrism produces its other (what Irigaray calls the feminine and what Butler terms the abject). This is a complex space, much more complex than Butler's zonality. Irigaray argues that the feminine is constituted as the unbounded space against which phallocentrism asserts its self, as formless and fluid matter: 'if there is no more "earth" to press down/repress, to work, to represent, but also and always to desire (for one's own), no opaque matter in which theory does not know herself, then what pedestal remains for the ex-sistence of the "subject"?' (1985b: 133). She also argues that the feminine is constituted through a containing space which can protect the phallocentric self against that matter: space can be 'a play to achieve mastery through an organized set of signifiers that surround, besiege, cleave, out circle, and out-flank the dangerous, the embracing, the aggressive mother/body' (Irigaray, 1985b: 37). Irigaray's geo-morphology refuses this mastering of femininity into either volume or amorphousness. And in early essays she wrote about, re-embodied, the female lips as corporeal signs of a differently spatialized relationship between self and other. She has also used other figures to serve similar ends: thresholds, mucus, hysterics, angels ... 'in my view, there are no a priori principles' (in Whitford, 1991: 191). The lips (of) which (she) speak(s) are corporealized but not essentially so. They perform constantly: 'woman "touches herself"' all the time, and moreover no one can forbid her to do so, for her genitals are formed of two lips in constant contact'. The lips are thus 'neither one nor two', they have an 'incompleteness of form' that evades phallocentrism's mechanics of solids and its other, its flow of liquid matter (1985a: 26). Neither active nor passive, neither completely fused nor absolutely distinct, this morphology eludes the bipolar spatiality divided between tumescent solid and abject liquid. 'No ground subsists. But no abyss either' (1985a: 213). The lips are a figure that performs an imaginary geography between women: it articulates a space that allows women, decontained yet differentiated, to speak among themselves in a way which is not a simple reversal of phallocentrism:

> Between our lips, yours and mine, several voices, several ways of speaking resound endlessly, back and forth. Once is never separable from the other. You/I: we are always several at once. And how could one dominate the other? impose her voice, her tone, her meaning? One cannot be distinguished from the other, which does not mean that they are indistinct. You don't understand a thing? No more than they understand you. (Irigaray, 1985a: 209)

Irigaray is trying to work through a space in which the separateness of identity does not entail closure, exclusion and imprisonment, where women can be separate yet still connect, 'without eternal strife and without a lethal fusion' (in Whitford, 1991: 115). The bodily in its fleshiness becomes a resource for that project, material that can be used to articulate a space different from the arrangements of phallocentric discourse. Thus there may be a geography of corporealized space that does not entail solid shape, boundaries, fixity, property and possession, whether of the self or of others. It may be possible to embody a space that allows a different kind of betweenness.

What impels Irigaray's discussion? Desire.

For Butler, that answer is both 'a cultural impossibility and a politically impracticable dream' (1990: 30). Butler (1990) adopts Foucault's critique of psychoanalytic accounts of desire and claims that desire is not outside the arena of symbolic law since that law itself produces desire; it follows that, for her, placing political faith in anything extradiscursive is an absurdly utopian strategy. She implies that psychoanalytic feminists follow the logic of that law too slavishly, both by believing that desire is beyond discourse and by overestimating the efficacy of the phallocentric law of the symbolic. I have already suggested though that Butler's allegiance to discourse reproduces in her own work the subject, who both is intelligible and makes others intelligible, that she aims to disrupt by citing its unintelligible other. I now want to suggest again that to distort this pernicious dualism, the performative does indeed require theorizing beyond, as well as in, the discursive.

As Copjec points out, Butler's position leaves her with no means to explain the imperative of discursive performance:

> What we are provided with . . . is a description of the effect of the inherent failure of discourse – a riot of sense in which one meaning constantly collides with another; a multiplication of the possibilities of each discourse's meaning – but no real acknowledgement of its cause: the impossibility of saying everything in language. We repeat, Freud taught us, because we cannot remember. And what we cannot remember is that which we never experienced, never had the possibility of experiencing, since it was never present as such. It is the deadlock of language's conflict with itself that produces this experience of the inexperienceable (which can neither be remembered nor spoken); it is this deadlock which thus necessitates repetition. (Copjec, 1994: 24)

Copjec insists that the subject is not fully knowable, not fully discursive, because it is formed at the limits of discourse; it is thus marked by the finitude of discourse.

These comments remind me of Irigaray's labours at the edge of discourse. Irigaray is enough of a psychoanalyst not to attempt to erase that edge; it is constitutive of meaning after all, and without it all would be psychotic confusion. However, I think she is interested in reworking the way sexual difference is currently structured around it, and she is certainly interested in disrupting that particular structuring by reimagining the strategies and tactics it induces. If 'their stories constitute the locus of our displacement. It's not that we have a territory of our own; but their fatherland, family, home, discourse, imprison us in enclosed spaces where we cannot keep on moving, living, as ourselves' (Irigaray, 1985a: 212). Irigaray instead is searching for something else, 'acceptance of an open sea that cannot be mastered, of a multiplicity irreducible to one' (in Whitford, 1991: 215). She might be looking, for example, for a space of desire.

> Our age will have failed to realize the full dynamic reserve signified by desire if it is referred back to the economy of the *interval*, if it is situated in the attractions, the tensions, and actions occurring between *form and matter*, but also in the *remainder* that subsists after each creation or work, *between* what has been identified and what has still to be identified, and so on. (Irigaray, 1993b: 8)

Irigaray's discussion of the lips may be understood as an articulation of desire. Not of identification, the desire to be the other; but of desire, the wish to be in relation to the other because she is different.

In her book *The Practice of Love*, Teresa de Lauretis elaborates this distinction. In so doing, she offers another spatial articulation of desire as a relation between difference as part of her attempt to explain why, if it takes two to make a lesbian, lesbian lovers are not 'simply, so to speak, two women in the same bed' (1994: 232). 'Desire', she says, 'is a tension toward the other(s), a drive toward something or someone outside the self' (1994: 234). Desire is the impossible-to-satisfy relation towards what Copjec describes as 'that which we never experienced', the 'experience of the inexperienceable'. De Lauretis goes on:

> The signification and representation of that tension necessitates a signifier ... it is this sign that signifies, for the subject, the object's existential otherness, difference and distance from the self. Or so it seems to me, not in deference to psychoanalytic theory, but by the long-mediated intellectual conviction that Freud's theory of desire, for the most part and as I now understand it, does account for my experience. (de Lauretis, 1994: 234)

As in so much of her work, de Lauretis implies here that the spatial articulates (sexual) difference and desire. 'Difference' becomes 'distance' from the self. Yet this distance and its placing 'outside the self' are not an interval, to use Irigaray's term. This is not a distance measured in the space between the sovereign phallocentric subject and his bounded other. De Lauretis theorizes this distance not through the phallocentric desire for control, but through a fantasized desire that produces (at least) two lesbian women. In her use of 'fantasy', de Lauretis follows Laplanche and Pontalis and explores the particular spatiality of lesbian fantasy. The specific fantasy in question is hers, a point I will return to: the fantasy performed by Sheila McLauglin's film *She Must Be Seeing Things*, and in particular a scene in which two lovers parody heterosexual roles. De Lauretis describes her own pleasure in this scene, with its 'symbolic space of excess and contradiction that the role, the lack of fit, the disjuncture, the difference between characters and roles make apparent in each of them, and the scenario or imaginary space in which that difference configures a lesbian subject-position' (1994: 110). Fantasy is that 'imaginary space'. Fantasies are the *mise-en-scène* of desire; they are the scenarios, the settings, the articulations of desire, impelled by the search for an irretrievably lost object. De Lauretis is particularly interested in the space of the subject as the spectator of her 'own' lesbian fantasy. She argues that since the subject is at once watching the fantasy and participating in it, the subject is simultaneously inside and outside the scene. The spectator is 'a subject seeing herself and yet not seeing herself, a subject not placed in either one of the terms of fantasy but looking on, outside the fantasy scenario and nonetheless involved, present in it' (de Lauretis, 1994: 96). The fantasy thus both divides and is permeable, and the subject is correspondingly both doubled and split. De Lauretis suggests that it is this structure, this doubling-and-splitting space, that articulates lesbian desire in contemporary heterocentric conditions. Like Butler, then, de Lauretis suggests that the excessive parodying of straight masculinities and femininities can be reframed as a lesbian fantasy – as her own relation to that scene in *She Must Be Seeing Things* suggests. Desire may deregulate (heterocentric) discourse, deform and displace its spaces.

But, unlike Butler, de Lauretis argues that this re-vision is undertaken by a particular kind of spectator in a specific performative relation: a spectator who herself desires such a scene, and in desiring performs the divided and permeable space that articulates her as lesbian. For de Lauretis, the lesbian spectator must be able to see the gap between her desire and the parodied hetero desire; the spectator is herself doubled by her participation in the performance yet split by her knowledge that it is just that, a performance of something not quite right for her. And while thus formally specifying the spatiality of relational lesbian desire, de Lauretis is also quite clear that there will be some spectators, including lesbian spectators, whose desire remains quite unmoved by the content of a particular scenario; she refuses to generalize the effects of any particular fantasy, and this is an important moment in her argument, given the ethical criticisms of Butler's performative subject. The particular forms of disruptive, perverse desires, de Lauretis suggests, are relationally performed depending on the specificities of the subject:

> her or his psychic and fantasmatic configuration, the places or positions she or he may be able to assume in the structure of desire, but also the ways in which she or he is located in the social relations of sexuality, race, class, gender, etc., the places she or he may be able to assume in the social. (de Lauretis, 1994: 129)

In this more ethical account, the subversive success or failure of a performance rests on the specificities of the performance and its spectators. A particular performance of fantasy may disrupt certain of the laws of heterocentric discourse for some people, while leaving them intact for others.

Moreover, de Lauretis takes care to emphasize that fantasies are always imagined through culturally available signs. Indeed, in the final pages of *The Practice of Love*, she turns to Foucault and suggests that while he describes discursive practices that 'implant sexuality into the social subject', she is more concerned in her psychoanalytic account with the 'subjective mechanisms through which implantation takes' (de Lauretis, 1994: 309). She wants to know how lesbian desire is performed and her answer involves, but does not elide, discourse and desire in the spatiality of their particular lesbian intersection. Nor does she neglect the bodily. In her effort to shift the phallocentrism of psychoanalytic theorizing, she simply claims that the lesbian is performed not in some kind of relationship with the phallus, but in relation to a desire for an other woman's body: 'what the lesbian desires in a woman ... is indeed not a penis but a part or perhaps the whole of the female body, or something metonymically related to it, such as physical, intellectual or emotional attributes, stance, attitude, appearance, self-presentation – and hence the importance of clothing, costume, performance, etc. in lesbian subcultures' (de Lauretis, 1994: 228). The body too, in its discursive, psychic and corporeal modalities.

The body then is entangled with fantasy and discourse; fantasy mobilizes bodies and is expressed through discourse; and discourse, well, discourse is disrupted by fantasy and interrupted by the bodily. And all of these relations are articulated spatially; their performance produces space. I make this suggestion not because I think it may be true, but because it seems useful. I find it useful both as a means of understanding complex performances of phallocentric space and as a way of thinking, dreaming and practising other spaces that carry other ways of producing differential relations.

Acknowledgements

This chapter owes a great deal to conversations with postgraduate students; I would like to thank Sally Hodgson, Sue Lilley and, especially, David Woodhead.

References

Butler, Judith (1990) *Gender Trouble: Feminism and the Subversion of Identity*. London, Routledge.

Butler, Judith (1993) *Bodies That Matter: On the Discursive Limits of 'Sex'*. London, Routledge.

Copjec, Joan (1994) 'Sex and the euthanasia of reason'. In Joan Copjec (ed.), *Supposing the Subject*. London, Verso, 16–44.

de Lauretis, Teresa (1994) *The Practice of Love: Lesbian Desire and Perverse Sexuality*. Bloomington, Indiana University Press.

Dhairyam, Sagri (1994) 'Racing the lesbian, dodging white critics'. In Laura Doan (ed.), *The Lesbian Postmodern*. New York, Columbia University Press, 25–46.

Foucault, Michel (1977) *Discipline and Punish: The Birth of the Prison* (trans. Alan Sheridan). London, Allen Lane.

Foucault, Michel (1980) *Power/Knowledge: Selected Interviews and Other*

Writings 1972–77: Michel Foucault (ed. Colin Gordon, trans. Colin Gordon, Leo Marshall, John Mepham and Kate Soper). Brighton, Harvester Press.

Huffer, Lynne (1995) '*Luce et veritas*: towards an ethics of performance'. *Yale French Studies*, 87: 20–41.

Irigaray, Luce (1985a) *This Sex Which Is Not One* (trans. Catherine Porter). Ithaca NY, Cornell University Press.

Irigaray, Luce (1985b) *Speculum of the Other Woman* (trans. Gillian C. Gill). Ithaca NY, Cornell University Press.

Irigaray, Luce (1993a) *Sexes and Genealogies* (trans. Gillian C. Gill). New York, Columbia University Press.

Irigaray, Luce (1993b) *An Ethics of Sexual Difference* (trans. Carolyn Burke and Gillian C. Gill). London, Athlone Press.

Whitford, Margaret (ed.) (1991) *The Irigaray Reader*. Oxford, Blackwell.

13
Thirdspace: Expanding the Scope of the Geographical Imagination

Edward W. Soja

My purpose here, and in the writing of *Thirdspace: Journeys to Los Angeles and Other Real-and-Imagined Places* (1996), is to encourage the development of a different way of thinking about space and the many associated concepts that compose, comprise and infuse both the inherent spatiality of human life and what is being described in this volume as 'Human Geography Today'. In encouraging geographers and others to 'think differently' about such familiar notions as space, place, territory, city, region, location and environment, I am not suggesting that you discard your old and familiar ways of thinking, but rather that you question them in new ways that are aimed at opening up and expanding the scope and critical sensibility of your already established spatial or geographical imaginations.

In this chapter, I compress what I have written in *Thirdspace* into five summative arguments or theses. Each is rather boldly stated, addressed specifically to an audience of human geographers, and expansive and open in its implications for human geography today. The brief commentaries following each statement amplify and I hope help to clarify the fundamental points being made, while at the same time providing cumulative and fugue-like variations on the many ways of defining Thirdspace. There is no singular definition presented for this different way of thinking about space and spatiality, but rather an open-ended set of defining moments, every one of which adds potential new insights to the geographical imagination and helps to stretch the outer boundaries of what is encompassed in the intellectual domain of critical human geography.

THESIS I: Contemporary critical studies in the humanities and social sciences have been experiencing an unprecedented spatial turn. In what may in retrospect be seen as one of the most important intellectual developments in the late twentieth century, scholars have begun to interpret space and the spatiality of human life with the same critical insight and interpretative power as have traditionally been given to time and history (the historicality of human life) on the one hand, and to social relations and society (the sociality of human life) on the other.

Few would deny that understanding the world is, in the most basic sense, a simultaneously historical and social project. Whether in writing the biography of a particular individual or interpreting a momentous event or simply dealing with the intimate routines of our everyday lives, the closely associated historical and social (or sociological) imaginations have always been at the forefront in the effort to gain practical and informative knowledge of the subject at hand. This has been especially true in the development of critical thinking within the broadly defined human sciences, where the express purpose is to gain knowledge that is useful and beneficial, if not emancipatory, in its cumulative effect.

Without reducing the significance of life's inherent historicality and sociality, or dimming the creative and critical imaginations that have developed around their practical and theoretical understanding, a third critical perspective, associated with an explicitly spatial imagination, has in recent years begun to infuse the study of history and society with new modes of thinking and interpretation. As we approach the *fin de siècle*, there is a growing awareness of the simultaneity and interwoven complexity of the social, the historical *and the spatial*, their inseparability and often problematic interdependence. It is this important 'spatial turn', as it is now being described, that I associate with the emergence of a Thirdspace perspective and an expansion in the scope and critical sensibility of the geographical imagination.

These new developments revolve, in large part, around what can be described as an *ontological shift*, a fundamental change in the way we understand what the world must be like in order for us to obtain reliable knowledge of it. For the past two centuries, ontological discussion has focused primarily on the temporal and social characteristics of human existence, on what can be described as the existential relations between the historicality and sociality of being or, more concretely, of being-in-the-world. There were earlier attempts, by such critical philosophers as Martin Heidegger and Jean-Paul Sartre, to give to this existential being and to its dynamic expansion in the notion of 'becoming' a pertinent spatiality, but until very recently this spatiality remained fundamentally subordinated to the dominant dialectic of historicality-sociality, the interplay between what might more collectively be called the making of histories and the constitution of societies. Today, however, the inherent and encompassing spatiality of being and becoming is beginning to be more forcefully recognized than ever before, injecting an assertive third term into the ontology of human existence. This momentous development is creating what I have described, reflecting this assertive 'thirding', as an ontological *trialectic* of spatiality-sociality-historicality, or more simply, a three-sided rather than two-sided way of conceptualizing and understanding the world. Stated somewhat differently, the social production of human spatiality or the 'making of geographies' is becoming as fundamental to understanding our lives and our life worlds as the social production of our histories and societies.

Figure 13.1 is an attempt to capture this now three-sided relation in visual form. A different rendering appears in primary colours on the cover of *Thirdspace*. Within this configuration are three interactive relationships that apply not only to ontology, but also equally well to all other levels of knowledge formation: epistemology, theory building, empirical analysis and praxis, the transformation of knowledge into action. There is not only the longstanding historicality–sociality relation that has been the dominant focus of Western critical thought for at least the past two hundred years, but also the relation between sociality and spatiality that I described some years ago as the 'socio-spatial dialectic'; and the relation between historicality and spatiality, time and space, that gives rise to a substantive spatio-temporal or geohistorical dialectic that I explored in some detail in *Postmodern Geographies* (1989) and again in *Thirdspace*, most directly in chapter 6, 'Re-Presenting the Critique of Historicism'.

The key to understanding the 'trialectics of being', and a major reason why the reassertion of critical spatial thinking is of transdisciplinary importance and not just confined in its impact to geographers, architects, urbanists, and others for whom spatial thinking is a primary professional preoccupation, lies in the absence of any *a priori* privileging of the three terms. Studying the historicality of a particular event, person, place or social group is not intrinsically any more insightful than studying its sociality or spatiality. The three terms and the complex interactions between them should be studied together as fundamental and intertwined knowledge sources, for this is what being-in-the-world is all about. Making theoretical and practical sense of the world is best accomplished by combining historical, social and spatial perspectives. Specialists (historians, geographers, sociologists) may focus more deeply on one of these modes of thinking, but when this is done in ways that exclude significant attention to the other two existen-

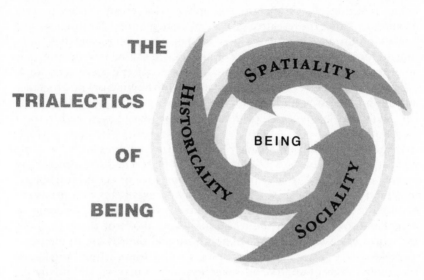

THE

TRIALECTICS

OF

BEING

Figure 13.1 The trialectics of being
Originally published in Soja, *Thirdspace* (1996), p. 71.

tial dimensions there is the danger of silencing too much of what matters in human life, of falling into narrow-minded historical, social or spatial-geographical determinisms. Practicality and inclination may dictate that we emphasize one of the three fields over the others, but we must always try to maintain a critical consciousness that is aware of and open to the potentially equivalent powers of all three working interdependently together.

The very nature and social timing of this ontological 'restructuring', however, involve at least a temporary highlighting, if not a cautious privileging, of spatiality. This is not because spatiality is intrinsically more important but because it has until recently been relatively peripheralized in the humanities and social sciences and especially in the construction of critical social theory. In *Postmodern Geographies* and in *Thirdspace*, I pointed specifically to a deep tradition of historicism as a primary reason for the diminishment of critical spatial thinking. Unfortunately, this has been frequently interpreted, most often by geographers I might add, either as an attempt to reduce the importance of historical analysis, a kind of anti-history that verges on spatialism; or else as a failure to recognize that good historians have always been sensitive to space and geographical analysis. I cannot emphasize enough that my spatial critique of historicism is not an anti-history, an intemperate rejection of critical historiography or the emancipatory powers emanating from the creative historical imagination. Historians have always produced some of the best human geographies and they continue to do so today. My critique of historicism can be best described as an attempt to *rebalance* the fundamental trialectic of historicality-sociality-spatiality, to make all three modes of thinking operate together at 'full throttle' at every level of knowledge formation, without any one being inherently privileged, or diminished for that matter, with respect to the others.

If the current transdisciplinary spatial turn continues with the same intensity as it has in the 1990s, a point may be reached when there may no longer be a need to accentuate the importance of the critical spatial imagination or to emphasize the space-blinkering effects of a persistent historicism or sociologism. In the same way that we have come to accept that everything in the world and every mode of thinking about the world has a significant social and historical dimension, to the point where we have historians and sociologists of science, of philosophy, of geography, even of sports and sexuality, so too may we eventually recognize the inherent and encompassing spatiality of everything and every mode of thought, with human geographers accepted on equal terms with social scientists and historians as critical analysts of the human condition. But this moment has not yet arrived. The project of rebalancing the trialectic still has a long way to go, and the persistent powers of historicism and sociologism (or should we describe it as 'socialism'?) in constraining the development and expanding scope of the geographical imagination continue to be worth fighting against. But are the geographical imagination and human geography today up to this challenge? This brings me to my second argument.

THESIS II: The geographical imagination, especially as it has developed within the spatial disciplines, continues to be confined by an encompassing dualism, or binary logic, that has tended to polarize spatial thinking around such fundamental oppositions as objectivity v. subjectivity, material v. mental, real v. imagined, things in space v. thoughts about space. Expanding the scope of the geographical imagination to the breadth and depth that have been achieved for historicality and sociality, and hence rebalancing their critical empowerment, requires a creative deconstruction and rethinking of this bifurcation into two modes of spatial thinking and analysis.

Figure 13.2 summarizes visually a central argument in *Thirdspace* that pertains to what I call, following the ontological triad mentioned earlier, the

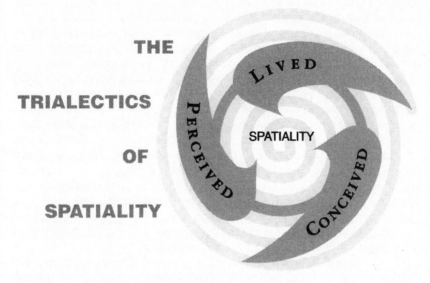

THE

TRIALECTICS

OF

SPATIALITY

Figure 13.2 The trialectics of spatiality
Originally published in Soja, *Thirdspace* (1996), p. 74.

'trialectics of spatiality'. It identifies in Thirdspace, here defined by Henri Lefebvre's notion of *espace vécu*, or 'lived space', an alternative mode of spatial enquiry that extends the scope of the geographical imagination beyond the confining dualism of what I describe as Firstspace and Secondspace epistemologies – or what Lefebvre refers to as spatial practices or 'perceived space' on the one hand, and the representations of space or 'conceived space' on the other. A few simple definitions help to explain the diagrammed relations, which mirror closely those of figure 13.1.

'Firstspace' (Perceived Space) refers to the directly experienced world of empirically measurable and mappable phenomena. This materialized spatiality, which presents human geographies primarily as outcomes, has been the dominant and familiar focus for geographical analysis, often to the exclusion of other ways of thinking about space and geography. For many, especially those who see geography as a formal science, this has been the only objective or 'real' space worth studying. It forms the geographer's primary 'text' or subject matter, and can be 'read' or explained in two broad ways. Endogenous approaches explain Firstspace geographies through accurate descriptions of patternings and distributions (as in the study of areal differentiation), the search for recurrent empirical regularities (the foundation of specifically spatial science), and the correlation or spatial covariation of one geographical configuration with another (the basic method of both idiographic and nomothetic geographies). The key point here is that empirical analysis, theory building and explanation remain internal to geography, that is, geographies are used to explain other geographies. Exogenous approaches explain material geographies by focusing on the underlying social or physical processes that produce them. Human geographies are seen here as the product or outcome of forces which are not in themselves geographical or spatial, but are derived from the inherent sociality and historicality that lie behind the empirical patternings, distributions, regularities and covariations. These approaches are particularly well developed in most critical forms of geographical thinking and interpretation, such as in the application of class analysis in Marxist geography or the analysis by feminist geographers of the space-shaping impact of patriarchy and masculinism. But various kinds of exogenous analysis, including those that use the physical environment as an explanatory variable, infuse all fields of human geographical enquiry.

'Secondspace' (Conceived Space), in contrast, is more subjective and 'imagined', more concerned with images and representations of spatiality, with the thought processes that are presumed to shape both material human geographies and the development of a geographical imagination. Rather than being entirely fixed on materially perceivable spaces and geographies, it concentrates on and explores more cognitive, conceptual and symbolic worlds. It thus tends to be more idealist than materialist, at least in its explanatory emphasis. If Firstspace is seen as providing the geographer's primary empirical text, then Secondspace represents the geographer's major ideational and ideological 'discourses', the ways we think and write about this text and about geography (literally 'earth-writing') in general. Although there is an epistemology to the study of Firstspace, it is in Secondspace that epistemological discourse receives the greatest attention. In the long history of geographic thought, Secondspace approaches have been turned to most often when mainstream Firstspace approaches have become too rigidly materialist and 'scientistic', as with the various critiques that emerged in response to the epistemological closures of positivist human geography. For Henri Lefebvre, however, Secondspace is not so secondary. He argues in *The Production of Space* (1991) that 'conceived space' is the dominant space in that it powerfully controls the way we think about, analyse, explain, experience and act upon or 'practice' human spatiality (or the 'making' of geographies). I cannot dwell on his argument here, but I suggest that it provides a very different way of approaching the subject matter that conventionally comprises what is called the history of geographic thought.

Most human geographers do not work at the extremes of these two approaches, but somewhere in between, conceiving of 'pure' material-ism/objectivity and idealism/subjectivity as opposite poles of a contin-uum of approaches. There has been a persistent tendency, however, to see Firstspace and Secondspace as together defining the whole of the geographical imagination, as encompassing in their varying admixtures all possible ways of conceptualizing and studying human geography and the spatiality of human life. This 'bicameral' confinement of the geo-graphical imagination, or what I call a Firstspace–Secondspace dualism, has been primarily responsible for the difficulty many geographers and other spatial thinkers have in understanding and accepting the deeper meaning of the ontological restructuring discussed earlier, and hence in comprehending 'Thirdspace' (Lived Space) as representing a call for a different way of thinking about human geographies. Instead of respond-ing to the growing spatial turn as a profound challenge to develop a new mode of understanding the spatiality of human life (human geo-graphy in its broadest sense) that is commensurate in scope and critical insight with life's intrinsic historicality and sociality, many geographers, pleased with the growing attention being given to their discipline, simply pour the new wine into the same old double-barrelled contain-ers, thus reinforcing the constraints and illusions of the Firstspace–Secondspace dualism. It is not surprising then that many of the primary sources for the reconceptualization of spatiality and the expansion in scope of the geographical imagination have been coming from outside the traditionally spatial disciplines. To find where this challenge to think differently about space was first and most cogently asserted brings us to my third argument.

THESIS III: A radical break from this confining dualism was initiated in France in the late 1960s, largely through the works of Michel Fou-cault and Henri Lefebvre. I describe their method of criticizing the Firstspace–Secondspace dualism as a 'critical thirding-as-Othering', and I attribute to their challenging geographical imaginations the origins of Thirdspace as a radically different way of looking at, interpreting, and acting to change the embracing spatiality of human life.

Drawing primarily from Lefebvre's major work *The Production of Space* (for a discussion of Foucault's 'heterotopologies', see chapter 5 in *Thirdspace*), we can see a very different picture of the scope and substance of the geographical imagination. For Lefebvre, the persis-tent dualism between mental and materialist approaches to space, or between what he called spatial practice and the representation of space, was a form of reductionism that was akin to that produced by many other 'Big Dichotomies' that run through the history of Western philosophy and social theory: subject–object, abstract–concrete, agency–structure, real–imagined, local–global, micro–macro, nature–culture, centre–periphery, man–woman, black–white, bourgeoisie–proletariat, capitalism–socialism. Confined in such a way, the geographical imagination could never capture the experiential complexity, fullness and perhaps unknowable mystery of actually *lived space*, or what he described somewhat cryptically (by intent?) as the Spaces of Representation (translated from the French as Representational Spaces).

Whenever faced with such Big Dichotomies, Lefebvre sought to break them open to new and different possibilities. As he would repeatedly say, two terms are never enough to deal with the real and imagined world. *Il y a toujours l'Autre.* There is always an-Other term, a third possibility that works to break down the categorically closed logic of the 'either–or' in favour of a different, more flexible and expansive logic of the 'both-and-also'. Note that this approach differs from seeking an 'in-between' position along the presumed continuum that connects the opposite extremes of the dichotomy, for such a positioning still remains within the totalizing dualism. Lefebvre seeks instead to break out from the constraining Big Dichotomy by introducing an-Other, a different alternative that both reconstitutes and expands upon the original opposition.

Such thinking was not unique to Lefebvre. It has been a feature of dialectical thinking from the ancient Greeks to Hegel and Marx, and has featured prominently in the more recent development of postmodern, poststructuralist, post-colonial and feminist critiques of modernism, of the persistent constraints and closures of modernist epistemologies, and of such 'closed' binarizations as those between agency and structure, man and woman, colonizer and colonized, etc. But Lefebvre was the first to apply this critical method comprehensively to the ways we think about, and practise, what he described as the production of space, or, in other words, the making of human geographies. In doing so, he also engaged in another philosophical (and political) project: the spatialization of dialectical thinking itself. Lefebvre called his approach *une dialectique de triplicité.* I have chosen to describe it as a *critical thirding-as-Othering*, retaining the capitalized emphasis on the Other.

Critical thirding-as-Othering creatively expands upon the dialectics of Hegel and Marx, moving beyond the presumed completeness and strict temporal sequencing of its classical framing in the form of thesis-antithesis-synthesis. Rather than a culminatory synthesis or a conclusive statement that can itself trigger another dialectical round of thesis-antithesis-synthesis, thirding introduces a disruptive 'other-than' choice.

This Othering does not derive simply and sequentially from the original binary opposition and/or contradiction, but seeks instead to disorder, deconstruct and tentatively reconstitute in a different form the entire dialectical sequence and logic. It shifts the 'rhythm' of dialectical thinking from a temporal to a more spatial mode, from a linear or diachronic sequencing to the configurative simultaneities and synchronies I have attempted to capture visually in the diagrams of figures 13.1 and 13.2. As Lefebvre described it, 'the dialectic today no longer clings to historicity and historical time, or to a temporal mechanism such as "thesis-antithesis-synthesis" ... To recognise space, to recognise what "takes place" there and what it is used for, is to resume the dialectic.' To underline his point and to avoid reducing the 'contradictions of space' only to the Firstspace–Secondspace dualism, he adds: '*We are not speaking of a science of space but of a knowledge (a theory) of the production of space* ... this most general of products' (Lefebvre, 1976: 18; emphasis in the original).

Lefebvre saw this thirding as the beginning of a heuristic chain of 'approximations' that builds cumulatively in an ever-expanding process of knowledge formation. There are no closures, no permanent structures of knowledge, no intrinsically privileged epistemologies. One must always be moving on, nomadically searching for new sources of practical knowledge, better approximations, carrying along only what was most usefully learned from earlier voyages. To avoid the dangers of hyper-relativism and a freewheeling 'anything goes' philosophy that is often attached to such radical epistemological openness, one must be guided by and committed to a challenging intellectual and political project. Thirding thus does not end with the assertion of a third term or with the construction of what some might describe as a holy trinity. Making practical and theoretical sense of the world requires a continuous expansion of knowledge formation, a radical openness that enables us to see beyond what is presently known, to explore 'other spaces' (see Foucault's *des espaces Autres* and 'heterotopologies') that are both similar to and significantly different from the real-and-imagined spaces we already recognize.

In this sense, Thirdspace (as Lived Space) is simultaneously (1) a distinctive way of looking at, interpreting, and acting to change the spatiality of human life (or, if you will, human geography today); (2) an integral, if often neglected, part of the trialectics of spatiality, inherently no better or worse than Firstspace or Secondspace approaches to geographical knowledge; (3) the most encompassing spatial perspective, comparable in scope to the richest forms of the historical and sociological imaginations; (4) a strategic meeting place for fostering collective political action against all forms of human oppression; (5) a starting point for new and different explorations that can move beyond the 'third term' in a constant search for other spaces; and still more to come.

> THESIS IV: Over the past decade, the most creative explorations of Thirdspace, and hence the most accomplished expansions in the scope of the geographical imagination, have come from the broadly defined field of critical cultural studies. Particularly prominent here has been the work of feminist and post-colonial critics who approach the new cultural politics of class-race-gender from a radical postmodernist perspective. One of the accomplishments of these scholars and activists has been to make human geography today more transdisciplinary than it ever has been before.

The African American writer and social critic bell hooks occupies a special place in widening the scope of the spatial imagination. Drawing inspiration and insight from the works of both Lefebvre and Foucault, she creatively enriches our understanding of lived space by infusing it with a radical cultural politics and new political strategies to deal with the multiple axes of oppression built around race, class and gender. Although she speaks specifically as a radical woman of colour, her words resonate with much broader implications for contemporary politics as well as for the practice of human geography. hooks does this in part by empowering *lived space* with new communicative meaning and strategic significance. For hooks, lived space and what I would describe as a Thirdspace consciousness provide a new political grounding for collective struggles against all forms of oppression, whatever their sources and at whatever geographical scale they are expressed, from the intimacies of the human body (what the poet Adrienne Rich once called the 'geography closest in') to the entrapments built in to the global political economy. What follows is a series of passages from hooks's most spatial work, *Yearning: Race, Gender and Cultural Politics* (1990), and especially from a chapter evocatively titled 'Choosing the Margin as a Space of Radical Openness':

> As a radical standpoint, perspective, position, 'the politics of location' necessarily calls those of us who would participate in the formation of counter-hegemonic cultural practice to identify the spaces where we begin the process of re-vision ... For many of us, that movement requires pushing against oppressive boundaries set by race, sex, and class domination. Initially, then, it is a defiant political gesture. (p. 145)

> For me this space of radical openness is a margin – a profound edge. Locating oneself there is difficult yet necessary. It is not a 'safe' place. One is always at risk. One needs a community of resistance. (p. 149)

I am located in the margin. I make a definite distinction between that marginality which is imposed by oppressive structures and that marginality one chooses as site of resistance – as a location of radical openness and possibility. This site of resistance is continually formed in that segregated culture of opposition that is our critical response to domination. We come to this space through suffering and pain, through struggle ... We are transformed, individually, collectively, as we make radical creative space which affirms and sustains our subjectivity, which gives us a new location from which to articulate our sense of the world. (p. 153)

It was this marginality that I was naming as a central location for the production of a counter-hegemonic discourse that is not just found in words but in habits of being and the way one lives. As such, I was not speaking of a marginality one wishes to lose, to give up, but rather as a site one stays in, clings to even, because it nourishes one's capacity to resist. It offers the possibility of radical perspectives from which to see and create, to imagine alternatives, new worlds. (p. 152)

Postmodern culture with its decentered subject can be the space where ties are severed or it can provide the occasion for new and varied forms of bonding. To some extent, ruptures, surfaces, contextuality, and a host of other happenings create gaps that make space for oppositional practices which no longer require intellectuals to be confined to narrow separate spheres with no meaningful connection to the world of the everyday ... [A] space is there for critical exchange ... [and] this may very well be 'the' central future location of resistance struggle, a meeting place where new and radical happenings can occur. (p. 31)

Radical postmodernism calls attention to those shared sensibilities which cross the boundaries of class, race, gender, etc., that could be fertile ground for the construction of empathy – ties that would promote recognition of common commitments, and serve as a base for solidarity and coalition ... To change the exclusionary practice of postmodern critical discourse is to enact a postmodernism of resistance. (pp. 27, 30)

Spaces can be real and imagined. Spaces can tell stories and unfold histories. Spaces can be interrupted, appropriated, and transformed through artistic and literary practice. As Pratibha Parmar notes, 'The appropriation and use of space are political acts.' (p. 152)

This is an intervention. A message from that space in the margin that is a site of creativity and power, that inclusive space where we recover ourselves, where we move in solidarity to erase the category colonizer/colonized. Marginality is the space of resistance. Enter that space. Let us meet there. Enter that space. We greet you as liberators. (p. 152)

In these eye-opening passages, there are many glimpses of a different kind of human geography, one that combines the grounded and politically conscious materialism of Firstspace analyses and the rich, often metaphorical representations of space and spatiality characteristic of Secondspace geographies; and at the same time stretches beyond their mere additive combination to create 'Other' spaces that are radically open and openly radicalized, that are simultaneously material-and-metaphorical, real-and-imagined, concretely grounded in spatial practices yet also represented in literary and aesthetic imagery, imaginative recombinations, epistemological insight, and so much more. hooks literally cracks open lived space to new insights and new expectations that extend well beyond the long-established boundaries of the traditional geographical imagination.

But it is to the specifically political implications of hooks's emphasis on 'choosing the margin as a space of radical openness' and her explicit but cautious adoption of a radical postmodernism that I wish to draw your attention, for it is this combination of an expansive Thirdspatial imagination, a strategic attachment to a new cultural politics of difference and identity, and a radical postmodernist critical positioning that has become the source of some of the best new writings emanating not just from radical women of colour such as bell hooks but from the wider fields of feminist and post-colonial criticism. Here is a brief sampling from chapter 4 of Soja (1996), 'Increasing the Openness of Thirdspace'. Page numbers refer to that chapter, not the original sources.

From the artist and urban critic Rosalyn Deutsche (1988), on the significance of geographically uneven development within the city and 'spatial design' as a tool for the social control of class, race and gender:

> Lefebvre's analysis of the spatial exercise of power as a construction and conquest of difference, although it is thoroughly grounded in Marxist thought, rejects economism and predictability, opening up possibilities for advancing analysis of spatial politics into realms of feminist and anti-colonialist discourse and into the theorization of radical democracy. More successfully than anyone of whom I am aware, Lefebvre has specified the operations of space as ideology and built the foundations for cultural critiques of spatial design as a tool of social control. (p. 106)

From Teresa de Lauretis's *Technologies of Gender* (1987), on moving the 'subject of feminism' beyond a simple Man/Woman dichotomy into a wider frame of cultural representations related to class, race and sexuality. Note how de Lauretis, like hooks, intertwines the material and metaphorical to define the importance of spaces on the margin:

> [We are looking at] the elsewhere of discourse here and now, the blind spots or space-off, of its representations. I think of it as spaces in the margins of hegemonic discourses, social spaces carved in the interstices of institutions and in the chinks and cracks of the power–knowledge appar-

ati ... It is a movement between the (represented) and what the representation leaves out or, more pointedly, makes unrepresentable. It is a movement between the (represented) discursive space of the positions made available by hegemonic discourses and the space-off, the elsewhere of these discourses ... These two spaces are neither in opposition to one another nor strung along a chain of signification, but they exist concurrently and in contradiction. (pp. 111–12)

Another newcomer to the spatial disciplines, Barbara Hooper, focuses her work on the disruptive interplay of bodies, cities and texts in an unpublished manuscript that focuses on 'The case of citizen Rodney King' (1994):

[T]he space of the human body is perhaps the most critical site to watch the production and reproduction of power ... It is a concrete physical space of flesh and bone, of chemistries and electricities; it is a highly mediated space, a space transformed by cultural interpretations and representations; it is a lived space, a volatile space of conscious and unconscious desires and motivations – a body/self, a subject, an identity: it is, in sum, a social space, a complexity involving the workings of power and knowledge and the workings of the body's lived unpredictabilities ... Body and body politic, body and social body, body and city, body and citizen-body, are intimately linked productions ... These acts of differentiation, separation, and enclosure involve material, symbolic, and lived spaces ... and are practiced as a politics of difference. (p. 114)

The geographer Gillian Rose brings home the critical power of the spatial feminist critique to break down the masculinist hegemony that continues to dominate the discipline. From *Feminism and Geography* (1993):

Social space can no longer be imagined simply in terms of a territory of gender. The geography of the master subject and the feminism complicit with him has been ruptured by the diverse spatialities of different women. So, a geographical imagination is emerging within feminism which, in order to indicate the complexity of the subject of feminism, articulates a 'plurilocality.' In this recognition of difference, two-dimensional social maps are inadequate. Instead, spaces structured over many dimensions are necessary. (p. 124)

Rose adds her own expansion of hooks's space of radical openness and what I have been describing as Thirdspace:

The subject of feminism, then, depends on a paradoxical geography in order to acknowledge both the power of hegemonic discourses and to insist on the possibility of resistance. This geography describes that subjectivity as that of both prisoner and exile; it allows the subject of feminism to occupy both the centre and the margin, the inside and the outside. It is a geography structured by the dynamic tension between such poles, and it is also a multidimensional geography structured by the simultaneous contradictory diversity of social relations. It is a geography which is as multiple and contradictory and different as the subjectivity imagining it ... a different kind of space through which difference is tolerated rather than erased. (pp. 124–5)

Gloria Anzaldúa, a poet and cultural critic of the lived spaces found along the US–Mexico borderlands, creates another form of 'plurilocality' around what she calls the consciousness of the *mestiza*, or *mestizaje* (1987), another way of being outside and inside at the same time:

> As a *mestiza*, I have no country, my homeland casts me out; yet all countries are mine because I am every woman's sister or potential lover. (As a lesbian I have no race, my own people disclaim me: but I am all races because there is the queer of me in all races.) ... I am an act of kneading, of uniting and joining that not only has produced both a creature of darkness and a creature of light, but also a creature that questions the definitions of light and dark and gives them new meanings. (pp. 128–9)

Anzaldúa's poetics also journey into theorizing space (1990):

> We need theories that will rewrite history using race, class, gender and ethnicity as categories of analysis, theories that cross borders, that blur boundaries ... Because we are not allowed to enter discourse, because we are often disqualified or excluded from it, because what passes for theory these days is forbidden territory for us, it is *vital* that we occupy theorizing space, that we not allow white men and women solely to occupy it. By bringing in our own approaches and methodologies, we transform that theorizing space. (p. 129)

Of all the cultural critics of Eurocentrism and post-colonialism, Edward Said has probably received the greatest attention from human geographers. Derek Gregory's excellent expansion upon Said's 'Imaginative geographies' (1995) provides us with the following observations from Said:

> Just as none of us is outside or beyond geography, none of us is completely free from the struggle over geography. That struggle is complex and interesting because it is not only about soldiers and cannons but also about ideas, about forms, about images and imaginings ... What I find myself doing is rethinking geography ... charting the changing constellations of power, knowledge, and geography. (pp. 137–8)

Finally, some passages from Homi Bhabha, whose fascinating work on the 'location of culture' and the notion of 'hybridity' is framed by his own conceptualization of a 'third space', similar to yet different from what is being defined as Thirdspace in this chapter. From 'The third space' (1990):

> All forms of culture are continually in a process of hybridity. But for me the importance of hybridity is not to be able to trace two original moments from which the third emerges, rather hybridity to me is the 'third space' which enables other positions to emerge. This third space displaces the histories that constitute it and sets up new structures of authority, new political initiatives, which are inadequately understood through received wisdom ... The process of cultural hybridity gives rise to something different, something new and unrecognisable, a new area of negotiation of meaning and representation. (p. 140)

Bhabha grounds his third space in the perspectives of postmodernism, post-colonialism and post-feminism, but urges us to be ready to go 'beyond', to cross boundaries, 'to live somehow beyond the border of our times'. From *The Location of Culture* (1994):

> It is significant that the productive capacities of the Third Space have a colonial or postcolonial provenance. For a willingness to descend into that alien territory – where I have led you – may reveal that the theoretical recognition of the split-space of enunciation may open the way to conceptualizing an *inter*national culture, based not on the exoticism of multiculturalism or the *diversity* of cultures, but on the inscription and articulation of culture's *hybridity*. To that end we should remember that it is the 'inter' – the cutting edge of translation and negotiation, the *in-between* space – that carries the burden of the meaning of culture ... And by exploring this Third Space, we may elude the politics of polarity and emerge as others of ourselves. (p. 141)

THESIS V: Continuing the project initiated by Lefebvre and expanding it in new directions that resound with more contemporary relevance, the new human geographers emerging from critical cultural studies are explicitly spatializing radical subjectivity and political practice, imbuing both with a critical spatial consciousness that extends far beyond what has existed in the past. Reflecting what was earlier described as an ontological shift and a critical thirding-as-Othering, these scholars are opening up a new and still relatively unexplored realm of radical political action centred and sited in the *social production of lived space*, a strategic choice that is aimed at constituting a community of resistance which can be as empowering and potentially emancipatory as those formed around the making of history and the constitution of human societies.

Never before have human geographies been given such transdisciplinary attention. But the best are human geographies of a different sort, more comprehensive in scope, more empowered and potentially empowering, more explicitly politicized at many different levels of knowledge formation, from ontology to praxis, from the materially concrete to the imaginatively abstract, from the body to the planet. They are made more 'real' by being simultaneously 'imagined'. The metaphorical use of space, territory, geography, place and region rarely floats very far from a material grounding, a 'realandimagined' that signals its intentional Otherness from more conventional geographies. Thirdspace as Lived Space is portrayed as multi-sided and contradictory, oppressive and liberating, passionate and routine, knowable and unknowable. It is a space of radical openness, a site of resistance and struggle, a space of multiplicitous representations, investigatable through its binarized oppositions but also where *il y a toujours l'Autre*, where there are always 'other' spaces, heterotopologies, paradoxical geographies to be explored. It is a meeting ground, a site of hybridity and *mestizaje* and moving beyond entrenched boundaries, a margin or edge where ties can be severed and also where new ties can be forged. It can be mapped but never captured in conventional cartographies; it can be creatively imagined but obtains meaning only when practised and fully *lived*.

For the past two centuries, radical subjectivity and progressive political action with regard to the unequal power relations associated with class, race and gender have revolved primarily around conscious interventions into the historicality and sociality of human life, around how societies make histories and organize their social relations and modes of production. For the most part, these struggles have tended to remain relatively confined to separate channels of collective identity and consciousness, with either class or race or gender (codified in such Big Dichotomies as Capital v. Labour, White v. Black, Man v. Woman) occupying entrenched and essentialized positions so politically and theoretically privileged that forming effective coalitions between these often chauvinistic and exclusive channels was extremely difficult. Even when linkages were formed, they tended to remain unstable, as each radical movement retained a distinctive and exclusive prioritization of its own particular binarized axis of oppression.

Inspired by the breakdown of these totalizing modernist political epistemologies (that is, the orthodoxies of Marxism, radical feminism and black nationalism) and the possibility of a radical postmodernism (a possibility which many on the left still refuse to recognize), a new socio-spatial movement or 'community of resistance' is beginning to develop around what I am describing as a Thirdspace consciousness and a progressive cultural politics that seeks to break down and erase the specifically spatial power differentials arising from class, race, gender, and many other forms of the marginalizing or peripheralizing (both pre-eminently spatial processes) of particular groups of people. Rather than operating in separate and exclusive channels, this new movement/community is insistently inclusive (radically open) and recombinative, searching for new ways of building bridges and effective political coalitions across all modes of radical subjectivity and collective resistance. In this coalition building, it is a *shared spatial consciousness* and a collective determination to take greater control over the *production of our lived spaces* that provide the primary foundation – the long-missing 'glue' – for solidarity and political praxis.

Coalition building is a long-established political strategy, but these progressive coalitions have formerly been mobilized in the largest sense primarily around taking collective control over the making of history and the way social relations of power and status are constituted and maintained; that is, to redress the inequalities and oppression produced in the historical course of societal development. The new coalitions retain these empowering sources of mobilization and political identity, but add to them a reinvigorated spatial consciousness and subjectivity, an awareness that the spatiality of human life, the making of human geographies, the nexus of space–knowledge–power also contain the sources of continued oppression, exploitation and domination.

This newly spatialized form of individual and collective struggle is still in its earliest stages and not yet a formidable force in contemporary politics. And it must be recognized that the new spatial politics is not exclusively confined to progressive forces. Indeed, conservative and neoliberal approaches to spatial politics in the new information age of globalization and economic restructuring have been significantly empowered all over the world over the past thirty years. This makes it all the more important for progressive thinkers and activists to set aside their internal conflicts over postmodernism (and geography) to find new ways to contend strategically with the postmodern right in the struggle to shape our contemporary worlds. We must recognize and participate in the expanding sites and communities of resistance and assertion that bell hooks and others invite us to enter, to move in consciously spatial solidarity and begin a process of re-visioning the future. This opportunity to reassert the expanded theoretical and strategically political importance of the critical spatial imagination may be what is most new and different – and most challenging and exciting – about human geography today.

References

Anzaldúa, Gloria (1987) *Borderlands/La Frontera*. San Francisco, Aunt Lute Press.

Anzaldúa, Gloria (ed.) (1990) *Making Face/Making Soul*. San Francisco, Aunt Lute Press.

Bhabha, Homi K. (1990) 'The third space: interview with Homi Bhabha'. In Jonathan Rutherford (ed.), *Identity, Community, Culture, Difference*. London, Lawrence & Wishart, 207–21.

Bhabha, Homi K. (1994) *The Location of Culture*. New York and London, Routledge.

de Lauretis, Teresa (1987) *Technologies of Gender: Essays on Theory, Film and Fiction*. London, Macmillan.

Deutsche, Rosalyn (1988) 'Uneven development'. *October*, 47: 3–52.

Gregory, Derek (1995) 'Imaginative geographies'. *Progress in Human Geography*, 19: 447–85.

hooks, bell (1990) *Yearning: Race, Gender and Cultural Politics*. Boston, South End Press.

Hooper, Barbara (1994) 'Bodies, cities, texts: the case of citizen Rodney King'. 80-p. unpublished ms.

Lefebvre, Henri (1976) *The Survival of Capitalism*. London, Allison and Busby.

Lefebvre, Henri (1991) *The Production of Space*. Oxford and Cambridge MA, Blackwell (trans. by Donald Nicholson-Smith of Lefebvre (1972) *La production de l'espace*. Paris, Anthropos).

Rose, Gillian (1993) *Feminism and Geography*. Cambridge, Polity Press.

Soja, Edward W. (1989) *Postmodern Geographies: The Reassertion of Space in Critical Social Theory*. London, Verso.

Soja, Edward W. (1996) *Thirdspace: Journeys to Los Angeles and Other Real-and-Imagined Places*. Oxford and Cambridge MA, Blackwell.

14
Spaces of Politics

Doreen Massey

Changing politics, imagining space

There are, of course, many ways of imagining space/spatiality. What I should like to imagine here is a space for the politics of our times. And in that context I want to explore some propositions about spatiality.[1]

What do I mean by a politics for our times? Briefly (for it will be elaborated later), I mean a radical commitment to the openness of the future, a recognition of multiplicities and difference, and a general alertness to the dangers of essentialist modes of conceptualization. There are other things of course, but for the purpose of this chapter I shall take these to be of prime significance.

Moreover, I want to argue, to be able to think this politics seriously it is necessary both to take spatiality seriously and to conceptualize it in a particular way. There are three elements to this reimagining of space (they do not map simply on to the three aspects of politics outlined above, but they are related).

1 I want to imagine that space is a product of interrelations. That is – probably uncontroversially – space is constituted through a process of interaction.

2 I want to imagine space as the sphere of the possibility of the existence of multiplicity; space as the sphere in which distinct narratives co-exist; space as the sphere of the possibility of the existence of more than one voice. Without space, multiplicity would be impossible. Moreover, the converse is also the case:

without multiplicity there can be no space. If space is the product of interrelations (my first point) then it must be predicated upon the existence of plurality. The very fact of interrelation entails the notion of multiplicity. Multiplicity and space are co-constitutive.

3   I want to imagine space as disrupted and as a source of disruption. That is, even though it is constituted out of relations, spatiality/space is not a totally coherent and interrelated system of interconnections.

It is worth dwelling for a moment on this set of propositions. For, although they may at least to some seem intuitively obvious, in fact, actually, space is often not thought of in this way at all. This is just the kind of idea at which, when put forth as a set of abstract propositions, the assembled company might nod and say yes of course and think no more about it. And this thinking no more about it is precisely a problem; because we then tend often *in practice* to adopt other approaches, other implicit conceptualizations, altogether at odds with what we have just so fervently agreed with in theory.

It is very common, for instance, to think of spatial variation but without really imagining co-existing difference. We talk and write often, for instance, of 'variations over space', income levels between regions, perhaps, or degrees of 'development' between countries. On the one hand – the minor point at this juncture – this implies space as a 'thing', 'over which' there can be variation. It implies a space which exists in its own right. And on the other hand – the more important point – it raises the question of how we conceive of those variations. In practice, implicitly, and often against our own theoretical pronouncements, such variations are often conceived as temporal rather than spatial. That is to say that regions with a lower per capita income are thought of as being 'behind' or 'backward', and countries with lower levels of 'development' (precisely!) are conceived as being underdeveloped, developing or newly industrializing. (It is a way of thinking clearly more typical of human geography than physical and, within human geography, is particularly characteristic of, though by no means exclusive to, economic geography.) What is going on in this kind of geographical imagination of spatial variation is that spatial differences are being thought of as temporal. Spatial differences are being reconvened in temporal terms.

This way of conceiving of spatial difference by occluding it is typical of many of the great modernist understandings of the world. The stories of progress, of development, of modernization, of the evolution through revolution from pre-capitalist through capitalist to socialist/Communist, share a geographical imagination which rearranges spatial differences into temporal sequence. In these geographical imaginations, countries of, say, the South (for these are generally imaginations emanating from the North) are conceived of not as different but as backward; or rather their difference consists (only) in the fact of their 'backwardness'. It is a powerful imaginary geography which – ironically – serves to occlude the real significance of geography. This reordering of co-existing (that is to say, spatial) differences into temporal sequence has important effects. Most significantly, it obliterates, or at least reduces, the real import and the full measure of the real differences which are at issue. It closes down multiplicity and the possibility of alternative voices. It is a kind of geographical imagination which fails to recognize the full import of spatiality.[2] Truly recognizing spatiality – I want to argue – necessitates acknowledging a genuinely co-existing multiplicity – a different kind of difference from any which can be compressed into a supposed temporal sequence.

For that kind of acknowledgement of multiplicity (and thus that kind of definition of difference) is, after all, no more than a kind of temporo-spatial version of that understanding of difference which sees others as really only a variation on oneself, where the 'oneself' is the one constructing the imagination. So, the countries of, say, the South of the planet, in these imaginations of progress emanating from the North, are not *really* different: they are just backward versions of us. A spatial (rather than a temporal) recognition of difference, in contrast, would acknowledge that 'the South' might not just be following us but might have its own story to tell. It would grant the other, the different, at least a degree of autonomy in that sense; it would grant the possibility of at least relatively autonomous trajectories. In other words, it would entertain the possibility of the existence of a multiplicity of narratives.[3]

Thus, on this reading, what is required for the constitution of the spatial is a degree of mutual autonomy, a genuine plurality. Above all, it implies the existence of trajectories which are not simply alignable into one linear story. It implies the necessary existence in the definition of spatiality/space of (previously) independent trajectories – that is to say, a multiplicity of narratives. An understanding of spatiality, in other words, entails the recognition that there is more than one story going on in the world and that these stories have, at least, a relative autonomy.

Moreover, the stress here is on 'relative'. The reference to independent trajectories does not imply a total lack of connection. Interconnection and relative independence are not simply opposed to each other. Rather, what is ruled out is the simple teleology of the one and only story.

Not all understandings of space, then, recognize it as the sphere of co-existing multiplicity. Indeed not infrequently the notion of 'difference' has been more associated with temporality, and read as difference-through-time. In consequence, the spatial is not appreciated as a sphere of active interaction. For a whole lineage of philosophers, space has been the realm of stasis, of the dead. For Bergson, for example (who remains a significant influence, for instance on Deleuze), it is time which is the dimension of the emergence of novelty, while space is the realm of fixity. For Bergson, space became associated with the 'science' with which he was embattled: a science which denied the open temporality he was struggling to assert and whose process of scientific production he came to interpret as 'spatialization'. Indeed, representation as a generic activity became associated with the spatial, an association which lives on strongly to this day. For Bergson 'the rational mind merely spatializes'; he thought in terms of 'the immobilizing (spatial) categories of the intellect' (Gross, 1981–2: 66, 62):

> For Bergson, the mind is by definition spatially oriented. But everything creative, expansive and teeming with energy is *not*. Hence, the intellect can never help us reach what is essential because it kills and fragments all that it touches. . . . We must, Bergson concluded, break out of the spatialization imposed by mind in order to regain contact with the core of the truly living, which subsists only in the time dimension. (Gross, 1981–2: 62)

Bergson asked himself 'what is the role of time?' and replied 'Time prevents everything from being given at once. . . . Is it not the vehicle of creativity and choice? Is not the existence of time the proof of indeterminism in nature?' (1959: 1331). 'Indeterminism', here, stands precisely for the openness of the future. However, although we might agree that time may be the medium within which change occurs, that does not mean that it is its cause. Why is there this 'creativity'? How does it happen? It cannot emerge from the immanent unfolding of some unitary, undifferentiated identity, because in that case the terms would already be given in the initial conditions. More than this, that kind of interpretation would be thoroughly essentialist. For a non-essentialist interpretation of difference-as-change, change must emerge from interrelations, and for there to be interrelations there must be multiplicity. Bergson may be right that time stops everything being given at once, but he takes his case too far. For there to be temporality (change) there must be interaction and therefore, in Bergson's terms, 'more than one thing'. And for there to be more than one thing (multiplicity) there must be space. Space and time (space-time) come into existence together.

And finally, and given that we imagine space in terms of interrelated multiplicities, there is still the third point: that these relations do not form a single, closed and interconnected system. Here, too, there is a counter-tradition. In this case, the strongest line of inheritance probably derives from structuralism. The early structuralists, in an attempt to escape the assumptions of cause in narrativity, and of 'progression from the savage to the civilized', turned to the concepts of structure, space and synchrony. Instead of narrative, structure; instead of diachrony, synchrony; instead of time, space. It was a move made with the best of intentions. And yet, in relation to space, it has left a legacy of assumptions and taken-for-granted understandings which have continued to this day to bedevil debate. For the structuralists' structures were not really spatial; they were analytical schemas. As Osborne puts it, 'Synchrony is not con-temporality, but a-temporality' (1995: 27). Moreover, the reason that these analytical structures are dubbed spatial is that they are established as a-temporal, as without time. It is, primarily, a negative definition and, again, one which reduces space to stasis. Further, the conceptual synchronies of structuralism, although based on 'relations', are relations imagined in a highly particular way. Above all, they are characterized by links within them, between their constituent elements, such that they form a completely interlocked system. They are closed systems. It is this aspect of the conceptualization which does most damage. For it robs 'the spatial' (when it is called such) of one of its most creative and disruptive characteristics: its happenstance arrangement-in-relation-to-each-other of multiple narratives. It is this crucial characteristic of 'the spatial' which constitutes it as one of the vital moments in the production of those dislocations which are necessary to the existence of an open politics and temporality.

The way space is being imagined in this chapter, then, flies in the face of some powerful and well-established positions. Space/spatiality in the argument of this chapter is the sphere of the meeting up (or not) of multiple trajectories, the sphere where they co-exist, affect each other, maybe come into conflict. It is the sphere both of their independence (*co*-existence) and of their interrelation. Subjects/objects are constructed through the space of those interrelations (and, although that is not addressed in this chapter, have their own internal space-times).

This mode of constitution, moreover, has further implications. It is now widely accepted in 'Western' human geography that 'space is socially constituted'. It is the product of the intricacies and the complexities, the interlockings and the non-interlockings, of relations from the unimaginably cosmic to the intimately tiny. And precisely because it is the product of relations, relations which are active practices, material and embedded, practices which have to be carried out, space is always in a process of becoming. It is always being made (see Massey, 1992). It is always, therefore, also in a sense unfinished. There are always connections yet to be made, juxtapositions yet to flower into interaction (or not), potential links which may never be established. 'Space', then, can never be that completed simultaneity in which all interconnections have been established, in which everywhere is already (and at that moment unchangingly) linked to everywhere else. There are always loose ends in space. It is always integrally space-*time*.

'Space/spatiality', then, (in the sense of a simultaneity) is not a closed system. Moreover it is also an 'open system' (or, better, not a 'system' at all) which entails a certain degree of the unexpected, of the unpredictable. There is always an element of 'chaos' in space. It is a chaos which results from those happenstance juxtapositions, those accidental separations, the often paradoxical character of geographical configurations in which – precisely – a number of distinct trajectories interweave and, sometimes, intersect. Space, then, as well as having loose ends, is also inherently disrupted.

Now, I want to go on in a moment to present a case for the relevance of this way of imagining space to what might be seen as recent shifts in the conceptualization of the political. But before doing that I want to point to one phenomenon which, in that context, must be seen as anomalous. This is that, for all the maligning of grand narratives that has gone on in recent years, there are many, even amongst those who would count themselves as amongst the most anti of the anti-modernists, who none the less have an easy recourse to what are, in effect, grand-narrative forms of thinking and – the real point in terms of the present argument – their concomitant effects in the suppression of the real force of co-existing spatial difference, and its attendant openness of the future.

Our brief example illustrates this point. 'Globalization' must be one of the most powerful terms in our current geographical imaginations. Most current accounts of this phenomenon, especially but not only in social and cultural studies, take economic globalization as a given. There may be debates about its degree, but there is no doubt 'it' is under way. With 'history' – for which read 'technological change' – 'globalization' is seen to be inevitable. It is just like modernity's story of progress: it has the inexorable inevitability of a grand narrative. And with that in turn comes yet again, just as in modernity's discourse, an imagining of spatial differences as temporal. Parts of the world's 'South' are not 'yet' drawn into the global village of electronic communications? Never mind; they soon will be. Soon they will, in this regard, be like 'us'. Once again, spatial differences are convened under the sign of temporal sequence. And once again the potential openness of the future is foreclosed in a tale of inevitability.

These, moreover, are not just conceptual effects; they are also political. For the impact of understanding spatial differences as 'really' a matter of being advanced or backward works to deny the possibility that there might be alternative stories. That, indeed, may be part of the political *point* in seeing things this way. The World Trade Organization, while it strives mightily to achieve globalization (in its particular neoliberal form), is also engaged in the maintenance of a discourse of its inevitability. In stories of this sort there is no space – precisely – to tell different stories, to try to follow another path (whether that be autarchic, Islamicist, socialist, or whatever). Neither, in the case of globalization for instance, are the 'differences' understood as being inequalities and structural divides produced within the very process of 'globalization' itself. This is not in fact simply a question of 'backwardness'; it is co-production. Even *within* globalization there are different trajectories. Conceptual and political can therefore come together. Imagining space as constituted out of difference and interrelations enables the political recognition of the possibility of alternative trajectories.

New spaces for new politics

Arguing about the meaning of concepts can have a variety of rationales. Soper (1995), among others, presents a strong argument against legislating (or trying to legislate, for the attempt will never succeed) on the meaning of concepts, and that position is accepted here too. However, as Soper also argues, one needs some kind of justification for adopting and arguing for one meaning over another. That too is agreed here. Soper's sphere of justification lies entirely within the realm of correspondence with the 'real' itself. However, I should like to add something else – that particular understandings of certain concepts become appropriate in specific moments of space-time and from particular political perspectives. That is to say that old ways of thinking can run into the ground, become blockages to change, indeed be actively mobilized *as* blockages to change. On this ground, the reason for advocating this particular way of imagining space is not because it is eternally true or correct, but because it refuses the entrapments of previously hegemonic formulations and opens up the ground for new questions which – politically – need urgently to be posed. This way of thinking about space conceptualizes it in immediate connection to questions of the constitution of difference, a non-essentialist politics of interrelationships, and an imagined openness of the future.

But I also want to make a further claim: it is that this kind of recognition of this kind of spatiality is particularly adequate for – indeed necessary for – some contemporary changes in the way in which 'politics' itself is imagined. These changes were indicated briefly at the beginning of this chapter. Let us begin this stage of the argument by picking up on two of them. First, there is today a much greater insistence upon the acknowledgement of difference and of a multiplicity of voices. It has been the work of many versions of post-colonial and feminist theorizing to put this on the agenda, and poststructuralism has contributed to a stronger understanding of what might be meant by 'difference'. Coole, for instance, bemoans 'a collapse of wild differences into tamed others' and argues for the recognition of 'differences beyond the imagination of liberal eccentricity' (1996: 27). Second, there has been in recent years a shift towards a fuller understanding of politics as requiring a genuine openness of the future (the kind of openness, indeed, which Bergson used so to insist upon). Derrida's poststructuralism, Deleuze and Guattari's nomadism (Deleuze and Guattari, 1984), the insistent openness of queer theory (Golding, 1997), and Laclau and Mouffe's proposals for radical democracy (1985) have all contributed to this move. Laclau and Mouffe, for instance, maintain that our politics cannot be guaranteed by resort to a universal rationalism but only through recognition of our thorough-going contingency. And the wider condition for this contingent politics genuinely to be exercised is that the future is genuinely open: this is the meaning of the core concept of 'dislocation' – that we do not live in a grand closed system where 'everything that happens can be explained *internally* to this world ... and everything acquires an absolute intelligibility within the grandiose scheme' (Laclau, 1990: 75). Rather we inhabit an environment through which the genuinely novel may emerge.

All this is very different from the dominant forms of progressive politics (whether liberal or Marxist) which have characterized the recent Enlightenment era.

Of course, in some ultimate sense any notion of political activity must evidently engage with a notion of openness – that there is some possibility of changing things. Yet there was always an implicit ambiguity about this (known but not so much directly referred to) in dominant forms of 'modernist' politics of the left. On the one hand we were involved in histories of which grand narratives guaranteed the broader sweep and general direction; on the other hand we were still engaged (or felt we ought to be engaged) in daily, weekly, struggles to bring this about; in some way to 'realize' the achievement of the narrative. The future was both open and not. (The 'debate' around structure and agency of course took off from some sense of this ambiguity.)

As I have argued, one of the characteristics of grand narratives, whether imperialist/colonialist, liberal progressive or socialist/Communist, is that they read spatial difference in terms of place within an overall story (some societies were 'primitive', some economies were 'advanced capitalist'). Two things followed from this. First, they *under*-read the effectivity of spatial difference. At the extreme, there was only one grand temporality (one story) and no real spatiality in the sense of difference. That is what singular narratives do; they suppress that 'multiplicity/difference/alterity' aspect of spatiality. Second, such narratives were not really open; the future was already inscribed in the stories they were telling.

Now, from what has been said above, it will be evident that imagining space in terms of interrelations and of constitutive difference can provide one of the preconditions for this openness, for the possibility of the emergence of genuine novelty. Both the endless openness of spatiality (its loose ends) and its inherent disruptedness (its conflicting co-existences, its unexpected distancings, its dissonant or congenial juxtapositions . . .) establish the grounds for such newness. Imagining space in terms of multiplicity and the possibility of interrelations guarantees the openness of the outcome of any interaction (or lack of interaction). This space is neither stasis nor closure (nor is it 'smooth'). It is disruptive, active and generative. In other words, it provides a source for Laclau's 'dislocations'.[4] Spatializing those grand narratives, in other words, completely changes their character. Precisely through its multiplicity, and through those happenstance juxtapositions and sometimes paradoxical positionings, it opens them up to the generation of novelty, to the emergence of new narratives, to a future which is less predictably inscribed in the past. This 'spatial' is the very product of multiplicity and thus a source of dislocation, of radical openness, and so of the possibility of the kind of creative politics which these writers seek.

Rethinking space in terms of difference and interrelations, then, runs compatibly with a shift in (much) political thinking on the left away from the surety of single, linear narratives, whether liberal modernist or Marxist. That quotation from Laclau, above, about 'the grandiose scheme' in which 'everything that happens can be explained *internally*' is followed by 'This is the Hegelian-Marxist moment' (Laclau, 1990: 75). None of this means that we forget Marx, but it does mean that we have to find ways of breaking out of systemic closures and singular narratives which – in one and the same gesture – occluded the real potential meaning of spatiality-as-difference and, in fact, shut down the possibility of novelty and thus, really, of politics as a genuinely open process. Perhaps, then, what I have been trying to think through here is the related and dual current reconceptualization – of both politics and space. That is, we only get to thinking space as multiplicity if we imagine it interrelationally, and we only get to thinking this is politics (or a condition of politics) if we understand politics in terms not of single grand narratives, but of a plural and radical openness.

There is, however, also more to the rethinking both of space and of politics, and of the relation between them, than this: the content of left politics in the Western world has over recent decades also shifted in other ways. In particular there is a greater concern not just with 'difference', but with the nature of the constitution of difference, and the constitution of identity.

These developments too have parallels with changes over the same period in how we think about space. Thinking space in terms of interrelations, and imagining places/regions as interlockings of those interrelations, clearly reflect a shift of a similar kind to that involved in conceptualizing difference/identity as constituted not through the closures of counterpositional boundedness, but through an understanding of the links and relations by which 'entities' more generally are constructed. Just as places may be thought of as open articulations of connections so too may constructions of difference and identity. Both are moves primarily motivated by the effort to imagine the world in a manner which is non-essentialist: identities of subjects and identities of places constructed through interrelations not only challenge notions of past authenticities but also hold open the possibility of change in the future.

Both these reconceptualizations, in other words, are intimately imbued with politics. And they are so in ways which maintain that essential 'openness' of the new imaginations of the political. This is what much of the debate has been about. Indeed Mouffe (1993) argues that reconstituting the identity of 'the citizen' in this relational way is essential for the establishment of a radically democratic and plural politics. In this reading, the political is not the ground on which meet up in contestation already-constituted identities; rather those identities are themselves relationally constructed as part of the process of politics. In this politics, subject-objects and their interrelations are co-constitutive. I would agree. But I would also add a third term, and would argue that it is a necessary one. For there to be interrelations (so that political subjects, for instance, can be constructed) there must be multiplicities (a multiplicity of potential subjects) and for there to be a multiplicity there must be space. Objects (with their internal space-times), relations *and space*, then, are co-constitutive. Non-essentialist identities require spatiality.

It is important, however, to be precise about the formulation of this space/politics. One trap which can be fallen into is that envisaging the world in terms of interrelations can be read as a sufficient politics in itself. Thus, everything is related to everything else, and recognizing that – so the scenario occasionally runs – will lead to a world which is immediately more co-operative and benign. This is not what is meant here. Recognizing interrelatedness does *not* mean that we emerge, having seen the light of our interrelatedness, on to a happy sunlit plain where all relationships are positive. The point is not this. Rather it is that recognizing our interrelatedness enables us to examine our interrelations.

There has been debate about this within feminism. Thus, Jean Grimshaw (1986: 183) has worried that:

> an unclear or idealised version of female relatedness and connectedness can lead both to unrealistic expectations of community or harmony among women, and sometimes to a sort of coerciveness, a denial of the needs of individual women to forge their own path and develop their own understanding and goals.

What I intend by a focus on 'relatedness and connectedness', however, by no means implies that all those relations are benign or egalitarian. 'Relations' means real relations – material practices which change over time (and this constant production of practices is of course one of the reasons for the never-ending openness of this space and this politics – the impossibility of holistic closure). Recognizing our interrelatedness means recognizing that these relations are power relations of a variety of sorts and that they may well be in some sense unequal or oppressive. The argument is that such inequalities can only meaningfully be addressed when they have been adequately recognized. As Judith Butler argues, one of the problems with bounded identities is precisely that the construction of the boundaries can be a manoeuvre designed to *repress* the fact of the connections through which all identities are constructed:

> To the extent that subject-positions are produced in and through a logic of repudiation and abjection, the specificity of identity is purchased through the loss and degradation of connection, and the map of power which produces and divides identities differentially can no longer be read. (1993: 114).

It is the recognition of the 'maps of power', or the power geometries, within which and through which we are all constructed that opens up the possibility of a politics of renegotiating those identities.

Marx's conceptualization of capital and labour was much along these lines. Capital and labour are co-constituted through the fact and the nature of their interrelationship. They do not (they simply cannot) exist prior to that interrelationship. The purpose of any politics must be to address that interrelationship, rather than only one or other of the subjects which it constructs. And their mutual interdependence means that one cannot change one without at the same time necessarily affecting the other: famously – you cannot abolish the bourgeoisie without at the same time abolishing the proletariat. What is at issue is the conditions of production (through interrelation) of the constituted identities.

That mode of thinking has now been much more explicitly extended to a wider field of politics, and most importantly to the 'extra-human' field of the natural and the machinic and to a recognition of the hybridity of most entities. The significant point here, however, is that that conceptualization can be brought full circle: that what is involved here is not just a rethinking of entities in relational terms as hybrid beings and quasi-objects, but that in the very construction of these things a space (and a space of a particular kind) is also constituted. And that that space is precisely the space of the maps of power, the power geometries, which can provide a field for politics.

Moreover there is a further point here about the nature of this space. The second part of the quotation from Grimshaw made reference to a kind of closure which may be inferred from a reconceptualization of the world in terms of interrelationships. One of the problems with certain kinds of relational thinking is that it can lead to a totalizing (at its worst totalitarian) claustrophobia. One is locked into a structure (like the structures of the structuralists) in which everything is related to everything else. And yet, as was argued earlier, in the way in which I wish to imagine space there is no closure; on the contrary there are always loose ends and disruptiveness. This is a space neither of holistic closure nor of individualistic reductionism. It entails what in another context Butler (and indeed the situationists) refer to as the productiveness of incoherence.[5]

It can also be read as the ground of the possibility of radical democracy. Mouffe (1993, 1998) argues strongly, and in just these terms, against the revitalization of 'pre-modern' holistic conceptions of society, against the organicist closures of the new communitarianism, and against the totalizing tendencies inherent in emerging notions of 'the radical centre'. 'It is', she argues, 'the very characteristic of modern democracy to impede such a final fixation of the social order and to preclude the possibility for a discourse to establish a definite suture' (1993: 52). It is 'this aspect of nonachievement, incompleteness and openness' which is peculiarly characteristic of a radical democratic politics (1993: 110).

For we make, and constantly remake, the spaces and places and identities through which we live our lives. This applies to the ways in, and the terms on, which we construct our personal and communal identities, it applies to the renegotiation of that mixture of open flows and attempts to bound spaces which we currently refer to as globalization, it applies to how we construct the spaces of 'home' and of 'employment' and how we negotiate the power relations and the boundaries which exist between them. All of these involve the co-constitution of spaces and of identities where the spaces can be thought of as 'geometries' (in the most informal sense of that word) of a variety of forms of power.

'Identities', in this formulation, are temporary (in the sense of not eternal) constellations, always interrelationally hybrid but none the less, and to varying degrees, with viably different stories to tell. To cite some classically geographical examples: indigenous groups, nation states, diaspora communities and economic blocs are all different kinds of coherences (with their own internal space-times) – held together by different relations, with varying degrees of longevity, and so forth. What is (or could be) at issue politically is the power relations through which such identities are constituted and those through which they interact with each other and the wider world. It is the fact of their plurality and interrelation which keeps the future open for politics.

A politics of space?

And in this complexity, can there be a politics of space? Or a politics of space and place? It seems to me that the answer must be double-sided.

On the one hand, I would argue, there cannot be any universal political spatial 'rules'. That is to say, to give an obvious example, we cannot argue either for total freedom of movement about the planet or for some immutable right of local people to their own inviolable places. On the political left, we might in certain debates be tempted to argue for freedom of movement (when faced with racist, or even just restrictive, international immigration rules, for instance); but what then when the case concerns the untrammelled entry of multinational corporations into every nook and cranny of 'local cultures'? If we cannot use a principle of freedom of movement in both cases, then we should not use it in either. What is different between the two cases is precisely the construction of their power geometries – in the first case it is the relatively 'weak' who want to move, in the second it is their places that look set to be invaded by the mobility of the relatively powerful. We cannot make a judgement on the basis of a spatiality abstracted from power relations – always what is at issue is *spatialized social* power: it is the power relations in the construction of the spatiality, rather than the spatiality alone, which must be addressed. (In fact, of course, in the context of today's global power geometries, matters work quite the other way around: multinationals get to move around the world far more easily than economic migrants or political refugees – a situation legitimized by the appeal, in different settings, precisely to quite contradictory universal spatial principles: see Massey, 1996.)

Or again, what are these 'local cultures' but hybrids of varying longevity, geography and power? Is the local culture of Fortress Europe to be made equivalent in political discourse to the local culture of the Zapatistas of Chiapas? No: because the power relations through which both their hybrid identities and their relations with the 'outside world' are constructed are vastly different, as is the content of those relations. So maybe there cannot be any 'rights of local people' outside of the context of the particular power geometries in which they are constructed and set. Or – one final example involving different modalities of power – do we want the spaces of daily life to be closed and compartmentalized (a place for leisure, a place for the domestic, a place for paid employment) or would it be better to blur the boundaries and integrate our lives? In writing up some recent research, even as I was railing against the closed and purified compartments (though of course they can never *really* be purified) within which so much intellectual labour is performed, and in which so much that is legitimized by the labels of 'science' and 'knowledge' is produced, I was also aware of Virginia Woolf's impassioned plea for a room of her own, and too of the fact that to write this stuff I had retreated to that most closed and elitist of spaces, the Reading Room at the British Museum.

So, no simple rules maybe, but many responsibilities – and those responsibilities are for the character of the social relations through which we constantly construct all identities and all spaces.

But – finally – there is also, as I said above, an 'on the other hand'. For if there are few if any abstract universal political spatial rules, it is none the less true that the politics of the various forms of social power is constituted spatially. At one level, all of the above examples bear some kind of empirical witness to this. But at another and more general level conceptualizations of space and conceptualizations of politics are related. To return to my theoretical starting point, the essence of, the very constitution of, a reformulated politics and space revolves around the openness of the future, the interrelatedness of identities, and the nature of our relations with different others. Reformulating the way in which we imagine space/spatiality can be itself 'political'.

Notes

1 I am using the words 'space' and 'spatiality' interchangeably in this chapter, partly to avoid constant repetition. What both terms are striving to capture is how we think of 'the realm of the spatial', that particular spatial cut through our understanding of the world around us. As will be evident, the underlying position is that we should think in terms of space-*time* (Massey, 1992), but it is the specific element of spatiality (and how it has been imagined in social thought) which is addressed here.

2 It can be argued that one of the effects of some strands of post-colonialist thought has been more adequately to 'spatialize' some of these stories of modernism. This argument, and that concerning discourses of globalization, are spelled out fully in Massey (1998).

3 And, of course, there will be many trajectories within both 'North' and 'South'. Like the well-known folk story of the cosmology of turtles, this is a story of multiplicities 'all the way down' – some might call it 'fractal'.

4 It is, of course, ironic, given what I am arguing here, that in Laclau (1990) he labels all forms of dislocation 'temporality' and explicitly counterposes such dislocation to a spatiality which he conceives of as a closed system. The conceptualizations of temporality and spatiality are exactly the opposite of what is being proposed here, but the political impetus and spirit have much in common.

5 Deleuze and Guattari, too, struggle to maintain a constant openness within their concept of relatedness. It should be noted, though, that the term 'incoherence' may be misleading – according to theoreticians such as Prigogine (1997) it is precisely the openness of (dissipative) structures which maintains their 'stability' and 'coherence' – though these terms are understood in ways far more dynamic than heretofore.

References

Bergson, H. (1959) *Oeuvres*. Paris, Presses Universitaires de France.

Butler, J. (1993) *Bodies that Matter*. London, Routledge.

Coole, D. (1996) 'Wild differences and tamed others: postmodernism and liberal democracy, *Parallax*, 2, February: 23–36.

Deleuze, G. and F. Guattari (1984) *A Thousand Plateaus*. London, Athlone Press.

Golding, S. (ed.) (1997) *The Eight Technologies of Otherness*. London, Routledge.

Grimshaw, J. (1986) *Feminist Philosophers: Women's Perspectives on Philosophical Traditions*. Brighton, Wheatsheaf.

Gross, D. (1981–2) 'Space, time, and modern culture'. *Telos*, 50, Winter: 59–78.

Laclau, E. (1990) *New Reflections on the Revolution of Our Time*. London, Verso.

Laclau, E. and C. Mouffe (1985) *Hegemony and Socialist Strategy: Towards a Radical Democratic Politics*. London, Verso.

Massey, D. (1992) 'Politics and space/time'. *New Left Review*, 196: 65–84, and in D. Massey (1994) *Space, Place and Gender*. Oxford, Polity Press, 249–72.

Massey, D. (1996) 'Politicising space and place'. *Scottish Geographical Magazine*, 112/2: 117–23.

Massey, D. (1998) 'Imagining globalisation: power-geometries of time-space'. In A. Brah, M.J. Hickman and M. MacanGhaill (eds), *Future Worlds: Migration, Environment and Globalization*. Basingstoke, Macmillan.

Mouffe, C. (1993) *The Return of the Political*. London, Verso.

Mouffe, C. (1998) 'The radical centre: a politics without adversary'. *Soundings*, 9.

Osborne, P. (1995) *The Politics of Time: Modernity and Avant-Garde*. London, Verso.

Prigogine, I. (1997) *The End of Certainty: Time, Chaos and the Laws of Nature*. London, Free Press.

Soper, K. (1995) *What is Nature? Culture, Politics and the Non-Human*. Oxford, Blackwell.

15
Steps to an Ecology of Place

Nigel Thrift

Once at a show, a buttoned-down executive, frustrated by the [Grateful] Dead's usual chaos, demanded to know who was the boss. A roadie named Ramrod, who had unloaded equipment at nearly all of the Dead's many, many concerts, patiently explained one of the basic facts of rock 'n' roll life. 'The situation', he said; 'that's the boss'.

The Economist, 10 August 1996

[T]here is no longer anything special about representation.

Terry Eagleton, 'Self-undoing subjects'

Perhaps there is nothing except practices.

J. Law, 'Traduction/trahison'

It is not down in any map; true places never are.

Herman Melville, *Moby Dick*

The place

I have avoided writing much about place, even though it is often considered to be at the heart of project geography, because I have found real difficulties in knowing what to do with the idea. The more you think about place, the less it seems to offer. Richard Ford's protagonist, in *Independence Day* (1995: 151–2), sports writer-turned-realtor Frank Bascombe, beautifully captures this sense of disillusion, as he looks out over a beach he knows well:

On the beach, beyond the sandy concrete walk, moms under beach umbrellas lie fast asleep on their heavy sides, arms flung over sleepy babies. Secretaries with a half day off to start the long weekend are lying on their bellies, shoulder to shoulder, chatting, winking and smoking cigarettes in their two-pieces. Tiny stick-figure boys stand bare-chested at the margins of the small surf, moving their eyes as dogs trot by, tanned joggers jog and elderlies in pastel garb stroll behind them in the fractured light. Here is human hum in the barely moving air and surf-sign, the low scrim of radio notes and water subsiding over words spoken in whispers. Something in it moves me as though to a tear (but not quite); some sensation that I have been here, or nearby, been at dire pains here time-ago and am here now again, sharing the air just as then. Only nothing signifies, nothing gives a nod. The sea closes up, and so does the land.

I am not sure what chokes me up: either the place's familiarity or its rigid reluctance to act familiar. It is another useful theme and exercise of the Existence Period, and a patent lesson of the realty profession, to cease sanctifying places – houses, beaches, hometowns, a street corner where you once kissed a girl, a parade ground where you marched in time, a court house where you served a divorce on a cloudy day in July, but where there is now no sign of you, no mention in the air's breath that you were there or that you were ever, importantly you, or that you even *were*. We may feel they *ought* to, *should* confer something – sanction, again – because of events that transpired there once; light a warning fire to animate us when we're well nigh inanimate and sunk. But they don't. Places never cooperate by revering you back when you need it. In fact, they almost always let you down . . . Best just to swallow back your tear, get accustomed to the minor sentimentals and shove off to whatever's next, not whatever was. Place means nothing.

I do not so much want to claim that Ford has got it wrong here as, instead, to try to forge a dynamic sense of place, a sense of place in which 'nothing signifies' and which is able to 'shove off to whatever's next'. Using this sense of place, I can then argue that place *is* alive and well and that understanding place should be a crucial concern of the social sciences and humanities.

But this can only happen if we *stop looking at things in the usual way*. And that is difficult. In the well-known words of the touchstone of most of my work:

> The difficulty – I might say – is not that of finding a solution but rather of recognising as the solution something that looks as if it were only a preliminary to it . . . This is connected, I believe, with wrongly expecting an explanation, whereas the solution of the difficulty is description, if we give it the right place in our considerations. (Wittgenstein, 1958: 27e)

Giving the right place to description, which in turn can provide a place for the understanding of place that I want to construct, is the task of what I call non-representational 'theory' (Thrift, 1996). Non-representational theory arises from the simple (one might almost say commonplace) observation that we cannot extract a representation of

NRT.

the world from the world because we are slap bang in the middle of it, co-constructing it with numerous human and non-human others for numerous ends (or, more accurately, beginnings). We act to think, and we only think we think to act because we have let some quite specific forms of life colonize our notion of what constitutes 'humanity'. In other words, 'It is as if someone were to say: "A game consists in moving objects about on a surface according to certain rules ... " – and we replied: You seem to be thinking of board games, but there are others. You can make your definition correct by expressly restricting it to those games' (Wittgenstein, 1958: 3, p. 3e).

Three dislikes: three likes

In order to provide some sense of why I still think that place is important, I need to begin by providing a list of three theoretical 'dislikes'. These dislikes all point towards the possibility of producing an alternative to them which I call non-representational 'theory' – the 'theory' is in scare quotes since one of the purposes of non-representational theory is precisely to undo what we think of as theory (Thrift, 1996). Thus I also provide a mirror of my list of three dislikes in the form of three likes which are all a part of moving to other games.

Old worlds

My first dislike is what I have called *grand theory*, the kind of theory that wants to build systematic accounts of the world which aspire to rigorous standards of exactness, and which wants to understand the totality of social life in terms of those accounts, as stories that add up.

Why am I so uneasy in the face of this kind of theory? I will mention only four of the most pressing reasons. First, such thinking tends to produce a logocentric presence which then becomes the precondition (and confirmation) of further thinking. Merleau-Ponty called this the 'retrospective illusion' but earlier on, in the seventeenth century to be exact, John Wilmot, Earl of Rochester, put it just as well when he wrote about reasoners who 'frame deep mysteries, then find them out'. Second, it becomes too easy to relate a system of (theoretical) frames to scale. Theoretical categories are 'big' and human practices count for little except as the raw material of the categorical aggregate. Like the extras in another *Independence Day*, human figures are then just cannon fodder for alien forms from on high. Just as problematically, it can come to seem as though 'big' effects must have 'big' causes. Third, grand theory tends, by its very nature, to downgrade the 'domestic'. This is the equivalent of the tendency of avant-garde artists and architects who assert their accomplishments by contrasting them with domesticity. As Reed (1996: 8) puts it, with reference to the modernism characterized by Baudelaire's famous defence of Impressionism in his essay 'The Painter of Modern Life' (1859):

> this essay cast the modernist painter as a *flâneur*, 'a man of the crowd', who curses the hours he must spend indoors when a man could be out recording 'the landscapes of the great city'. It is significant that, despite the many Impressionist paintings with domestic subjects, the movement is best known for its treatment of landscapes and city scenes, supposedly rendered on the spot by artists from home and studio. As Griselda Pollock points out in reference to the work of women Impressionists, 'spaces of femininity' (which she catalogues as dining rooms, drawing-rooms, bedrooms, balconies, terraces, and private gardens – in short, the spaces of domesticity) were made subordinate to the theatres, night clubs, cafes and brothels, that constituted the urban pictorial realm of the male Impressionists. Pollock argues that even when men turned to domestic subjects, their images 'are painted from a totally different perspective'. The men, she says, present the home as spectacle to be witnessed by an audience of outsiders, rather than 'with a sureness of knowledge of the daily routine and rituals' that characterise the women for whom the domestic sphere was home-turf.

Fourth, grand theory does not usually understand its own cultural particularity, and therefore very often simply reproduces Euro-American cultural myths. For example, 'the person' is nearly always assumed to be synonymous with individual human beings, even though there are many examples of cultures where this is not held to be the case (Strathern, 1992, 1996). Again, it is often taken as for real that societies are running in a 'fast-forward' mode, continually speeding up (Thrift, 1995):

> What contributes to this? Why does [the] Euro-American have the sense that wherever society is going it is faster than it used to be? Is this simply its own exaggeration – that is, if everything is exaggerated then a sense of movement is too? From where is the exaggeration, then? There can be no single source to point to, but there is an enabling factor. This is the cultural place that is given to enablement itself. Euro-Americans imagine that they can do 'more' things than they once did, crystallised in the hypostatisation of technology as 'enabling' . . .
>
> I suspect that above all they take for granted, quite simply, that *given the technology* they can do anything. If technology is society made durable, it is at the same time ability made effective. The enabling effect of 'technology' is a guarantee of that. Choice comes afterwards. Sever

ourselves from our disabilities, and then we shall see how we want to live, and how we want to create the certain identity we feel, like children severing themselves from unsatisfactory parents. (Strathern, 1996: 46, 49)

If I dislike grand theory, I *really* dislike one of its main outputs. My second dislike, then, is the idea of *modernity*, a series of grand stories about the history (and geography) of Western cultures. Modernity is not an easy idea to criticize because it is diffuse. Osborne (1995), for example, suggests that it has three main meanings: as an historically specific quality of social consciousness or experience, as a category of historical periodization, and as an incomplete historical project. But, in so far as modernity can be treated as a single idea, my objections to it are five-fold.

1 I think that the cost of totalizing history to this extent is too high; it ends up as simply a way of doing 'shorthand' history, as part and parcel of a general trend in which 'one discipline after another in the human sciences [has] cut its ties to history, strengthened its autonomy with theory and produced its meanings without that pervasive historical perspective that in the 19th century had permeated the self-understanding of almost every branch of learning' (Schorske, 1990: 416).

2 Relatedly, there is what Anderson (1984: 98) calls the 'fundamentally planar' vision of time which the use of an idea like modernity entails; time becomes a continuous succession of the new of which notions like postmodernity are, in part, only an extension, since they accommodate any form of hesitancy about modernity by in effect declaring modernity anew. Thus 'postmodernity is . . . accorded the status of being the latest stage in a master logic of historical development, notwithstanding all the obligatory homilies paid to the critique of development' (Featherstone and Lash, 1995: 1).

3 The idea of modernity depends upon a geopolitical vision of a Western core which is propelled away from the mundane history/geography of the rest of the world. Again, recent postmodernist attempts to avoid the taint of what has always looked surprisingly like a developmentalist model, by stressing concepts like globalization, hybridization, multiple modernities and numerous new world orders, seem to me only to take the rough edges off this model and cannot escape the charge that the perspective is 'Western and white' (King, 1995: 120).

4 Modernity relies on accounts of Euro-American culture which are highly questionable. Thus, to refer back to the earlier discussion, they depend on notions of personhood which are usually highly

individualistic. And they cleave to notions of a generalized period of acceleration which makes a decisive break with a slower, and often tradition-bound, past (Gell, 1992). And they invoke other such accounts as well, of which the most insidious is probably the notion that we have seen the gradual triumph of ordered and secularized systems, rooted in the Enlightenment. At the level of everyday life, I suspect that nothing is further from the truth. As I have pointed out elsewhere (Thrift, 1996, 1997), I think that we live in a world which is still populated by myth and magic, in which people believe all manner of often contradictory things without batting an eyelid. From telepathy to precognition, from reincarnation to haunting, from angels to aliens, people appeal to all sorts of explanation that are often regarded as 'irrational' as they think the borders of the possible (Bennett, 1997; Cohen, 1996). In other words, it is difficult to avoid the conclusion that modernity is a story told by 'intellectuals' for intellectuals.

5   So, following on from this latter point, it seems that much of what is regarded as modernity is generated by intellectual forms of life which, because of their allegiance to a textualist model of the world which insists on the primacy of *representation*, systematically exaggerate transience, fragmentation and loss of meaning, consistently over-emphasize systematicity (and in any case are blind to the many creative acts which keep systematic orders as systematic as they are), and downgrade everyday life to residual Rabelaisian pockets of resistance in an ever more programmed and ever more frantic world. In particular, these forms of life give ground to what is written down. The danger is that by so doing they cancel out what is not written down, which tends to be the lives of those who have struggled to get by rather than get on. The point is not that these actors are mutes that then have to be made to speak, it is rather that their practices need to be valued *for themselves* as the somatic legacy we all live by, with and for.

My third dislike is a certain view of space, time and place which follows on from the previous two dislikes. This is the view that human beings are engaged in *building* discursive worlds by actively constructing webs of significance which are laid out over a physical substrate. In other words, human beings are located in a terrain which appears as a set of phenomena to which representations must be affixed prior to any attempt at engagement. Thus:

> For the non-human, every thread in the web is a relation between it and some object or feature of the environment, a relation that is set up

through its own partial immersion in the world and the bodily orientations that this entails. For the human, by contrast, the web – and the relations of which it consists – is inscribed in a separate plane of mental representations, forming a tapestry of meaning that covers over the world of environmental objects. Whereas the non-human animal perceives these objects as immediately available for use, to human beings they appear initially as occurrent phenomena to which potential uses must be affixed, prior to any attempt at engagement. The fox discovers shelter in the roots of a tree, but the forester sees timber only in his mind's eye, and has first to fit that image into his perception of the current object – the tree – before taking action. (Ingold, 1995: 63)

This is a classic declaration of what might be called the 'building perspective':

> For a founding statement, we could turn once again to Geertz, and to his assertion that culture . . . consists in the 'imposition of an arbitrary framework of symbolic meaning upon reality' (1964, p. 39). Reality, that which is imposed upon, is envisioned here as an external world of nature, a source of raw materials and sensations for diverse projects of cultural construction. Following from this, a distinction is commonly made between the 'real' environment that is given independently of the senses, and the 'perceived' environment as it is reconstituted in the mind through the ordering of sense data in terms of acquired, cognitive schemation. Other conventional oppositions that encode the same distinction are between 'etic' and 'emic', and between 'operational' and 'cognised'. The starting point in all such accounts is an imagined separation between the perceiver and the world, such that the perceiver has to reconstruct the world, in the mind, prior to any meaningful engagement with it.
>   Here, then, is the essence of the building perspective: that *worlds are made before they are lived in.* (Ingold, 1995: 66, my emphasis)

Note how, in the building perspective, space and time are neutral grids, or perhaps containers, over which and in which meaning is 'placed'. They are not a part of the play; they are onlookers. But, as authors as diverse as Bergson, Merleau-Ponty and Latour have all shown in their different ways, space and time are what we labour to produce as we go along. As Latour, for example, would have it, they are part of the construction of a network, not an outside.

In geography the building perspective is a remarkably common one. All the way from early research on mental maps to work on the idea of landscape as text to much of the recent post-colonial literature, it has retained a hold on the subject.[1] But, in geography, as in other disciplines, the perspective generates some obvious problems. For instance, it sets up a false and unsustainable division, between culture and nature, people and the environment, and humans and non-humans. Moreover, it generalizes out quite specific Western cultural constructions of space and time to the whole world. Yet there is plenty of evidence that shows that these constructions are only some out of the many that are possible (see, for example, Gell, 1992). And, then, it entirely neglects the ways in which space and time are practised as embodied and involved activity, as means of shoving off, in favour of what is ultimately a textualist model of the world, which over-emphasizes the cognitive, the contemplative and the representational.

New worlds

So let me now, from the springboard provided by these three dislikes, shove off to three likes which together begin to offer an account of what is involved in Wittgenstein's non-reductive 'explanation', which is really description, 'if we give it the right place in our considerations'.

My first like, then, is 'non-representational theory' (Thrift, 1996), a body of work which is 'due largely to the historical impact of the convergence between Wittgenstein and Heidegger', with other traditions (like American pragmatism) acting 'as a sounding board and amplifier' (Apel, 1996: 241; see figure 15.1). In other words, non-representational theory provides us with that taken-for-granted grip on the world which we can never take for granted.

Non-representational theory is anchored in an irreducible ontology in which the world is made up of billions of happy or unhappy encounters, encounters which describe a 'mindful connected physicalism' consisting of multitudinous paths which intersect. This is an ontology 'which works through things rather than imposes itself upon them from outside or above' (Brennan, 1993: 86). It follows that in this 'fibrous, thread-like, wiry, stringy, ropy, capillary' (Latour, 1997: 2) space-time of encounters and paths, paths and encounters, there are no stable and complete orders, only tentative and fractional orderings. Thus, to put it in the terms of actor network theory, instead of taking 'local contingencies as so many queer particularities that should be either eliminated or protected', this ontology starts from 'irreducible, incommensurable localities which then, at a great price, sometimes end in provisionally commensurable connections' (Latour, 1997: 2). Like Deleuze, then, I want to get away from the guilt-ridden, doom-laden and life-denying tone of much Western philosophical thought and 'reinvigorate the idea that living is bewildering, strange, and sometimes wonderful' (Probyn, 1996: 19) by emphasizing the Spinozan themes of 'active ... forms of life and the process of formation of composite bodies' (Armstrong, 1997: 50).

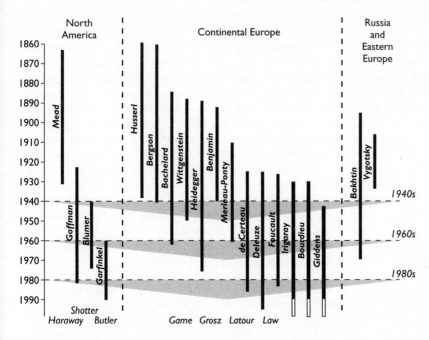

Figure 15.1   The life-time-lines of non-representational theory

This irreducible ontology is paralleled by a 'situated' epistemology which recognizes very strong limits on what can be known and how we can know it because of the way human subjects are embodied as beings in time-space, because of their interconnected position in multiple social relations, and because there are numerous perspectives on, and metaphors of, what counts as knowledge, or, more precisely, knowledges. Thus, 'there is no thought which embraces all our thought ... since we are in the world, and our reflections are carried out in the temporal flux on to which we are trying to seize' (Merleau-Ponty, 1962: xiv). Whether we like it or not, then, 'our condition condemns us to live among badly analyzed composites, and to be badly analyzed composites' (Deleuze, 1988: 21). I cannot therefore do much better than argue, as Haraway (1991: 195) does, for an archipelago of 'situated knowledges' (see also Serres, 1995; Serres and Latour, 1995):

> politics and epistemologies of location, positioning and situating, where partiality and not universality is the condition of being heard to make rational knowledge claims. These are claims on people's lives; the view from a body, always a complex, contradictory, structuring and structured body, versions of the view from above, from nowhere, from simplicity.

I take it that Haraway's geopoetics requires holding to a number of conditions. Of these, four seem particularly important. First, I take it that in a situated epistemology concepts have to be seen, in a Wittgensteinian way, as indefinite (since language is, by its nature, indefinite and involves metaphors which, in Game and Metcalfe's (1996: 50) felicitous phrase, 'keep blooming') and, in a Bergsonian way, as image-concepts whose main purpose is to resonate or, as Bachelard (1969) would have it, 'reverberate'. Second, in a situated epistemology knowledge is counted as always and everywhere contextual, most especially because it is rooted in embodiment. Then, third, I take it that reflexivity is an important component of a situated epistemology, but reflexivity of an 'infra-reflexive' kind (Latour, 1988). Thus, and fourth, the understanding of theory in a situated epistemology is really very different from the understanding of theory that is traditionally held. Theory becomes a *practical means of going on rather than something concerned with enabling us to see, contemplatively, the supposedly true nature of what something is.* Theory therefore acts as a 'reminder' which moves us towards:

> a new way of 'looking over' the play of appearances unfolding before us, such that, instead of seeing the events concerned, in terms of theories of what they supposedly represent, we see them 'relationally' – that is, we see them practically, as being embedded in a network of possible connections and relations with their surroundings, 'pointing toward' the (proper) roles they might actually play in our lives. (Shotter, 1995: 11)

This is, then, a very modest view of the role of theory which is intent on seeking *relational* rather than representational understandings; 'we are not seeking, as already developed individuals, to discover what something is, but different possible ways in which we might relate ourselves to our surroundings – how to be different in ourselves, *how to live in different worlds*' (Shotter, 1995: 14). In other words, we are seeking to develop disclosive *skills* (Spinosa et al., 1997).

That this is a practical kind of theory is crucial because non-representational 'theory' is the theory of practices. I take it that this theory, which is really more of a poetics, consists of a set of fundamental (and this is really the wrong word) tenets which I have summarized elsewhere (Thrift, 1996). Perloff (1996: xiv) has done a wonderful job of condensing them in her description of Wittgensteinian poetics:[2]

> First, its *dailyness*: for Dante's purgatorial staircase, for Yeats's 'ancient winding stair', Wittgenstein substitutes a mere ladder – a ladder, moreover, whose origin . . . is as equivocal as its destination. Second, the movement 'up' the ladder can never be more than what Gertrude Stein called 'Beginning again and again' – a climbing 'through', 'on' and 'over' its

rungs that is never finished. Hence Wittgenstein's suspicion of generalisa-
tion, of metalanguage, indeed of *theory* itself as an imposition on *practice*.

And third – and most important – one cannot (shades of Heraclitus!)
climb the same ladder twice. Which is to say that each philosophical
'proposition', however much it depends on the propositions that have laid
its foundations, always bears some sign of difference, even if the exact
same words are reported in the same order. Repetition, after all, always
entails a shift in context as well as in use.

There is, in other words, no vision – only revision – both for Wittgenstein himself and for his reader. And in the case of the climbing that
occurs, the rungs of the . . . ladder manifest their inherent strangeness.

A second like consists of notions of history which can be linked to
non-representational theory. These notions are necessarily based on
wide-ranging metaphors, each of which must be understood as *practical*
and *performative* – that is as productive, embodied, mimetic, partial
and contingent. This point is beautifully put by Game and Metcalfe
(1996: 50–1):

According to Aristotle, good metaphors have a vividness that makes
meaning lively. The child's metaphor of the ship taking a bath animates
the inanimate, making us participate in meaning by imaginatively playing
the role of the ship. By performing ship we lend our form to ship and
thereby bring shipness to life for us. The saucepan lid lets the child play
saucepan through his prior knowledge of hats. By having us act these
roles, metaphor makes a world of ships and saucepans to us; our acting
gives us an appreciation of how the world actually is.

Metaphoric actuality is not the same as the literal's reality, but we are
sceptical of the literal's claim to re-present reality. Reality cannot really be
seen, because we cannot see the world from the outside. Our knowledges
are *ours*, mediated through and projecting us into the world. We cannot
fix or imitate the world as it really is, but we can create our own simula-
tions of it through mime. As Benjamin noted; 'Perhaps there is none of
[man's] higher functions in which his mimetic faculty does not play a
decisive role. By letting us live(en) the world metaphors enliven our
understandings. Weber was too modest when claiming that the faculty for
compassion or empathy lets us understand other people: it underlines all
metaphoric truth.

We do not come empty-handed to our performances of metaphor.
When metaphor engages us, we respond through the emotions and memories that reverberate with the role. Our enactment of the world is a
method actively informed and energised by the previous experiences that
constitute us. We know ships because we remember the feeling of a bath;
we know sulky pants by momentarily reliving our own moods; we know
a growling boss because we have seen and imagined ourselves as lions.

When performing a role, we are its stuff; we know it through lending it our form. Metaphor is a full-bodied and embodied way of knowing.

In turn, this kind of understanding of metaphor – as provisional, contingent and constantly reworked – has led to a stress on metaphors which try to capture the 'dynamics of emergent creativity' (Goodwin, 1994: 184; see also Goodwin, 1997) by acknowledging that the world is complexly connected, constantly changing, and contingent; always 'these', never just 'this'. I will point to just three of many possible metaphors. Importantly each of them is inherently spatial, that is they are concerned with figuring the world as *distributed* rather than centred. Each of these metaphors is also inherently *dynamic*, that is they rely on notions of time which are multiple, open and open-ended. Thus, they are intended to simulate the process by which places can only become places through shoving off to what is next, both spatially and temporally.

The first of these geopoetic metaphors takes a leaf from the sciences of *complexity* which have arisen from a broad spectrum of work on self-organization, emergent order, chaotic behaviour, and dynamical systems in general. In other words, the metaphor arises from what is fast becoming an interdisciplinary methodology, which is intended to explain the emergence of certain macroscopic phenomena as becoming the result of the non-linear interaction of microscopic elements in complex systems. In principle, then, economies, organisms and ecosystems can all be metaphorized as self-organizing assemblages.

In many ways most important of all, complexity can be seen as a metaphor which replaces the old Darwinian metaphorical social associations that are familiar from the deployment of descriptive terms like 'survival of the fittest', 'competitive interactions between species', 'selfish genes', 'survival strategies' and the like:

> Complex systems do not follow the straight lines of historical narration or Darwinian evolution, but are comprised of multiple series of parallel processes, simultaneous emergences, discontinuities and bifurcations, anticipations and mutations of every variety. Regardless of the materials or scales on which they operate, their macroscopic, molar appearance belies a complexity of local interactions and molecular behaviours which proceed without any ... transcendent guides. There is no governor, no central processing unit, and no monolithic generating point, and neither genetic evolution nor the evolution of behaviour needs a global program like a supervisory divine will, a vital force, or a global strategy of evolutionary optimisation. (Plant, 1996: 210)

Thus the complexity metaphor is a statement, writes Plant (1996: 212) with characteristic hyperbole, that:

beyond spectacular society and speculative humanism there is an emergent complexity, an evolving intelligence in which all material life is involved, all theory, writing, dancing, engineering, creativity, social organisation, biological processing, economic interaction and communication of every kind. It is the matrix, the virtuality and the future of every separated thing, individuated organism, disciplined idea and social structure.

Rather more to the point, the altered perspective supplied by the complexity metaphor makes it possible to see organisms (of whatever kind) as *productive relational orders*:

> Organisms cease to be simply survival machines and assume intrinsic value, having worth in and of themselves, like art. Such a realisation arises from an altered understanding of the nature of organisms as centres of action and creativity, connected with a usual agency that cannot be described as mechanical. It is relational order *between* components that matters more than material composition in living processes, so that emergent qualities predominate over quantities. This consequence extends to social structure, where relationships, creativity and values are of primary significance. (Goodwin, 1994: xiv)

A second metaphor is the *surface* (Philo, 1994). This metaphor originated with the work of Foucault, thinking in 'terms of relations of proximity'. For Foucault, the world is 'a network in which each point is distant ... and has a position in relation to every other point in a space that simultaneously holds and separates them all' (Foucault, 1987: 12). The metaphor has been taken up and elaborated by other writers who are more concerned than Foucault to emphasize that connections have to be *made, they do not* just happen. For example, actor network theorists have tried to depict a world of overlapping networks all struggling to make themselves felt by making connections between all manner of things human and non-human. Writers like Deleuze and Guattari (1987) want to write of a world of the constant deterritorialization and reterritorialization of various machinic assemblages, while feminist theorists like Probyn (1996: 34) aim to remetaphorize debates on identity and belonging: 'conducted on the surface, this requires us to constantly place ourselves within relations of proximity of different forms of belonging. And at the edge of ourselves we mutate; we become other.'

Then, finally, there is the metaphor of the *messenger*. The figure of Hermes looms large in the work of writers like Serres as a means of conjuring up a world of communication through an 'argumentative operator' who brings things closer together, swiftly passing through a folded set of times, establishing connections:

We must conceive or imagine how Hermes flies and gets about when he carries messages from the gods – or how angels travel. And for this we must describe the spaces situated between things that are already marked out – spaces of interference.... This god or these angels pass through folded time, making millions of connections. *Between* has always struck me as a preposition of prime importance.

Follow the flight pattern of a fly. Doesn't time sometimes seem to flow according to the breaks and bends that this flight seems to follow? ... it's what we call in the most simplistic exercises to *explicate, that is*, to 'unpleat'. This is an extremely complex design, incomprehensible and appearing chaotic or random, but made admirably understandable by the movements of the baker kneading his dough. He makes folds, he *implicates* something that his movements then *explicate*. The most simple and mundane gesture can produce very complicated curves.

The intermediaries – Hermes, angels, I myself ... – we are forced to fly according to these curves. (Serres and Latour, 1995: 64–5)

The messenger brings light to texts or signs that are obscure. But she also induces a certain foreignness, even strangeness, because the message comes from afar.

In turn, these metaphors – and others like the network[3] – can be used to form new figurations, new subject positions which do not so much take in what has been left out, or leave in what has been taken out, as redefine what we mean by leaving in and taking out.

What these and other metaphors produce – and this is my third like – are new ways of looking at space and time which emphasize *distribution, dynamism, effort* and *friction*. In direct contrast to Kantian thinking, space and time are therefore folded into and are forms of the objects themselves and are not, as Kant would have it, forms of intuition (Genova, 1995). In turn, space is understood through what might be called, following Heidegger, a 'dwelling' perspective, based upon the primacy of practices. This perspective is founded on the work of Heidegger after the famous turn (or *Kehre*) of 1935 when he executed a major critical shift from his earlier work. His notion of space (see Heidegger, 1971; Franck, 1986; Villela-Petit, 1996) changed accordingly, from one in which, as in *Being and Time*, spatiality is founded upon temporality, to one in which space and time are co-equal (*Zeit – Raum*): the book *Sein und Zeit* becomes the 1968 essay 'Zeit und Sein'. The dwelling perspective is in exact contradiction to the building perspective:

'We do not dwell because we have built, but we build and have built because we dwell, that is because we are dwellers.... To build is in itself already to dwell.... *Only if we are capable of dwelling, only then can we build*' (Heidegger, 1971, p. 48, p. 146, p. 160, p. 160 original emphasis).

I take this to be the founding statement of the dwelling perspective. What it means is that the forms people build, whether in the imagination or on the ground, arise within the current of their involved activity, in the specific relational contexts of their practical engagement with their surroundings. Building, then, cannot be understood as a simple process of transcription, of a pre-existing design of the final product on to a raw material substrate. It is true that human beings – perhaps uniquely among animals – have the capacity to envision forms in advance of their implementation, but this envisioning is itself an activity carried on by real people in a real-world environment, rather than by a disembodied intellect moving in the subjective space delineated by the proposals it sets out to solve. In short, people do not import their ideas, plans or mutual representations into the world since that very world, to borrow a phrase from Merleau-Ponty, is the homeland of their thoughts. Only because they already dwell therein can they think the thoughts they do. (Ingold, 1995: 76)

Thus, we can say that:

human children, like the young of many other species, grow up in environments furnished by the work of previous generations, and as they do so *they come literally to carry the forms of their dwelling in their bodies – in specific skills, sensibilities and dispositions.* But they do not carry them in their genes, nor is it necessary to invoke some other kind of vehicle for the inter-generational transmission of information – cultural rather than genetic – to account for the diversity of human living arrangements. It is the very notion of information, that form is *brought in* to environmental contexts of development, that is at fault here. For as we have seen, it is within such contexts, in the movement of human beings' (or non-human animals') practical engagement with the components of their surroundings, that form is generated. (Ingold, 1995: 77, my emphasis)

With the turn, not only did Heidegger move from a building to a dwelling perspective but he also placed more emphasis on place rather than space. Thus, in *Being and Time*, the notion of place is present but it is simplistic; based upon the mode of involvement of the 'labour of the craftsman and the world which corresponds to it' (Villela-Petit, 1996: 142). In the later work, Heidegger goes beyond this kind of analysis. 'While in Sein und Zeit it was above all a question of "place" (*Platz*) and of a "network of places" (*Ganzheit von Plätzen*) seen as a function of the readiness to hand (*Zuhandenheit*) of an equipmental whole, it will from now on be a question of place (*Ort*) and of the relation between space and place' (Villela-Petit, 1996: 146). Place becomes 'an entire network of ways and significations which articulate its space and give a meaning to dwelling' (Villela-Petit, 1996: 146). In other words, what Heidegger has in mind is 'another way of thinking place, whereby it is both given and expressed at one and the same time as dwelling place' (Villela-Petit, 1996: 152). It follows that a place is not in space, but is a means by which space is produced as a *plenitude of different relations*.

However, Heidegger's later work is not by itself an adequate approach to place. Less seriously, since this was never Heidegger's intent, it never approaches the kind of ontic specificity that actually makes place into place (Thrift, 1996). But, more seriously, it suffers from an implicit romanticism – all that stuff about country pathways and peasant shoes – which associates certain practices with a transcendental authority in such dangerous ways. As Irigaray (1997) has pointed out, in part this retrogression is a function of a spatiality based on earth rather than air, with its implicit bias towards a masculine model of clearing a space in an existing world rather than taking flight into different worlds, thereby undoing the 'principle of a fixity of elements in separation' (Game, 1995: 194).

These criticisms suggest that we need to move back to where this chapter started, to the work of Wittgenstein. Like Heidegger's work, Wittgenstein's work lacks ontic specificity. But in principle, at least, that specificity can be recovered. Indeed, across a number of disciplines, a variety of authors have tried to do exactly that (see, for example, Bloor (1983) and Coulter (1987, 1993, 1996) in sociology, Schatzki (1996) in philosophy, Shotter (1995) in social psychology, Thrift (1996) in geography, and so on). Unlike Heidegger's work, Wittgenstein's work has no streak of the romantic. Rather, like actor network theory, its tone is tentative and anti-closural. It *is* about constructing disclosive spaces, different worlds, 'in which to take a deep breath' (Perloff, 1996: 23). It is, in other words, about how we question.

From board games to border games

So what place might the idea of place have in a Wittgensteinian scheme of things? I want to suggest that *places are 'passings' that 'haunt' 'us'*. What might I mean by such an elliptical, even enigmatic, statement?

I mean two things. The first, and most obvious, is that places must be seen as dynamic, as taking shape only in their passing. I do not mean by this just that places are a transitory part of practices and therefore must pass on, often lending their characteristics to other practices as they do so. I also mean that places can never be pre-ordained. Whilst places may be designed to elicit particular practices (including particular subject positions and emotional responses), all kinds of other practice may in fact be going on within them which they were never designed to admit (but which may become a vital part of those places' intelligibility). Places are, in other words, doubly incomplete.

Then, second, places haunt us (and we haunt them), but what I want to get at here is something rather more than terms like 'context' and 'setting' allow. I am nervous of the way in which these terms conjure up a building perspective in which practices take place *in* a setting. Wittgensteinian writers like Schatzki (1997: 115–16) have tried to surmount this obstacle by emphasizing that practices always *open* spaces. They are *disclosive*:

> An important aspect of world constitution is the opening of a space of places at which activities *can intelligibly be performed*. When a tree is understood as something to climb, for instance, it becomes a place at which climbing is intelligible; similarly, when a platform is understood as something from which to observe the landscape, it becomes a place at which observing is intelligible. In this way, beds are understood as places to sleep, tables as places to eat, and bus stops as places to catch the bus. A place to X is understood as a place where it is understood that X-ing occurs. Insofar, then, that the organisations of practices bestow interrelated meanings upon entities, practices open spaces of interrelated places at which their doings and sayings are correctly and acceptably performed. . . .
>
> A setting in which a given practice is to occur and which is laid out in accordance with the meanings that objects acquire in the practice's constituent actions anchors a space of places which similarly rests on practices, but their set-ups anchor spaces established by those practices. Practices, consequently, transpire in an objective space that devolves from the material arrangements of objects, while also themselves opening a type of space (the space of places) that differs from and is irreducible to objective space. Emphasising that practices lay out and course through settings combats the possible impression that practices on my account are ethereal constellations of meaning that lack any rootedness in or connection to materiality. . . . Emphasising that they open spaces, furthermore, signals that my earlier characterisation of spaces as spatio-temporal nexuses of behaviour, in an objective sense of 'spatio-temporal', does not exhaust the relations of practices to space and time.
>
> Finally, a person's understanding of Z, even abstractly, is likely to be complex and expressed in a variety of different types of action with regard to it. Z might be something to fell, to acquire, to climb, to examine, to prune, to sketch, and so on. Since these understandings are acquired in different practices, the resulting total understanding of Z is a many-coloured product. Usually, however, entities are encountered while engaged in a particular practice. This means (1) that they will have only these correct and acceptable meanings which are contained in that portion of a person's overall understanding of them that helps organise

the practice(s) involved; (2) that they will anchor only that space of places which is co-ordinate with those meanings; and (3) that people will (usually) talk about and act toward them solely in the correlated right and acceptable ways. Of course, people can suddenly alter those practices they are engaged in, such that entities can abruptly process different meanings, anchor different spaces of places and be acted toward differently. Moreover, in a situation where others are carrying out one practice, a person can intentionally understand and act towards entities in ways characteristic of another. Usually, however, people participate steadily in a given practice, meaning that they inhabit a world of stably meaningful objects, events, and people.

But I am not sure that Schatzki's account of disclosure quite gets at the elusive quality I want to identify, though it is a necessary and important building block in my argument. What I would regard as its mentalist overtones make it difficult for him to write of the extent to which, at one and the same time, places haunt us, and we haunt them.

These hauntings I take to be of four utterly interrelated kinds. The first is the world of *things*. Things are folded into the human world in all manner of active and inseparable ways, and most especially in the innumerable interactions between things and bodies which are placed at particular locations in particular configurations of action and value, which are themselves caught up in particular notions of the boundaries and capacities of things and bodies.[4] In turn, this insight leads to a project which tries:

> to render being intelligible in terms of the localisation of routes, habits and techniques within specific domains of action and value: libraries and studies; bedrooms and bathhouses; courtrooms and schoolrooms; consultancy rooms and museum galleries; markets and department stores.... To the apparent linearity and unidirectionality and irreversibility of time, we can [therefore] counterpoise the multiplicity of *places and practices*. And in each of these spaces, repertoires of conduct are cultivated that are not bounded by the closure formed by the human skin or found in an intense form in the interior of an individual: they are rather webs of tension across space that accord human beings capacities and powers to the extent that they catch them up in hybrid assemblages of knowledges, interests, vocabularies, systems of judgements and technical artefacts. (Rose, 1996: 143–4)

Latour, and actor network theorists, are good at seeing the power of things that dwell with us and their power to haunt us (and we them). Indeed one might argue that he and other actor network theorists have come closest to a coherent account of this haunting through their stories of constantly combining and recombining networks; a world of parts becoming wholes. But actor network theory also acts as a sign of trouble ahead. It does this in two ways, I think. First, the way in which things are mixed in can seem prosaic, and therefore misses much of their haunting quality especially as this relates to place, that sensuous mixture of object and experience that lies at the edge of semantic availability (Williams, 1977); what Toni 'Morrison sometimes just calls *the thing*, the sedimented conditions that constitute what is in place in the first place' (Gordon, 1997: 4). Waxing Benjaminian, Gordon (1997: 204–5) then points to what is lost:[5]

'There . . . are cross-roads where ghostly signals flash from the traffic and inconceivable analogies and connections between events are the order of the day' (Benjamin, 1978, p. 183). What are ghostly signals? We have encountered quite a few of them: a sunken couch, a hand, a photograph, a wolf, an open door, a hat. These are the flashing half-signs ordinarily overlooked until that one day when they become animated by the immense forces of atmosphere concentrated in them. These elements can be frightening and threatening; they are profane but nevertheless charged with the spirit that made them. . . . The profane illumination describes when 'thought presses close to its object, as if through touching, smelling, tasting, it wanted to transform itself' (Adorno in Taussig, 1992, p. 145). The profane illumination captures the medium by which we have a different kind of access to the 'density of experience'. . . . Proximate and vibrant, the profane illumination captures just that experience of the ghostly matter. Profane illumination is a kind of conjuring that 'initiates' (Benjamin, 1978, p. 192) because it is telling us something important we had not known; because it is leading us somewhere, or elsewhere.

But, and second, Latour and other actor network theorists might well want to criticize this kind of depiction as an understanding of the world of things based on an undercover humanism and a centred geographical connectedness which is just not there.[6] I think this is why (for all their studies of particular locations like laboratories) Latour and other actor network theorists often fail to see the importance of place: their vision of a radically symmetrical world of networks, consisting of different aspects like humans, animals and things, and mobiles like writing, print, paper and money constantly combining and recombining is an important corrective to simple humanisms and to simple notions of connectedness, but it also means that actor network theory cannot speak of certain things. In particular, Latour and other actor network theorists often fail to see the importance of place because they are reluctant to ascribe different competences to different aspects of a network or to understand the role of common ground in how networks echo back and forth, often unwittingly.

I think that certain human competences cannot be so easily reduced to this socio-spatial agnosticism and that these form much of what is passed through place and returns as hauntings (Black et al., 1989; Casey, 1993).[7] These competences all rely on *embodiment*, a tactile, 'elusory' (Radley, 1995) embodiment which cannot be reduced to just the constituent elements of different networks. This is, then, an embodiment which is folded into the world by virtue of the passions of the five senses and constant, concrete attunements to particular practices, which always involve highly attuned bodily stances as bodies move in relation to each other; ways of walking, standing, sitting, pushing, pulling, throwing, catching, each with its own cultural resources, each still to be seriously investigated:

> In his pioneering article on the techniques of the body, Marcel Mauss also paid attention to ways of moving, while drawing upon his own experience. In the first World War he had noted differences in walking between the French and the English and after observing nurses during a stay in a New York hospital he realised the influence of the American cinema on the way French girls walked. If he had lived today he would surely have noted the various ways in which models have started to move on the catwalk in recent years and the abolishment of the goose step by the East German ministry of defence in the summer of 1990, only months before the German reunification.... Mauss's investigations have hardly received the attention they deserve; indeed in most of the subjects he invented research has still to begin. (Bremmer, 1993: 15)

It follows that 'the materiality of place lives, is inscribed in our bodies' (Game, 1995: 202). These full-bodied competences are the source of the three other kinds of haunting I want to consider.

The first of these competences is *emotion*. Emotions provide us with a vital means of attunement, to use a Heideggerian phrase, to a situation. And they have a message. They are what matters. 'Things mattering is people being in particular moods and emotions, or having particular feelings, affects, and passions' (Schatzki, 1996: 123). The emotions produce one means of haunting, especially when they well up as passion:

> Passion is the form of mortal desire. The relation that rends my heart is the source of my joy. It is death's whisper that gives my life its scale and meaning, that tells me I'm alive. Passion is extreme not because of the extent or significance of our emotions, but because it deals with immeasurable, unmanageable and final things....
>
> Passion's association with life's limits can make it a rude and frightening force, especially in a century that has often prided itself on its techno-

logical and economic victory over finitude. Just as death is mediatised and quantified in western society, grand passion has come to seem an old fashioned idea. The implications of its power are repressed in the same way that civilisation is said to have tamed nature, the body, the primitive, and the irrational – the realms where passion supposedly resides. Modern sciences like psychology and sociology rarely talk about passions and certainly not their own. The closest they come is through the more anaemic concept of emotions. . . .

Yet our culture is not passionless, even if the dominant expressions are of a passion conveniently trimmed of grandeur and unreasonableness. Passion's darker, wilder forms still prowl unacknowledged around the outskirts of our rationality. (Game and Metcalfe, 1996: 3–4)

The second competence is *memory*. Memory may be produced by cultural forms like narrative and by various techniques and technologies of memorization which constantly make its practices anew, but it is a register of experience that cannot be escaped (Game, 1995). We live, then, in a world of 'cinders', which very often act like hauntings, cued to their present purpose by the reminders of particular places. These reminders of remainders may only leave the faintest of traces, but they still testify to the fire: 'trace destined, like everything, to disappear from itself, as much in order to lose the way, as to rekindle a memory' (Derrida, 1991: 57). In other words:

the cinder is nothing that can be in the world, nothing that remains as an entity (*étant*). It is the being (*être*), rather, that there is – this is a name of the being that there is but which, giving itself (*es gibt ashes*), is nothing . . . remains unpronounceable in order to make saying possible, although it is nothing. (Derrida, 1991: 57)

And this point brings us to the third competence, which is *language*. In non-representational theory language is, of course, *performative*, a virtual structure achieved through use, not a potential structure actualized by use. Thus, 'the meaning of a word is its *use* in the language' (Wittgenstein, 1958: 43, p. 20e):

Cultural living in its bare bones is talk, talk translated into all sorts of symbols. [But] the talk is not just talk. It is presentation. Timing makes it so; punchlines too; ambience; gestures; silences; presence; rhythm; fast flows and discontinuities; engagement with an audience; rhetorical forms, sometimes as old as culture itself, sometimes raw and new. (Dening, 1996: 34)

And this performativity extends to the text. As Schneider (1991: 38)[8] puts it:

I think that Freud, in his capacity as theoretician and interpreter of texts, disallows the childhood of language, if you like, everything about language which goes beyond the level of the text itself. Wittgenstein on the other hand allows you to re-hear the breathing element in language, everything which is genuinely alive in the text – its energy, the many gestures of information. So language is not locked into being nothing more than the statement it contains: on this view you can go much further than the traditional distinction between the subject of the stating and the subject of the statement. Wittgenstein enables us to go much further than just who makes the statement: making a statement is taken as a vital thing, and is not merely a matter of the subject.

On this view, language is no longer a prison house but an 'immense network of easily accessible wrong turnings' (Wittgenstein, 1980: 18), in which:

> Sense and nonsense are determined by a form of life, and that is reflected in the language-games we play. Contexts and situations often make the most grammatical remark nonsensical. To discover the limits of language, one must look beyond the method of representation to the pragmatic considerations which establish a language game. One obvious consequence of this new view of language is that it no longer makes sense to speak of the limits of language. Language is like a city: it grows, changes and reinvents itself constantly. There is no permanent boundary between the sayable and the unsayable. One can decide, that is, a form of life decides, to exclude certain combinations of words from the language and call them nonsense, but not because they violate some boundary . . . Concepts are not closed by a frontier: one draws boundaries when one needs to describe the situation and all the other pragmatic considerations of a language game, but the method is mute. (Genova, 1995: 122–3)

Further, threading through language is the extra-discursive which can now no longer be relegated to the sidelines but continually haunts us, both practically in particular contexts (each with its own configurations of action and value) and theoretically as a set of dilemmas concerning the extreme limits of the sayable with which we can never be reconciled: the impossibility of a complete description; the gap between what language does and what we want it to do; the unsettled relationship between what we see and what we know; and so on. In the famous words of Polanyi, 'we know more than we can tell'. Giving voice and giving a voice to this sensuous knowledge is, indeed, a ghostly matter but one with important political consequences, in terms of both how we value lives past and present and how we activate the potential for disclosing new ways of living (Spinosa et al., 1997).

Thus, the ecology of place is a rich and varied *spectral gathering*, an articulation of presence as 'the tangled exchange of noisy silences and seething absences' (Gordon, 1997: 206). It is, I think, no coincidence that one of the chief concerns of current social and cultural theory is the aspects of that tense gathering which both value and multiply anomaly, receptivity and imaginative capacity: ghosts, apparitions and monsters; magic, haunting and dreams; rites, rituals and raves. And it is this new style of describing becoming – with its accompanying baggage of only half-understood and sometimes inarticulate textual skills; the geopoetic metaphors, the paratextual plays with words (Genette, 1997), the new senses of semiosis (Gibson, 1997; Threadgold, 1997) – which is allow- ing a different and more open sense of place to make its way into the open. In turn, this change of style is beginning to change some of the premises of a cultural turn which has become too sure of itself, too smug in its uncertainties.

Conclusion

The account of place I have offered in this chapter is, like Law's (1994) and Massey's (1995a, 1995b) accounts, one based in a *relational mate- rialism* which depends upon conceiving of the world as associational, as an imbroglio of heterogeneous and more or less expansive hybrids per- forming 'not one but many worlds' (Law, 1997: 9) and weaving all manner of spaces and times as they do so. Place is still important because there is no other definition of these hybrids but a contextual one: it is how they matter and why they matter. Of course, this also means that there can be no single definition of place, especially as co- presence has become less important to successful associations.

It is no surprise, then, that place is both so pivotal and so hard to grasp. It comes with the weight of numerous past associations. Yet it always depends upon further works of association to activate these associations, let alone make new ones. It follows that it can never be completed. Yet it is often that part of a frighteningly contingent life that we most wish to complete. Surely *this* does not change? But it does, and in part because of the work of association we put into it. Like societies, places can be made durable but they cannot last. Frank Bascombe, scarred but still hopeful, knows this elementary lesson of the geopoetics of haunting only too well:

> And yet and yet, do I sense, as I sit here, a melancholy? The same scent of loss I suffered three nights ago at Sally's and almost shed a tear over, because I'd once *merely* been *near* there in a prior epoch of life and was in the neighbourhood again, feeling unwanted by the place? And so shouldn't I feel it even more here, because my story was longer, because I

loved here, buried a son nearby, lost a fine, permanent life here, lived alone until I couldn't stand it another minute and now find it changed to the Chaim Yankowicz Center, as indifferent to me as a gumdrop? Indeed, it's worth asking again, is there any case to think a place – any place – within its plaster and joists, its trees and plantings, in its putative essence *ever* shelters some spirit ghost of us as proof of its significance and ours?

No! Not one bit! Only other humans do that, and then only under special circumstances, which is a lesson of the Existence Period worth holding onto. We just have to be smart enough to quit asking places for what they can't provide, and begin to invent other options, the way Joe Markham has, at least temporarily, and my son Paul may be doing now – as gestures of our God-required but not God-assured independence. (Ford, 1995: 442)

Acknowledgements

I am happy to acknowledge Doreen Massey's generous help with trying to get this chapter right. Gillian Rose also provided some very helpful comments.

Notes

I have taken my chapter title from, and as a tribute to, *Steps to an Ecology of Mind*, Gregory Bateson's (1973) remarkably prescient book which has been so influential across such a wide range of disciplines.

1 Indeed what is remarkable is how pervasive it is in current cultural geography, which often seems to have taken representation as its central focus, to its detriment.
2 Critics of Perloff, like Kellogg (1996), seem to me to misunderstand her work by opposing it to 'theory'.
3 But see the work of Barry (1996a, 1996b), who has tried to place this figure in socio-historical perspective.
4 In what follows, I concentrate chiefly on the writings of Latour and Benjamin as examples of the folding of bodies and things, but clearly there are numerous other approaches such as object relations theory.
5 I am well aware that Latour is critical of Benjamin (see Hennion and Latour, 1997) but I believe that Latour's project has real failings of its own, which I explicate below. These, in certain senses, represent a failure of imagination in this direction (but see Latour, 1996).
6 Thus, in a recent paper Latour (1997) rails against geographical proximity, a variant of the separate worlds argument. But I believe that actor network theory is in danger of going too far the other way. Both proximate and network spaces are important (as indeed are other kinds of space: see Thrift and Olds, 1996; Law and Mol, 1995) and each of them can have its own form of placeness, though I cannot go into this in this brief chapter.

7 However, in referring to phenomenological work on place, as I do here, it is important to note that in non-representational theory subjectivity is not an isolated state based on the model of Euro-American individual action (as in much phenomenological work), but is distributed within particular situations amongst 'dividuals' of various kinds. Phenomenological accounts are therefore both an inspiration and, at the same time, highly problematic.

8 Schneider is one of the few French psychoanalyst-philosophers to acknowledge Wittgenstein. As she herself notes (Schneider, 1991: 36) 'in contemporary French psychoanalysis there is a kind of idolatry of the word' which has allowed textualism to become rampant. But note the remarkable work of Bouveresse (1973, 1984, 1991, 1995) on Wittgenstein. An alternative tradition of psychoanalytic work which attempts to get at place is represented by the work of writers like Vidler (1992), Benjamin (Gilloch, 1996) and Pile (1996). Rose's chapter in this volume is another telling example of this manner of thinking. There may be some chance of a certain degree of reconciliation between non-representational and psychoanalytic approaches based on a better understanding of the history of psychoanalysis. (I am thinking here of, for example, Lacan's interest in Heidegger (see Rockmore, 1994) and Merleau-Ponty and of the kind of interest in space and place found in writers like Irigaray (see Irigaray, 1987).)

References

Anderson, P. (1984) 'Modernity and revolution'. *New Left Review*, 144: 96–113.

Apel, K. (1996) 'Wittgenstein and Heidegger: language, games and life forms'. In C. Macann (ed.), *Critical Heidegger*. London, Routledge, 241–74.

Armstrong, A. (1997) 'Some reflections on Deleuze's Spinoza: composition and agency'. In K. Ansell-Pearson (ed.), *Deleuze and Philosophy: The Difference Engineer*. London, Routledge, 44–57.

Bachelard, G. (1969) *The Poetics of Space*. Boston, Beacon Press.

Barry, A. (1996a) 'Lines of communication and spaces of rule'. In A. Barry, T. Osborne and N. Rose (eds), *Foucault and Political Reason*. London, UCL Press, 123–42.

Barry, A. (1996b) 'The European network'. *New Formations*, 29: 26–38.

Bateson, G. (1973) *Steps to an Ecology of Mind*. London, Paladin.

Benjamin, W. (1978) *Reflections: Essays, Aphorisms, Autobiographical Writings*. New York, Harcourt Brace Jovanovich.

Bennett, J. (1997) 'The enchanted world of modernity: Paracelsus, Kant and Deleuze'. *Cultural Values*, 1: 1–28.

Black, D.W., J. Kunze and J. Pickles (eds) (1989) *Commonplaces: Essays on the Nature of Place*. Lanham MD, University Press of America.

Bloor, D. (1983) *Wittgenstein: A Social Theory of Knowledge*. London, Macmillan.

Bouveresse, J. (1973) *Wittgenstein: La Rime et la Raison*. Paris, Editions de Minuit.

Bouveresse, J. (1984) *La Force de la Règle: Wittgenstein et L'Invention de la Nécessité*. Paris, Editions de Minuit.

Bouveresse, J. (1991) *Wittgenstein et la Philosophe du Langage*. Paris, Editions de l'Eclat.

Bouveresse, J. (1995) *Wittgenstein Reads Freud: The Myth of the Unconscious*. Princeton NJ, Princeton University Press.

Bremmer, J. and Roodenburg, H. (eds) (1993) *A Cultural History of Gesture*. Cambridge, Polity Press.

Brennan, T. (1993) *History after Lacan*. Cambridge, Polity Press.

Casey, E.W. (1993) *Getting Back into Place*. Bloomington, Indiana University Press.

Cohen, J.J. (ed.) (1996) *Monster Theory: Reading Culture*. Minneapolis, University of Minnesota Press.

Coulter, J. (1987) 'Recognition in Wittgenstein and contemporary thought'. In M. Chapman and R. Dixon (eds), *Meaning and the Growth of Understanding: Wittgenstein's Significance for Developmental Psychology*. New York, Springer Verlag, 128–57.

Coulter, J. (1993) 'Consciousness: the Cartesian enigma and its contemporary resolution'. In S.G. Shanbeer and J. Canfield (eds), *Wittgenstein's Intentions*. Toronto, Garland Press, 64–85.

Coulter, J. (1996) 'Human practices and the observability of the macrosocial'. *Zeitschrift für Soziologie*, 25/5: 16–23.

Deleuze, G. (1988) *Bergsonism*. New York, Zone Books.

Deleuze, G. and F. Guattari (1984) *A Thousand Plateaus*. Minneapolis, University of Minnesota Press.

Dening, G. (1996) *Performances*. Chicago, Chicago University Press.

Derrida, J. (1991) *Cinders*. Lincoln NE, University of Nebraska Press.

Eagleton, T. (1997) 'Self-undoing subjects'. In R. Porter (ed.), *Rewriting the Self: Histories from the Renaissance to the Present*. London, Routledge, 262–9.

Featherstone, M. and S. Lash (1995) 'Globalisation, modernity and the spatialisation of social theory'. In M. Featherstone, S. Lash, and R. Robertson (eds), *Global Modernities*. London, Sage, 1–24.

Ford, R. (1995) *Independence Day*. London, Harvill Press.

Foucault, M. (1987) 'Maurice Blanchot: the thought from the outside'. In *Foucault/Blanchot*. New York, Zone Books.

Franck, D. (1986) *Heidegger et la Problème de l'Espace*. Paris, Editions de Minuit.

Game, A. (1995) 'Time, space, memory, with reference to Bachelard'. In M. Featherstone, S. Lash and R. Robertson (eds), *Global Modernities*. London, Sage, 192–208.

Game, A. and D. Metcalfe (1996) *Passionate Sociology*. London, Sage.

Geertz, C. (1964) 'The transition to humanity'. In S. Tax (ed.), *Horizons of Anthropology*. Chicago, Aldine.

Gell, A. (1992) *The Anthropology of Time*. Oxford, Berg.

Genette, G. (1997) *Paratexts: Thresholds of Interpretation*. Cambridge, Cambridge University Press.

Genova, A. (1995) *Wittgenstein*. New York, Routledge.

Gibson, A. (1997) *Towards a Postmodern Theory of Narrative*. Edinburgh, Edinburgh University Press.

Gilloch, G. (1996) *Myth and Metropolis: Walter Benjamin and the City*. Cambridge, Polity Press.

Goodwin, B.C. (1994) *How the Leopard Changed its Spots*. London, Weidenfeld and Nicolson.

Goodwin, B.C. (1997) 'Community, creativity and society'. *Soundings*, 5: 111–22.

Gordon, A.F. (1997) *Ghostly Matters: Haunting and the Sociological Imagination*. Minneapolis, University of Minnesota Press.

Haraway, D. (1991) *Simians, Cyborgs and Women*. London, Free Association Books.

Heidegger, M. (1971) *Poetry, Language, Thought*. New York, Harper and Row.

Hennion, A. and B. Latour (1997) 'L'art, l'aura et la distance selon Benjamin, ou comment devenir célèbre en faisant tant d'erreurs à la fois . . .'. http://www.ina.fr/CP/Mediologie/art26.htm.

Ingold, T. (1995) 'Building, dwelling, living: how people and animals make themselves at home in the world'. In M. Strathern (ed.), *Shifting Contexts: Transformations in Anthropological Knowledge*. London, Routledge, 57–80.

Irigaray, L. (1987) 'Sexual difference'. In T. Moi (ed.), *French Feminist Theory*. Oxford, Blackwell, 183–205.

Irigaray, L. (1997) *Forgetting Air*. London, Athlone Press.

Kellogg, D. (1996) 'Perloff's Wittgenstein: W(h)ither poetic theory?'. *Diacritics*, 26: 67–85.

King, A. (1995) 'The times and spaces of modernity or who needs postmodernism?'. In M. Featherstone, S. Lash and R. Robertson (eds), *Global Modernities*. London, Sage, 108–23.

Latour, B. (1988) 'The politics of explanation: an alternative'. In S. Woolgar (ed.), *Knowledge and Reflexivity*. London, Sage, 155–77.

Latour, B. (1996) *Aramis, or the Love of Technology*. Cambridge MA, Harvard University Press.

Latour, B. (1997) 'On actor-network theory: a few clarifications'. Centre for Social Theory and Technology, University of Keele. http://www.keele.ac.uk/depts/stt/ant/latour.htm.

Law, J. (1994) *Organising Modernity*. Oxford, Blackwell.

Law, J. (1997) 'Traduction/trahison: notes on ANT'. Centre for Social Theory and Technology, University of Keele. http://www.Keele.ac.uk/depts/stt/staff/jl/pubs-JL2.htm.

Law, J. and A. Mol (1995) 'Notes on materiality and sociality'. *Sociological Review*, 24: 641–71.

Massey, D. (1995a) 'Thinking radical democracy spatially'. *Environment and Planning D: Society and Space*, 18: 283–8.

Massey, D. (1995b) 'Making spaces, or, geography is political too'. *Soundings*, 1: 193–208.

Melville, H. (1973) *Moby Dick*. Harmondsworth, Penguin.

Merleau-Ponty, M. (1962) *The Phenomenology of Perception*. London, Routledge and Kegan Paul.

Osborne, P. (1995) *The Politics of Time*. London, Verso.

Perloff, M. (1996) *Wittgenstein's Ladder: Poetic Language and the Strangeness of the Ordinary*. Chicago, Chicago University Press.

Philo, C. (1994) 'Foucault's geography'. *Environment and Planning D: Society and Space*, 10: 137–61.

Pile, S. (1996) *The Body and the City*. London, Routledge.

Plant, S. (1996) 'The virtual complexity of culture'. In G. Robertson, M. Mash, L. Tickner, J. Bird, B. Curtis and T. Putnam (eds), *FutureNatural: Nature, Science, Culture*. London, Routledge, 203–17.

Probyn, E. (1996) *Outside Belongings*. London, Routledge.

Radley, A. (1995) 'The elusory body and social constructionist theory'. *Body and Society*, 1: 3–24.

Reed, C. (ed.) (1996) *Not at Home: The Suppression of Domesticity in Modern Art and Architecture*. London, Thames and Hudson.

Rockmore, T. (1994) *Heidegger and French Philosophy: Humanism, Anti-humanism and Being*. London, Routledge.

Rose, N. (1996) *Inventing Ourselves*. Cambridge, Cambridge University Press.

Schatzki, T.R. (1996) *Social Practices: A Wittgensteinian Approach to Human Activity and the Social*. Cambridge, Cambridge University Press.

Schneider, M. (1991) 'Interview'. In R. Mortley (ed.), *French Philosophers in Conversation*. London, Routledge, 29–44.

Schorske, K. (1990) 'History and society', *New German Critique*, 28: 13–26.

Serres, M. (1995) *Genesis*. Ann Arbor, University of Michigan Press.

Serres, M. and B. Latour (1995) *Conversations on Science, Culture and Time*. Ann Arbor, University of Michigan Press.

Shotter, J. (1995) *Cultural Politics of Everyday Life*. Milton Keynes, Open University Press.

Spinosa, C., H. Flores and H.L. Dreyfus (1997) *Disclosing New Worlds: Entrepreneurship, Democratic Action, and the Cultivation of Solidarity*. Cambridge, MIT Press.

Strathern, M. (1992) *Reproducing the Future: Anthropology, Kinship and the New Reproductive Technologies*. Manchester, Manchester University Press.

Strathern, M. (1996) 'Cutting the network'. *Journal of the Royal Anthropological Institute*, n.s., 2: 517–35.

Taussig, M. (1992) *The Nervous System*. New York, Routledge.

Threadgold, T. (1997) *Feminist Poetics: Poiesis, Performance, Histories*. London, Routledge.

Thrift, N.J. (1995) 'A hyperactive world'. In R.J. Johnston, P.J. Taylor and M. Watts (eds), *Geographies of Global Change*. Oxford, Blackwell, 18–35.

Thrift, N.J. (1996) *Spatial Formations*. London, Sage.

Thrift, N.J. (1997) 'The still point: resistance, expressive embodiment and dance'. In S. Pile and M. Keith (eds), *Geographies of Resistance*. London, Routledge, 124–51.

Vidler, A. (1992) *The Architectural Uncanny: Essays in the Modern Unhomely*. Cambridge MA, MIT Press.

Villela-Petit, M. (1996) 'Heidegger's conception of space'. In C. Macann (ed.) *Critical Heidegger*. London, Routledge, 134–58.

Williams, R. (1977) *Marxism and Literature*. Oxford, Oxford University Press.

Wittgenstein, L. (1958) *Philosophical Investigations* (second edition). Oxford, Blackwell.

Wittgenstein, L. (1980) *Culture and Value*. Chicago, University of Chicago Press.

Afterword: Open Geographies

John Allen with the collective

Human geography today is enjoying a welcome moment of fashion among those who pursue serious intellectual enquiry in the social sciences. Its central concerns – in particular with spatiality in all its different guises – are now seriously deserving of attention among cultural, political and social theorists alike. This moment will undoubtedly pass. Fashion is after all a feature of intellectual life, as it is of most other realms. What may persist and possibly retain a hold on intellectual life, however, is the understanding that geography makes a difference to the way that all manner of social relationships are conceived, especially in today's global and environmentally demanding times. Geography, it seems, turns up everywhere. Recently it has occupied a critical place in the enquiries of those who are trying to think through the changing political and social formation of the post-war period and its many worlds. The rise of post-colonial and feminist sensibilities to the place and power of knowledges, the contribution of poststructuralist thought to the construction of identity and the specificity of differences, and the growing geopolitical awareness of the networks of connections which cut across taken-for-granted blocks of territorial space are among those enquiries which, together, go some way towards signifying the hold that geography and its broad concerns now have on a range of thinking, especially outside of the discipline.

Thinking geographically

In this collection, the intention has been to push this critical thinking a step further. But not solely in the directions intimated above. As a form of intellectual engagement the chapters presented here were not written principally to address the imaginations of those outside the discipline. They were written by and for geographers, first and foremost, as an exercise which raised provocative and sometimes awkward questions of the nature of geography today and the responsibilities of those who practise it. Only on such a basis would it then be appropriate to intervene in wider debates which cut across the disciplines. This, then, has been a rather different type of enquiry from one which sees merit in merely adding a geographical twist to the familiar or the more pressing issues of the day – whether it be the meaning of identity in an age of migration and tumultuous mega-cities or the straightforward loss of a job in a local economy which has nose-dived in a global recession. Perhaps to belabour the point, there are indeed many important issues to consider, but to rethink them geographically actually involves more than 'adding on' space and place to an economic or cultural study. Thinking geographically can alter the way in which we understand events and issues, and it is this, above all else, that this collection has sought to demonstrate.

Questions of identity, of the nature of power, of the constitution of knowledge and its legitimation, for instance, are all recurrent themes in the social sciences. But what difference does it make to think them through geographically? The contributions to this collection differ in their substantive answer to such questions, yet they broadly coalesce around the view that the geographical refiguration of social enquiry alters not so much the objects of enquiry as it does how we conceive of them and what it is that we wish to know.

Take the example of difference considered in part III. Here, difference for the authors meant more than simply exploring the contexts in which differences are shaped. For them, the construction of difference and the marking of identities were something produced through their spatial relations: through their geographical positionings at, for instance, a differentiated core or periphery, or on the inside of a constructed border or perhaps beyond it, or wherever such variations 'placed' people. Moreover, the authors were not suggesting that geography exhausted all that there is to know about the construction of identity and difference. On the contrary, their aim was to show that what we want to know about people, identity and difference changes when the relations are conceived through their fixed and fluid geographies. Edward Said understood this well. It is demonstrated in much of his work through the careful exploration of geographical distinctions such as the terrains of 'ours' and 'theirs', the dividing lines of inside and outside, and relations of proximity more generally. What he pointed to with great clarity has been developed in this volume by authors, especially in part II, who have asked questions of the knowledge gained about peoples through their asserted spatial 'truths'; that is, through the imaginary geographies which make it difficult to see peoples, territories and everyday places in ways other than those which position us.

Various contributors to this volume have also had the equally ambitious aim of explicitly spatializing some of the social, political and cultural currents of theory which have recently entered the mainstream of geographical enquiry. As stressed in the introductory chapter, it is no longer adequate – if indeed it ever was – to import new ideas into the discipline without first subjecting their central claims to geographical scrutiny. Poor philosophy is not a substitute for geographical analysis, and nor for that matter is an unreflexive geography a substitute for critical enquiry. The likes of a Deleuze or a Foucault or a Latour, although not without their spatial vocabularies, spell out claims which may in turn be theorized spatially with an eye to producing new forms of understanding of not only their own material but also that of others. Part IV, on the spatialities of power, is an example of just such an examination, as indeed is much of part V, on the reformulations of space and place. In both parts, lines of thinking introduced into the discipline from outside are evaluated to establish what contribution a reframing of their central tenets along geographical lines has to offer.

In thinking about the state of human geography today, therefore, the concern of this collection has been not a preoccupation with notions of what its proper subject matter is or should be, but rather with what thinking geographically can add to our apprehension and comprehension of the major questions of the day.

Thinking openly

Many studies which have attempted to produce a broad overview of the discipline have had to wrestle with the issue of closure. If it is not around concerns of what is right and proper for the discipline to study, it is just as likely to be around the nature of the approach or the perspective (or perspectives) which best serve the discipline. In this collection we have tried to avoid such forms of closure. Inevitably, the selection of topics and questions which frame the collection serves to limit what is substantively raised and discussed. We have tried to maintain a degree of openness, however, in the manner in which the issues and questions are addressed. A number of the chapters involve authors who are working around issues and whose claims, by their own reckoning, must be seen as at best provisional. Others appear more certain, although their thoughts should not be regarded as in any sense final. Critically, however, we have tried to keep within view the overlaps, contrasts and differences that bring together and distinguish the chapters in their respective parts.

Where this works best is when an unforced dialogue emerges, as for example within part V, where the broad understanding that space is anything but transparent or fully knowable is distilled through the chapters in a number of ways. A feminist reading of space is coupled with a performative approach, which sits alongside a more strident rejection of representational theory, which in turn sits alongside an account which foregrounds the ideas of both Lefebvre and Foucault, among others. While there is much that is shared here in terms of approach, there are also inevitably points of disagreement – as indeed there are points of disagreement between authors across parts where common concerns arise. The nature and role of theory across the different collection, for example, ranges from the expectation that its use will involve the examined conceptualization of social processes to the more modest position that theory provides a useful means of getting by in the world. On this latter view, theory is regarded as something which helps us to relate to our surroundings, rather than an activity which seeks to provide an explanation of them. In fairness, neither sense actually rules out the other, but the adoption of a more practical approach to theorizing which plays down representation, whether in its mimetic or its constructionist form, inevitably takes us towards a different type of enquiry and opens up a different kind of geographical curiosity.

An openness in terms of enquiry, however, and a willingness to explore various ways in which our awareness of the world is constructed, naturally run the risk of eclecticism. The unpacking of performed meaning in one instance, and the appreciation of, say, globalization as a partial and uneven phenomenon in the next, does not necessarily lead to a 'pick 'n' mix' style of theorizing, however. It depends entirely upon how the different strands of enquiry come together; not as a totalizing synthesis made up of its (in)different parts, but rather as particular lines of thought engaged with particular geographical questions and concerns. There is no pretence here of 'wholeness' among the different authors, nor any attempt at amalgamation of the big philosophical 'isms', only a recognition that the specificity and the provisionality of findings are an advance in intellectual enquiry, not a regression or a sign of 'weak' thinking.

Thinking relationally

Having stressed the openness of thinking in this collection, however, it may seem odd then to prioritize the role of relational thinking. Is relational thinking just another form of closure, albeit one which has attempted to influence the discipline's mode of enquiry rather than its subject matter? Again the chapters in part I give a lead on this, although the answer to this question surfaces throughout the text. Clearly there is an attempt in many of the chapters to move beyond a type of binary thinking that traps us in a world of absolute rather than relative distinctions. In particular, there is a concern to escape situations where a clear-cut distinction forces us to theorize differences in either one way or the other. In such situations the act of choosing is itself a form of theoretical closure. We may be pressed to choose, for example, between either a local identity or a global identity, or between a natural process or a cultural process, or between a black self or a white self, depending upon the focus of enquiry, with little room given to think across such distinctions or to disturb them as conceptual benchmarks. When closure comes in this way, the breaking apart of such dualisms, the ability to think across and beyond them, represents a form of openness.

Each of the parts has something to contribute on this score. Part I thinks across the nature/culture divide, for example, whereas parts II and III highlight the importance of the connecting links between different territories and between different peoples. In a similar vein, part IV attempts to explode the power/resistance binary with its stress upon empowerment, and part V goes beyond simple oppositions of space and place to produce anti-essentialist accounts of both aspects. All in all, the various chapters prompt us to revise the closed thinking that is often associated with the borders and boundaries drawn around social processes, which act *as if* they were the last word on the subject.

It is hardly surprising, then, that a number of the contributions chime with sentiments of poststructuralist thought. However, it would be a mistake to impose such a label on the collection simply for its awareness of the constraints of binary thinking, as important as that recognition is. There are at least two reasons to resist such simplistic labelling. In the first place, certain authors in the book emphasize the importance of boundary construction and boundary maintenance as much as they do their diffusion. Power is a key issue here, running through the issues of identity and difference, space and place, and the construction of imaginative geographies more generally. Power in its various guises (and disguises) serves to freeze the language of 'us' and 'them' and to etch steadfastly the lines that divide those on the 'inside' from those on the 'outside'.

A second reason to resist an easy poststructionalist labelling is that the above reason reminds us that structures still exist in the form of material closures, no matter how much they may be wished away discursively. Thinking across binaries can aid the process of their dissolution, but their unquestioned imposition in the world at large is a testament to the solidity of power configurations and assemblages which are likely to be unmoved by theoretical nuances. We still live in a world of borders and boundaries, of fenced-off territories and exclusions, and, in Slater's words in this volume, of 'invasive imaginations'.

Thinking relationally, then, also involves a recognition of the connections drawn through material closure, as much as it does of those constructed through theoretical openings. Asking awkward questions of human geography today is simply not quite enough. We also have to take responsibility for the partiality of our answers and investigations, whether that partiality be discursive, Western or otherwise. Along the way, we might even find that we have made a quite different kind of geography. But in the meantime, we should perhaps just persist in making those connections across all kinds of line and barrier.

Index

Index compiled by Jackie B. McDermott